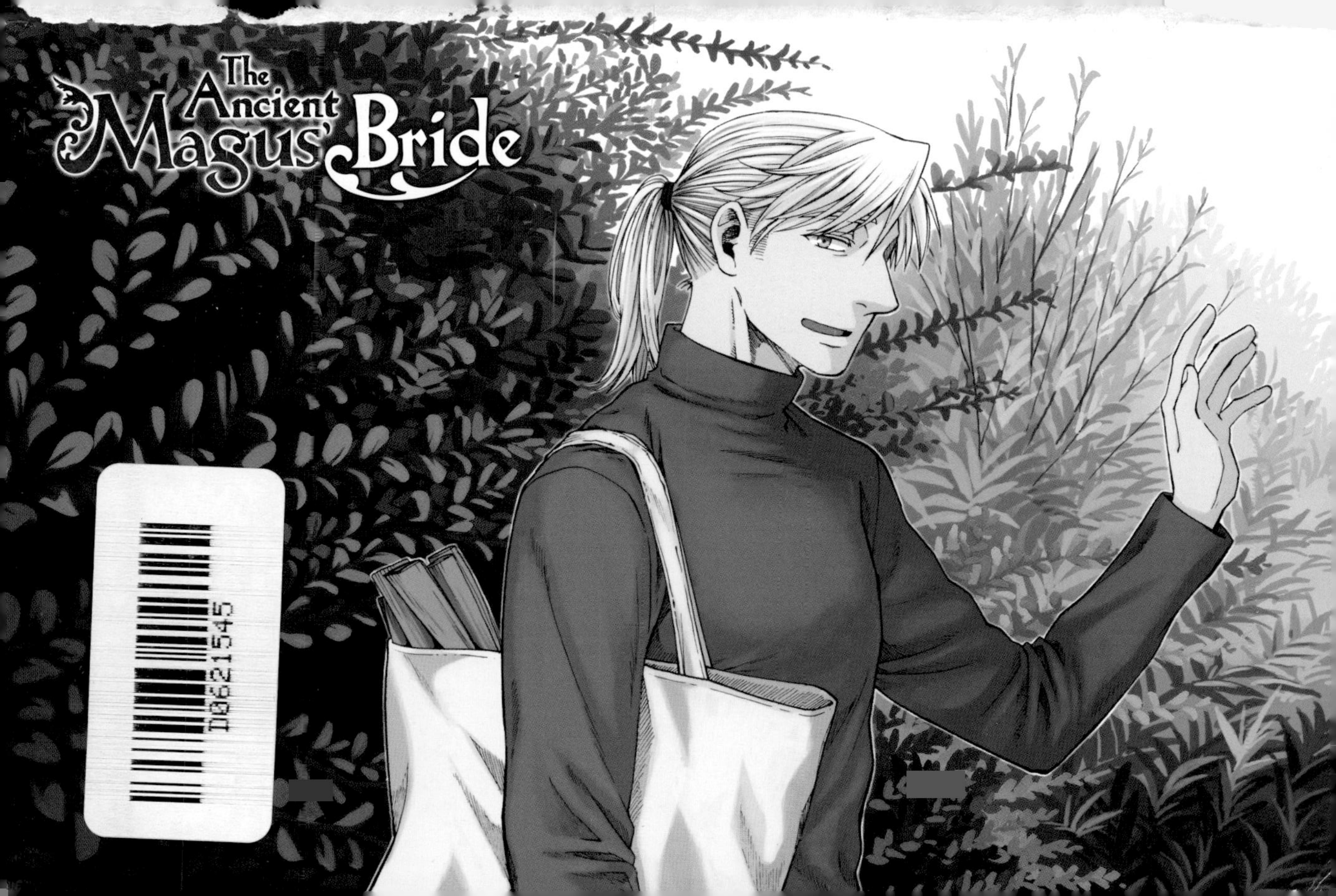
The Ancient Magus' Bride
D0621545

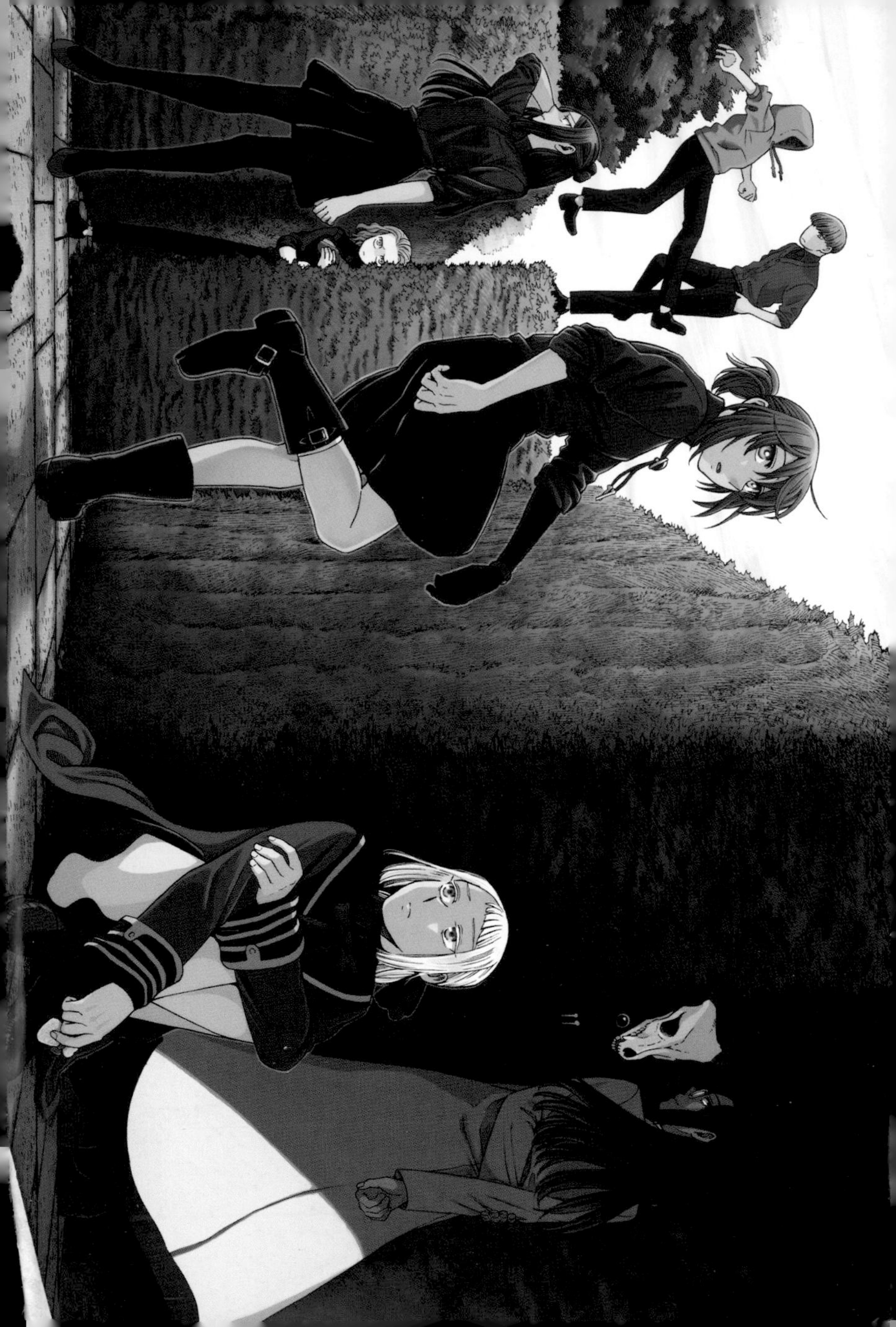

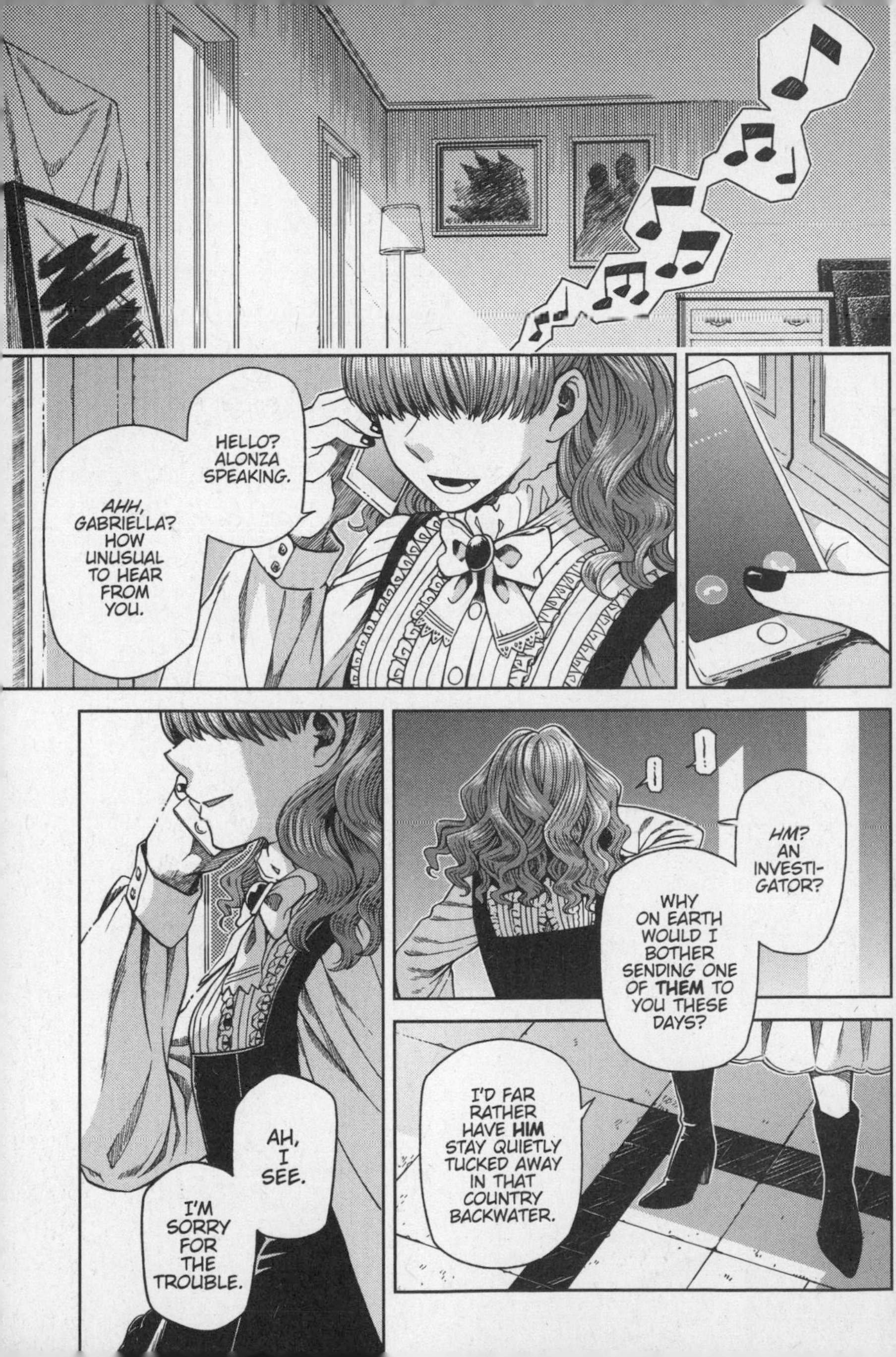
HELLO? ALONZA SPEAKING.
AHH, GABRIELLA? HOW UNUSUAL TO HEAR FROM YOU.
HM? AN INVESTI-GATOR?
WHY ON EARTH WOULD I BOTHER SENDING ONE OF **THEM** TO YOU THESE DAYS?
I'D FAR RATHER HAVE **HIM** STAY QUIETLY TUCKED AWAY IN THAT COUNTRY BACKWATER.
AH, I SEE.
I'M SORRY FOR THE TROUBLE.

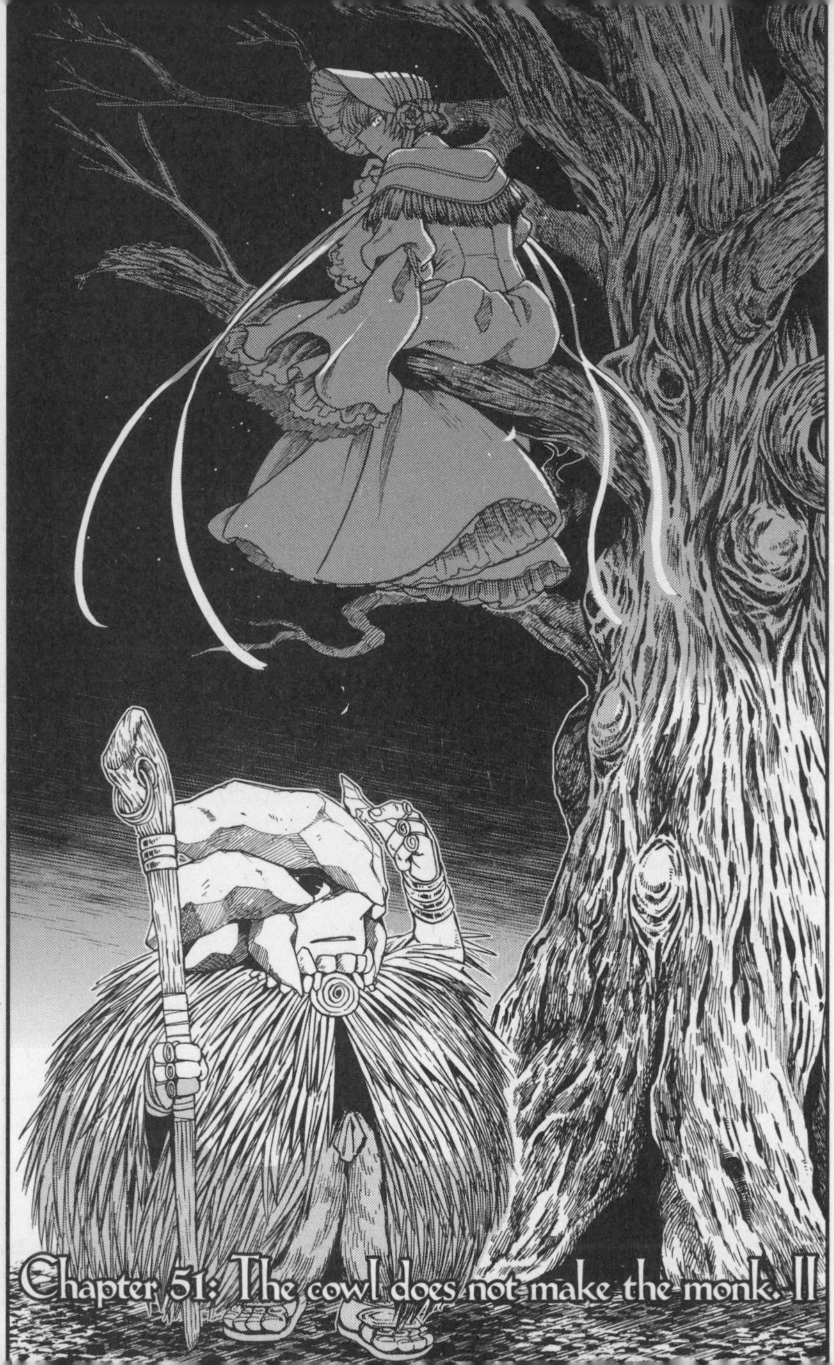
Chapter 51: The cowl does not make the monk. II

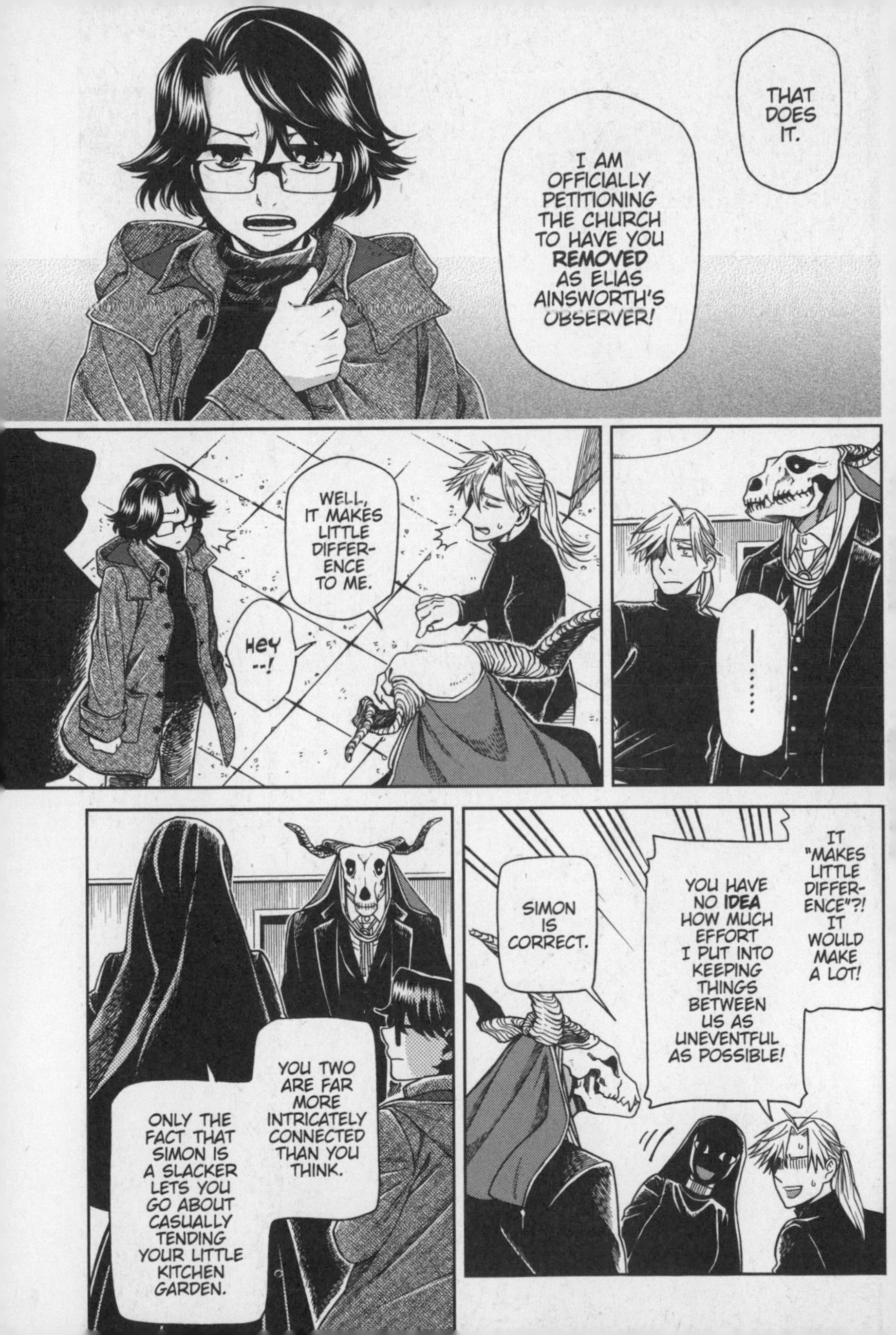
THAT DOES IT.
I AM OFFICIALLY PETITIONING THE CHURCH TO HAVE YOU **REMOVED** AS ELIAS AINSWORTH'S OBSERVER!
—......
WELL, IT MAKES LITTLE DIFFERENCE TO ME.
HEY --!
IT "MAKES LITTLE DIFFERENCE"?! IT WOULD MAKE A LOT!
YOU HAVE NO **IDEA** HOW MUCH EFFORT I PUT INTO KEEPING THINGS BETWEEN US AS UNEVENTFUL AS POSSIBLE!
SIMON IS CORRECT.
YOU TWO ARE FAR MORE INTRICATELY CONNECTED THAN YOU THINK.
ONLY THE FACT THAT SIMON IS A SLACKER LETS YOU GO ABOUT CASUALLY TENDING YOUR LITTLE KITCHEN GARDEN.

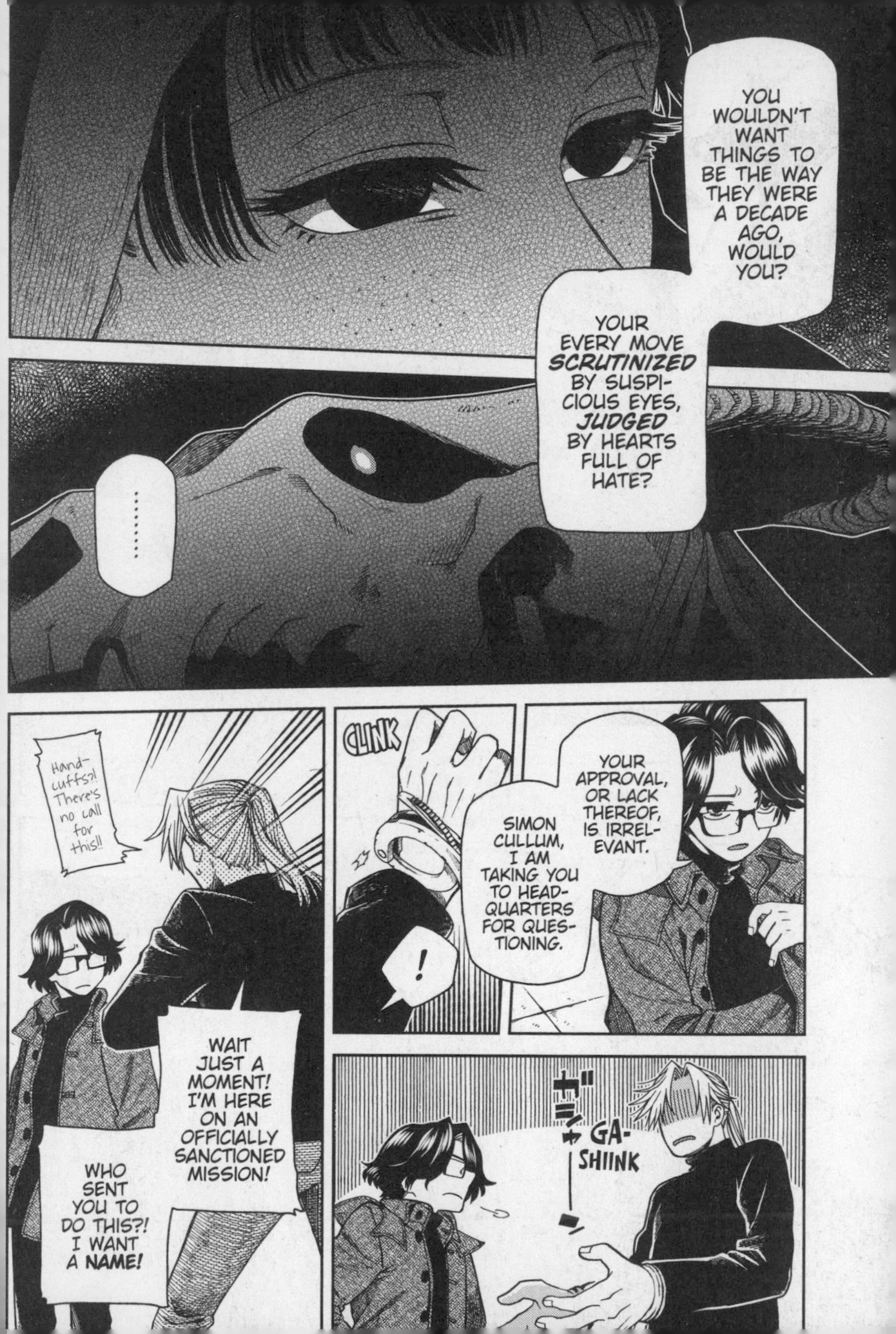
YOU WOULDN'T WANT THINGS TO BE THE WAY THEY WERE A DECADE AGO, WOULD YOU?
YOUR EVERY MOVE SCRUTINIZED BY SUSPICIOUS EYES, JUDGED BY HEARTS FULL OF HATE?
......
YOUR APPROVAL, OR LACK THEREOF, IS IRRELEVANT.
SIMON CULLUM, I AM TAKING YOU TO HEADQUARTERS FOR QUESTIONING.
CLINK
!
GA-SHIINK
Handcuffs?! There's no call for this!!
WAIT JUST A MOMENT! I'M HERE ON AN OFFICIALLY SANCTIONED MISSION!
WHO SENT YOU TO DO THIS?! I WANT A NAME!

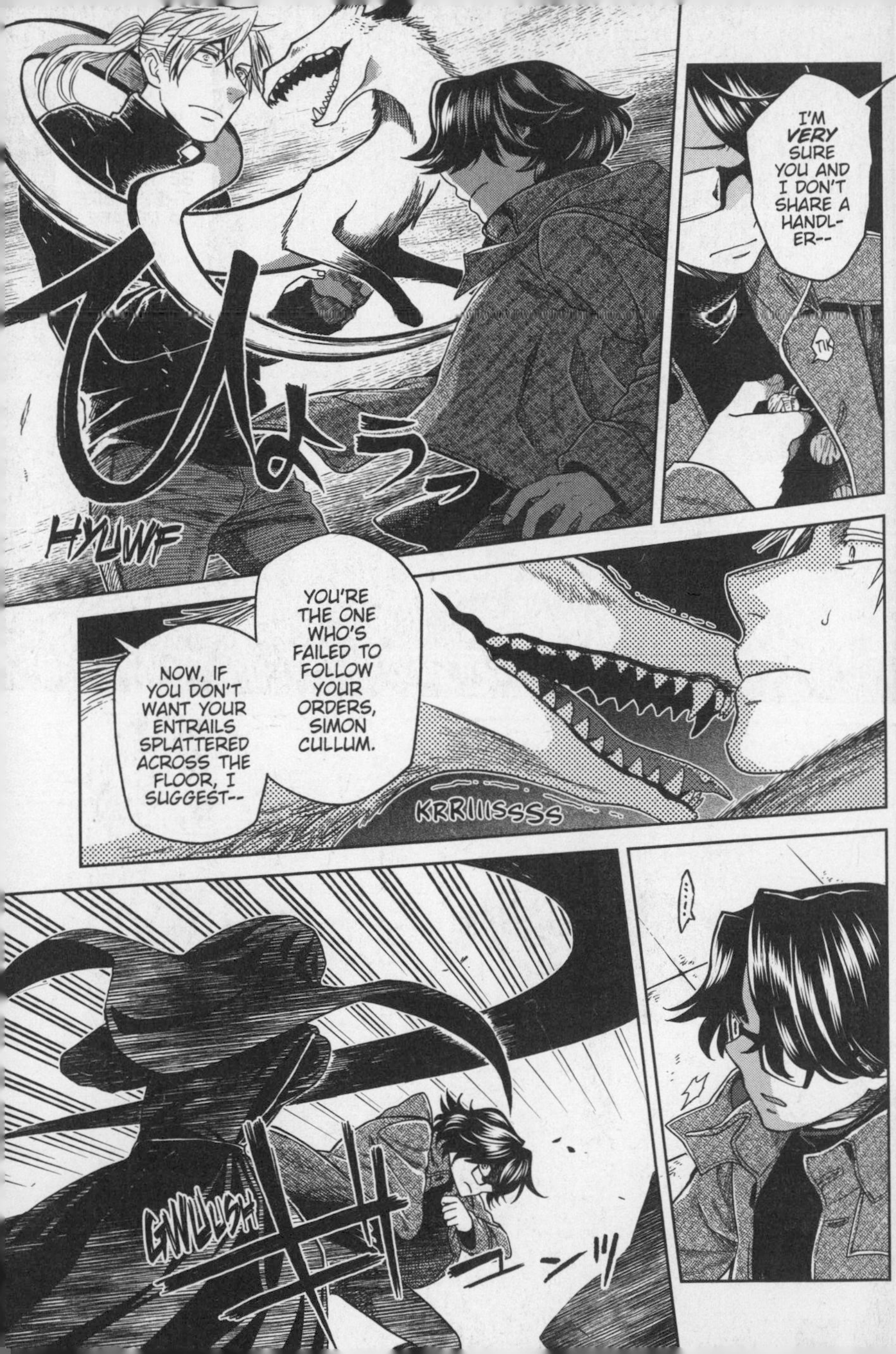
I'M VERY SURE YOU AND I DON'T SHARE A HANDLER--
TIK
HYUWF
YOU'RE THE ONE WHO'S FAILED TO FOLLOW YOUR ORDERS, SIMON CULLUM.
NOW, IF YOU DON'T WANT YOUR ENTRAILS SPLATTERED ACROSS THE FLOOR, I SUGGEST--
KRRIIISSSS
.....
GWULSH

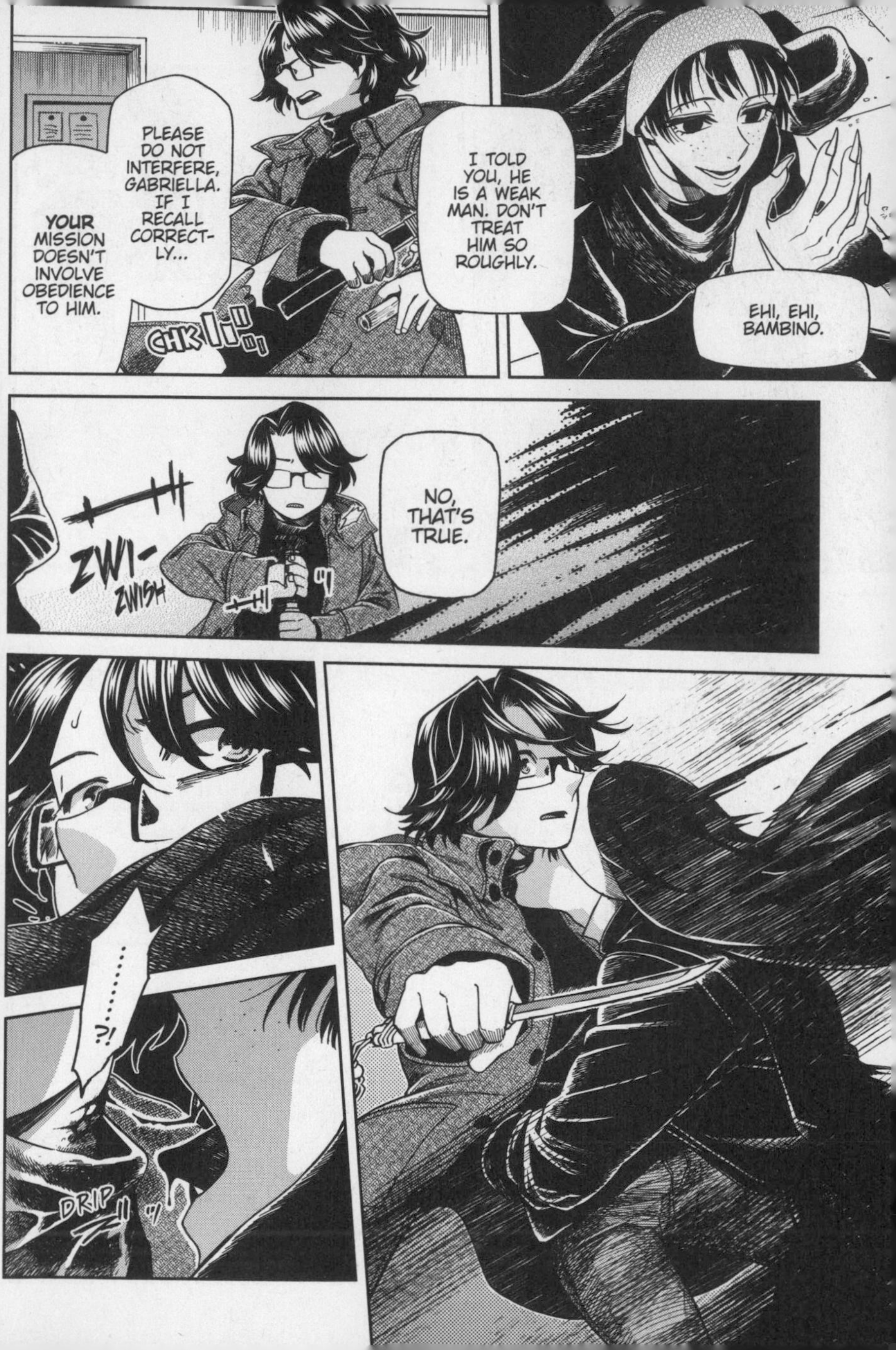
I TOLD YOU, HE IS A WEAK MAN. DON'T TREAT HIM SO ROUGHLY.
EHI, EHI, BAMBINO.
PLEASE DO NOT INTERFERE, GABRIELLA. IF I RECALL CORRECTLY...
YOUR MISSION DOESN'T INVOLVE OBEDIENCE TO HIM.
CHK
NO, THAT'S TRUE.
ZWI- ZWISH
......
?!
DRIP

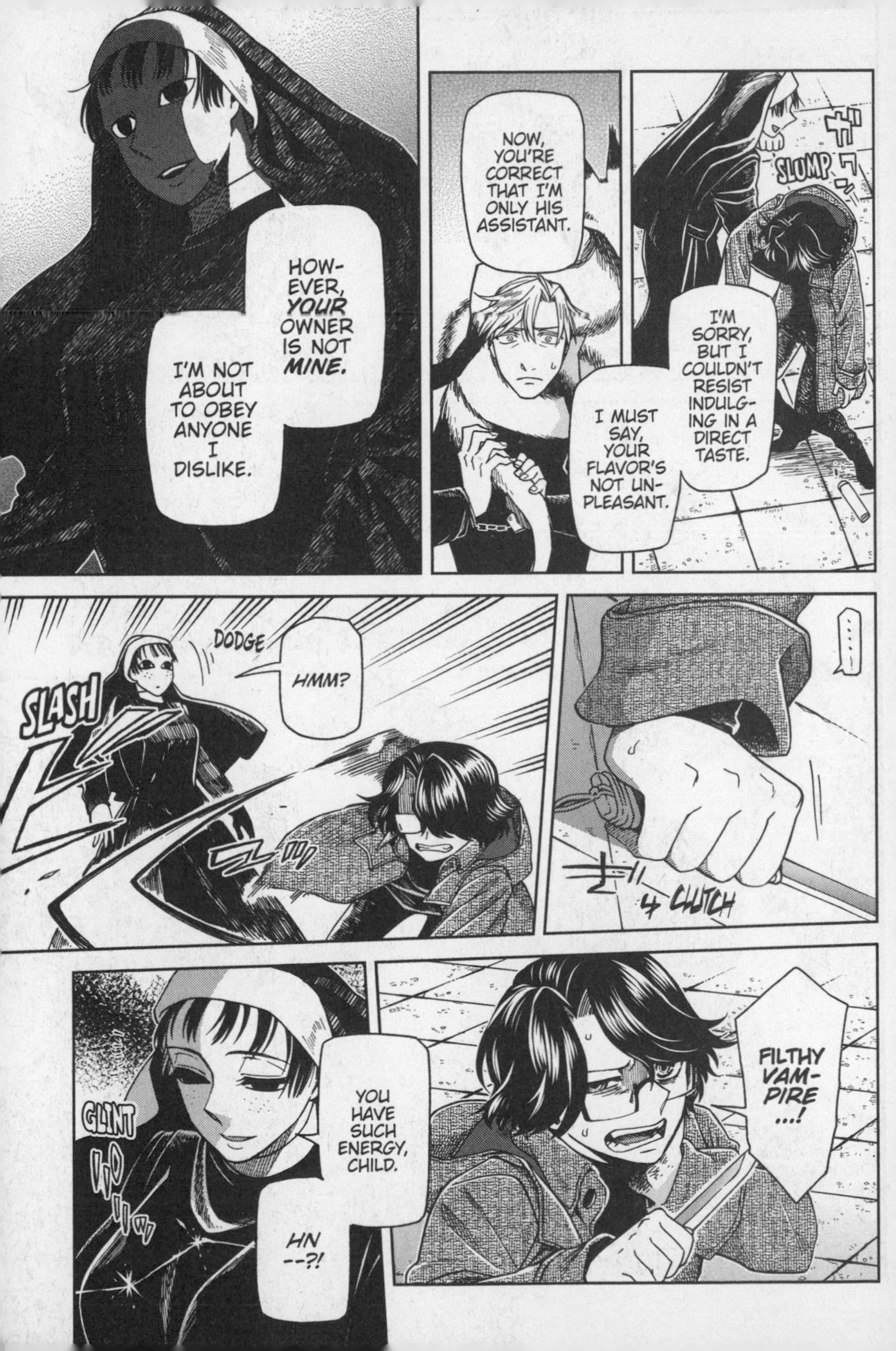
SLUMP
I'M SORRY, BUT I COULDN'T RESIST INDULGING IN A DIRECT TASTE.
I MUST SAY, YOUR FLAVOR'S NOT UNPLEASANT.
NOW, YOU'RE CORRECT THAT I'M ONLY HIS ASSISTANT.
HOW-EVER, *YOUR* OWNER IS NOT *MINE.*
I'M NOT ABOUT TO OBEY ANYONE I DISLIKE.
......!
CLUTCH
DODGE
HMM?
SLASH
FILTHY VAMPIRE...!
YOU HAVE SUCH ENERGY, CHILD.
GLINT
HN --?!

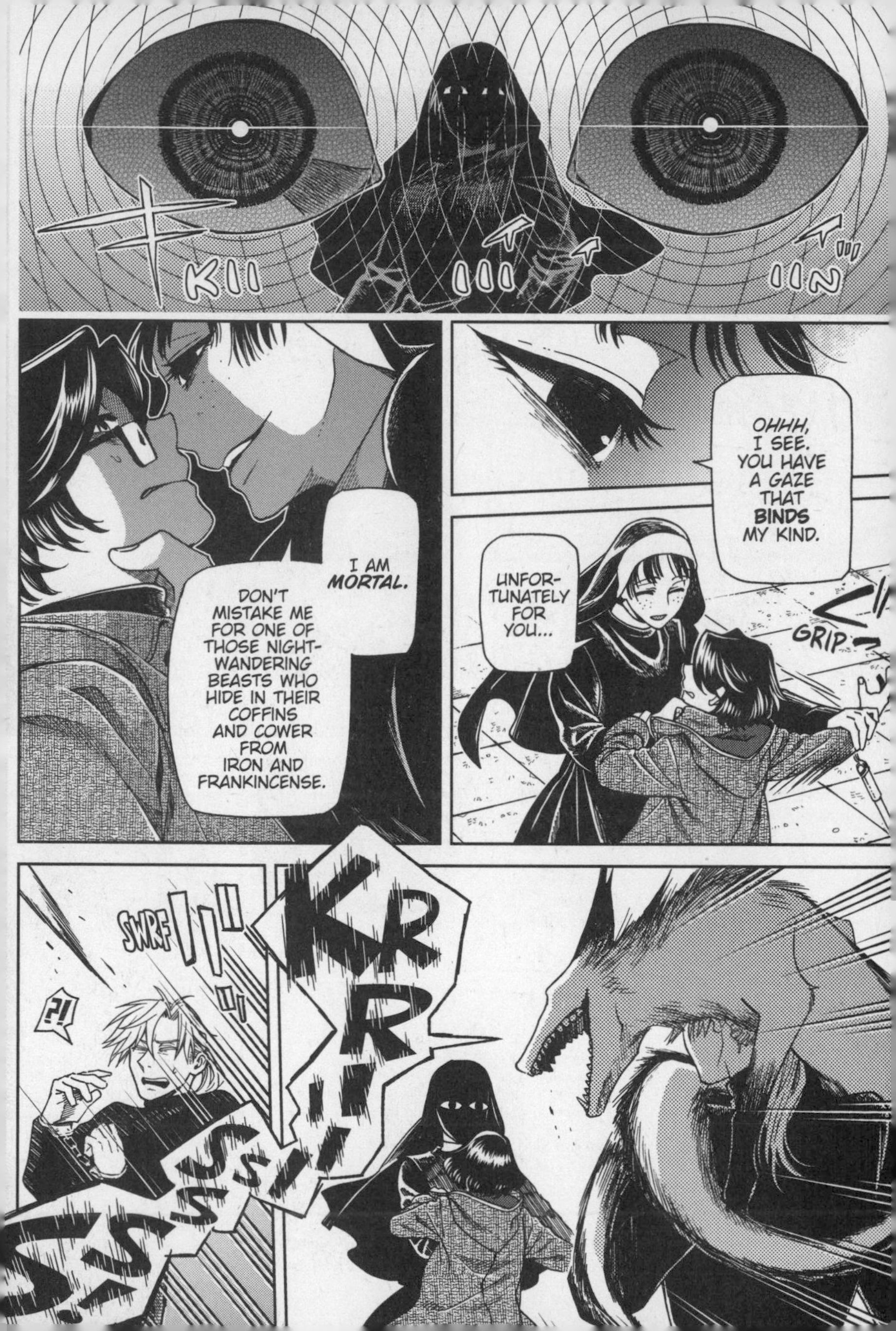
KII III IIN
OHHH, I SEE. YOU HAVE A GAZE THAT BINDS MY KIND.
UNFOR-TUNATELY FOR YOU...
GRIP
I AM MORTAL.
DON'T MISTAKE ME FOR ONE OF THOSE NIGHT-WANDERING BEASTS WHO HIDE IN THEIR COFFINS AND COWER FROM IRON AND FRANKINCENSE.
KRR!!
SWRF
?!
SSS

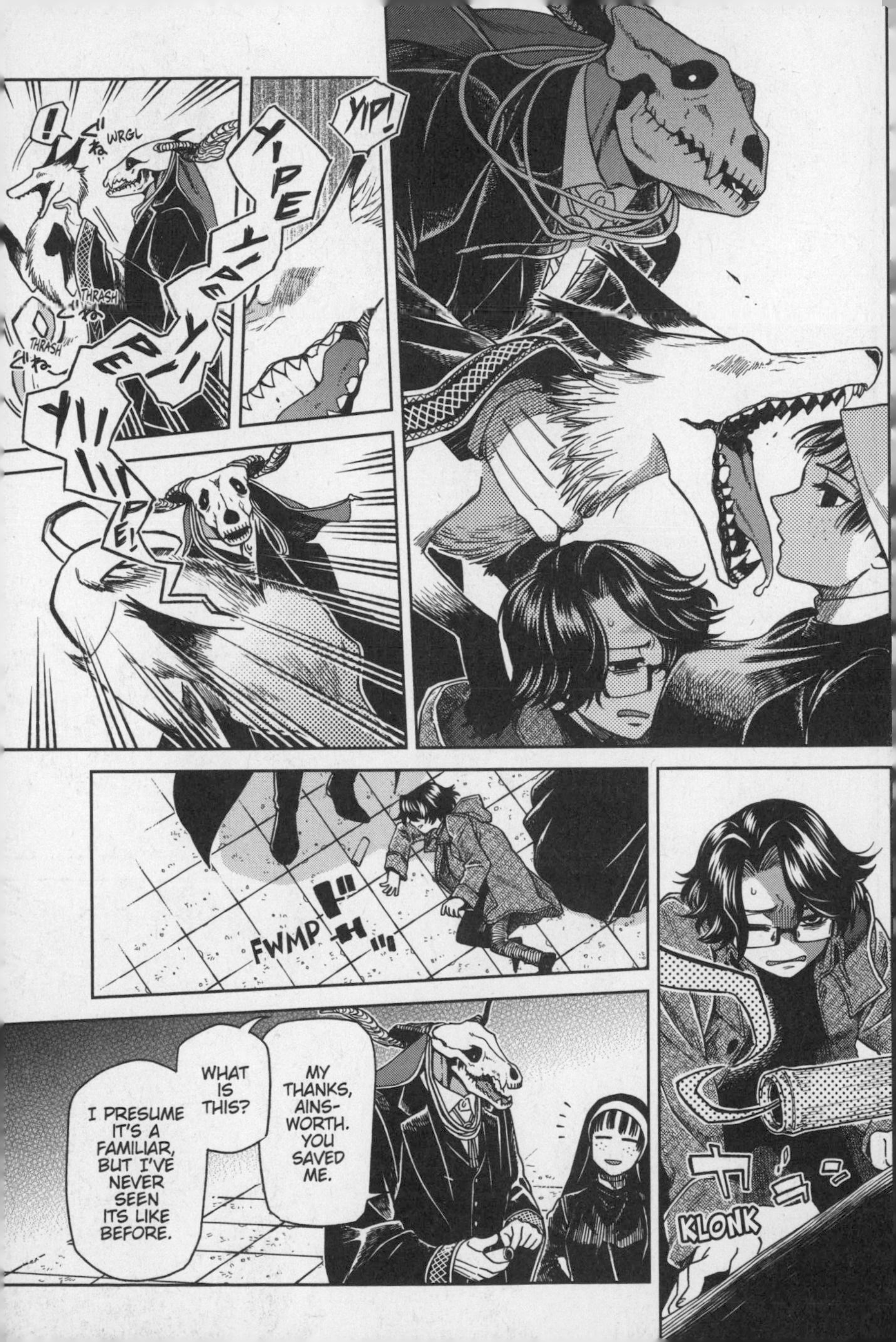
YIP!
!
WRGL
YIPE YIPE YIPE YIPPE!
THRASH
THRASH
!
KLONK
FWMP
MY THANKS, AINSWORTH. YOU SAVED ME.
WHAT IS THIS?
I PRESUME IT'S A FAMILIAR, BUT I'VE NEVER SEEN ITS LIKE BEFORE.

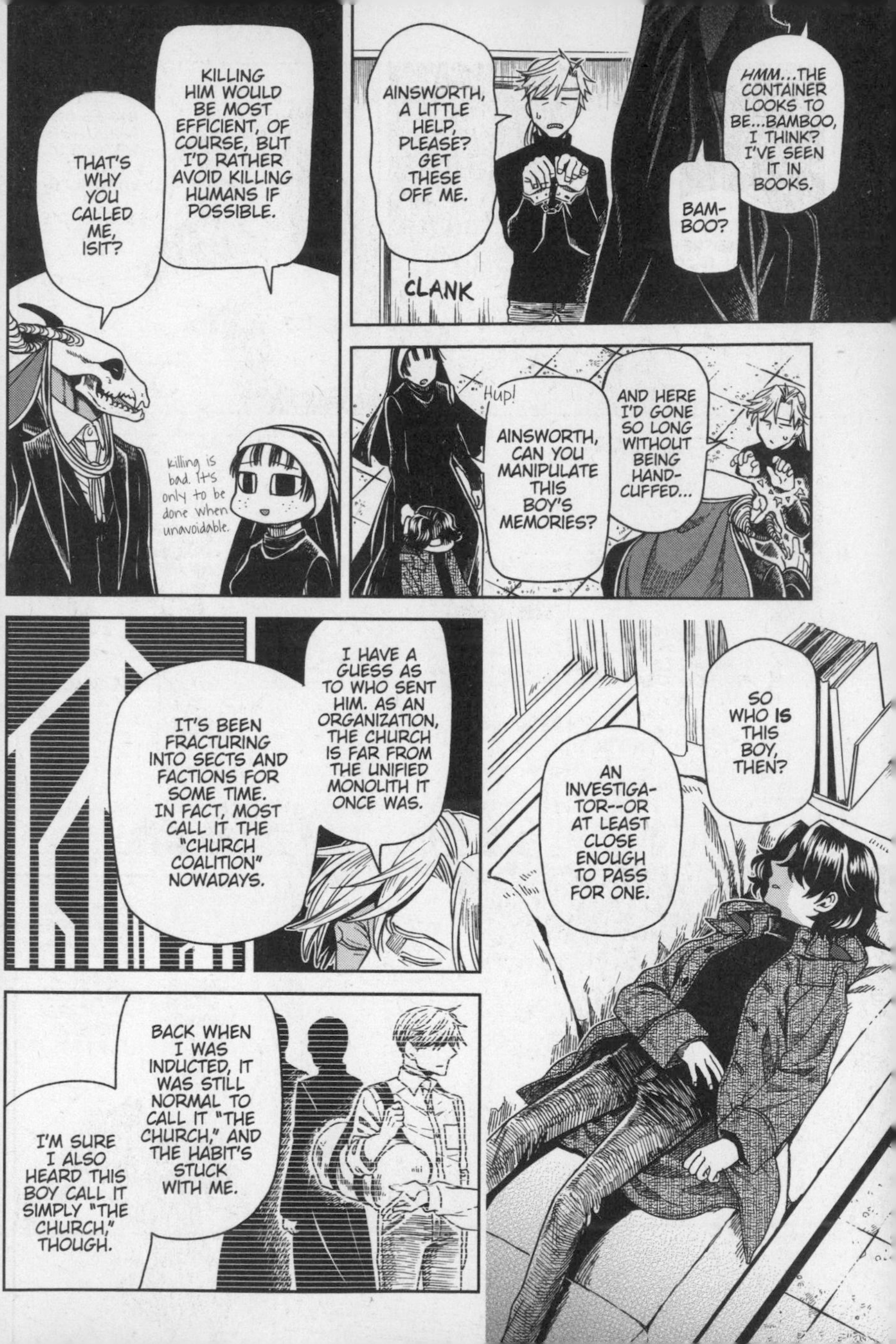
HMM...THE CONTAINER LOOKS TO BE...BAMBOO, I THINK? I'VE SEEN IT IN BOOKS.
BAM-BOO?
AINSWORTH, A LITTLE HELP, PLEASE? GET THESE OFF ME.
CLANK
AND HERE I'D GONE SO LONG WITHOUT BEING HAND-CUFFED...
Hup!
AINSWORTH, CAN YOU MANIPULATE THIS BOY'S MEMORIES?
KILLING HIM WOULD BE MOST EFFICIENT, OF COURSE, BUT I'D RATHER AVOID KILLING HUMANS IF POSSIBLE.
THAT'S WHY YOU CALLED ME, ISIT?
killing is bad. It's only to be done when unavoidable.
SO WHO IS THIS BOY, THEN?
AN INVESTIGA-TOR--OR AT LEAST CLOSE ENOUGH TO PASS FOR ONE.
I HAVE A GUESS AS TO WHO SENT HIM. AS AN ORGANIZATION, THE CHURCH IS FAR FROM THE UNIFIED MONOLITH IT ONCE WAS.
IT'S BEEN FRACTURING INTO SECTS AND FACTIONS FOR SOME TIME. IN FACT, MOST CALL IT THE "CHURCH COALITION" NOWADAYS.
BACK WHEN I WAS INDUCTED, IT WAS STILL NORMAL TO CALL IT "THE CHURCH," AND THE HABIT'S STUCK WITH ME.
I'M SURE I ALSO HEARD THIS BOY CALL IT SIMPLY "THE CHURCH," THOUGH.

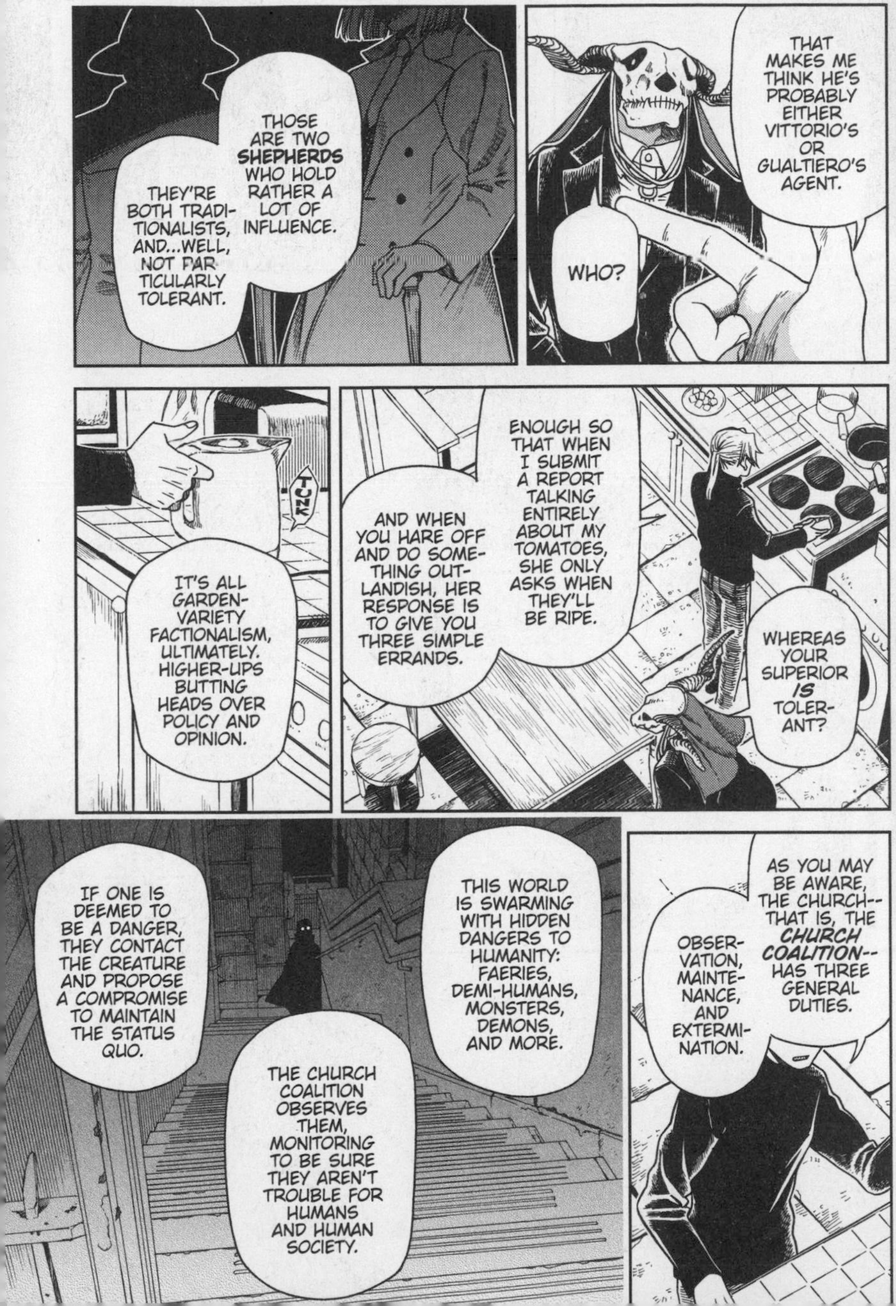

THAT MAKES ME THINK HE'S PROBABLY EITHER VITTORIO'S OR GUALTIERO'S AGENT.
WHO?
THOSE ARE TWO **SHEPHERDS** WHO HOLD RATHER A LOT OF INFLUENCE.
THEY'RE BOTH TRADITIONALISTS, AND...WELL, NOT PARTICULARLY TOLERANT.
WHEREAS YOUR SUPERIOR ***IS*** TOLERANT?
ENOUGH SO THAT WHEN I SUBMIT A REPORT TALKING ENTIRELY ABOUT MY TOMATOES, SHE ONLY ASKS WHEN THEY'LL BE RIPE.
AND WHEN YOU HARE OFF AND DO SOMETHING OUTLANDISH, HER RESPONSE IS TO GIVE YOU THREE SIMPLE ERRANDS.
TUNK
IT'S ALL GARDEN-VARIETY FACTIONALISM, ULTIMATELY. HIGHER-UPS BUTTING HEADS OVER POLICY AND OPINION.
AS YOU MAY BE AWARE, THE CHURCH--THAT IS, THE ***CHURCH COALITION***--HAS THREE GENERAL DUTIES.
OBSERVATION, MAINTENANCE, AND EXTERMINATION.
THIS WORLD IS SWARMING WITH HIDDEN DANGERS TO HUMANITY: FAERIES, DEMI-HUMANS, MONSTERS, DEMONS, AND MORE.
THE CHURCH COALITION OBSERVES THEM, MONITORING TO BE SURE THEY AREN'T TROUBLE FOR HUMANS AND HUMAN SOCIETY.
IF ONE IS DEEMED TO BE A DANGER, THEY CONTACT THE CREATURE AND PROPOSE A COMPROMISE TO MAINTAIN THE STATUS QUO.

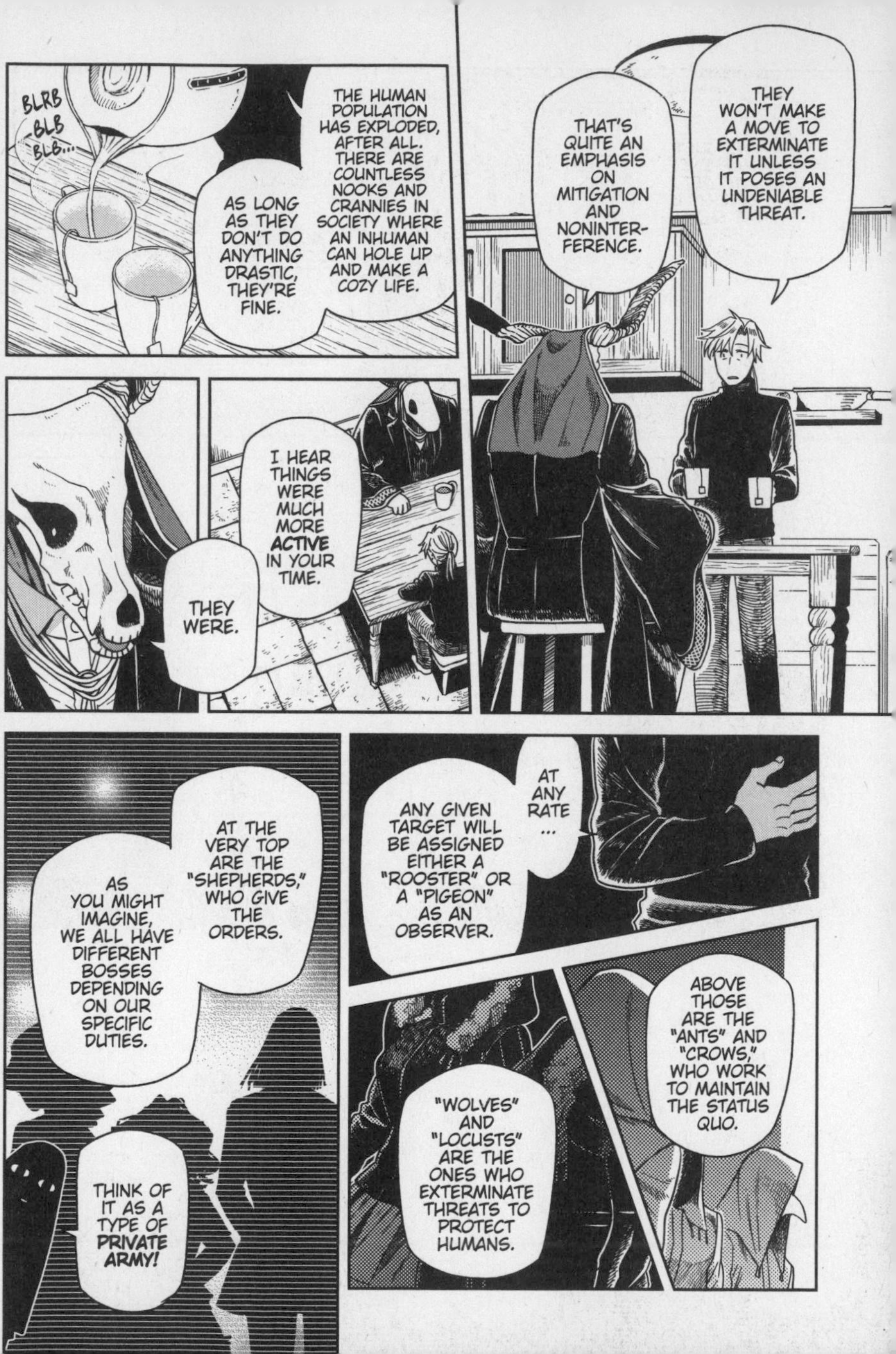

THEY WON'T MAKE A MOVE TO EXTERMINATE IT UNLESS IT POSES AN UNDENIABLE THREAT.
THAT'S QUITE AN EMPHASIS ON MITIGATION AND NONINTERFERENCE.
BLRB -BLB BLB...
THE HUMAN POPULATION HAS EXPLODED, AFTER ALL. THERE ARE COUNTLESS NOOKS AND CRANNIES IN SOCIETY WHERE AN INHUMAN CAN HOLE UP AND MAKE A COZY LIFE.
AS LONG AS THEY DON'T DO ANYTHING DRASTIC, THEY'RE FINE.
I HEAR THINGS WERE MUCH MORE **ACTIVE** IN YOUR TIME.
THEY WERE.
AT ANY RATE...
ANY GIVEN TARGET WILL BE ASSIGNED EITHER A "ROOSTER" OR A "PIGEON" AS AN OBSERVER.
ABOVE THOSE ARE THE "ANTS" AND "CROWS," WHO WORK TO MAINTAIN THE STATUS QUO.
"WOLVES" AND "LOCUSTS" ARE THE ONES WHO EXTERMINATE THREATS TO PROTECT HUMANS.
AT THE VERY TOP ARE THE "SHEPHERDS," WHO GIVE THE ORDERS.
AS YOU MIGHT IMAGINE, WE ALL HAVE DIFFERENT BOSSES DEPENDING ON OUR SPECIFIC DUTIES.
THINK OF IT AS A TYPE OF **PRIVATE ARMY!**

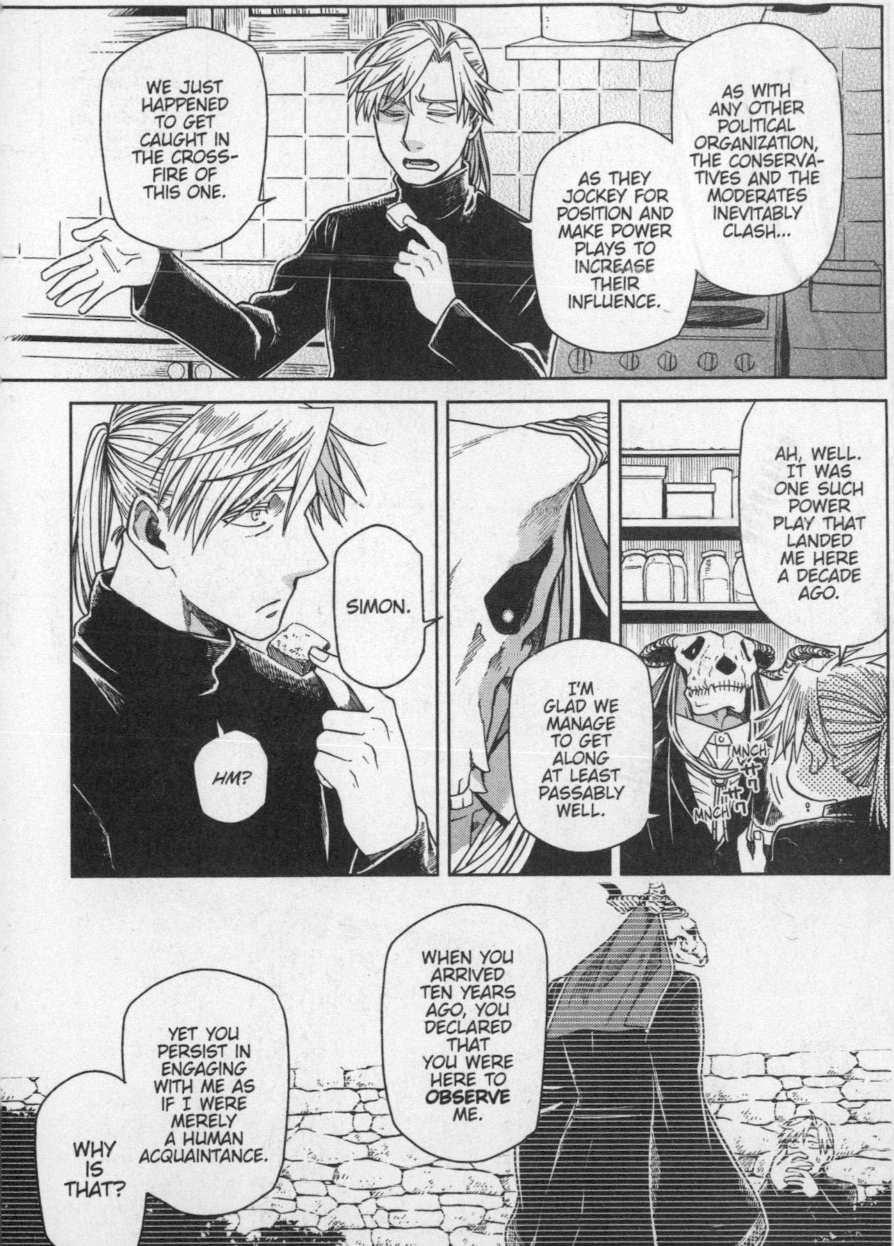
AS WITH ANY OTHER POLITICAL ORGANIZATION, THE CONSERVATIVES AND THE MODERATES INEVITABLY CLASH...
AS THEY JOCKEY FOR POSITION AND MAKE POWER PLAYS TO INCREASE THEIR INFLUENCE.
WE JUST HAPPENED TO GET CAUGHT IN THE CROSS-FIRE OF THIS ONE.
AH, WELL. IT WAS ONE SUCH POWER PLAY THAT LANDED ME HERE A DECADE AGO.
MNCH
MNCH
I'M GLAD WE MANAGE TO GET ALONG AT LEAST PASSABLY WELL.
SIMON.
HM?
WHEN YOU ARRIVED TEN YEARS AGO, YOU DECLARED THAT YOU WERE HERE TO **OBSERVE** ME.
YET YOU PERSIST IN ENGAGING WITH ME AS IF I WERE MERELY A HUMAN ACQUAINTANCE.
WHY IS THAT?

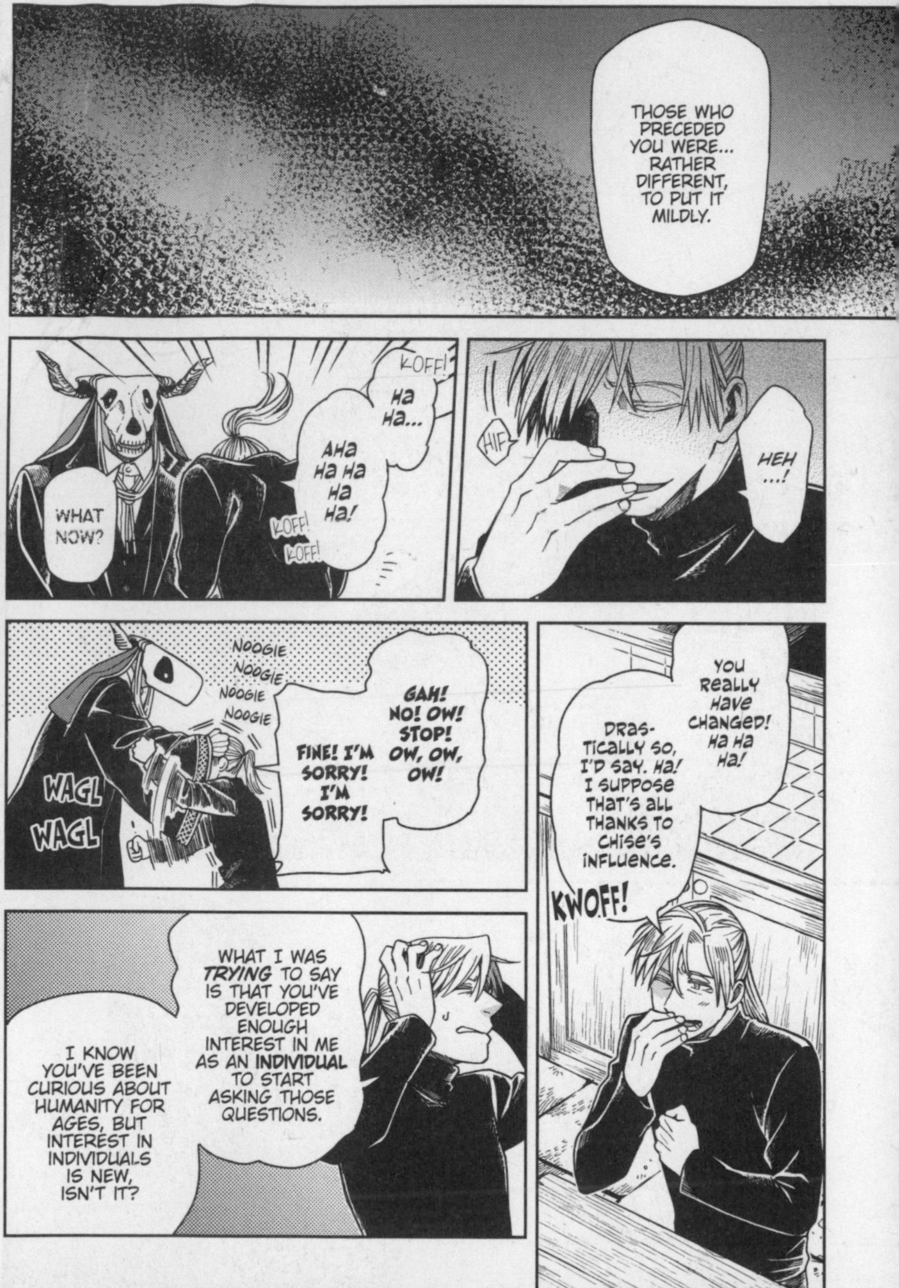
THOSE WHO PRECEDED YOU WERE... RATHER DIFFERENT, TO PUT IT MILDLY.
HEH ...!
HIF
KOFF!
HA HA...
AHA HA HA HA HA!
KOFF! KOFF!
WHAT NOW?
YOU REALLY HAVE CHANGED! HA HA HA!
DRAS-TICALLY SO, I'D SAY. HA! I SUPPOSE THAT'S ALL THANKS TO CHISE'S INFLUENCE.
KWOFF!
GAH! NO! OW! STOP! OW, OW, OW!
FINE! I'M SORRY! I'M SORRY!
NOOGIE NOOGIE NOOGIE NOOGIE
WAGL WAGL
WHAT I WAS TRYING TO SAY IS THAT YOU'VE DEVELOPED ENOUGH INTEREST IN ME AS AN INDIVIDUAL TO START ASKING THOSE QUESTIONS.
I KNOW YOU'VE BEEN CURIOUS ABOUT HUMANITY FOR AGES, BUT INTEREST IN INDIVIDUALS IS NEW, ISN'T IT?

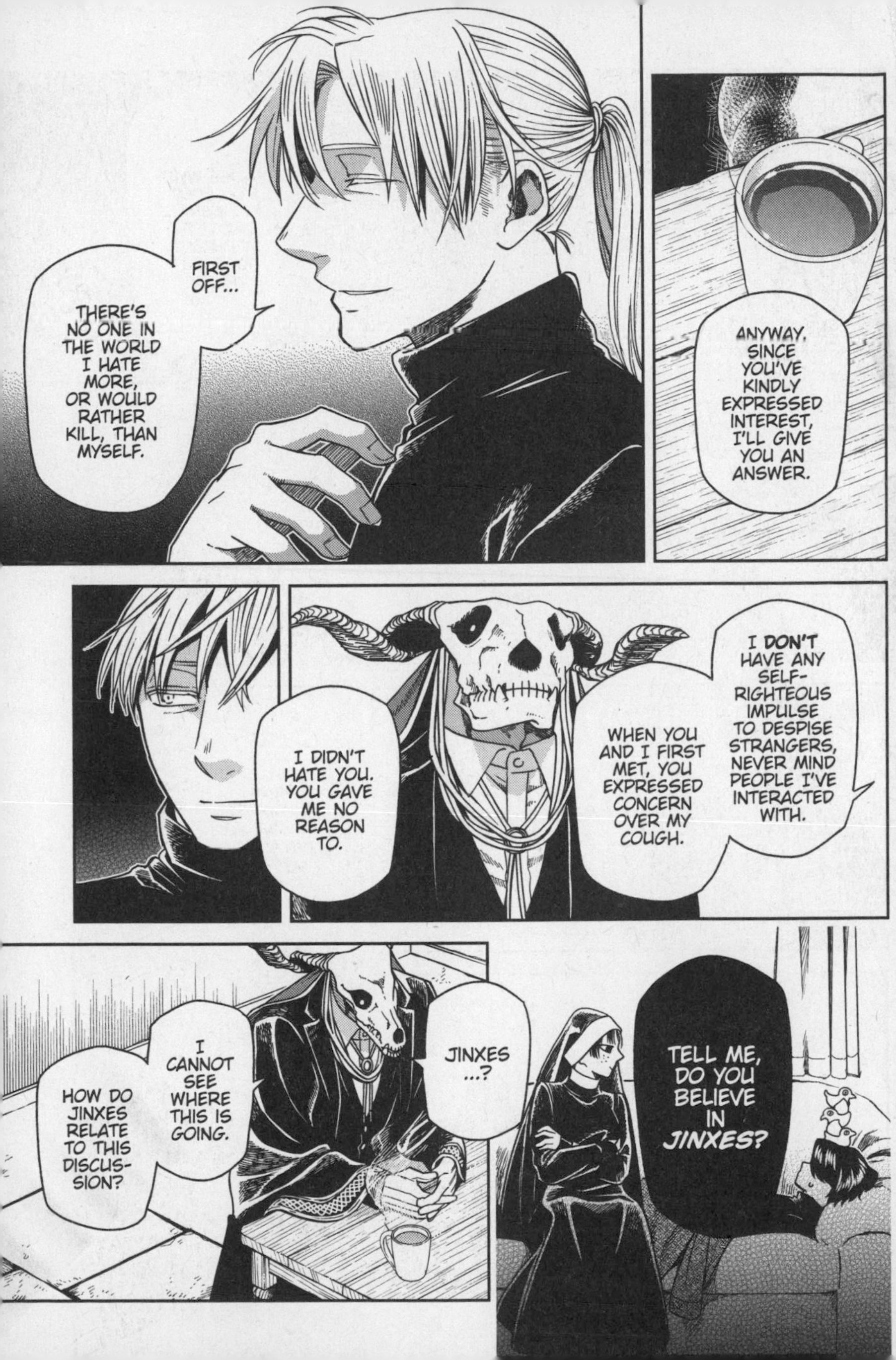
ANYWAY, SINCE YOU'VE KINDLY EXPRESSED INTEREST, I'LL GIVE YOU AN ANSWER.
FIRST OFF...
THERE'S NO ONE IN THE WORLD I HATE MORE, OR WOULD RATHER KILL, THAN MYSELF.
I **DON'T** HAVE ANY SELF-RIGHTEOUS IMPULSE TO DESPISE STRANGERS, NEVER MIND PEOPLE I'VE INTERACTED WITH.
WHEN YOU AND I FIRST MET, YOU EXPRESSED CONCERN OVER MY COUGH.
I DIDN'T HATE YOU. YOU GAVE ME NO REASON TO.
TELL ME, DO YOU BELIEVE IN *JINXES?*
JINXES ...?
I CANNOT SEE WHERE THIS IS GOING.
HOW DO JINXES RELATE TO THIS DISCUSSION?

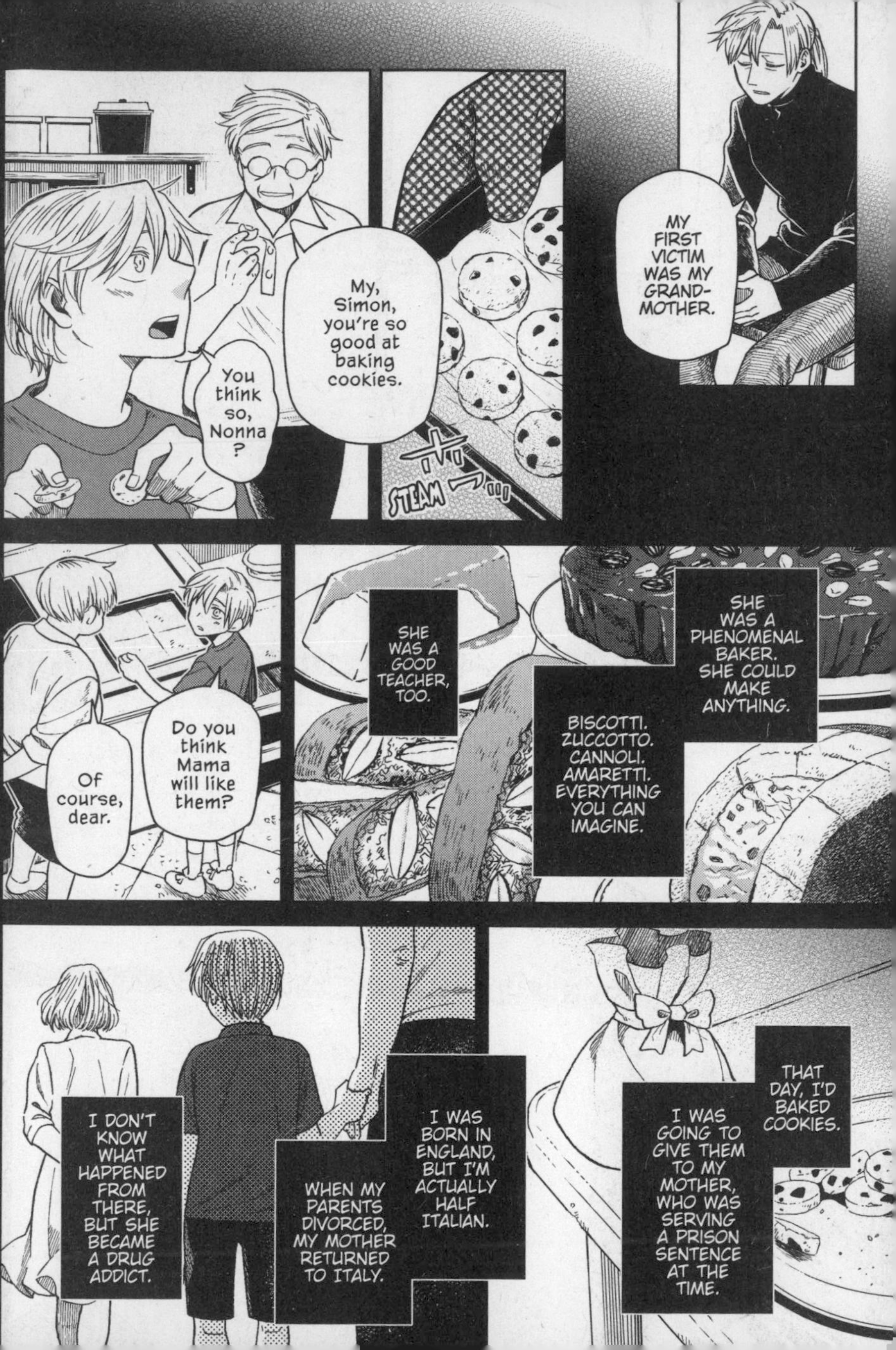
MY FIRST VICTIM WAS MY GRANDMOTHER.
STEAM
My, Simon, you're so good at baking cookies.
You think so, Nonna?
SHE WAS A PHENOMENAL BAKER. SHE COULD MAKE ANYTHING.
BISCOTTI. ZUCCOTTO. CANNOLI. AMARETTI. EVERYTHING YOU CAN IMAGINE.
SHE WAS A GOOD TEACHER, TOO.
Do you think Mama will like them?
Of course, dear.
THAT DAY, I'D BAKED COOKIES.
I WAS GOING TO GIVE THEM TO MY MOTHER, WHO WAS SERVING A PRISON SENTENCE AT THE TIME.
I WAS BORN IN ENGLAND, BUT I'M ACTUALLY HALF ITALIAN.
WHEN MY PARENTS DIVORCED, MY MOTHER RETURNED TO ITALY.
I DON'T KNOW WHAT HAPPENED FROM THERE, BUT SHE BECAME A DRUG ADDICT.

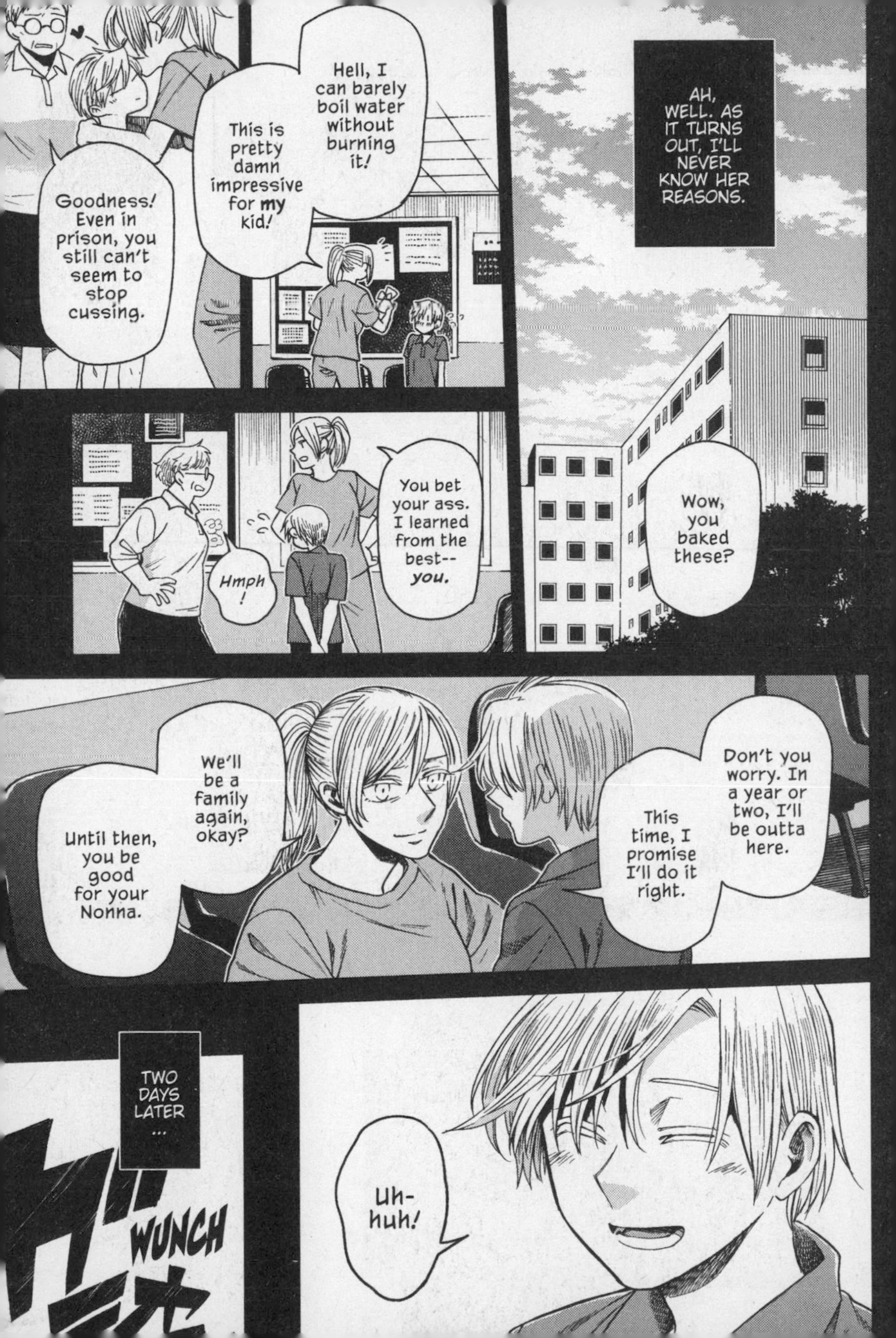
AH, WELL. AS IT TURNS OUT, I'LL NEVER KNOW HER REASONS.
Wow, you baked these?
Hell, I can barely boil water without burning it!
This is pretty damn impressive for my kid!
Goodness! Even in prison, you still can't seem to stop cussing.
You bet your ass. I learned from the best-- you.
Hmph!
Don't you worry. In a year or two, I'll be outta here.
This time, I promise I'll do it right.
We'll be a family again, okay?
Until then, you be good for your Nonna.
Uh-huh!
TWO DAYS LATER ...
WUNCH

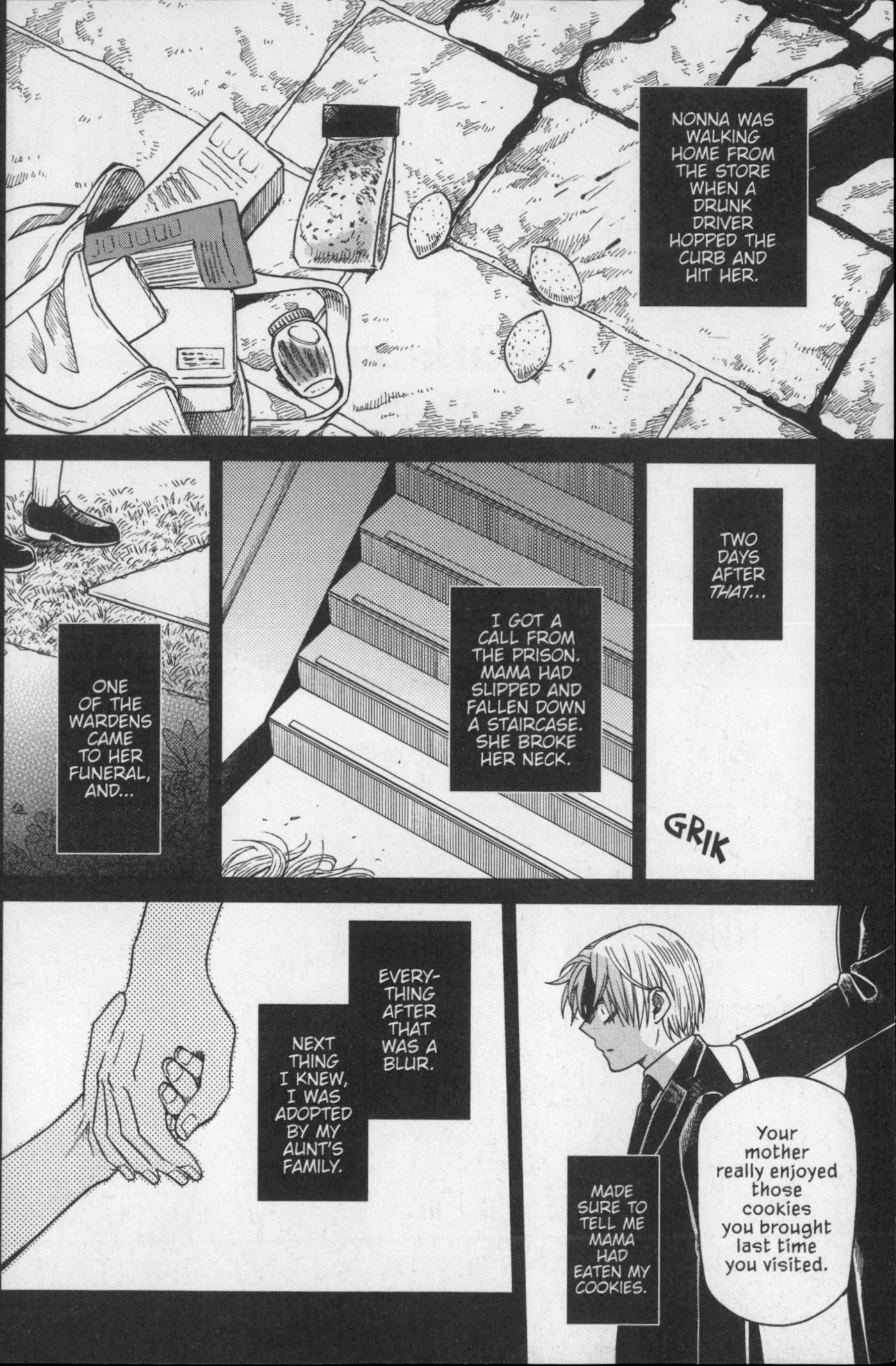
NONNA WAS WALKING HOME FROM THE STORE WHEN A DRUNK DRIVER HOPPED THE CURB AND HIT HER.
TWO DAYS AFTER *THAT*...
GRIK
I GOT A CALL FROM THE PRISON. MAMA HAD SLIPPED AND FALLEN DOWN A STAIRCASE. SHE BROKE HER NECK.
ONE OF THE WARDENS CAME TO HER FUNERAL, AND...
MADE SURE TO TELL ME MAMA HAD EATEN MY COOKIES.
Your mother really enjoyed those cookies you brought last time you visited.
EVERY-THING AFTER THAT WAS A BLUR.
NEXT THING I KNEW, I WAS ADOPTED BY MY AUNT'S FAMILY.

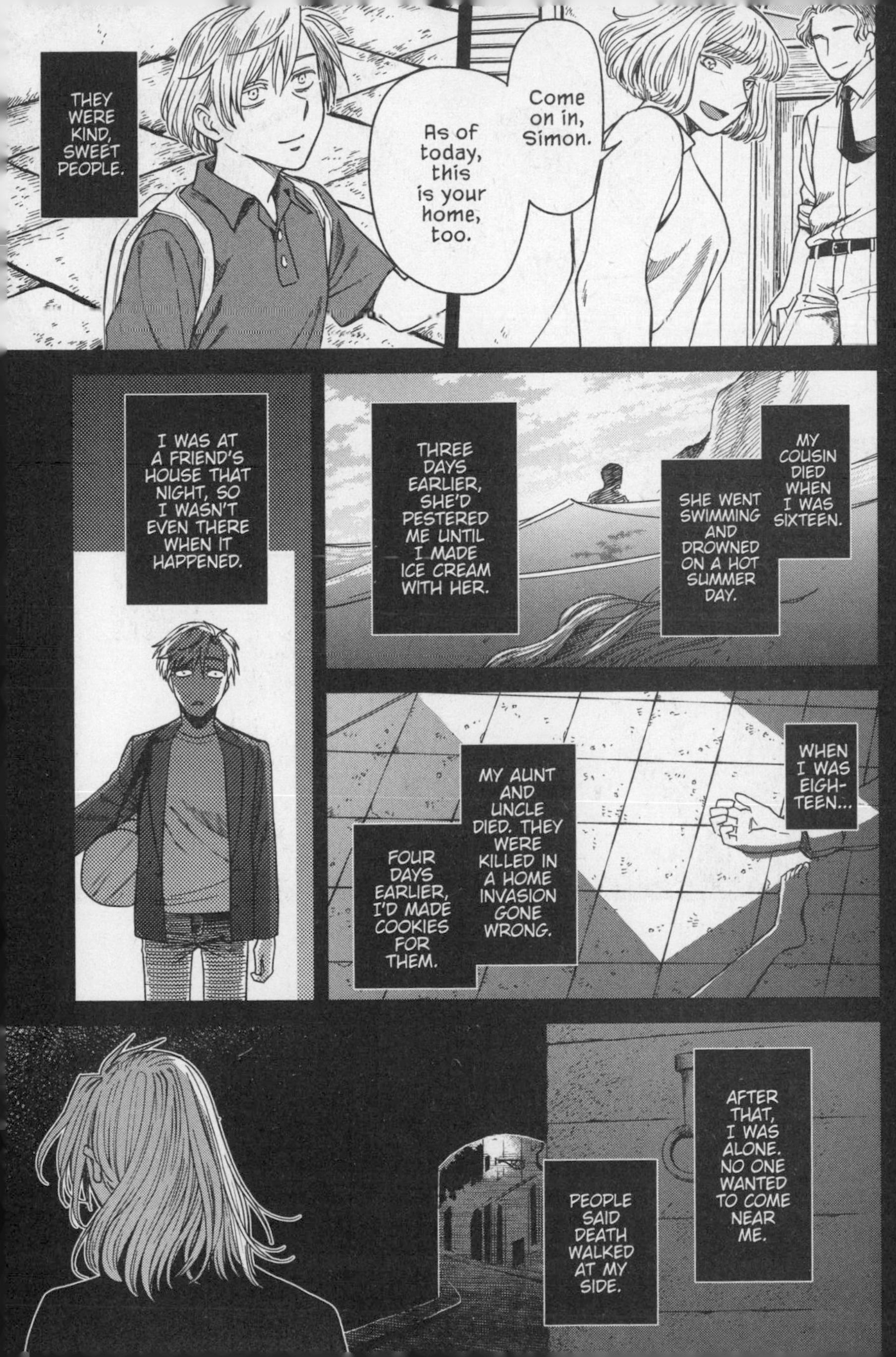
Come on in, Simon.
As of today, this is your home, too.
THEY WERE KIND, SWEET PEOPLE.
MY COUSIN DIED WHEN I WAS SIXTEEN.
SHE WENT SWIMMING AND DROWNED ON A HOT SUMMER DAY.
THREE DAYS EARLIER, SHE'D PESTERED ME UNTIL I MADE ICE CREAM WITH HER.
WHEN I WAS EIGH-TEEN...
MY AUNT AND UNCLE DIED. THEY WERE KILLED IN A HOME INVASION GONE WRONG.
FOUR DAYS EARLIER, I'D MADE COOKIES FOR THEM.
I WAS AT A FRIEND'S HOUSE THAT NIGHT, SO I WASN'T EVEN THERE WHEN IT HAPPENED.
AFTER THAT, I WAS ALONE. NO ONE WANTED TO COME NEAR ME.
PEOPLE SAID DEATH WALKED AT MY SIDE.

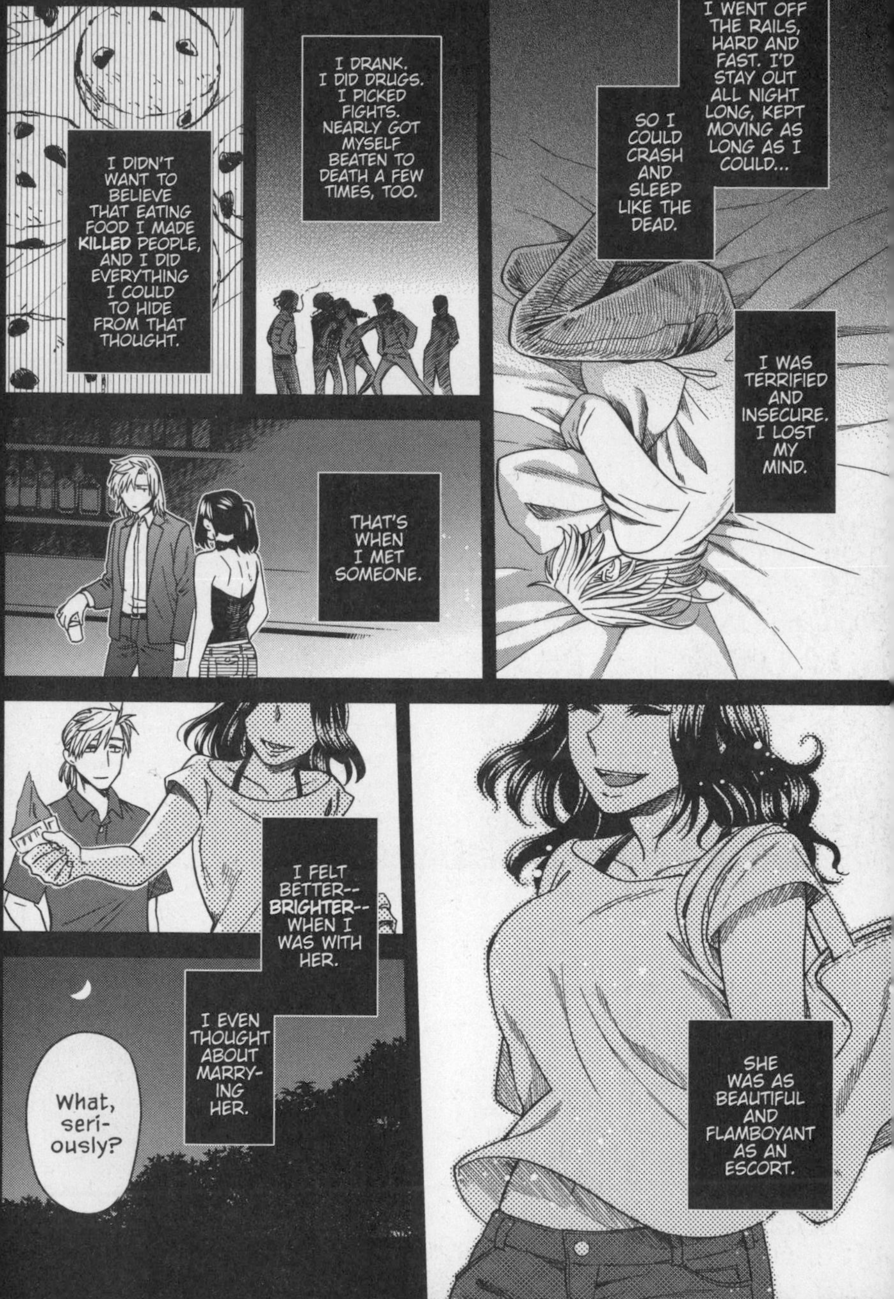
I WENT OFF THE RAILS, HARD AND FAST. I'D STAY OUT ALL NIGHT LONG, KEPT MOVING AS LONG AS I COULD...
SO I COULD CRASH AND SLEEP LIKE THE DEAD.
I WAS TERRIFIED AND INSECURE. I LOST MY MIND.
I DRANK. I DID DRUGS. I PICKED FIGHTS. NEARLY GOT MYSELF BEATEN TO DEATH A FEW TIMES, TOO.
I DIDN'T WANT TO BELIEVE THAT EATING FOOD I MADE **KILLED** PEOPLE, AND I DID EVERYTHING I COULD TO HIDE FROM THAT THOUGHT.
THAT'S WHEN I MET SOMEONE.
SHE WAS AS BEAUTIFUL AND FLAMBOYANT AS AN ESCORT.
I FELT BETTER-- **BRIGHTER**-- WHEN I WAS WITH HER.
I EVEN THOUGHT ABOUT MARRY-ING HER.
What, seri-ously?

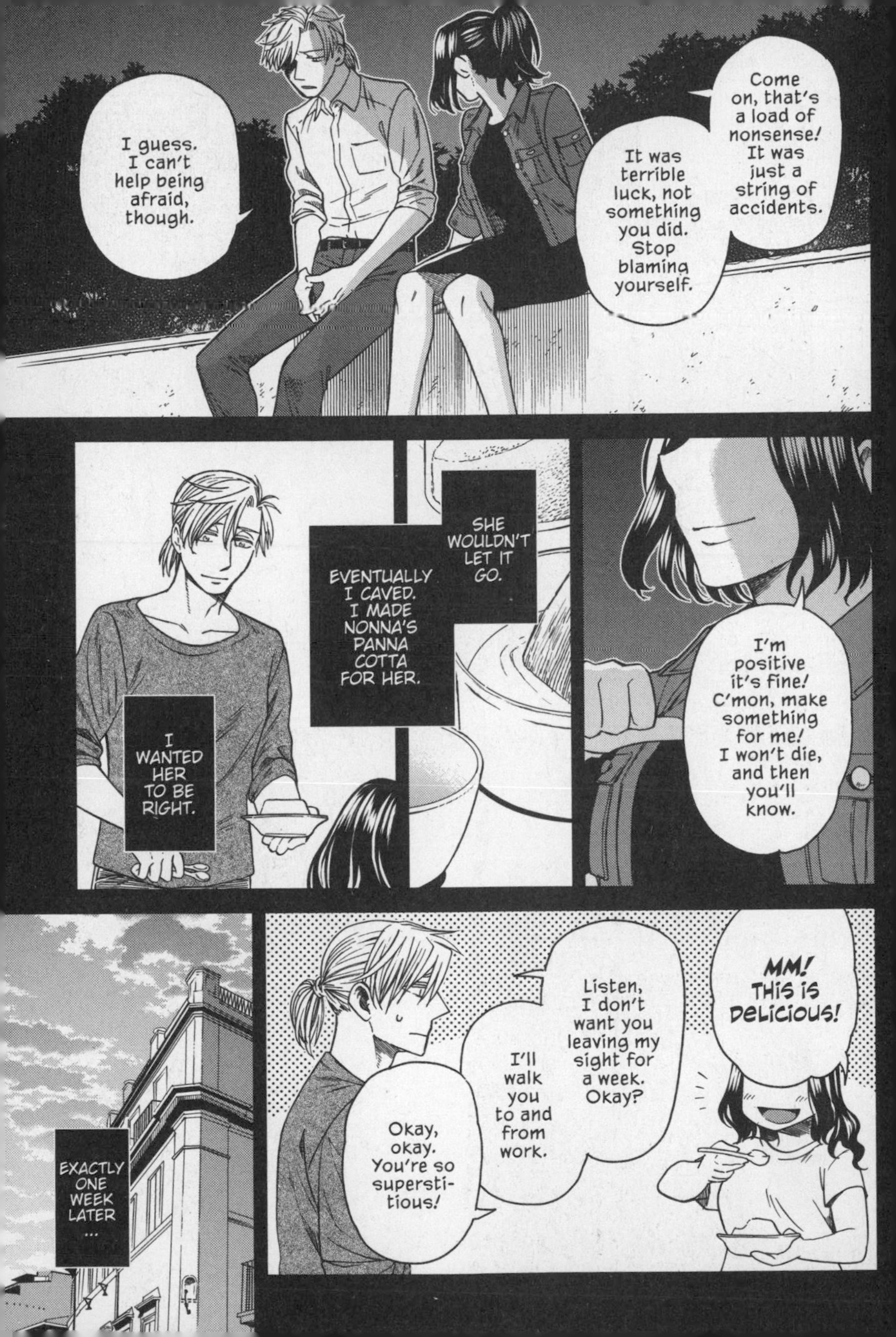
Come on, that's a load of nonsense! It was just a string of accidents.
It was terrible luck, not something you did. Stop blaming yourself.
I guess. I can't help being afraid, though.
I'm positive it's fine! C'mon, make something for me! I won't die, and then you'll know.
SHE WOULDN'T LET IT GO.
EVENTUALLY I CAVED. I MADE NONNA'S PANNA COTTA FOR HER.
I WANTED HER TO BE RIGHT.
MM! THIS IS DELICIOUS!
Listen, I don't want you leaving my sight for a week. Okay?
I'll walk you to and from work.
Okay, okay. You're so supersti-tious!
EXACTLY ONE WEEK LATER ...

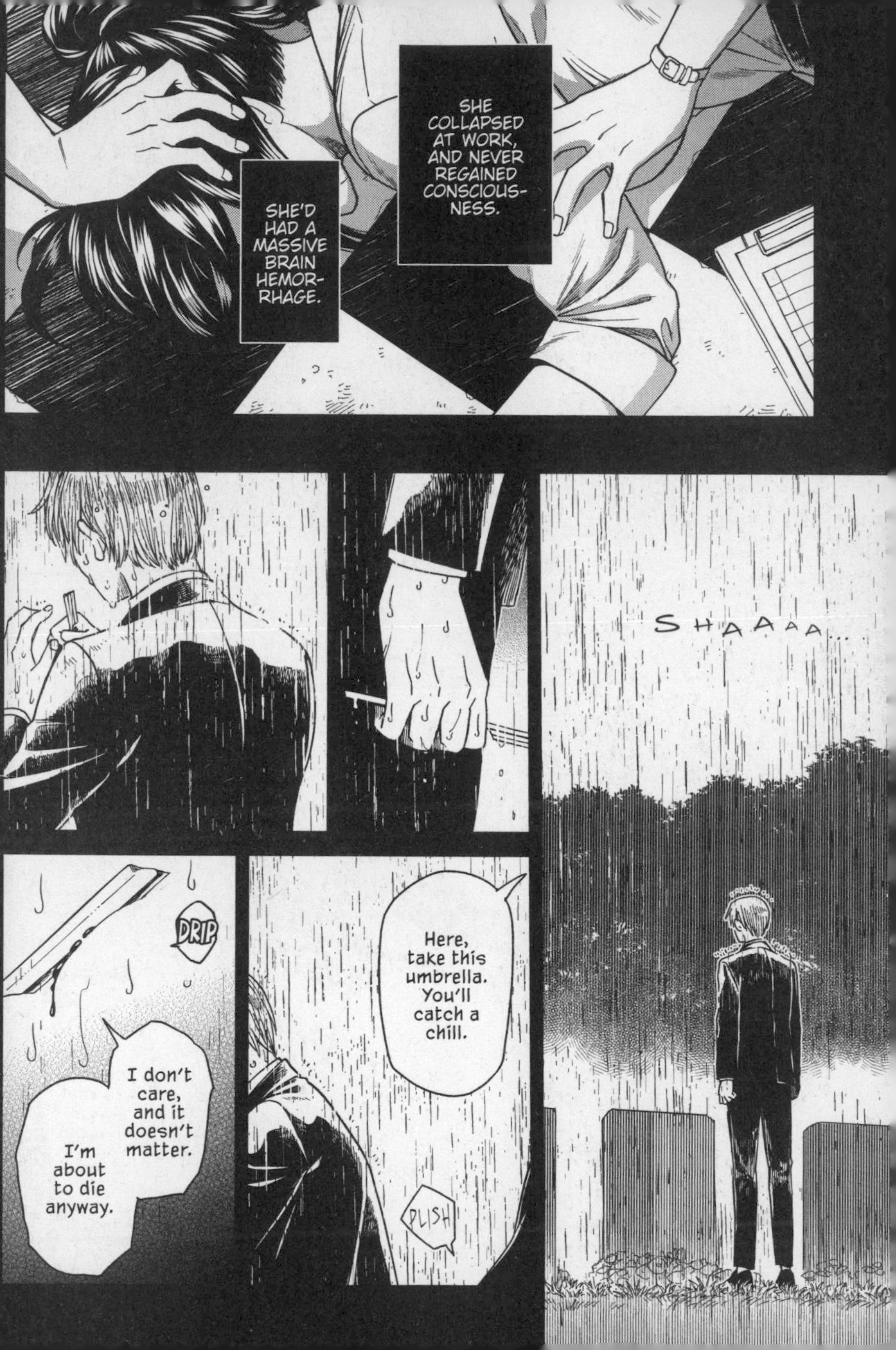
SHE COLLAPSED AT WORK, AND NEVER REGAINED CONSCIOUS-NESS.
SHE'D HAD A MASSIVE BRAIN HEMOR-RHAGE.
SHAAAA...
Here, take this umbrella. You'll catch a chill.
PLISH
DRIP
I don't care, and it doesn't matter.
I'm about to die anyway.

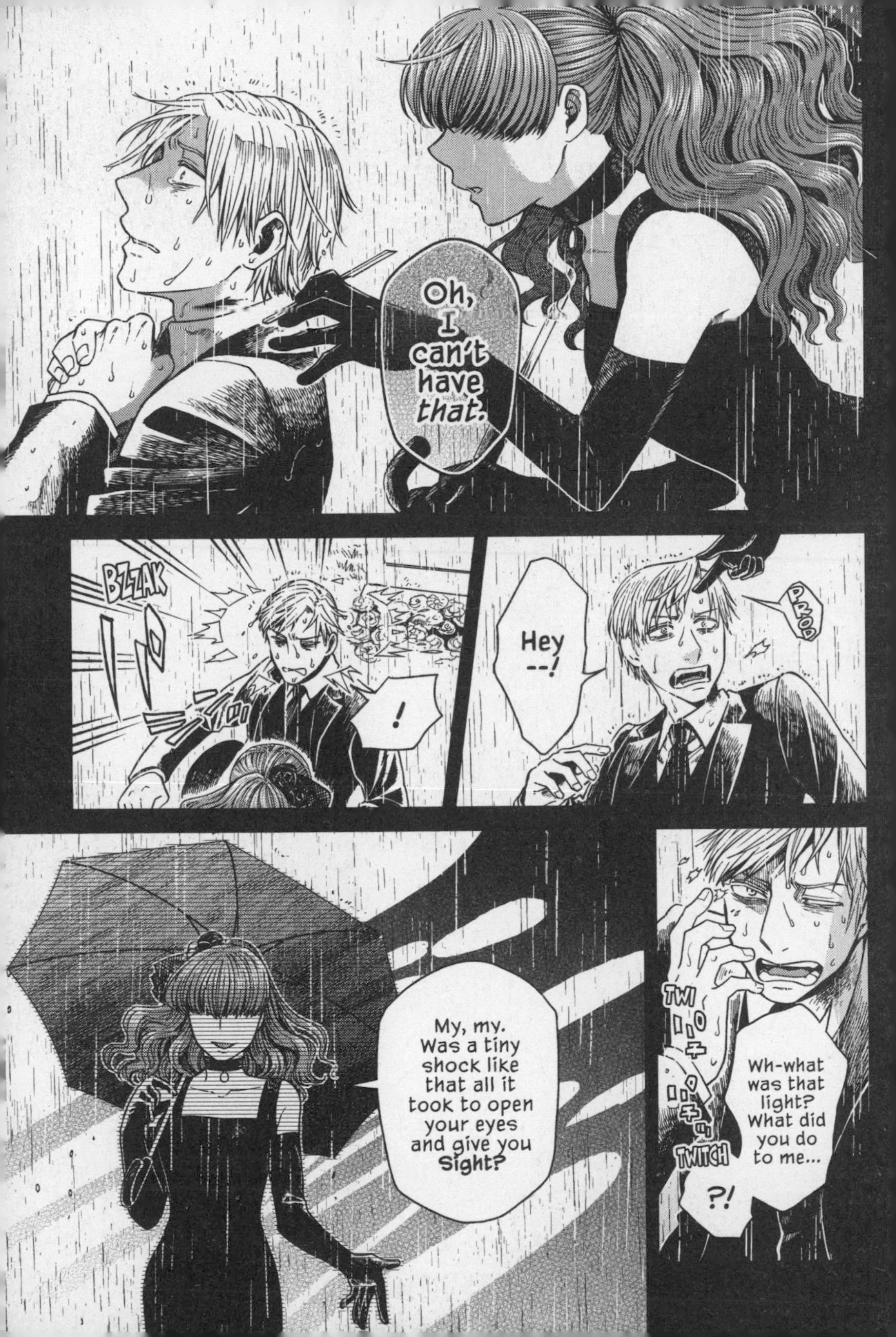
Oh, I can't have that.
PROD
Hey --!
BZZAK
!
TWI
TWITCH
Wh-what was that light? What did you do to me...
?!
My, my. Was a tiny shock like that all it took to open your eyes and give you Sight?

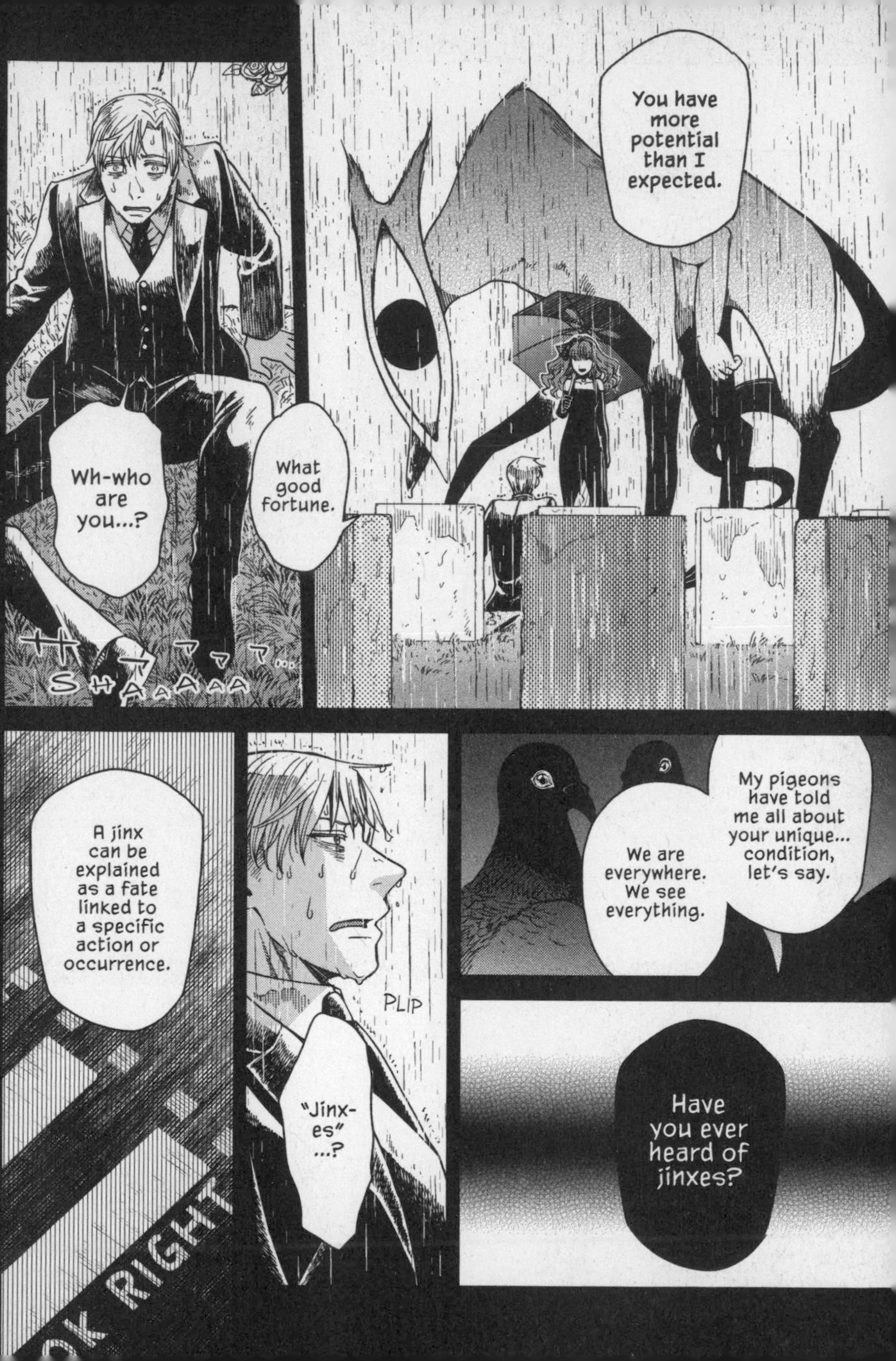

You have more potential than I expected.
What good fortune.
Wh-who are you...?
SHAAAAA
My pigeons have told me all about your unique... condition, let's say.
We are everywhere. We see everything.
Have you ever heard of jinxes?
PLIP
"Jinx-es" ...?
A jinx can be explained as a fate linked to a specific action or occurrence.

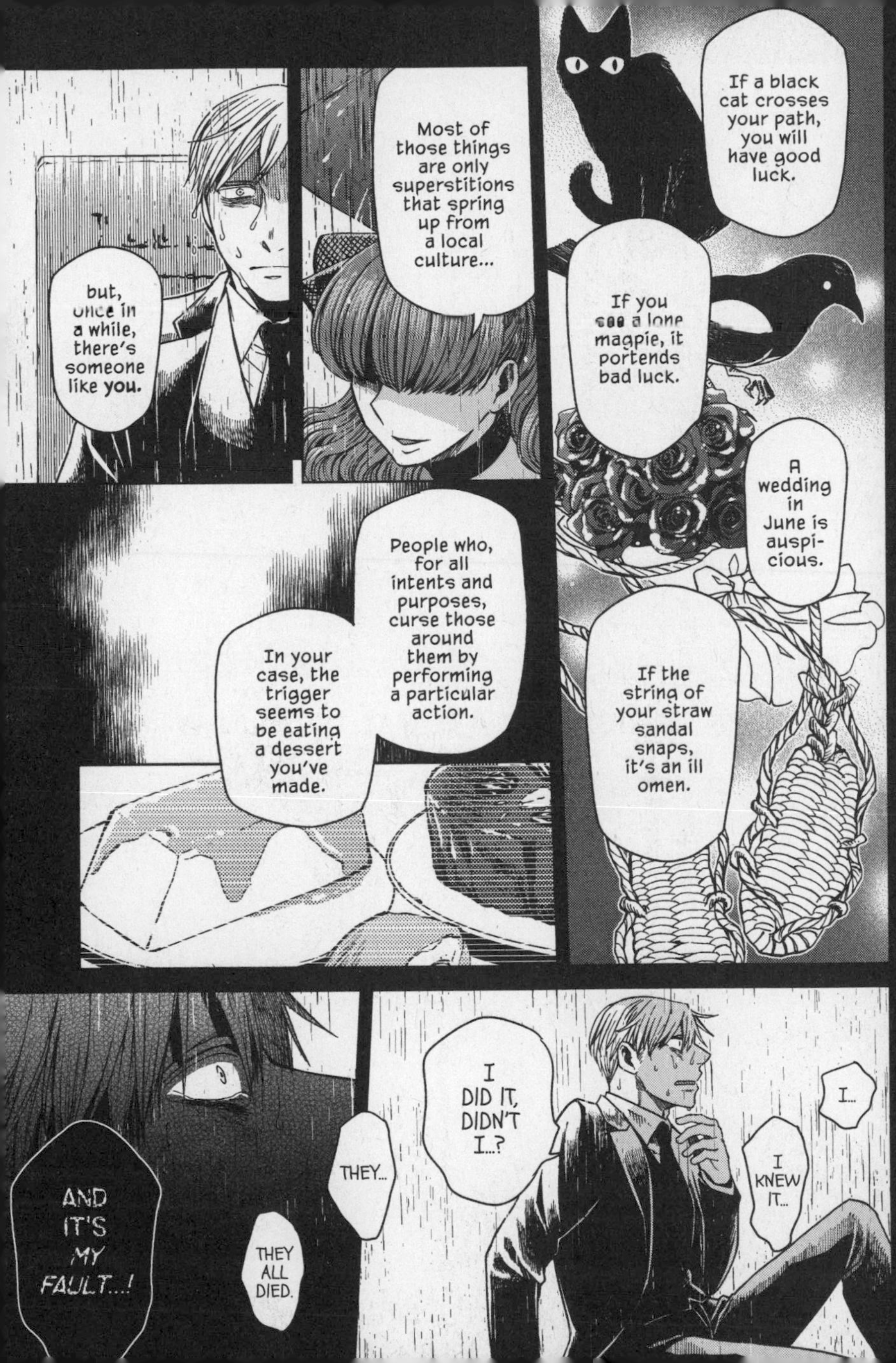

If a black cat crosses your path, you will have good luck.
If you see a lone magpie, it portends bad luck.
A wedding in June is auspicious.
If the string of your straw sandal snaps, it's an ill omen.
Most of those things are only superstitions that spring up from a local culture...
but, once in a while, there's someone like you.
People who, for all intents and purposes, curse those around them by performing a particular action.
In your case, the trigger seems to be eating a dessert you've made.
I...
I KNEW IT...
I DID IT, DIDN'T I...?
THEY...
THEY ALL DIED.
AND IT'S MY FAULT...!

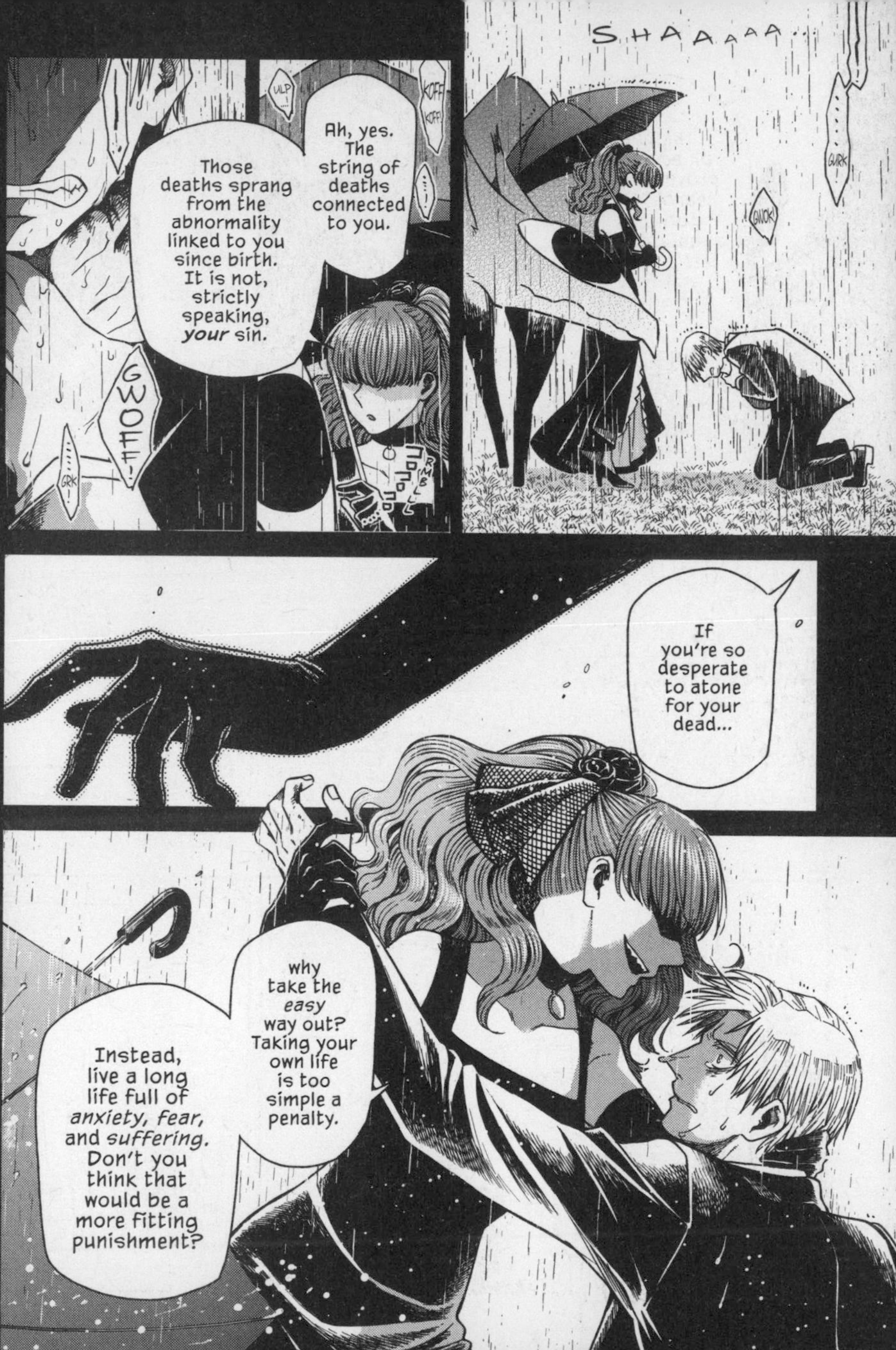

SHAAAAA...
GURK
GWOK!
ULP
KOFF KOFF
Ah, yes. The string of deaths connected to you.
Those deaths sprang from the abnormality linked to you since birth. It is not, strictly speaking, *your* sin.
RMBL
GWOFF!
GRK
If you're so desperate to atone for your dead...
why take the *easy* way out? Taking your own life is too simple a penalty.
Instead, live a long life full of *anxiety, fear,* and *suffering.* Don't you think that would be a more fitting punishment?

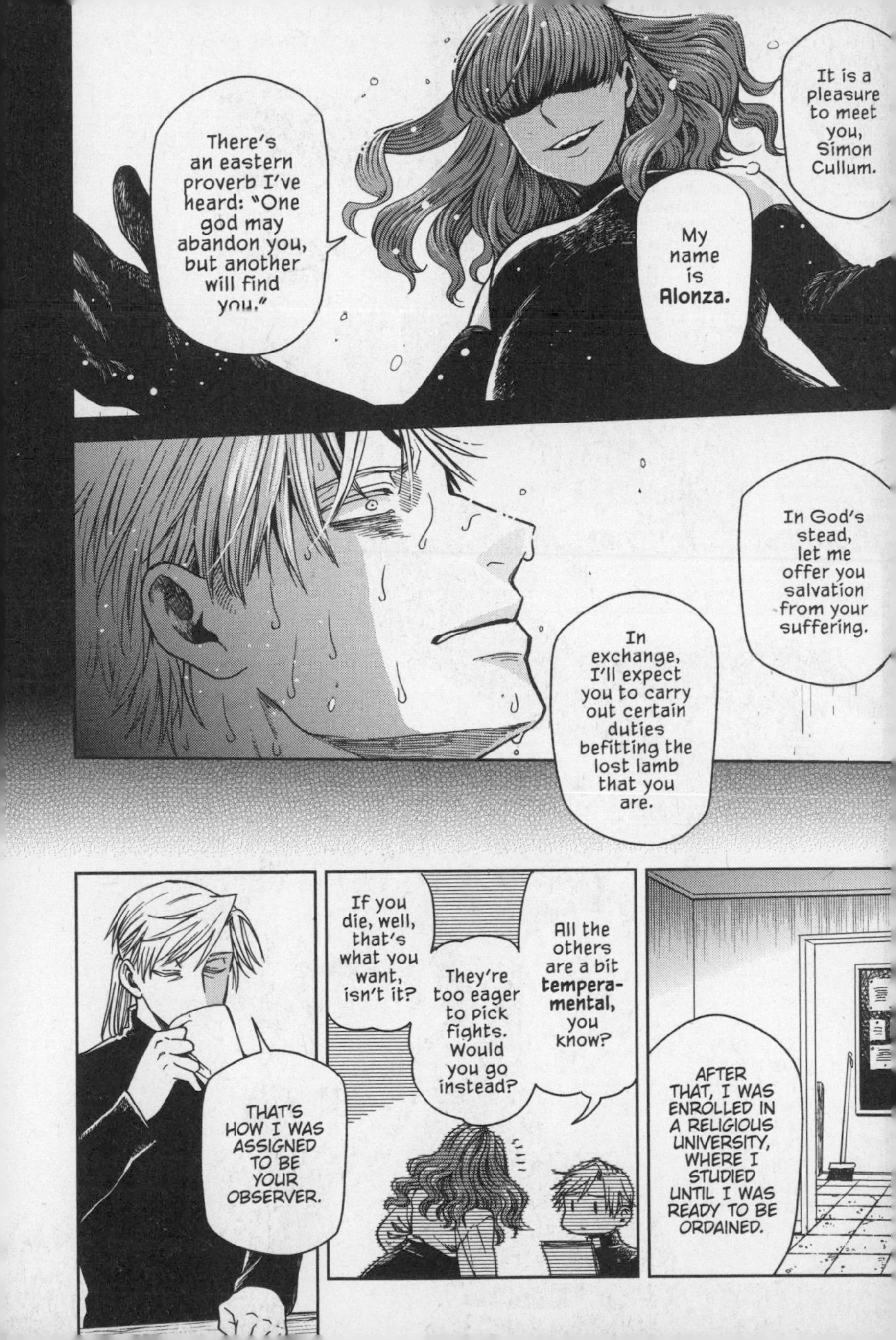
It is a pleasure to meet you, Simon Cullum.
My name is Alonza.
There's an eastern proverb I've heard: "One god may abandon you, but another will find you."
In God's stead, let me offer you salvation from your suffering.
In exchange, I'll expect you to carry out certain duties befitting the lost lamb that you are.
AFTER THAT, I WAS ENROLLED IN A RELIGIOUS UNIVERSITY, WHERE I STUDIED UNTIL I WAS READY TO BE ORDAINED.
All the others are a bit temperamental, you know?
They're too eager to pick fights. Would you go instead?
If you die, well, that's what you want, isn't it?
THAT'S HOW I WAS ASSIGNED TO BE YOUR OBSERVER.

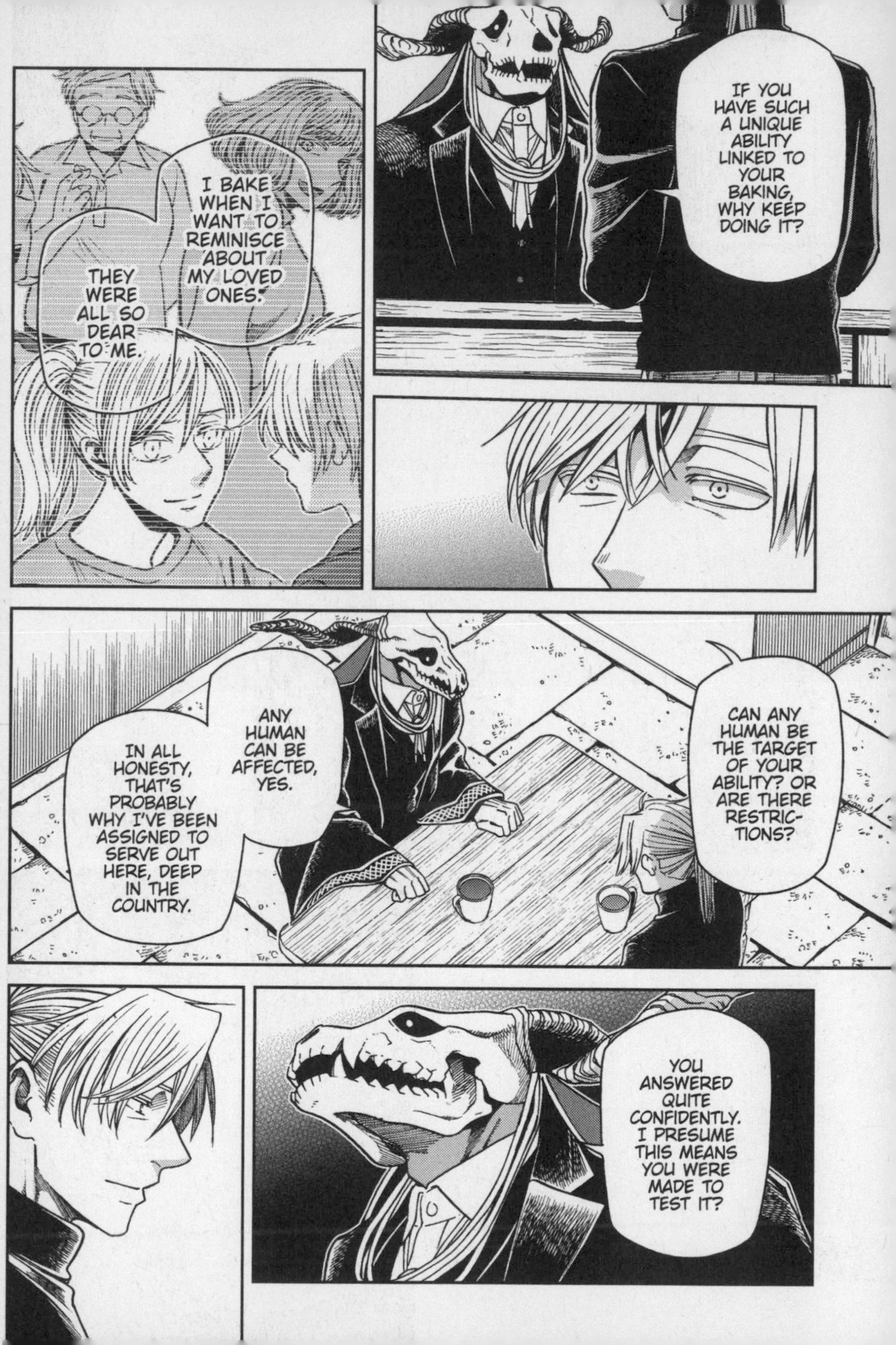
IF YOU HAVE SUCH A UNIQUE ABILITY LINKED TO YOUR BAKING, WHY KEEP DOING IT?
I BAKE WHEN I WANT TO REMINISCE ABOUT MY LOVED ONES.
THEY WERE ALL SO DEAR TO ME.
CAN ANY HUMAN BE THE TARGET OF YOUR ABILITY? OR ARE THERE RESTRIC-TIONS?
ANY HUMAN CAN BE AFFECTED, YES.
IN ALL HONESTY, THAT'S PROBABLY WHY I'VE BEEN ASSIGNED TO SERVE OUT HERE, DEEP IN THE COUNTRY.
YOU ANSWERED QUITE CONFIDENTLY. I PRESUME THIS MEANS YOU WERE MADE TO TEST IT?

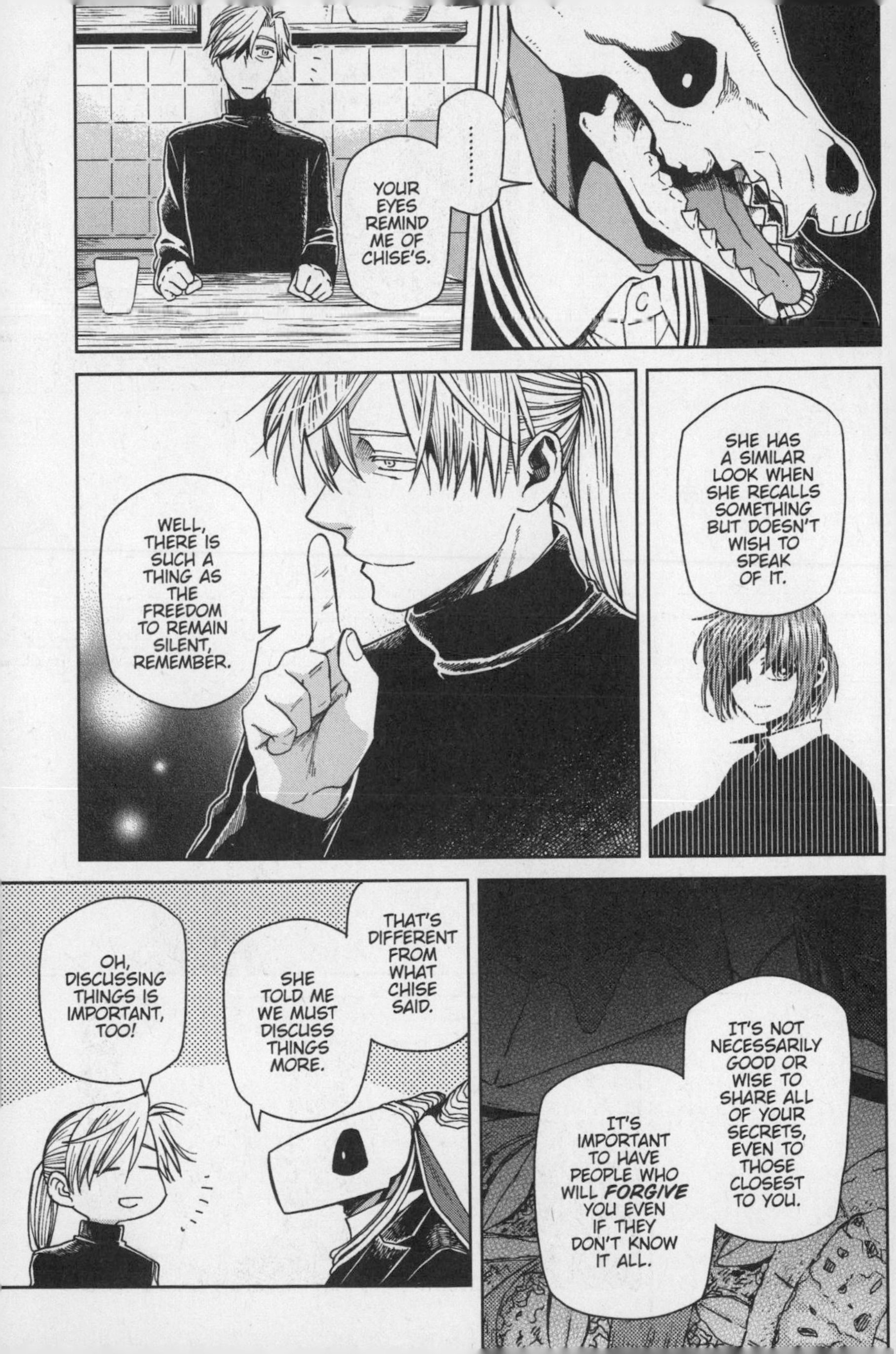
......
YOUR EYES REMIND ME OF CHISE'S.
SHE HAS A SIMILAR LOOK WHEN SHE RECALLS SOMETHING BUT DOESN'T WISH TO SPEAK OF IT.
WELL, THERE IS SUCH A THING AS THE FREEDOM TO REMAIN SILENT, REMEMBER.
IT'S NOT NECESSARILY GOOD OR WISE TO SHARE ALL OF YOUR SECRETS, EVEN TO THOSE CLOSEST TO YOU.
IT'S IMPORTANT TO HAVE PEOPLE WHO WILL *FORGIVE* YOU EVEN IF THEY DON'T KNOW IT ALL.
THAT'S DIFFERENT FROM WHAT CHISE SAID.
SHE TOLD ME WE MUST DISCUSS THINGS MORE.
OH, DISCUSSING THINGS IS IMPORTANT, TOO!

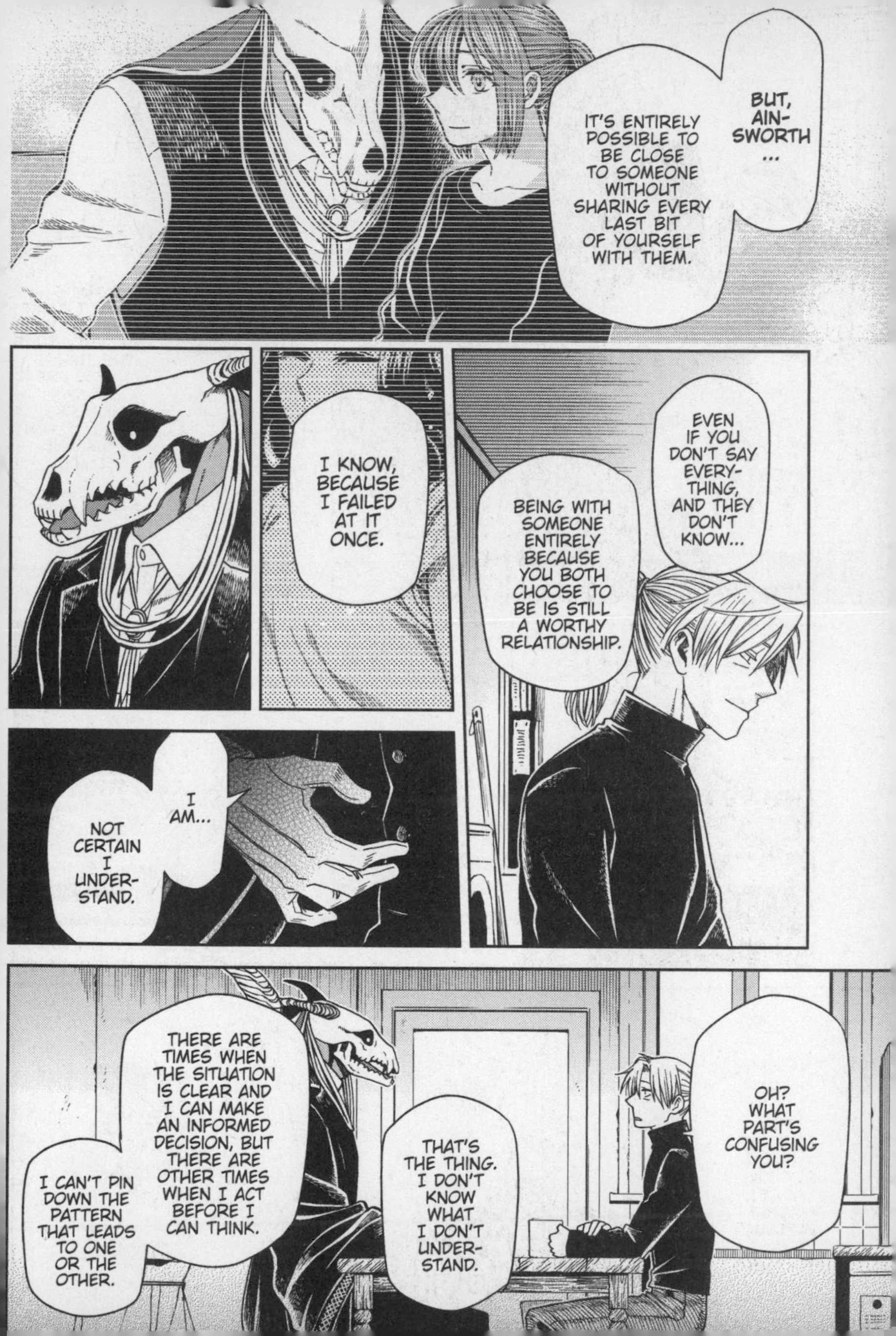
BUT, AINSWORTH...
IT'S ENTIRELY POSSIBLE TO BE CLOSE TO SOMEONE WITHOUT SHARING EVERY LAST BIT OF YOURSELF WITH THEM.
EVEN IF YOU DON'T SAY EVERYTHING, AND THEY DON'T KNOW...
BEING WITH SOMEONE ENTIRELY BECAUSE YOU BOTH CHOOSE TO BE IS STILL A WORTHY RELATIONSHIP.
I KNOW, BECAUSE I FAILED AT IT ONCE.
I AM...
NOT CERTAIN I UNDERSTAND.
OH? WHAT PART'S CONFUSING YOU?
THAT'S THE THING. I DON'T KNOW WHAT I DON'T UNDERSTAND.
THERE ARE TIMES WHEN THE SITUATION IS CLEAR AND I CAN MAKE AN INFORMED DECISION, BUT THERE ARE OTHER TIMES WHEN I ACT BEFORE I CAN THINK.
I CAN'T PIN DOWN THE PATTERN THAT LEADS TO ONE OR THE OTHER.

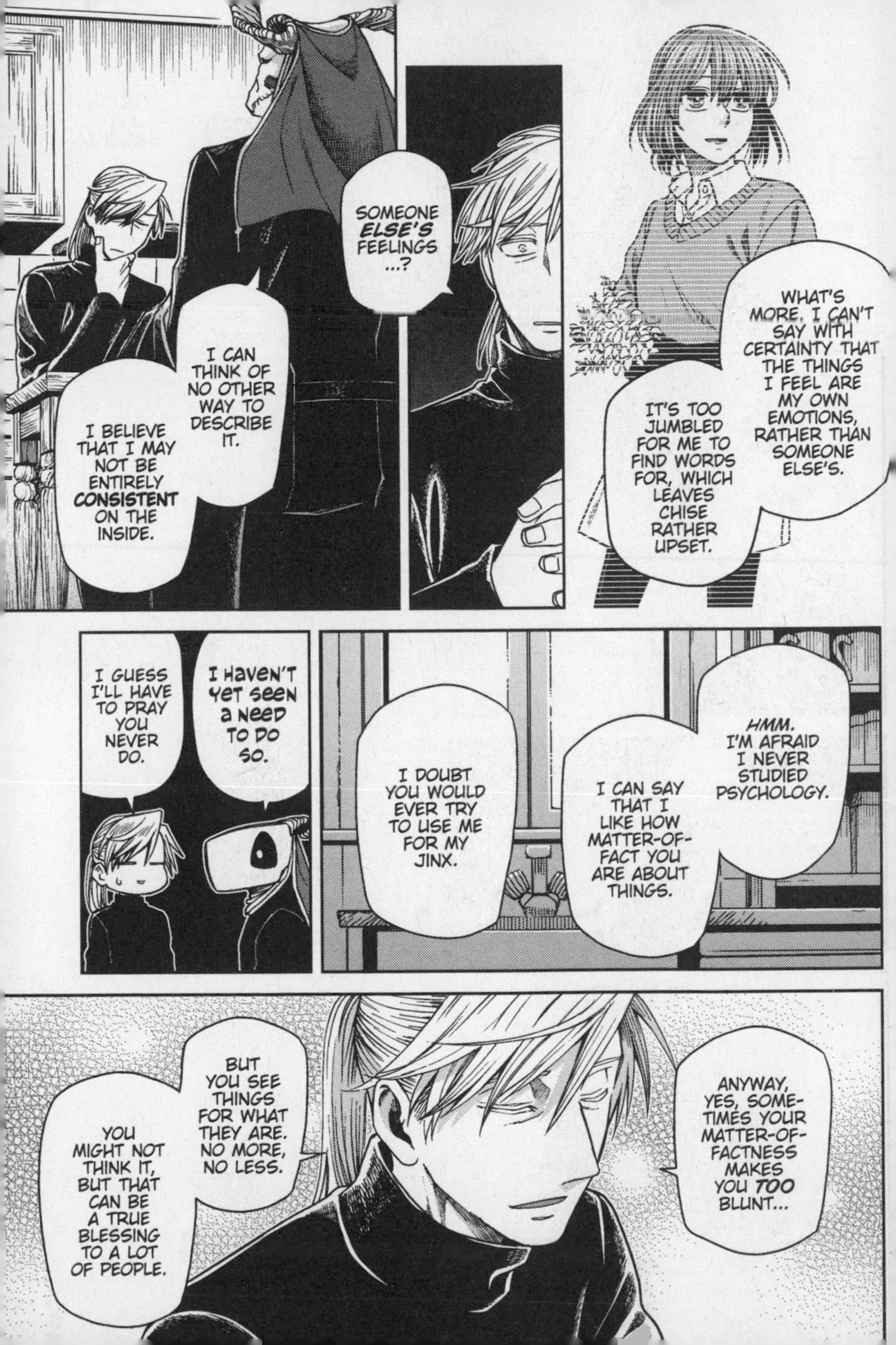
WHAT'S MORE, I CAN'T SAY WITH CERTAINTY THAT THE THINGS I FEEL ARE MY OWN EMOTIONS, RATHER THAN SOMEONE ELSE'S.
IT'S TOO JUMBLED FOR ME TO FIND WORDS FOR, WHICH LEAVES CHISE RATHER UPSET.
SOMEONE *ELSE'S* FEELINGS ...?
I CAN THINK OF NO OTHER WAY TO DESCRIBE IT.
I BELIEVE THAT I MAY NOT BE ENTIRELY **CONSISTENT** ON THE INSIDE.
HMM. I'M AFRAID I NEVER STUDIED PSYCHOLOGY.
I CAN SAY THAT I LIKE HOW MATTER-OF-FACT YOU ARE ABOUT THINGS.
I DOUBT YOU WOULD EVER TRY TO USE ME FOR MY JINX.
I HAVEN'T YET SEEN A NEED TO DO SO.
I GUESS I'LL HAVE TO PRAY YOU NEVER DO.
ANYWAY, YES, SOME-TIMES YOUR MATTER-OF-FACTNESS MAKES YOU *TOO* BLUNT...
BUT YOU SEE THINGS FOR WHAT THEY ARE. NO MORE, NO LESS.
YOU MIGHT NOT THINK IT, BUT THAT CAN BE A TRUE BLESSING TO A LOT OF PEOPLE.

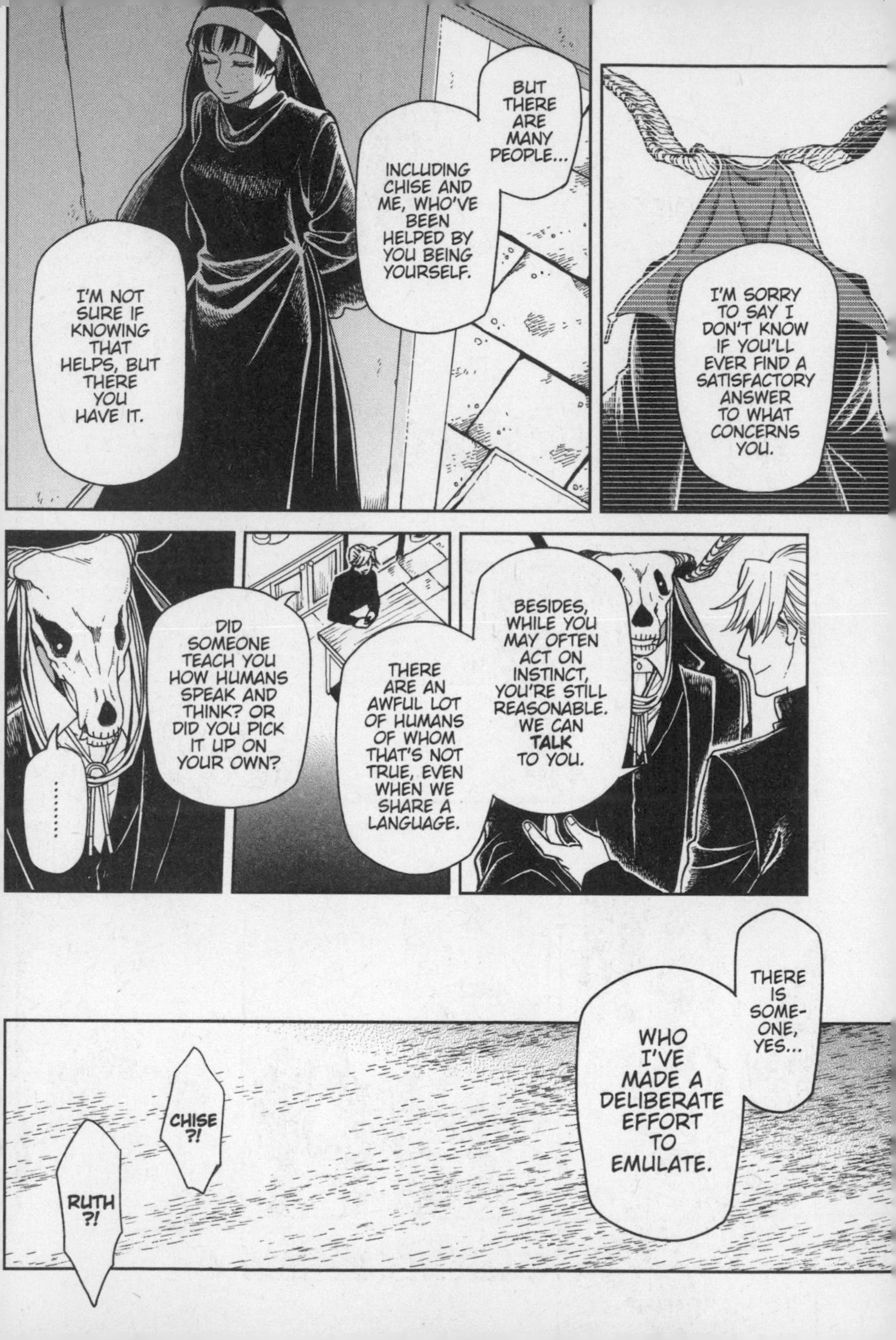
I'M SORRY TO SAY I DON'T KNOW IF YOU'LL EVER FIND A SATISFACTORY ANSWER TO WHAT CONCERNS YOU.
BUT THERE ARE MANY PEOPLE...
INCLUDING CHISE AND ME, WHO'VE BEEN HELPED BY YOU BEING YOURSELF.
I'M NOT SURE IF KNOWING THAT HELPS, BUT THERE YOU HAVE IT.
BESIDES, WHILE YOU MAY OFTEN ACT ON INSTINCT, YOU'RE STILL REASONABLE. WE CAN **TALK** TO YOU.
THERE ARE AN AWFUL LOT OF HUMANS OF WHOM THAT'S NOT TRUE, EVEN WHEN WE SHARE A LANGUAGE.
DID SOMEONE TEACH YOU HOW HUMANS SPEAK AND THINK? OR DID YOU PICK IT UP ON YOUR OWN?
......
THERE IS SOME-ONE, YES...
WHO I'VE MADE A DELIBERATE EFFORT TO EMULATE.
CHISE ?!
RUTH ?!

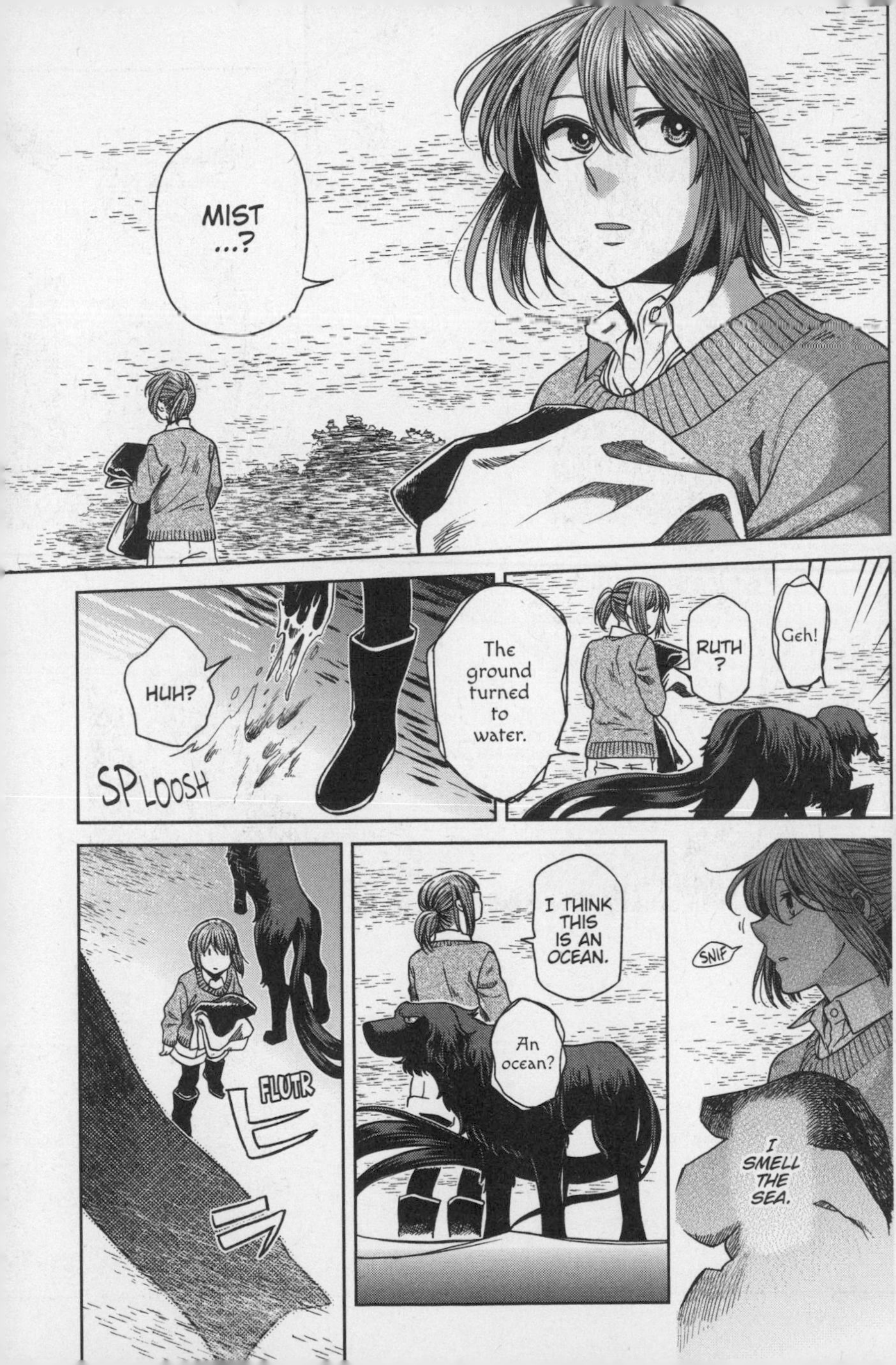
MIST ...?
Geh!
RUTH ?
The ground turned to water.
HUH?
SPLOOSH
SNIF
I SMELL THE SEA.
I THINK THIS IS AN OCEAN.
An ocean?
FLUTR

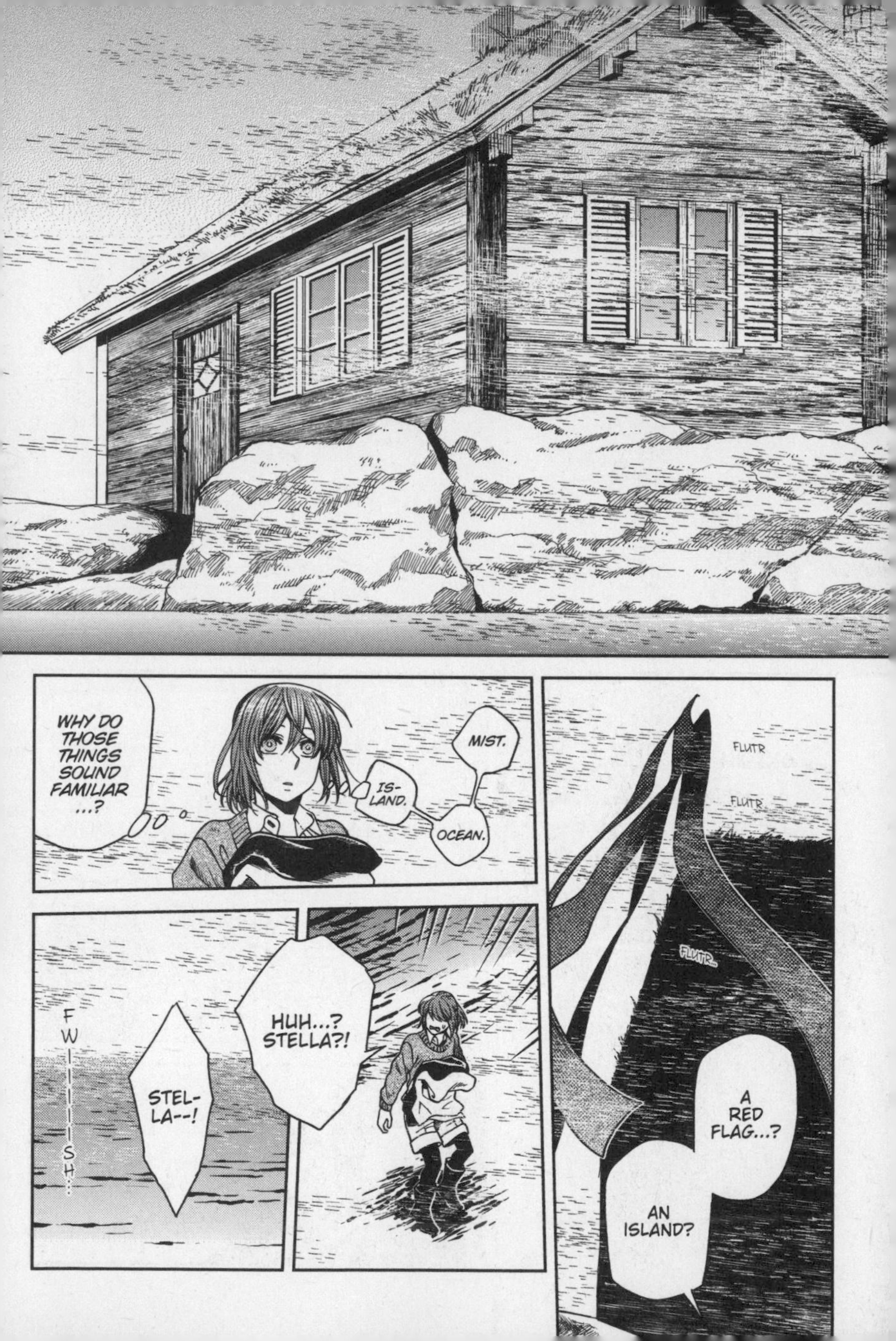
FLUTR
FLUTR
FLUTR...
A RED FLAG...?
AN ISLAND?
MIST.
IS-LAND.
OCEAN.
WHY DO THOSE THINGS SOUND FAMILIAR ...?
HUH...? STELLA?!
STEL-LA--!
FWIIIISH...

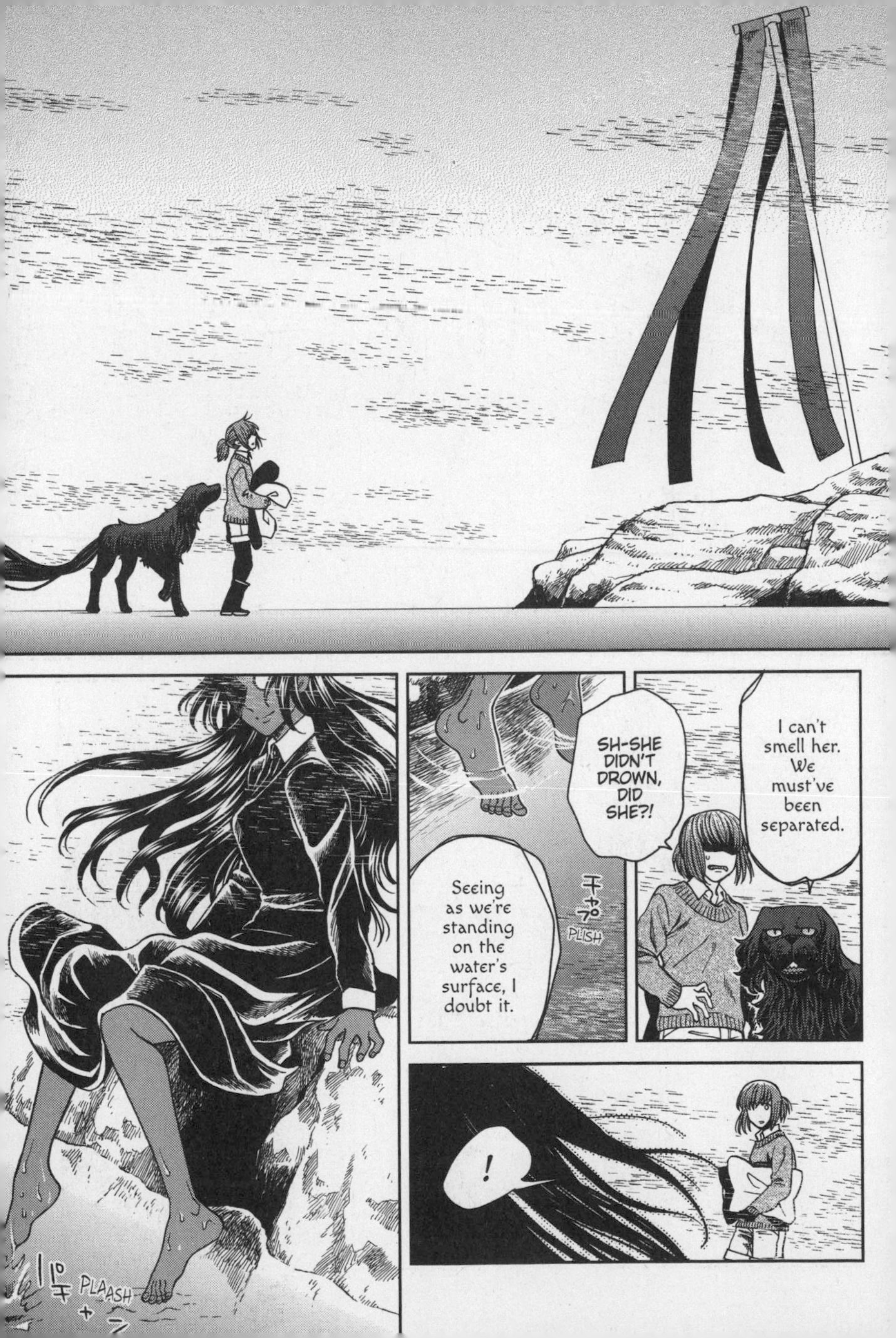

I can't smell her. We must've been separated.
SH-SHE DIDN'T DROWN, DID SHE?!
Seeing as we're standing on the water's surface, I doubt it.
PLISH
!
PLAASH

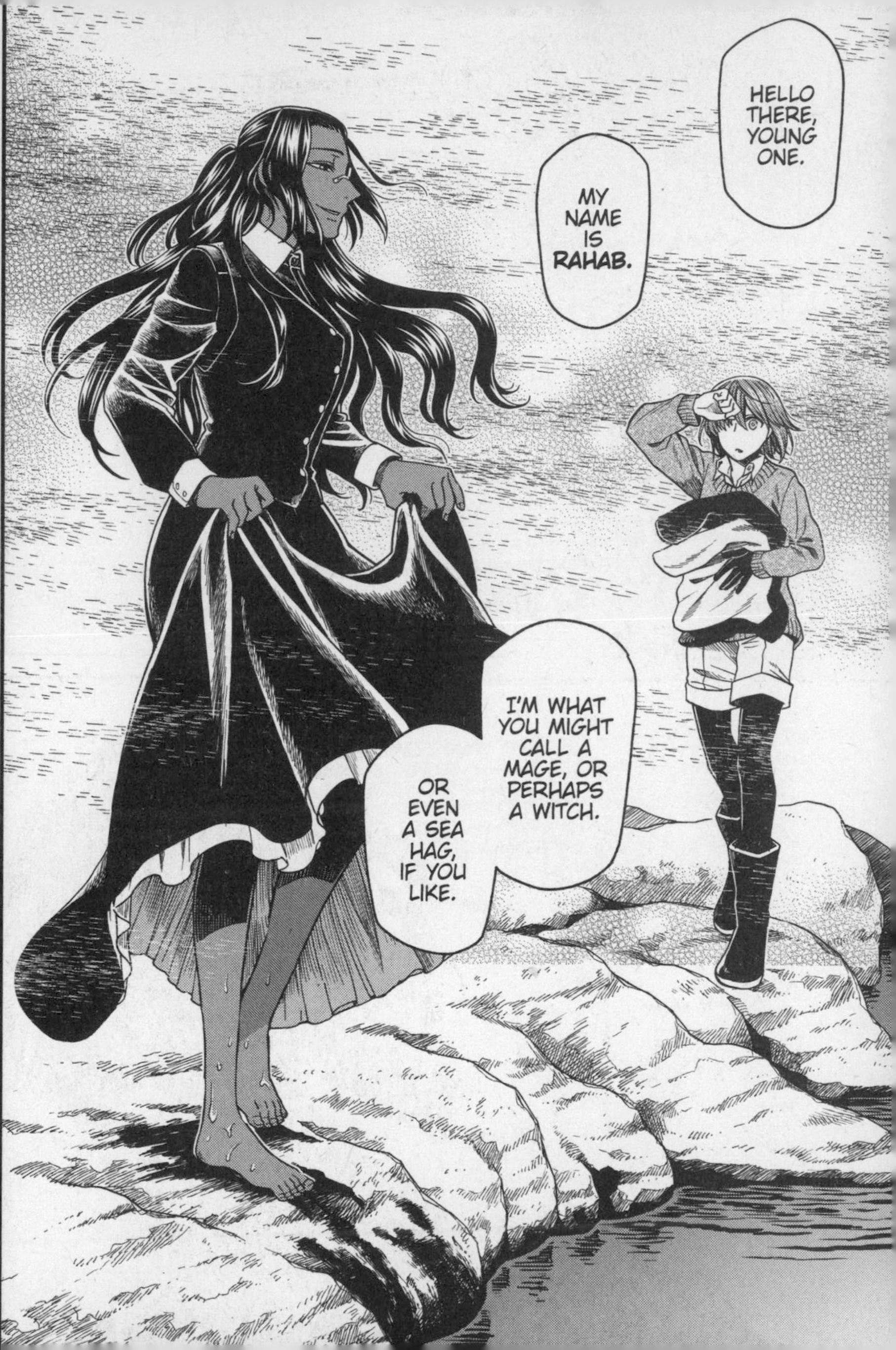
HELLO THERE, YOUNG ONE.
MY NAME IS RAHAB.
I'M WHAT YOU MIGHT CALL A MAGE, OR PERHAPS A WITCH.
OR EVEN A SEA HAG, IF YOU LIKE.

Chapter 52: The cowl does not make the monk: III

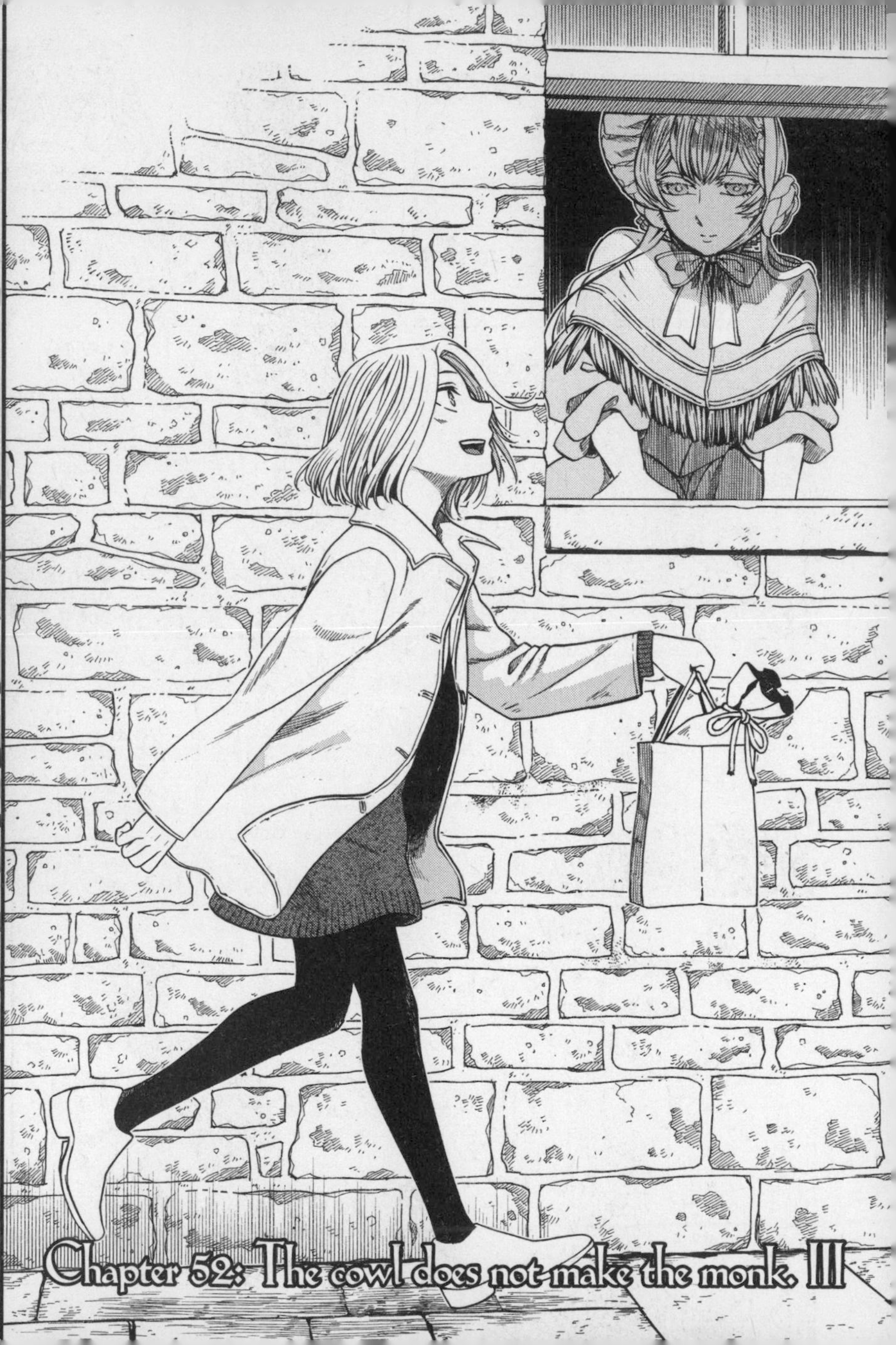
Chapter 52: The cowl does not make the monk. III

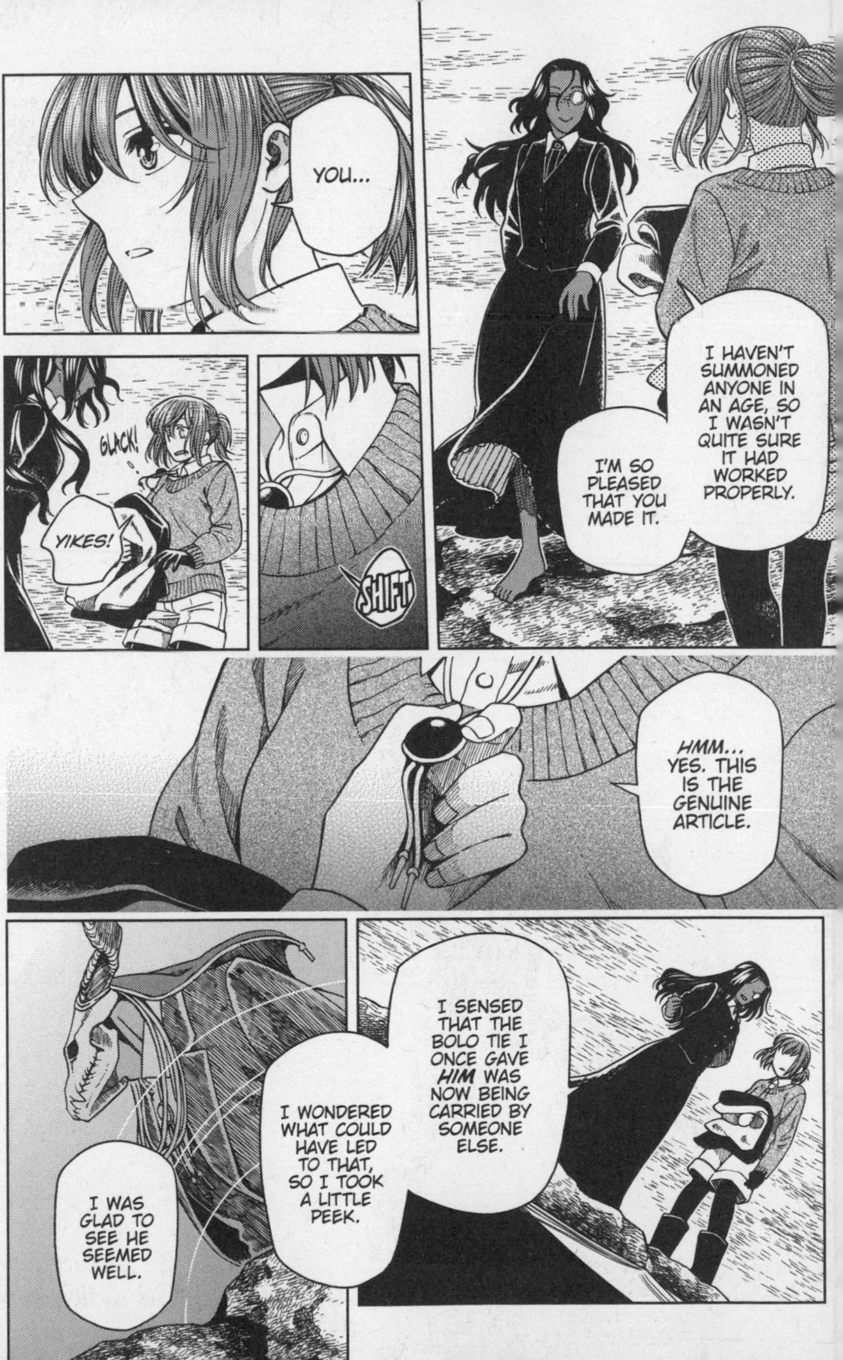
I HAVEN'T SUMMONED ANYONE IN AN AGE, SO I WASN'T QUITE SURE IT HAD WORKED PROPERLY.
I'M SO PLEASED THAT YOU MADE IT.
YOU...
SHIFT
GLACK!
YIKES!
HMM... YES. THIS IS THE GENUINE ARTICLE.
I SENSED THAT THE BOLO TIE I ONCE GAVE ***HIM*** WAS NOW BEING CARRIED BY SOMEONE ELSE.
I WONDERED WHAT COULD HAVE LED TO THAT, SO I TOOK A LITTLE PEEK.
I WAS GLAD TO SEE HE SEEMED WELL.

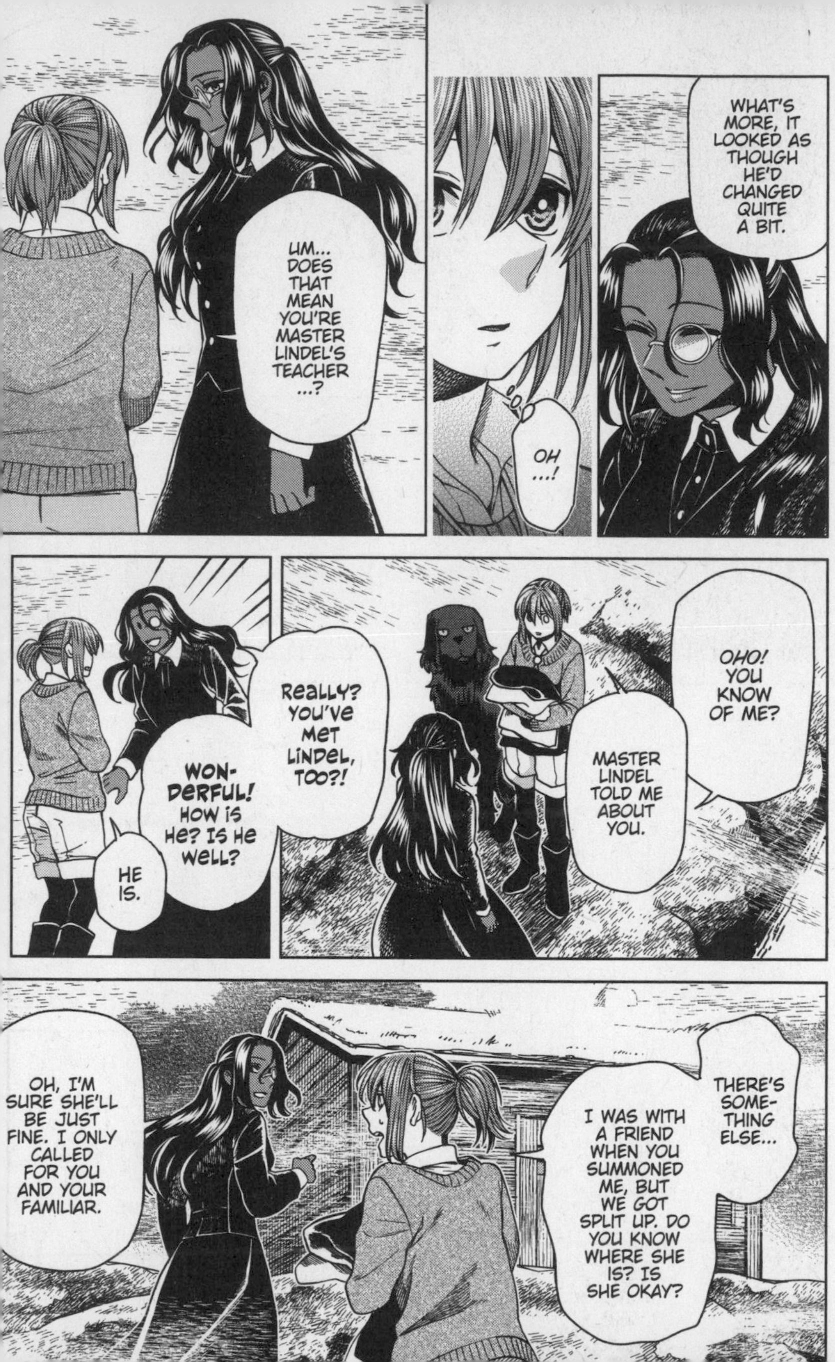
WHAT'S MORE, IT LOOKED AS THOUGH HE'D CHANGED QUITE A BIT.
OH ...!
UM... DOES THAT MEAN YOU'RE MASTER LINDEL'S TEACHER ...?
OHO! YOU KNOW OF ME?
MASTER LINDEL TOLD ME ABOUT YOU.
REALLY? YOU'VE MET LINDEL, TOO?!
WON-DERFUL! HOW IS HE? IS HE WELL?
HE IS.
THERE'S SOME-THING ELSE...
I WAS WITH A FRIEND WHEN YOU SUMMONED ME, BUT WE GOT SPLIT UP. DO YOU KNOW WHERE SHE IS? IS SHE OKAY?
OH, I'M SURE SHE'LL BE JUST FINE. I ONLY CALLED FOR YOU AND YOUR FAMILIAR.

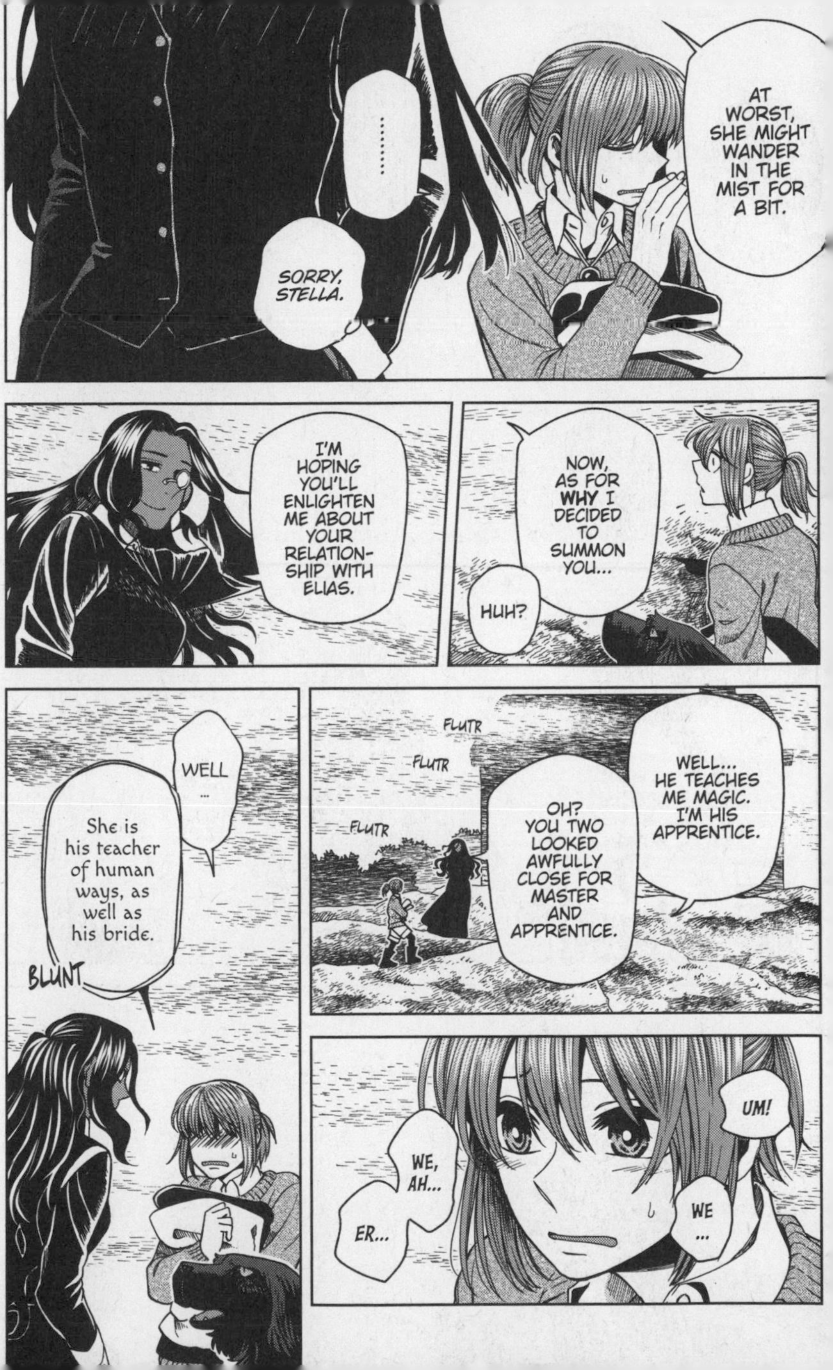
AT WORST, SHE MIGHT WANDER IN THE MIST FOR A BIT.
......
SORRY, STELLA.
NOW, AS FOR WHY I DECIDED TO SUMMON YOU...
HUH?
I'M HOPING YOU'LL ENLIGHTEN ME ABOUT YOUR RELATIONSHIP WITH ELIAS.
WELL... HE TEACHES ME MAGIC. I'M HIS APPRENTICE.
FLUTR
FLUTR
FLUTR
OH? YOU TWO LOOKED AWFULLY CLOSE FOR MASTER AND APPRENTICE.
UM!
WE ...
WE, AH...
ER...
WELL ...
She is his teacher of human ways, as well as his bride.
BLUNT

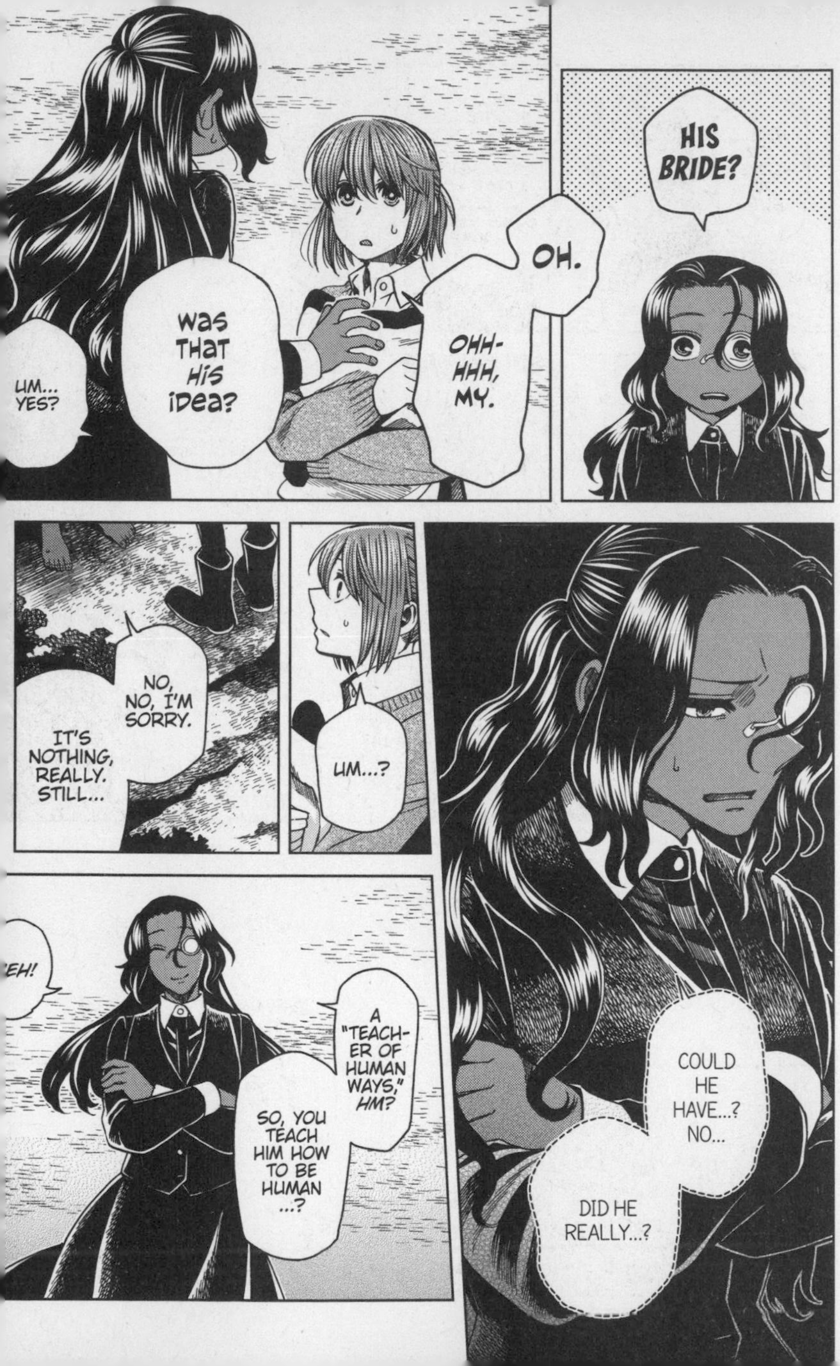
HIS BRIDE?
OH.
OHHHHH, MY.
Was THAT His idea?
UM... YES?
COULD HE HAVE...? NO...
DID HE REALLY...?
UM...?
NO, NO, I'M SORRY.
IT'S NOTHING, REALLY. STILL...
A "TEACHER OF HUMAN WAYS," HM?
SO, YOU TEACH HIM HOW TO BE HUMAN...?
EH!

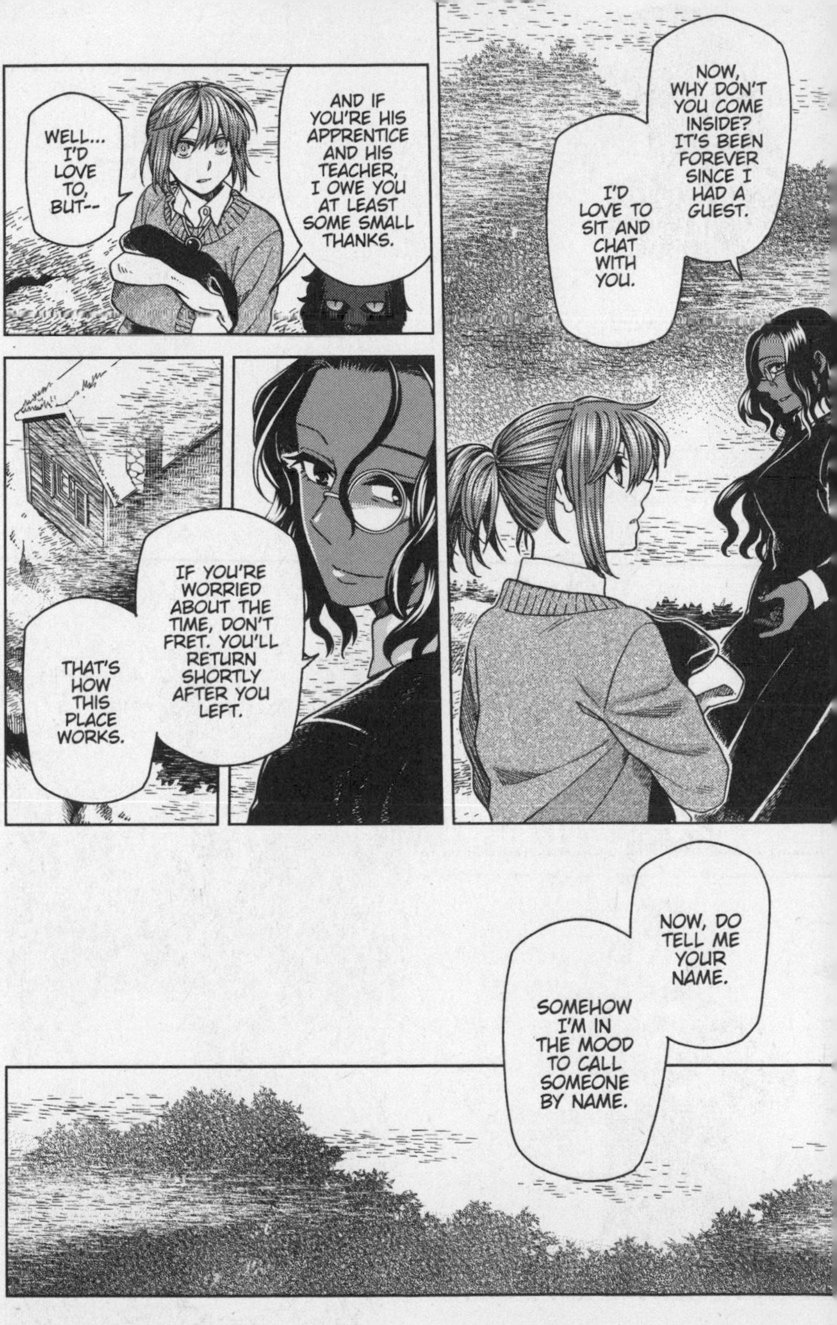
NOW, WHY DON'T YOU COME INSIDE? IT'S BEEN FOREVER SINCE I HAD A GUEST.
I'D LOVE TO SIT AND CHAT WITH YOU.
AND IF YOU'RE HIS APPRENTICE AND HIS TEACHER, I OWE YOU AT LEAST SOME SMALL THANKS.
WELL... I'D LOVE TO, BUT--
IF YOU'RE WORRIED ABOUT THE TIME, DON'T FRET. YOU'LL RETURN SHORTLY AFTER YOU LEFT.
THAT'S HOW THIS PLACE WORKS.
NOW, DO TELL ME YOUR NAME.
SOMEHOW I'M IN THE MOOD TO CALL SOMEONE BY NAME.

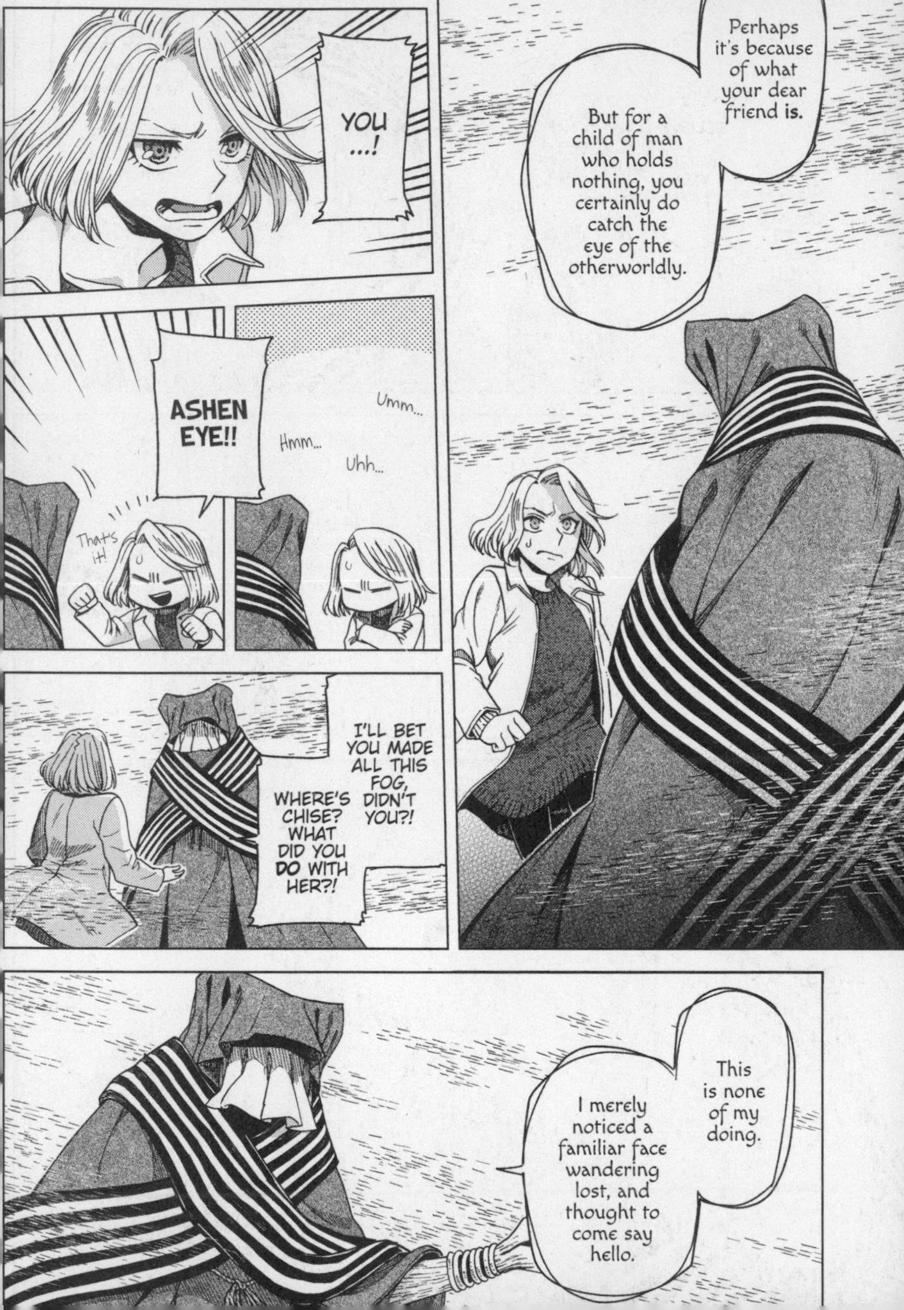
Perhaps it's because of what your dear friend **is.**
But for a child of man who holds nothing, you certainly do catch the eye of the otherworldly.
YOU ...!
Umm...
Hmm...
Uhh...
ASHEN EYE!!
That's it!
I'LL BET YOU MADE ALL THIS FOG, DIDN'T YOU?!
WHERE'S CHISE? WHAT DID YOU DO WITH HER?!
This is none of my doing.
I merely noticed a familiar face wandering lost, and thought to come say hello.

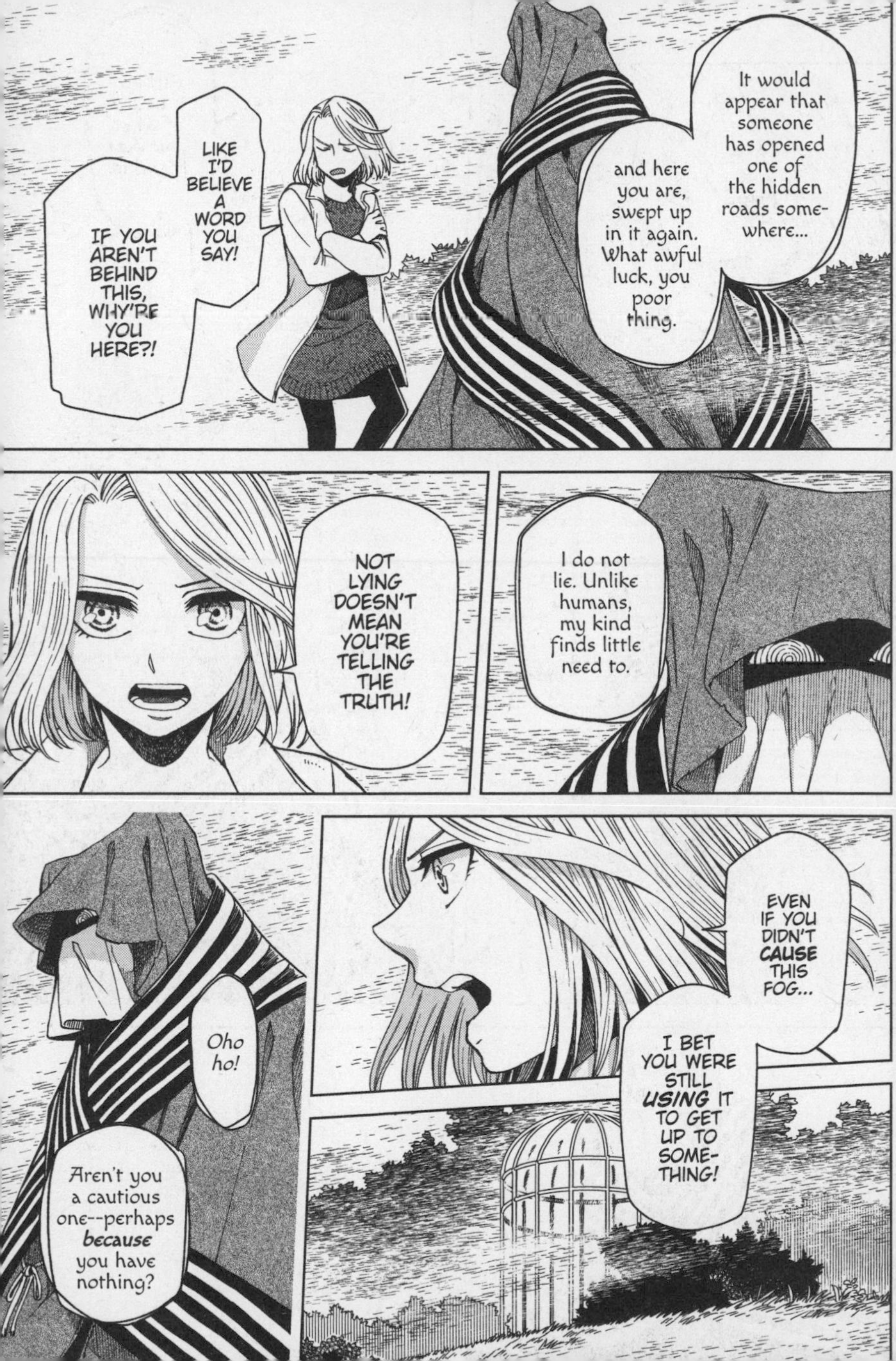
It would appear that someone has opened one of the hidden roads somewhere...
and here you are, swept up in it again. What awful luck, you poor thing.
LIKE I'D BELIEVE A WORD YOU SAY!
IF YOU AREN'T BEHIND THIS, WHY'RE YOU HERE?!
I do not lie. Unlike humans, my kind finds little need to.
NOT LYING DOESN'T MEAN YOU'RE TELLING THE TRUTH!
EVEN IF YOU DIDN'T CAUSE THIS FOG...
I BET YOU WERE STILL USING IT TO GET UP TO SOMETHING!
Oho ho!
Aren't you a cautious one--perhaps because you have nothing?

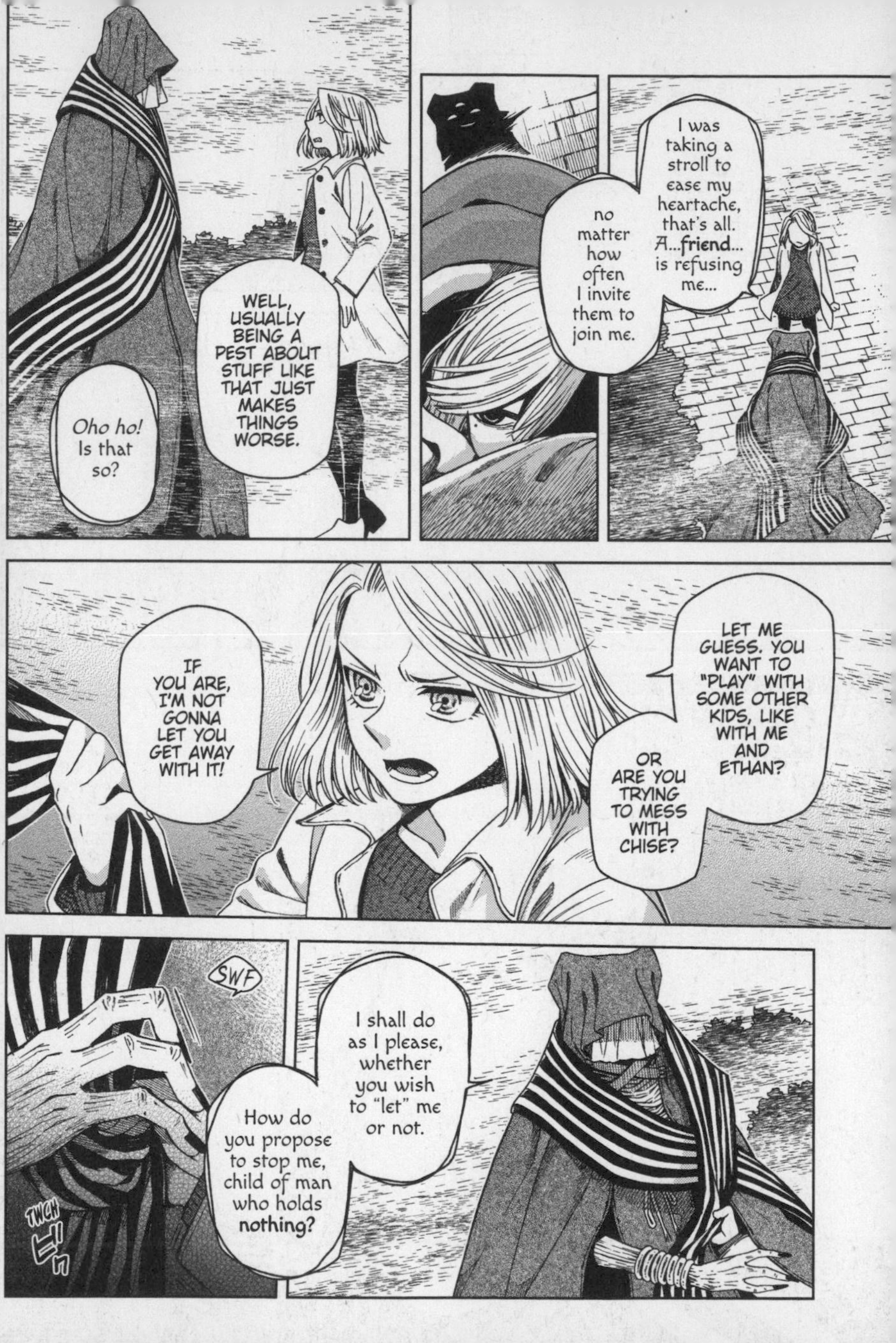
I was taking a stroll to ease my heartache, that's all. A...**friend**... is refusing me...
no matter how often I invite them to join me.
WELL, USUALLY BEING A PEST ABOUT STUFF LIKE THAT JUST MAKES THINGS WORSE.
Oho ho! Is that so?
LET ME GUESS. YOU WANT TO "PLAY" WITH SOME OTHER KIDS, LIKE WITH ME AND ETHAN?
OR ARE YOU TRYING TO MESS WITH CHISE?
IF YOU ARE, I'M NOT GONNA LET YOU GET AWAY WITH IT!
I shall do as I please, whether you wish to "let" me or not.
How do you propose to stop me, child of man who holds **nothing?**
SWF
TWCH

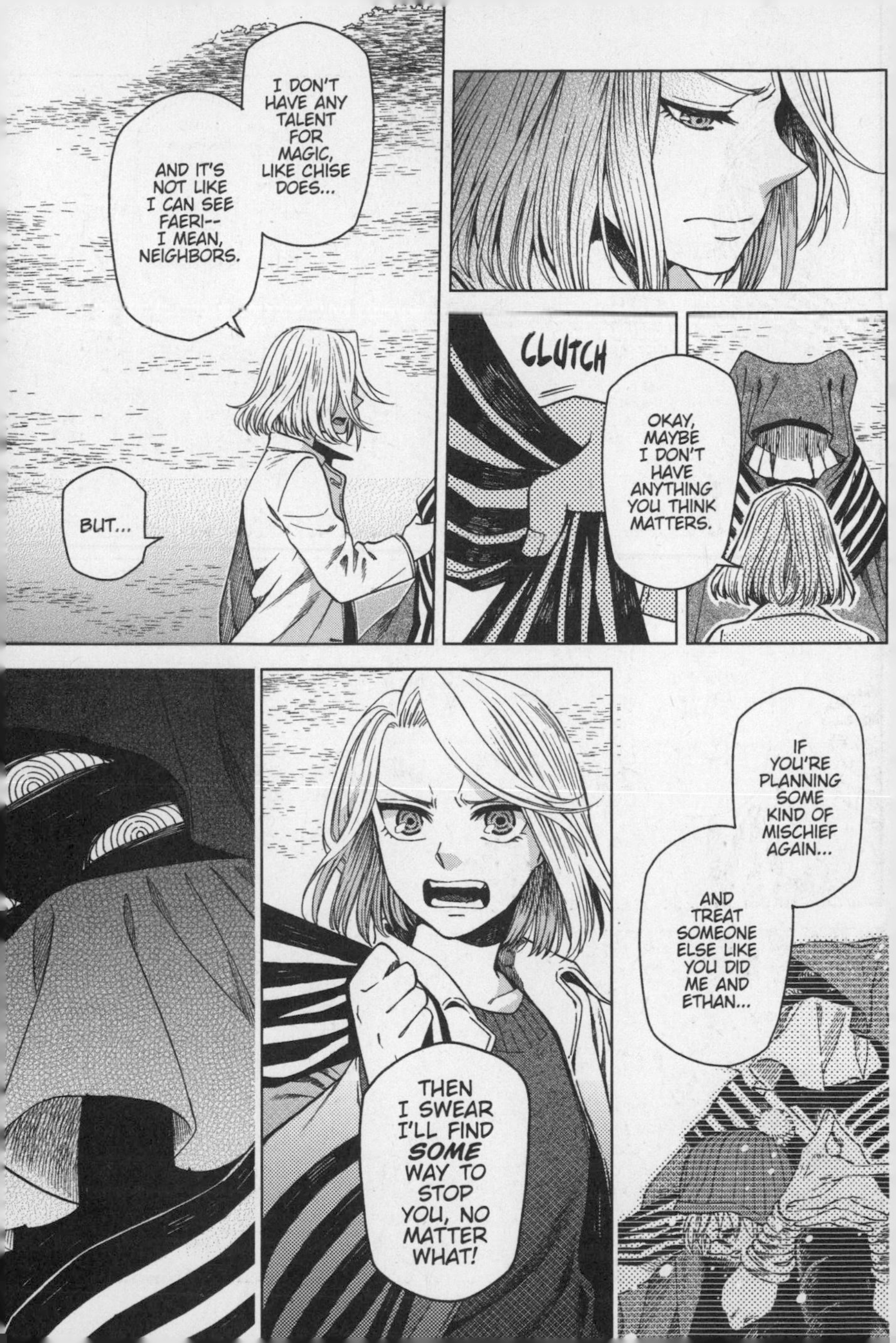
OKAY, MAYBE I DON'T HAVE ANYTHING YOU THINK MATTERS.
CLUTCH
I DON'T HAVE ANY TALENT FOR MAGIC, LIKE CHISE DOES...
AND IT'S NOT LIKE I CAN SEE FAERI-- I MEAN, NEIGHBORS.
BUT...
IF YOU'RE PLANNING SOME KIND OF MISCHIEF AGAIN...
AND TREAT SOMEONE ELSE LIKE YOU DID ME AND ETHAN...
THEN I SWEAR I'LL FIND *SOME* WAY TO STOP YOU, NO MATTER WHAT!

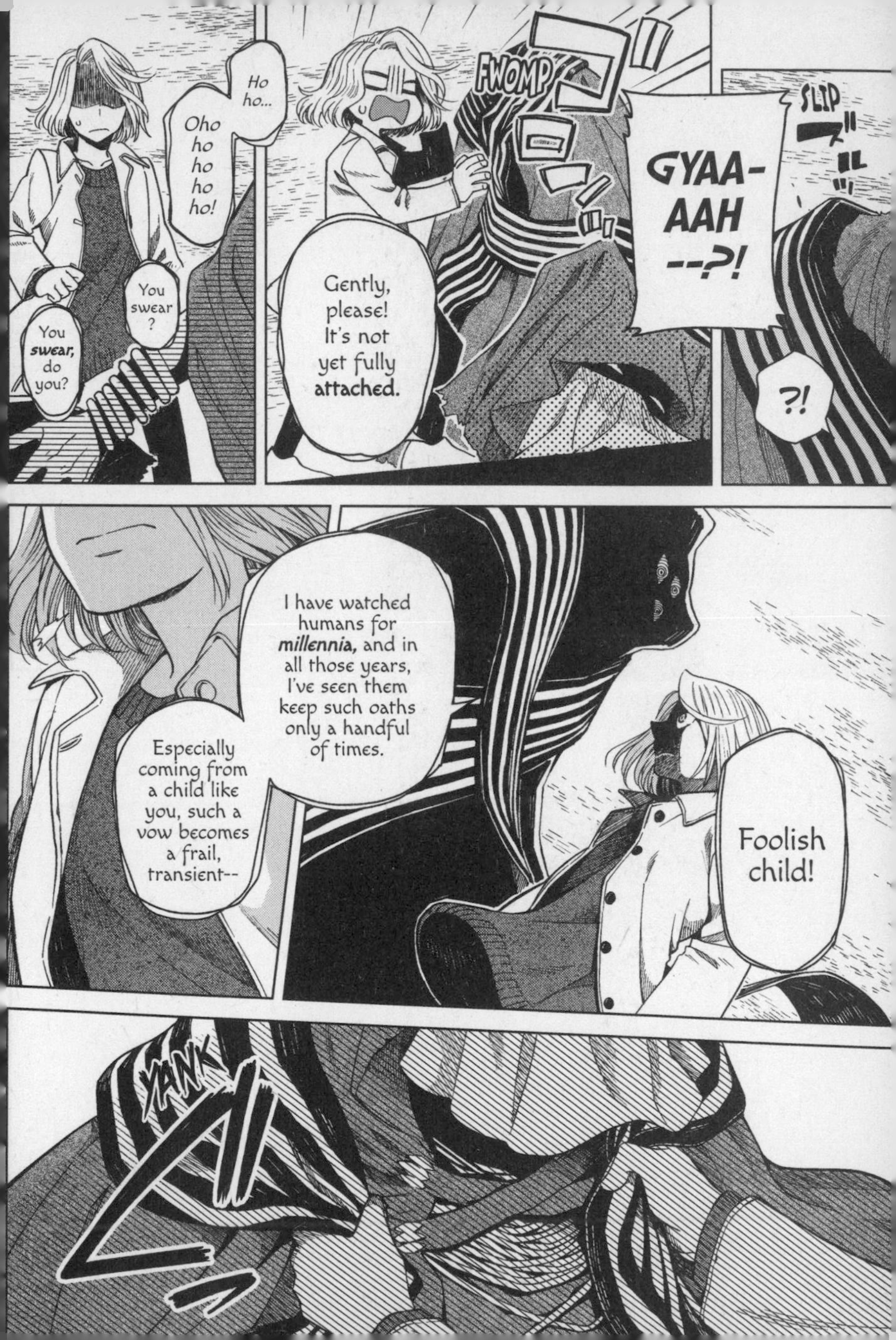
SLIP
?!
FWOMP
GYAA-AAH--?!
Gently, please! It's not yet fully attached.
Ho ho...
Oho ho ho ho ho!
You swear?
You swear, do you?
I have watched humans for millennia, and in all those years, I've seen them keep such oaths only a handful of times.
Especially coming from a child like you, such a vow becomes a frail, transient--
Foolish child!
YANK

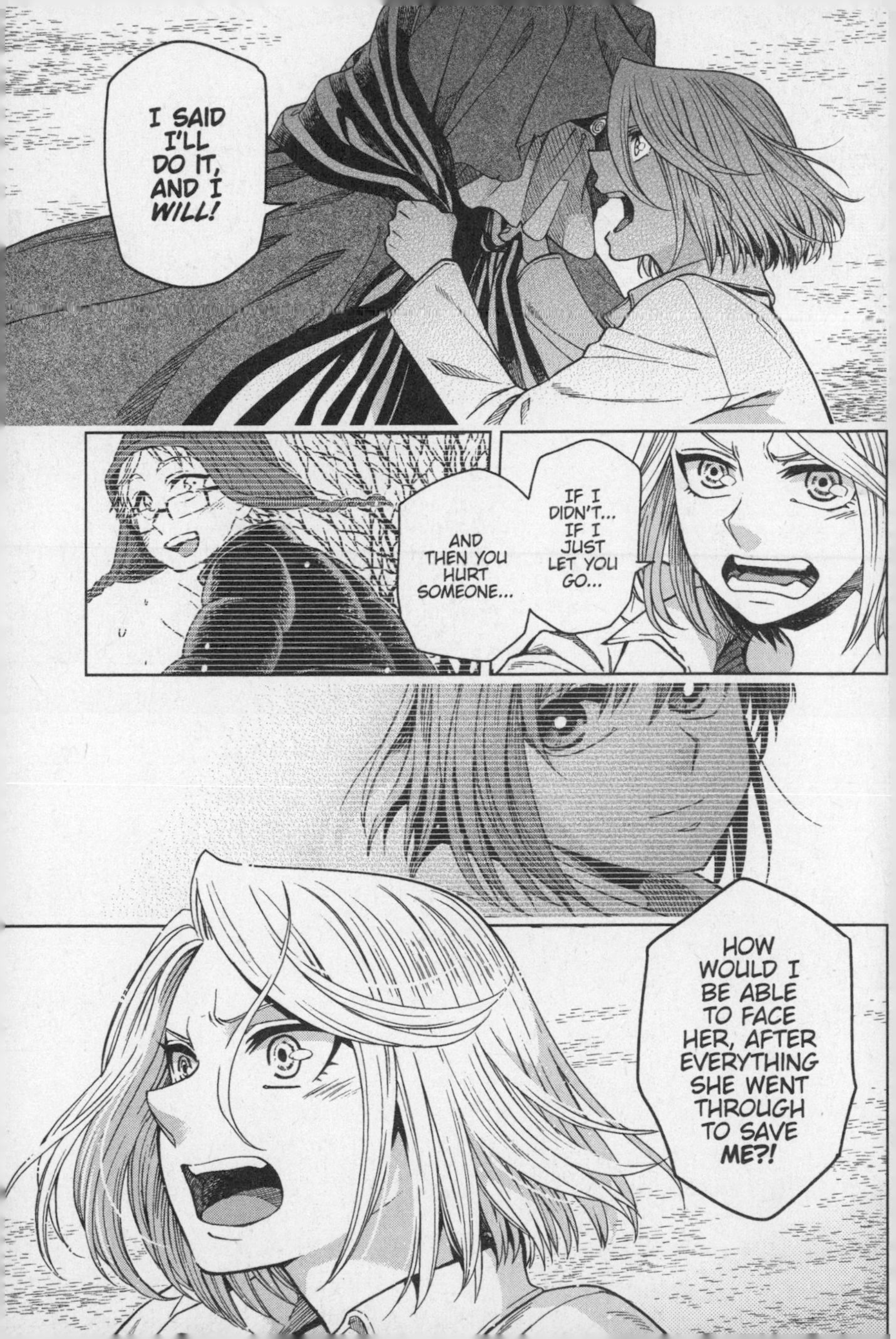
I SAID I'LL DO IT, AND I WILL!
IF I DIDN'T... IF I JUST LET YOU GO...
AND THEN YOU HURT SOMEONE...
HOW WOULD I BE ABLE TO FACE HER, AFTER EVERYTHING SHE WENT THROUGH TO SAVE ME?!

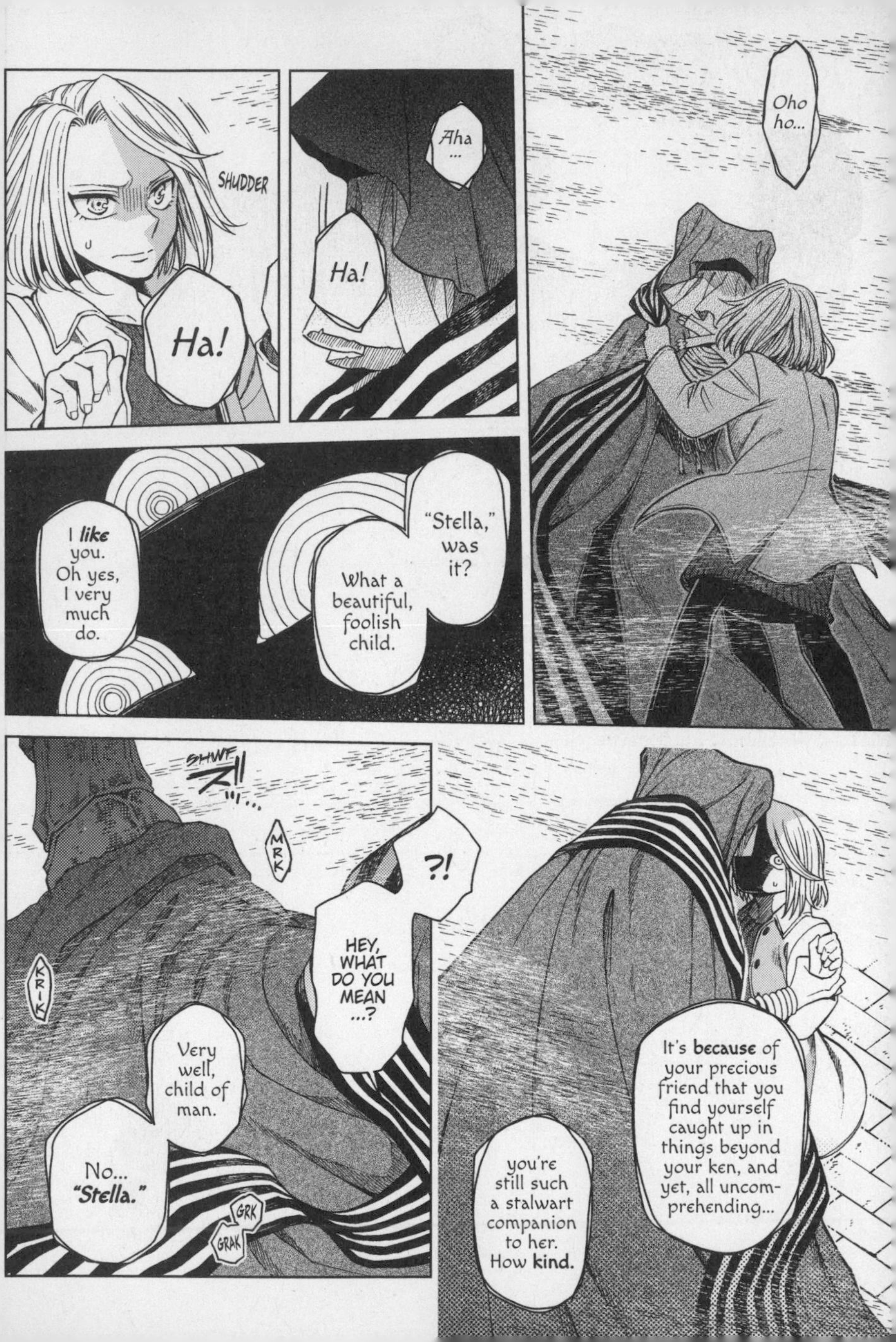
Oho ho...
Aha ...
Ha!
SHUDDER
Ha!
"Stella," was it?
What a beautiful, foolish child.
I like you. Oh yes, I very much do.
It's because of your precious friend that you find yourself caught up in things beyond your ken, and yet, all uncomprehending...
you're still such a stalwart companion to her. How kind.
?!
SHWF
MRK
HEY, WHAT DO YOU MEAN ...?
Very well, child of man.
No... "Stella."
KRIK
GRK
GRAK

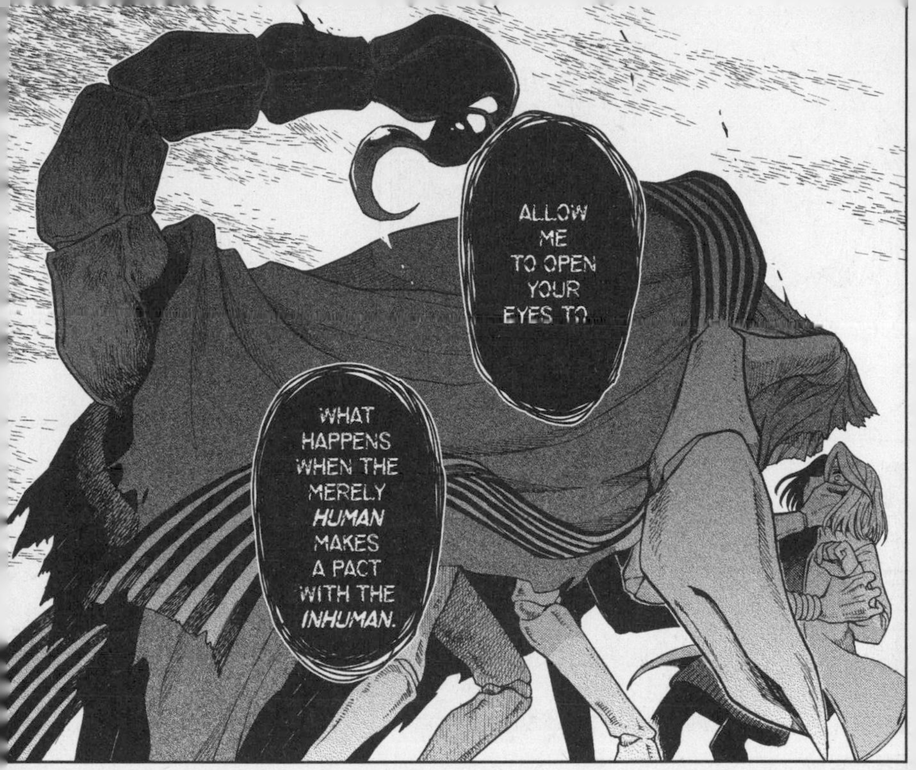
ALLOW ME TO OPEN YOUR EYES TO...
WHAT HAPPENS WHEN THE MERELY *HUMAN* MAKES A PACT WITH THE *INHUMAN*.
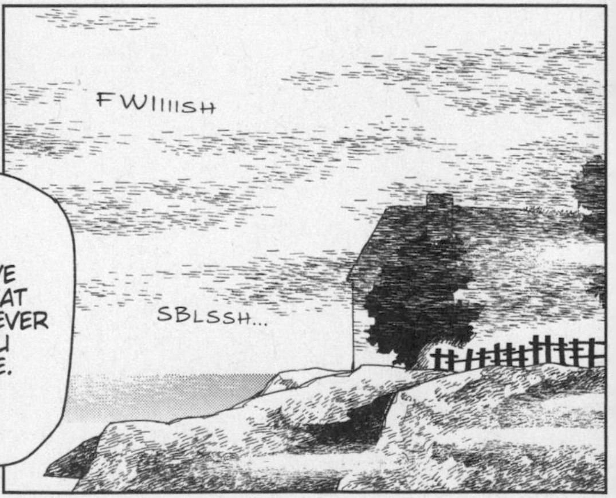
FWIIIISH
SBLSSH...
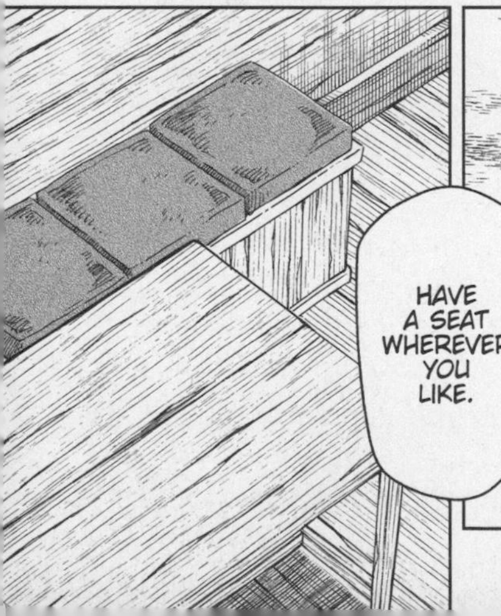
HAVE A SEAT WHEREVER YOU LIKE.

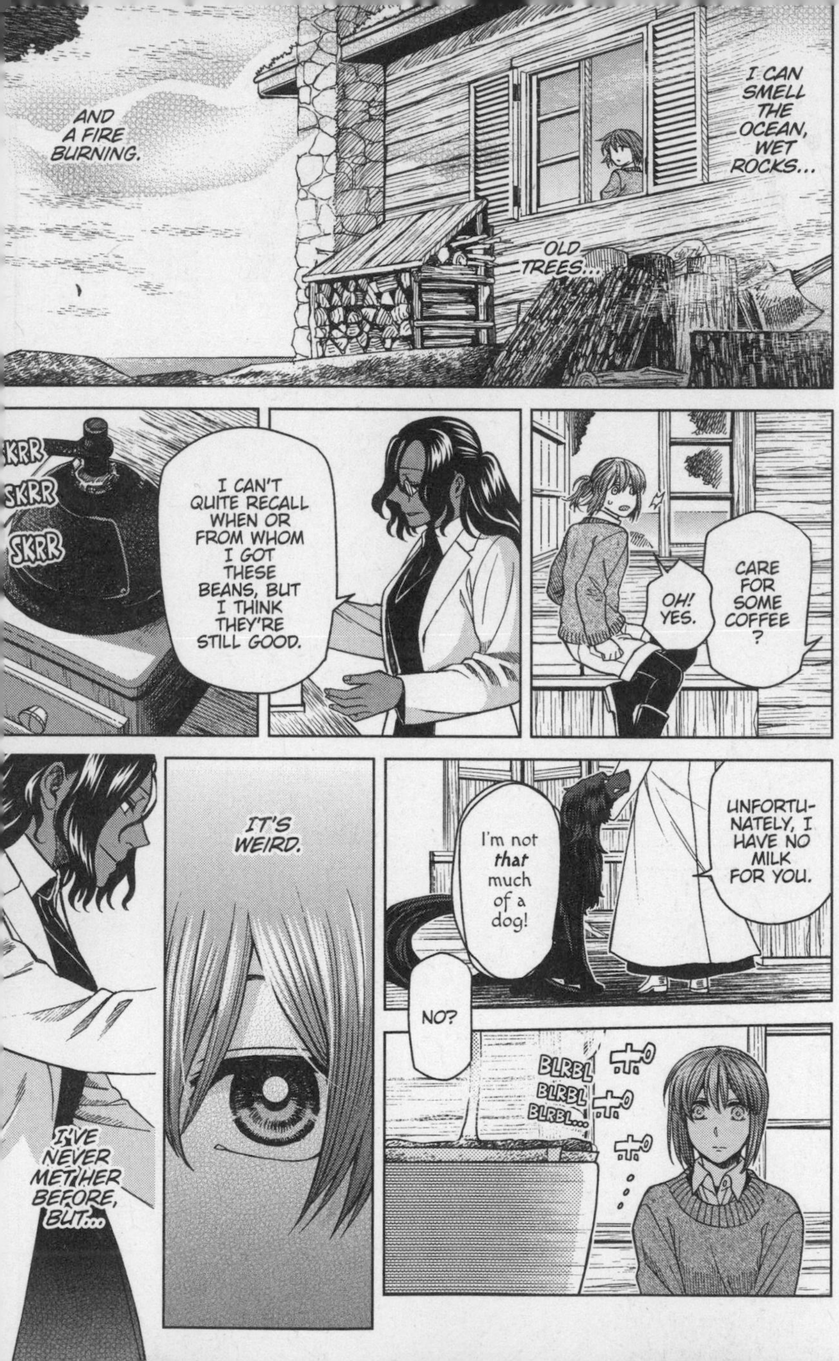
I CAN SMELL THE OCEAN, WET ROCKS...
OLD TREES...
AND A FIRE BURNING.
CARE FOR SOME COFFEE?
OH! YES.
I CAN'T QUITE RECALL WHEN OR FROM WHOM I GOT THESE BEANS, BUT I THINK THEY'RE STILL GOOD.
SKRR
SKRR
SKRR
UNFORTUNATELY, I HAVE NO MILK FOR YOU.
I'm not *that* much of a dog!
NO?
BLRBL
BLRBL
BLRBL...
IT'S WEIRD.
I'VE NEVER MET HER BEFORE, BUT...

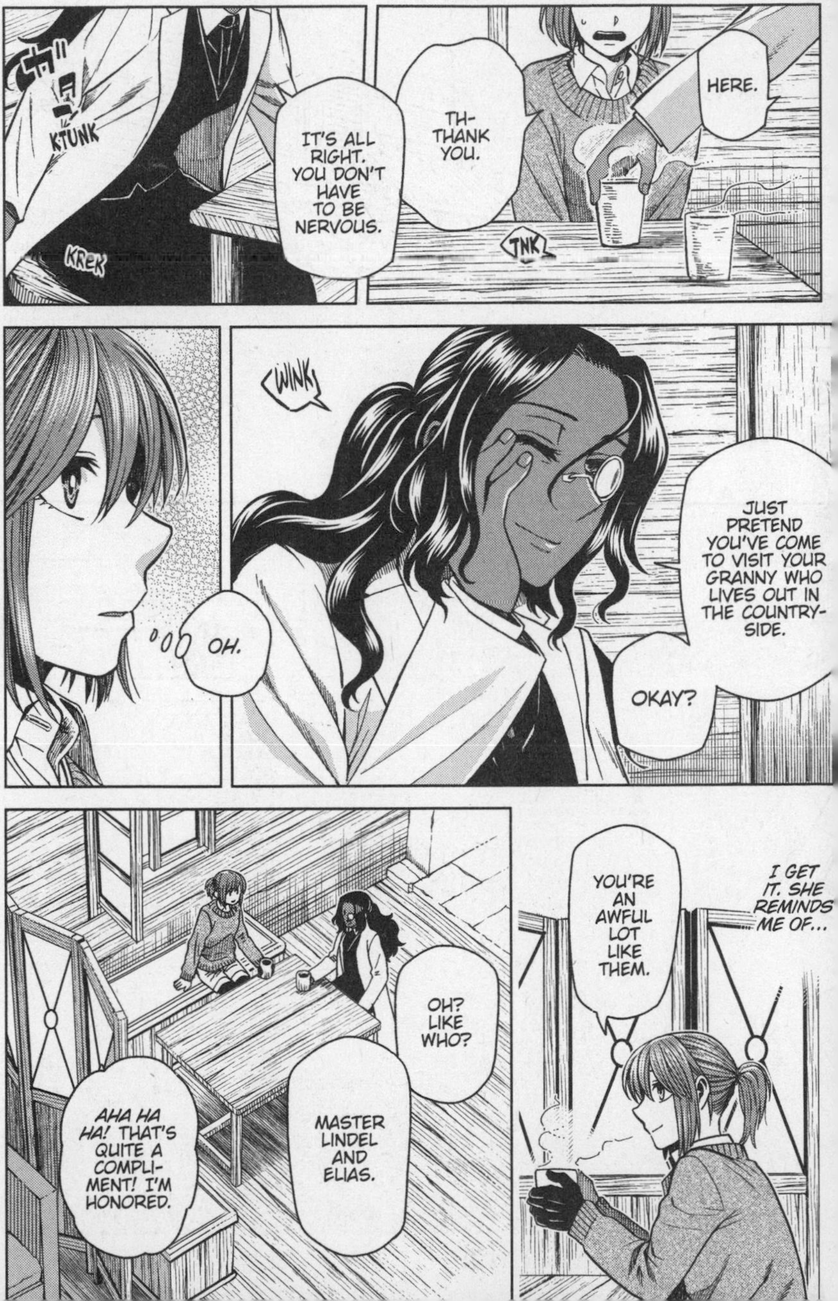
HERE.
TH- THANK YOU.
TNK
IT'S ALL RIGHT. YOU DON'T HAVE TO BE NERVOUS.
KTUNK
KREK
WINK
JUST PRETEND YOU'VE COME TO VISIT YOUR GRANNY WHO LIVES OUT IN THE COUNTRY-SIDE.
OKAY?
OH.
I GET IT. SHE REMINDS ME OF...
YOU'RE AN AWFUL LOT LIKE THEM.
OH? LIKE WHO?
MASTER LINDEL AND ELIAS.
AHA HA HA! THAT'S QUITE A COMPLI-MENT! I'M HONORED.

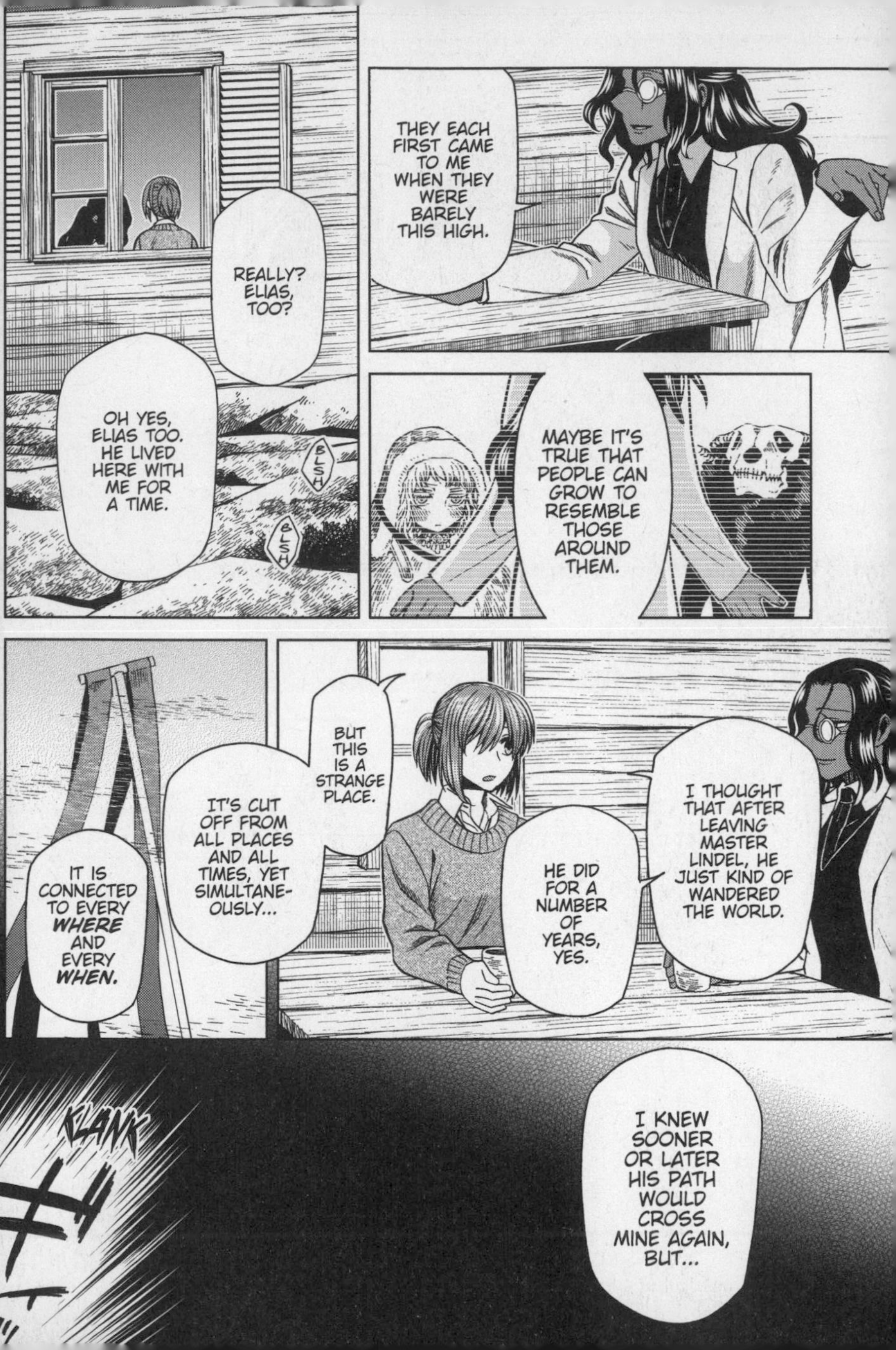
THEY EACH FIRST CAME TO ME WHEN THEY WERE BARELY THIS HIGH.
MAYBE IT'S TRUE THAT PEOPLE CAN GROW TO RESEMBLE THOSE AROUND THEM.
REALLY? ELIAS, TOO?
OH YES, ELIAS TOO. HE LIVED HERE WITH ME FOR A TIME.
BLSH
BLSH
I THOUGHT THAT AFTER LEAVING MASTER LINDEL, HE JUST KIND OF WANDERED THE WORLD.
HE DID FOR A NUMBER OF YEARS, YES.
BUT THIS IS A STRANGE PLACE.
IT'S CUT OFF FROM ALL PLACES AND ALL TIMES, YET SIMULTANE-OUSLY...
IT IS CONNECTED TO EVERY ***WHERE*** AND EVERY ***WHEN.***
I KNEW SOONER OR LATER HIS PATH WOULD CROSS MINE AGAIN, BUT...
KLANK

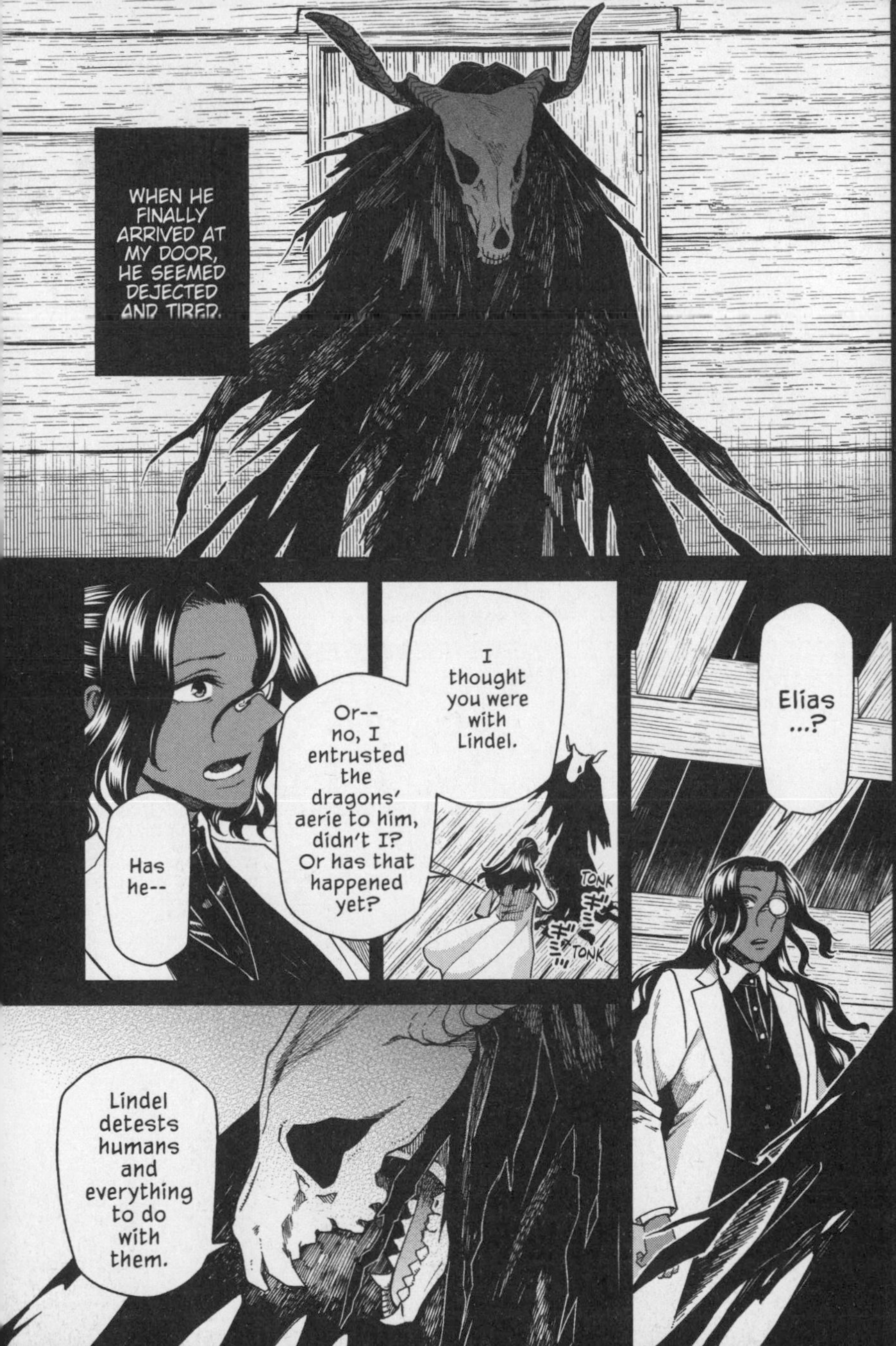
WHEN HE FINALLY ARRIVED AT MY DOOR, HE SEEMED DEJECTED AND TIRED.
Elias ...?
I thought you were with Lindel.
Or-- no, I entrusted the dragons' aerie to him, didn't I? Or has that happened yet?
TONK
TONK
Has he--
Lindel detests humans and everything to do with them.

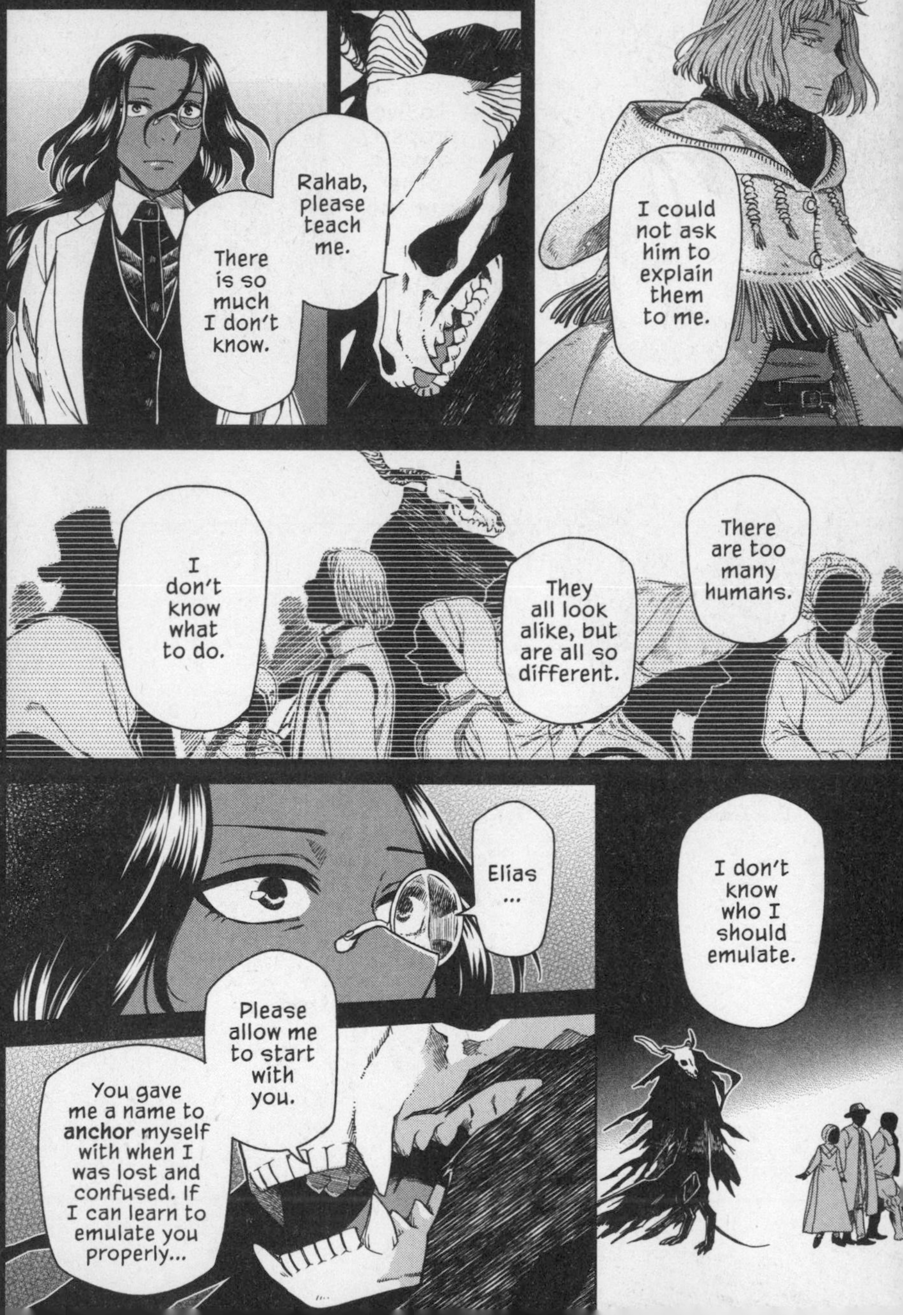
I could not ask him to explain them to me.
Rahab, please teach me.
There is so much I don't know.
There are too many humans.
They all look alike, but are all so different.
I don't know what to do.
I don't know who I should emulate.
Elias ...
Please allow me to start with you.
You gave me a name to **anchor** myself with when I was lost and confused. If I can learn to emulate you properly...

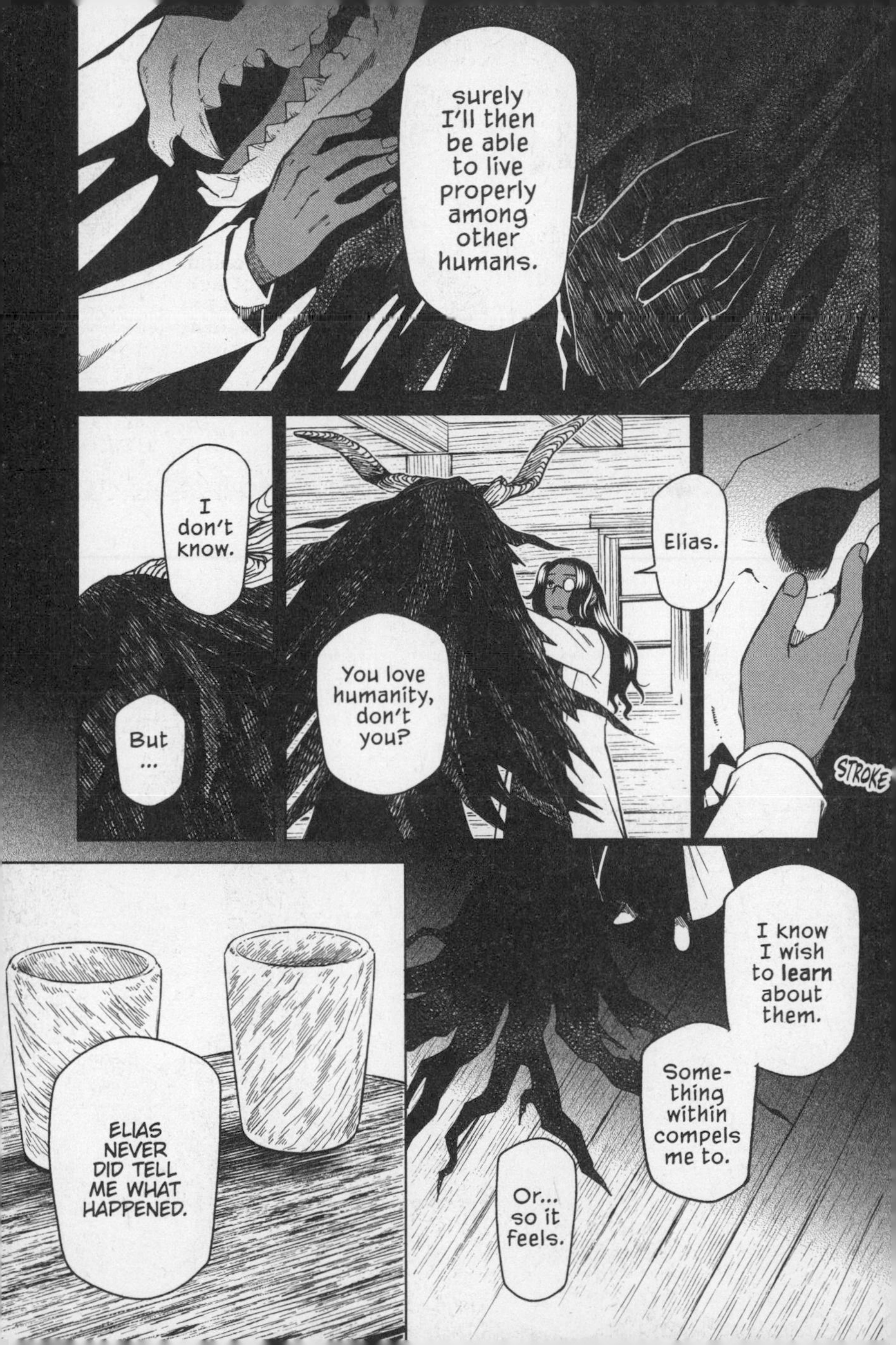
surely I'll then be able to live properly among other humans.
Elias.
STROKE
You love humanity, don't you?
I don't know.
But ...
I know I wish to **learn** about them.
Some-thing within compels me to.
Or... so it feels.
ELIAS NEVER DID TELL ME WHAT HAPPENED.

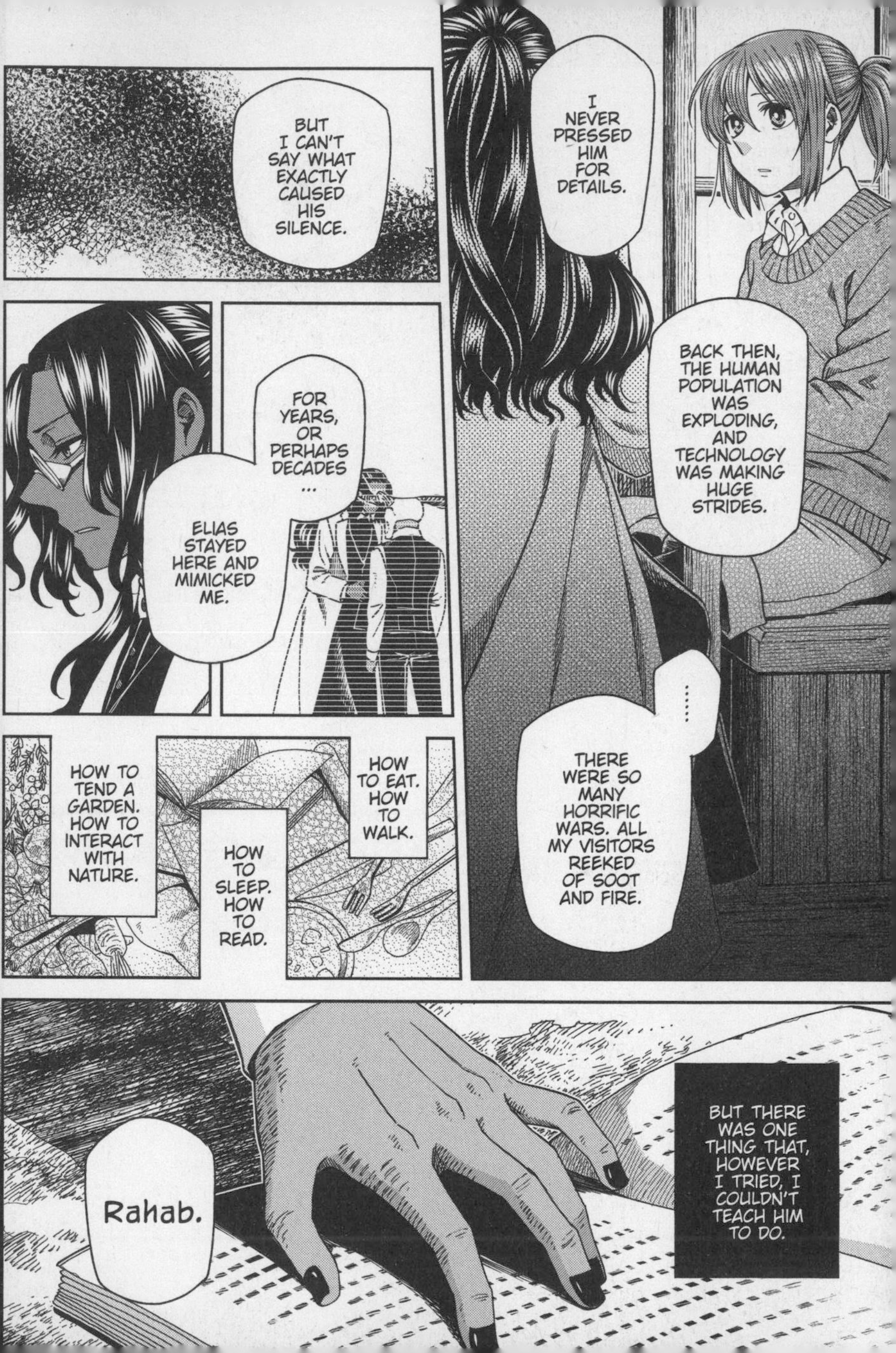
I NEVER PRESSED HIM FOR DETAILS.
BACK THEN, THE HUMAN POPULATION WAS EXPLODING, AND TECHNOLOGY WAS MAKING HUGE STRIDES.
......
THERE WERE SO MANY HORRIFIC WARS. ALL MY VISITORS REEKED OF SOOT AND FIRE.
BUT I CAN'T SAY WHAT EXACTLY CAUSED HIS SILENCE.
FOR YEARS, OR PERHAPS DECADES ...
ELIAS STAYED HERE AND MIMICKED ME.
HOW TO EAT. HOW TO WALK.
HOW TO SLEEP. HOW TO READ.
HOW TO TEND A GARDEN. HOW TO INTERACT WITH NATURE.
BUT THERE WAS ONE THING THAT, HOWEVER I TRIED, I COULDN'T TEACH HIM TO DO.
Rahab.

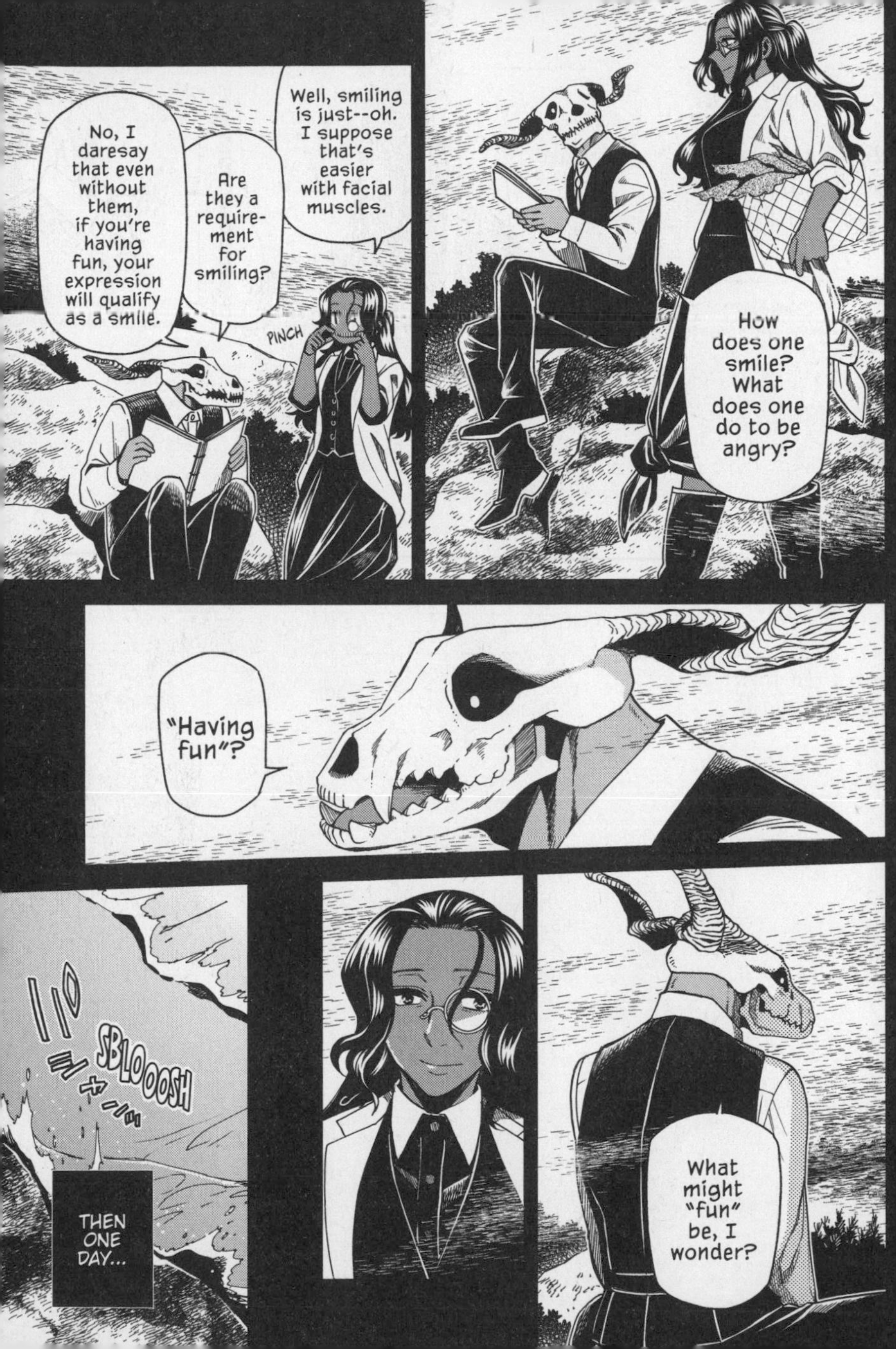
How does one smile? What does one do to be angry?
Well, smiling is just--oh. I suppose that's easier with facial muscles.
Are they a requirement for smiling?
No, I daresay that even without them, if you're having fun, your expression will qualify as a smile.
PINCH
"Having fun"?
What might "fun" be, I wonder?
SBLOOOSH
THEN ONE DAY...

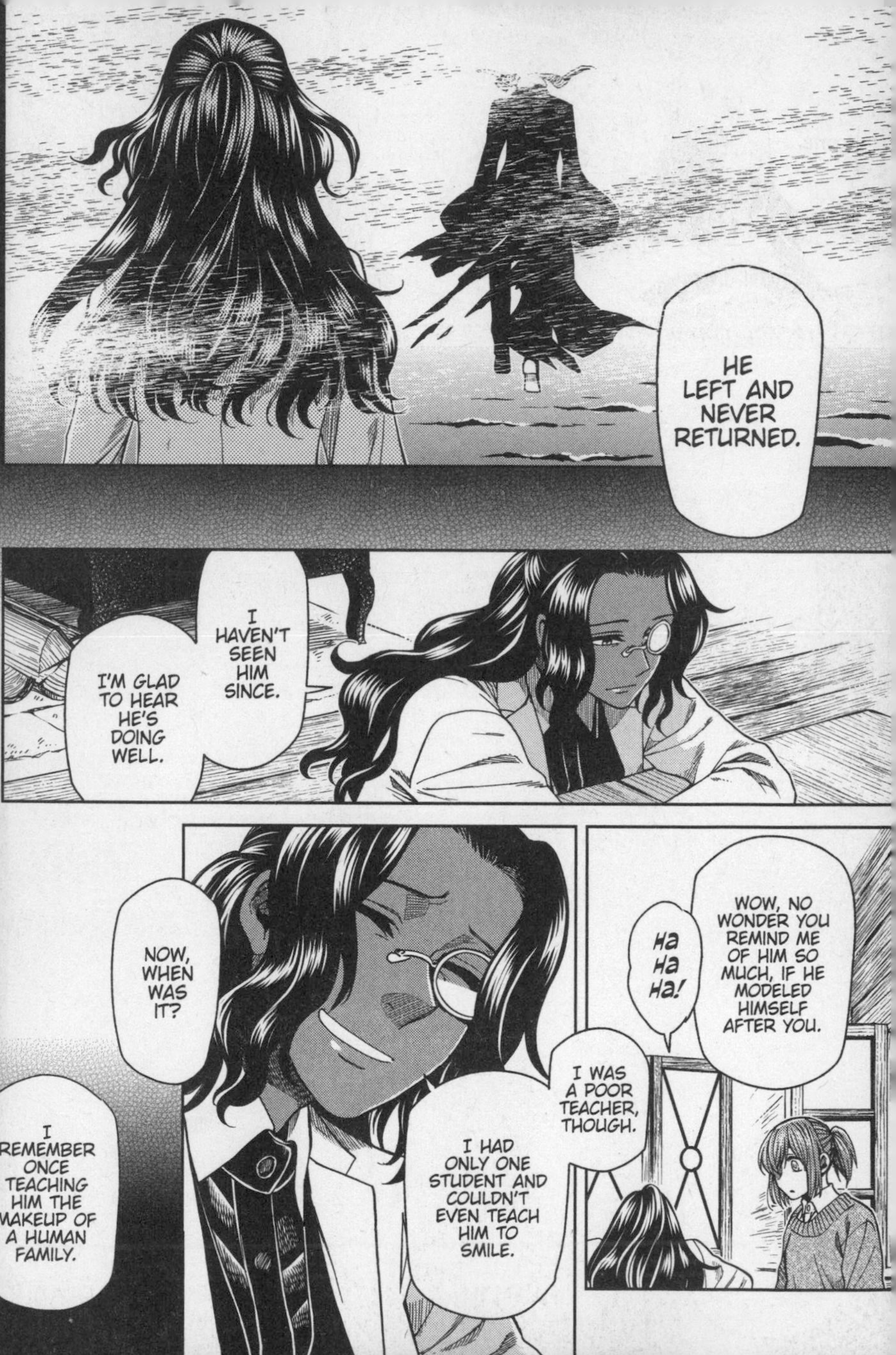
HE LEFT AND NEVER RETURNED.
I HAVEN'T SEEN HIM SINCE.
I'M GLAD TO HEAR HE'S DOING WELL.
WOW, NO WONDER YOU REMIND ME OF HIM SO MUCH, IF HE MODELED HIMSELF AFTER YOU.
Ha Ha Ha!
I WAS A POOR TEACHER, THOUGH.
I HAD ONLY ONE STUDENT AND COULDN'T EVEN TEACH HIM TO SMILE.
NOW, WHEN WAS IT?
I REMEMBER ONCE TEACHING HIM THE MAKEUP OF A HUMAN FAMILY.

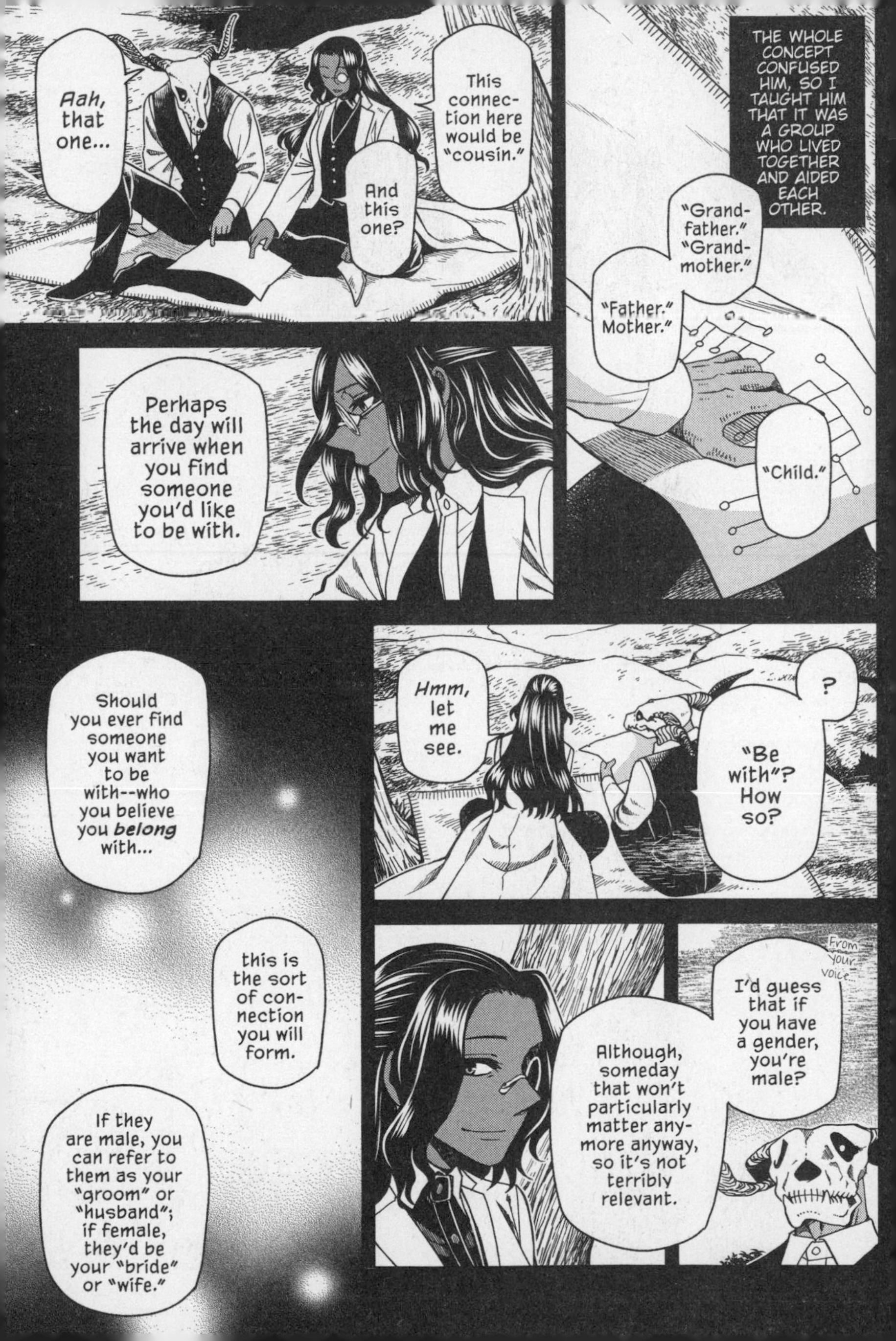

THE WHOLE CONCEPT CONFUSED HIM, SO I TAUGHT HIM THAT IT WAS A GROUP WHO LIVED TOGETHER AND AIDED EACH OTHER.
"Grand-father." "Grand-mother."
"Father." Mother."
"Child."
This connec-tion here would be "cousin."
And this one?
Aah, that one...
Perhaps the day will arrive when you find someone you'd like to be with.
?
"Be with"? How so?
Hmm, let me see.
From your voice...
I'd guess that if you have a gender, you're male?
Although, someday that won't particularly matter any-more anyway, so it's not terribly relevant.
Should you ever find someone you want to be with--who you believe you *belong* with...
this is the sort of con-nection you will form.
If they are male, you can refer to them as your "groom" or "husband"; if female, they'd be your "bride" or "wife."

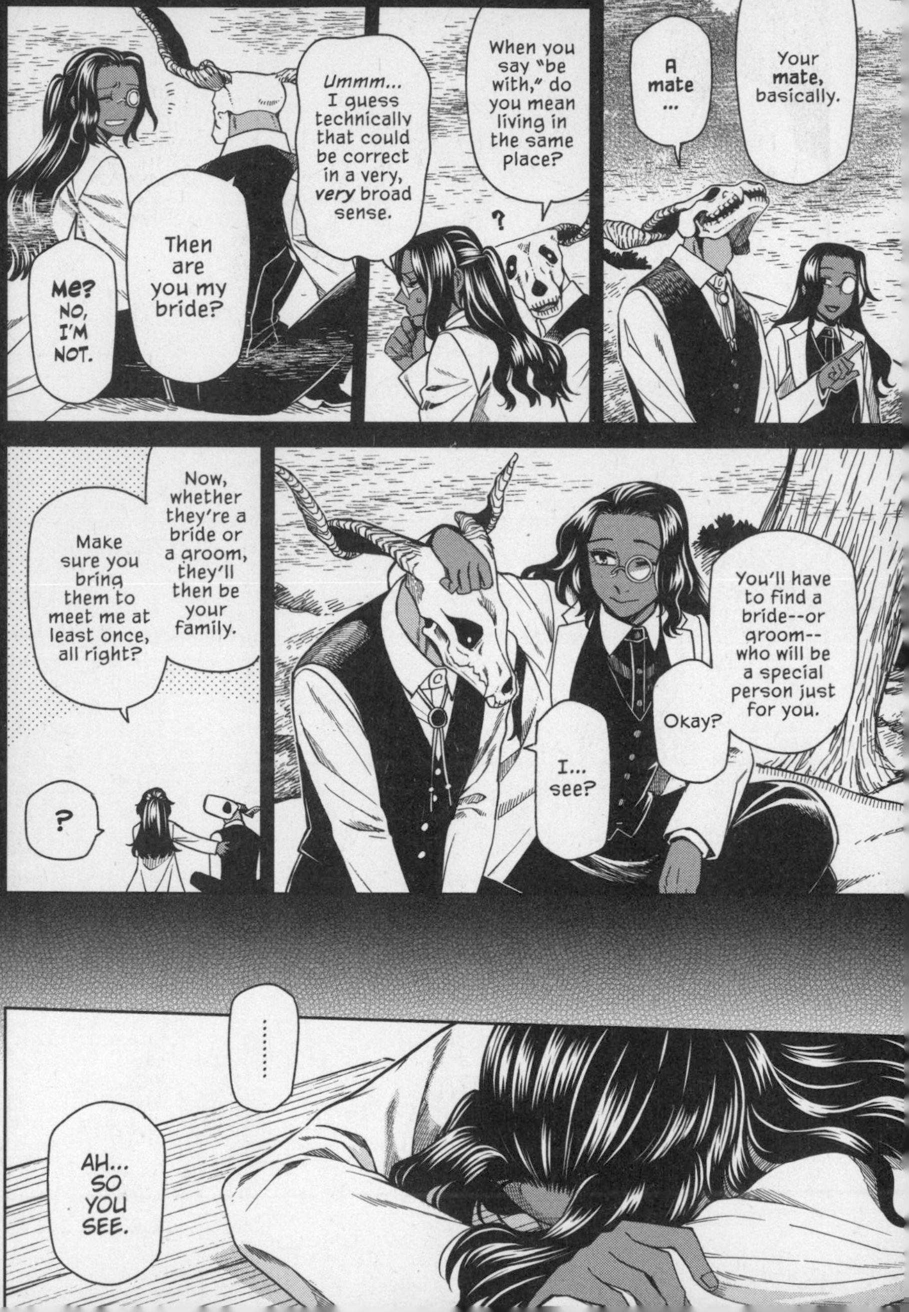

Your **mate**, basically.
A **mate**...
When you say "be with," do you mean living in the same place?
?
Ummm... I guess technically that could be correct in a very, *very* broad sense.
Then are you my bride?
Me? NO, I'M NOT.
You'll have to find a bride--or groom--who will be a special person just for you.
Okay?
I... see?
Now, whether they're a bride or a groom, they'll then be your family.
Make sure you bring them to meet me at least once, all right?
?
......
AH... SO YOU SEE.

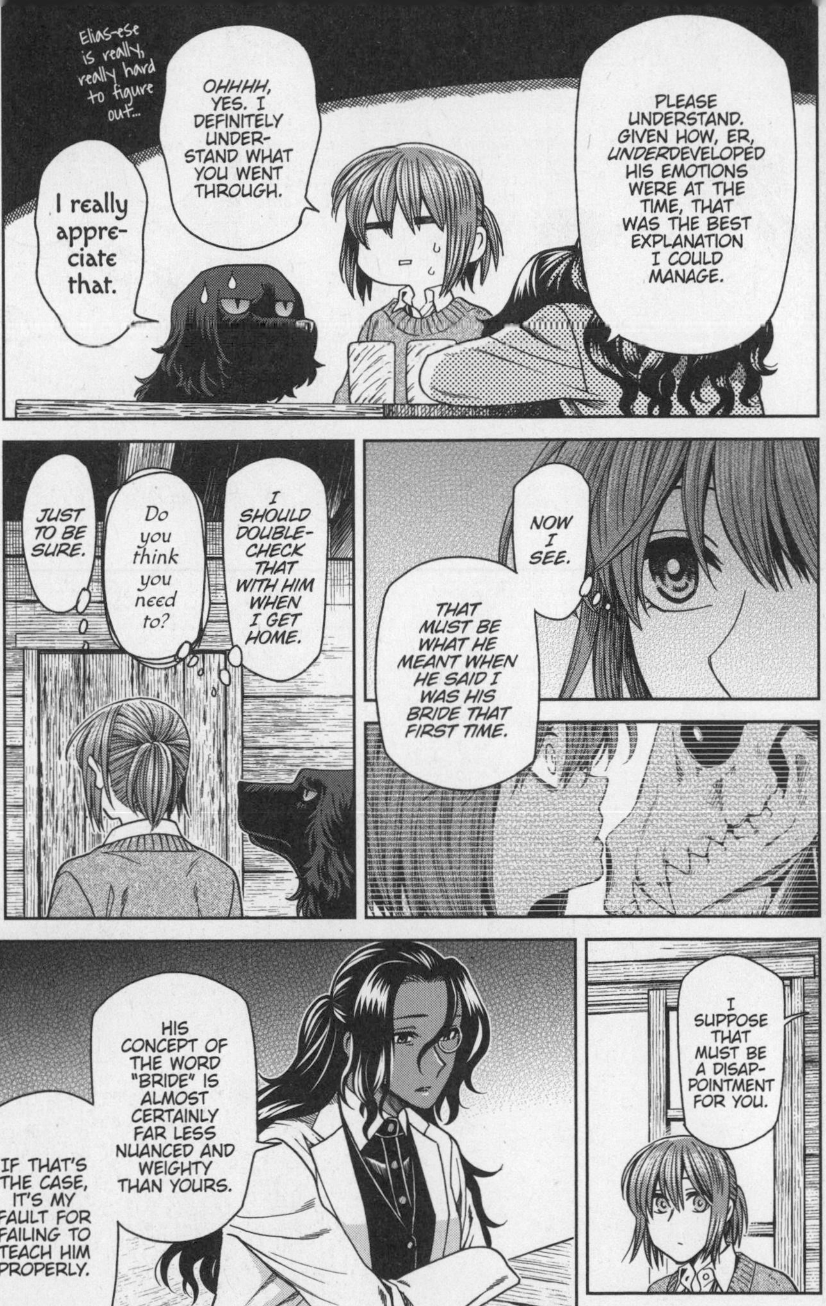
PLEASE UNDERSTAND. GIVEN HOW, ER, *UNDERDEVELOPED* HIS EMOTIONS WERE AT THE TIME, THAT WAS THE BEST EXPLANATION I COULD MANAGE.
OHHHH, YES. I DEFINITELY UNDER-STAND WHAT YOU WENT THROUGH.
Elias-ese is really, really hard to figure out...
I really appre-ciate that.
NOW I SEE.
THAT MUST BE WHAT HE MEANT WHEN HE SAID I WAS HIS BRIDE THAT FIRST TIME.
I SHOULD DOUBLE-CHECK THAT WITH HIM WHEN I GET HOME.
Do you think you need to?
JUST TO BE SURE.
I SUPPOSE THAT MUST BE A DISAP-POINTMENT FOR YOU.
HIS CONCEPT OF THE WORD "BRIDE" IS ALMOST CERTAINLY FAR LESS NUANCED AND WEIGHTY THAN YOURS.
IF THAT'S THE CASE, IT'S MY FAULT FOR FAILING TO TEACH HIM PROPERLY.

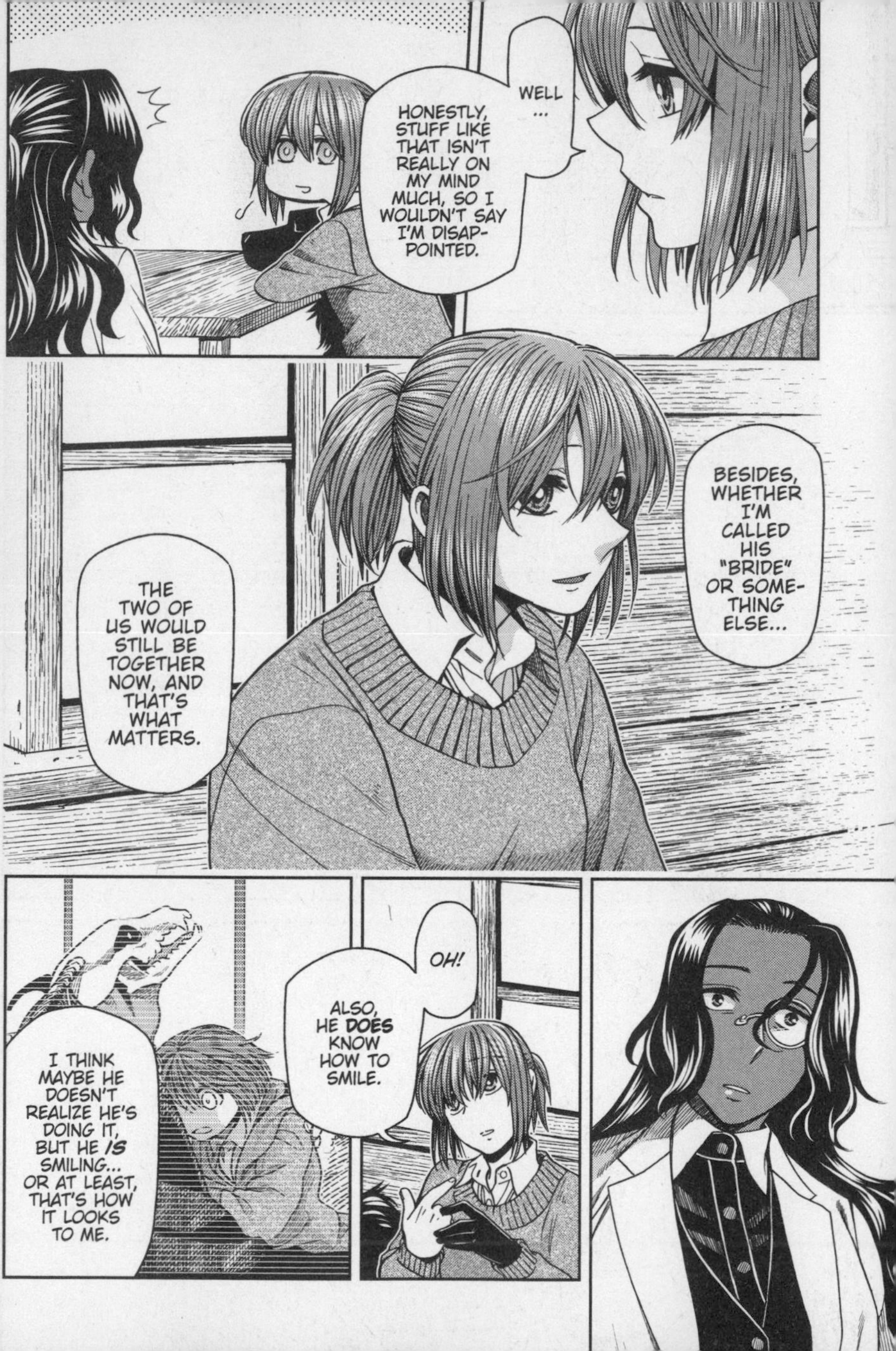
WELL ...
HONESTLY, STUFF LIKE THAT ISN'T REALLY ON MY MIND MUCH, SO I WOULDN'T SAY I'M DISAP-POINTED.
BESIDES, WHETHER I'M CALLED HIS "BRIDE" OR SOME-THING ELSE...
THE TWO OF US WOULD STILL BE TOGETHER NOW, AND THAT'S WHAT MATTERS.
OH!
ALSO, HE **DOES** KNOW HOW TO SMILE.
I THINK MAYBE HE DOESN'T REALIZE HE'S DOING IT, BUT HE *IS* SMILING... OR AT LEAST, THAT'S HOW IT LOOKS TO ME.

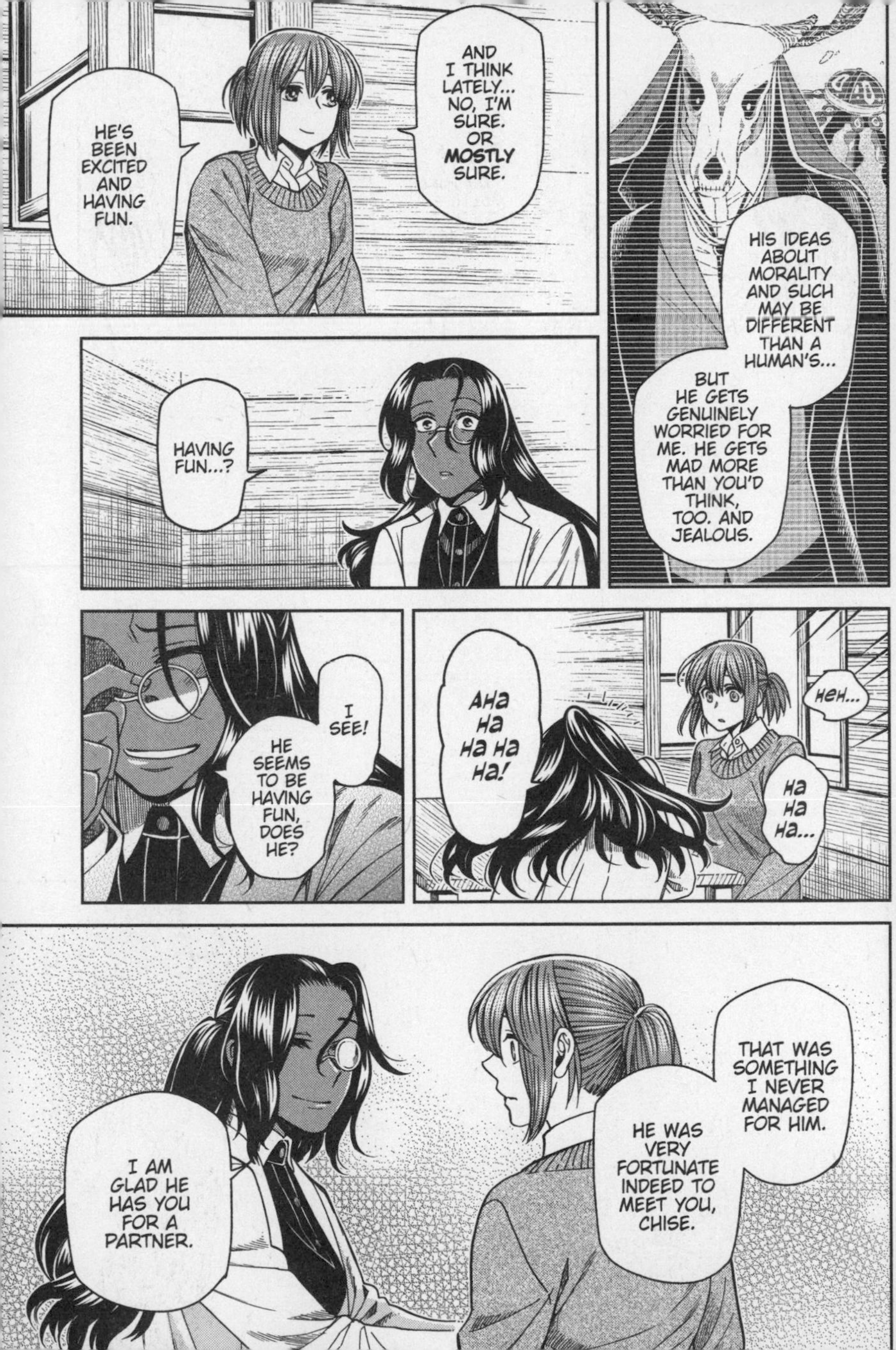
HIS IDEAS ABOUT MORALITY AND SUCH MAY BE DIFFERENT THAN A HUMAN'S...
BUT HE GETS GENUINELY WORRIED FOR ME. HE GETS MAD MORE THAN YOU'D THINK, TOO. AND JEALOUS.
AND I THINK LATELY... NO, I'M SURE. OR **MOSTLY** SURE.
HE'S BEEN EXCITED AND HAVING FUN.
HAVING FUN...?
HEH...
AHA HA HA HA HA!
HA HA HA...
I SEE!
HE SEEMS TO BE HAVING FUN, DOES HE?
THAT WAS SOMETHING I NEVER MANAGED FOR HIM.
HE WAS VERY FORTUNATE INDEED TO MEET YOU, CHISE.
I AM GLAD HE HAS YOU FOR A PARTNER.

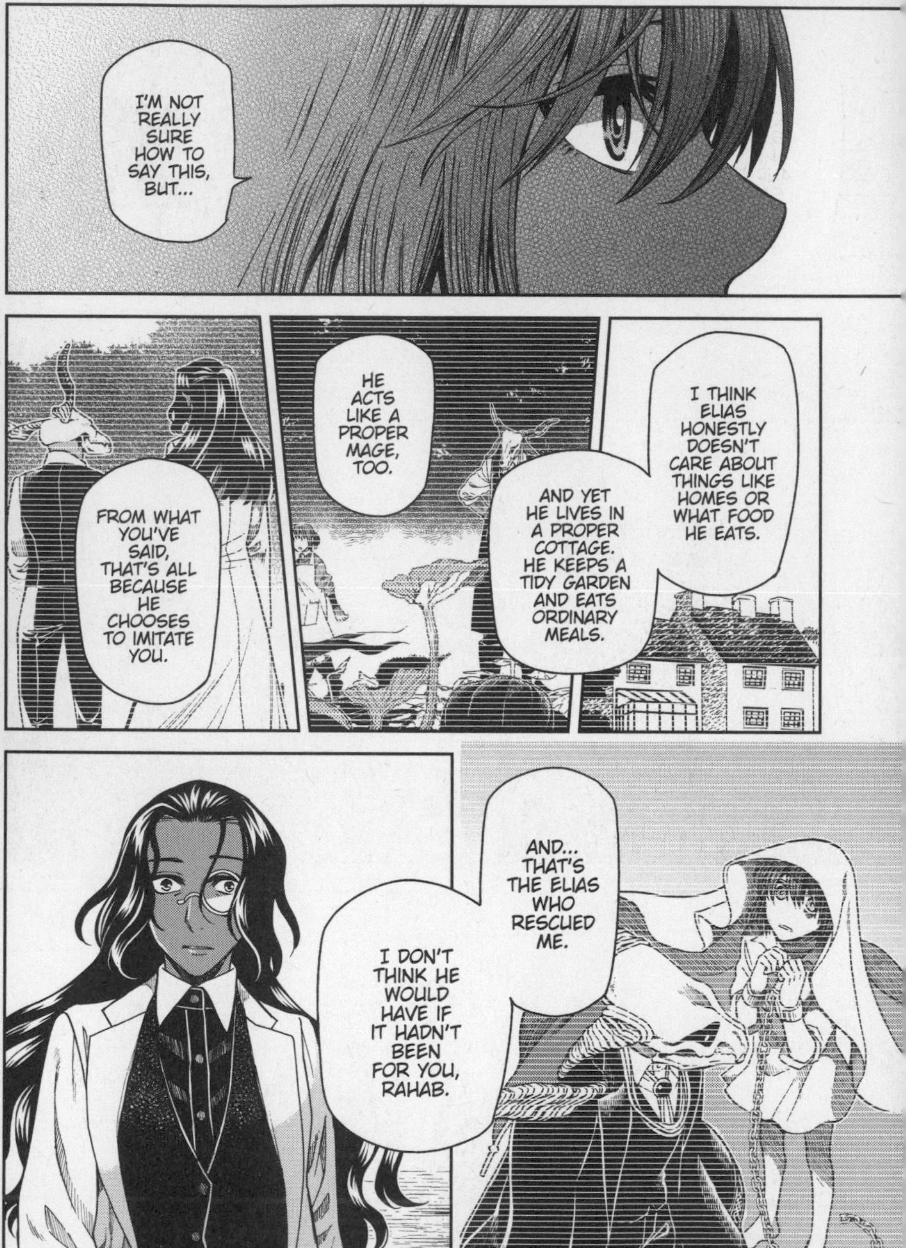
I'M NOT REALLY SURE HOW TO SAY THIS, BUT...
I THINK ELIAS HONESTLY DOESN'T CARE ABOUT THINGS LIKE HOMES OR WHAT FOOD HE EATS.
AND YET HE LIVES IN A PROPER COTTAGE. HE KEEPS A TIDY GARDEN AND EATS ORDINARY MEALS.
HE ACTS LIKE A PROPER MAGE, TOO.
FROM WHAT YOU'VE SAID, THAT'S ALL BECAUSE HE CHOOSES TO IMITATE YOU.
AND... THAT'S THE ELIAS WHO RESCUED ME.
I DON'T THINK HE WOULD HAVE IF IT HADN'T BEEN FOR YOU, RAHAB.

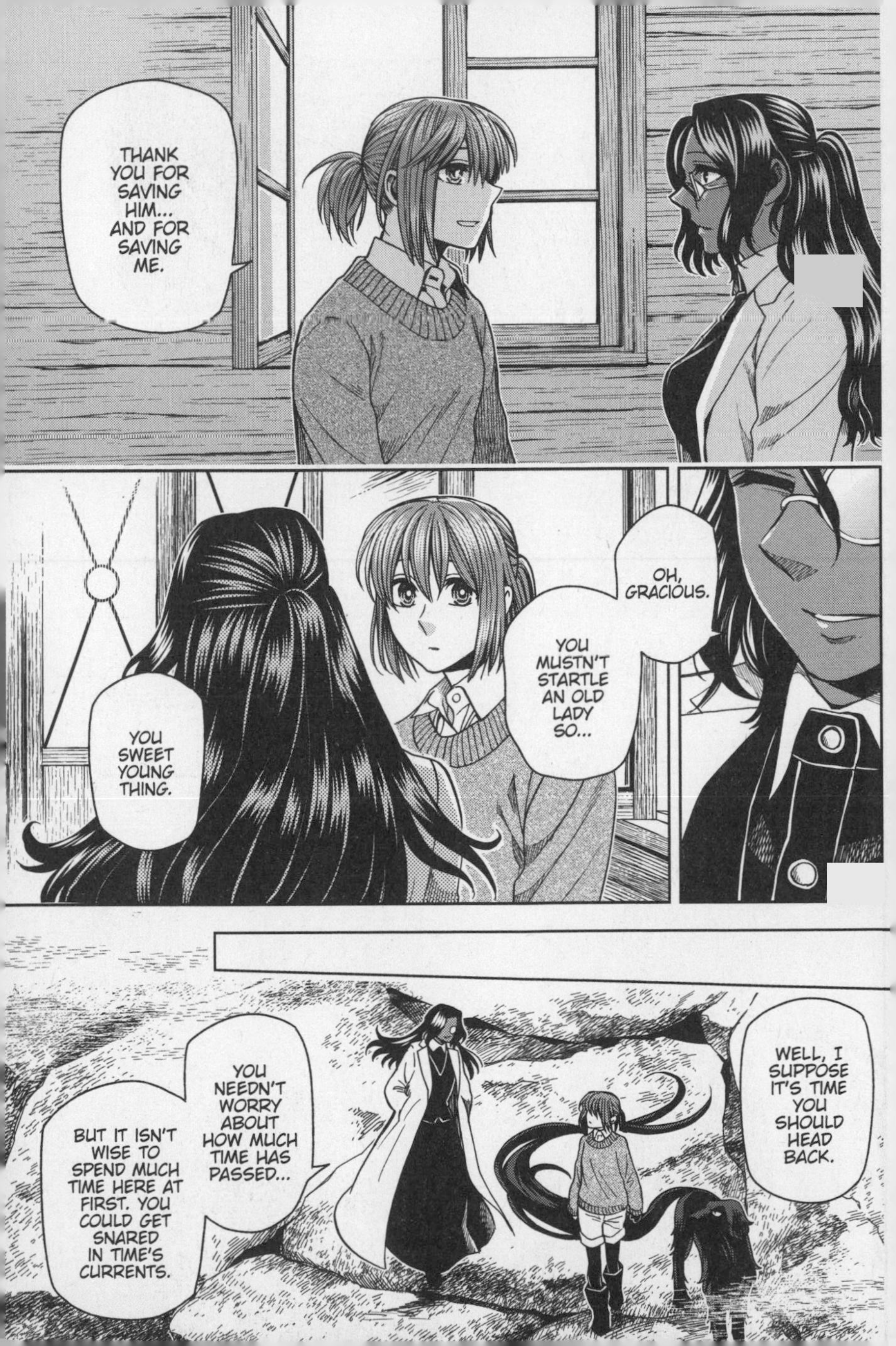
THANK YOU FOR SAVING HIM... AND FOR SAVING ME.
OH, GRACIOUS.
YOU MUSTN'T STARTLE AN OLD LADY SO...
YOU SWEET YOUNG THING.
WELL, I SUPPOSE IT'S TIME YOU SHOULD HEAD BACK.
YOU NEEDN'T WORRY ABOUT HOW MUCH TIME HAS PASSED...
BUT IT ISN'T WISE TO SPEND MUCH TIME HERE AT FIRST. YOU COULD GET SNARED IN TIME'S CURRENTS.

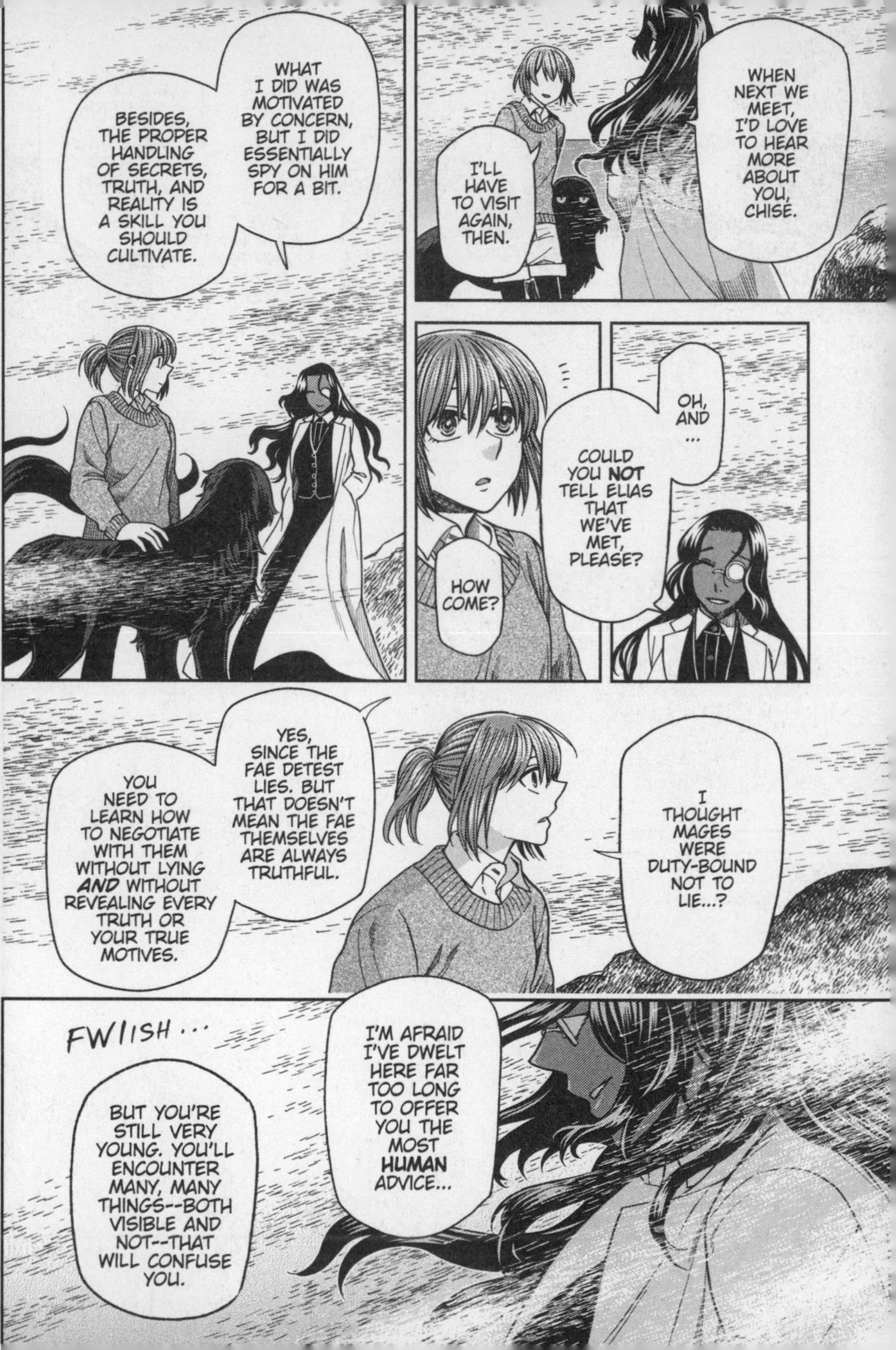
WHEN NEXT WE MEET, I'D LOVE TO HEAR MORE ABOUT YOU, CHISE.
I'LL HAVE TO VISIT AGAIN, THEN.
OH, AND ...
COULD YOU **NOT** TELL ELIAS THAT WE'VE MET, PLEASE?
HOW COME?
WHAT I DID WAS MOTIVATED BY CONCERN, BUT I DID ESSENTIALLY SPY ON HIM FOR A BIT.
BESIDES, THE PROPER HANDLING OF SECRETS, TRUTH, AND REALITY IS A SKILL YOU SHOULD CULTIVATE.
I THOUGHT MAGES WERE DUTY-BOUND NOT TO LIE...?
YES, SINCE THE FAE DETEST LIES. BUT THAT DOESN'T MEAN THE FAE THEMSELVES ARE ALWAYS TRUTHFUL.
YOU NEED TO LEARN HOW TO NEGOTIATE WITH THEM WITHOUT LYING *AND* WITHOUT REVEALING EVERY TRUTH OR YOUR TRUE MOTIVES.
I'M AFRAID I'VE DWELT HERE FAR TOO LONG TO OFFER YOU THE MOST **HUMAN** ADVICE...
BUT YOU'RE STILL VERY YOUNG. YOU'LL ENCOUNTER MANY, MANY THINGS--BOTH VISIBLE AND NOT--THAT WILL CONFUSE YOU.
FWIISH ...

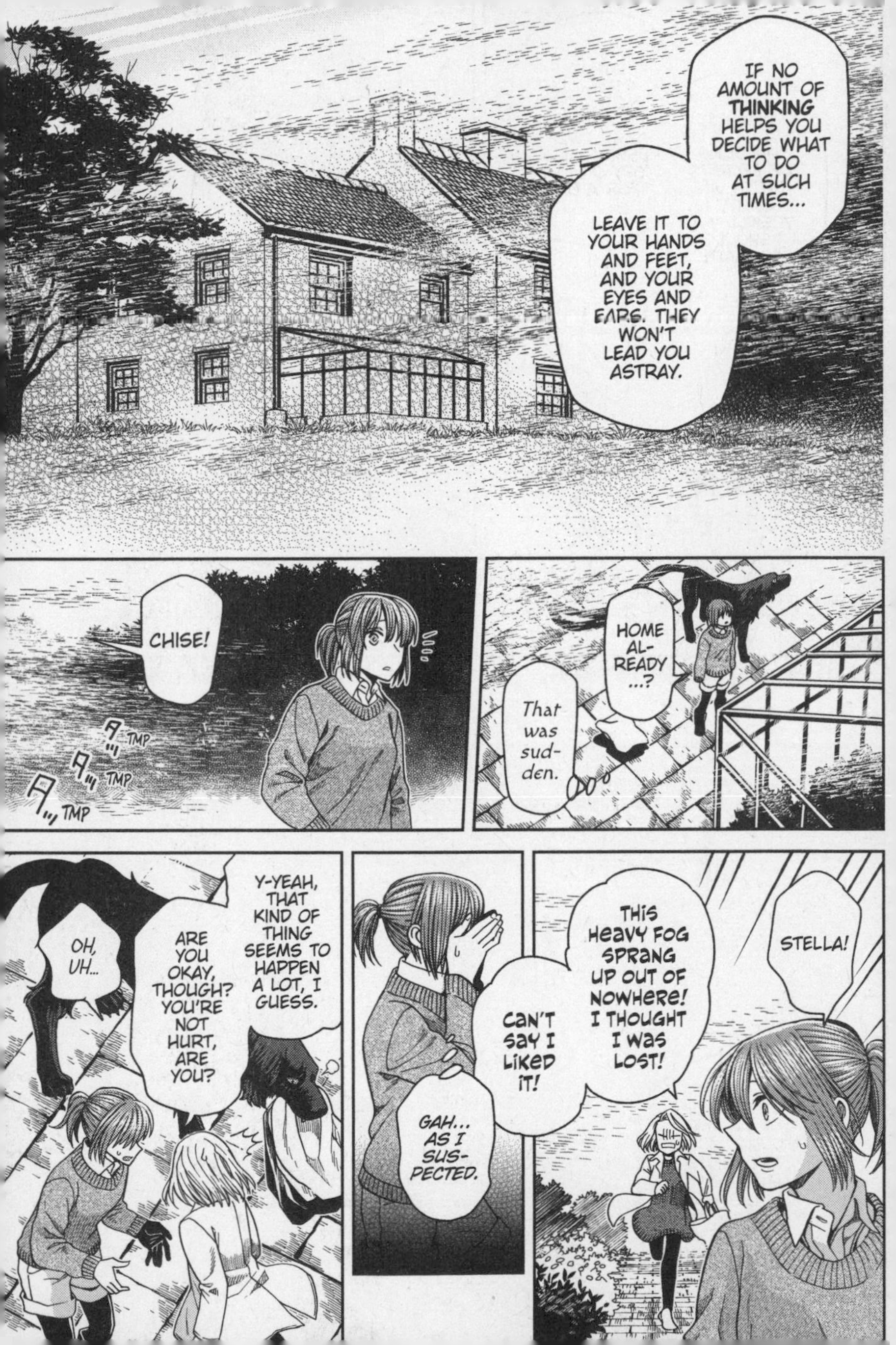
IF NO AMOUNT OF THINKING HELPS YOU DECIDE WHAT TO DO AT SUCH TIMES...
LEAVE IT TO YOUR HANDS AND FEET, AND YOUR EYES AND EARS. THEY WON'T LEAD YOU ASTRAY.
HOME AL-READY ...?
That was sud-den.
CHISE!
TMP
TMP
TMP
STELLA!
THIS HEAVY FOG SPRANG UP OUT OF NOWHERE! I THOUGHT I WAS LOST!
CAN'T SAY I LIKED IT!
GAH... AS I SUS-PECTED.
Y-YEAH, THAT KIND OF THING SEEMS TO HAPPEN A LOT, I GUESS.
ARE YOU OKAY, THOUGH? YOU'RE NOT HURT, ARE YOU?
OH, UH...

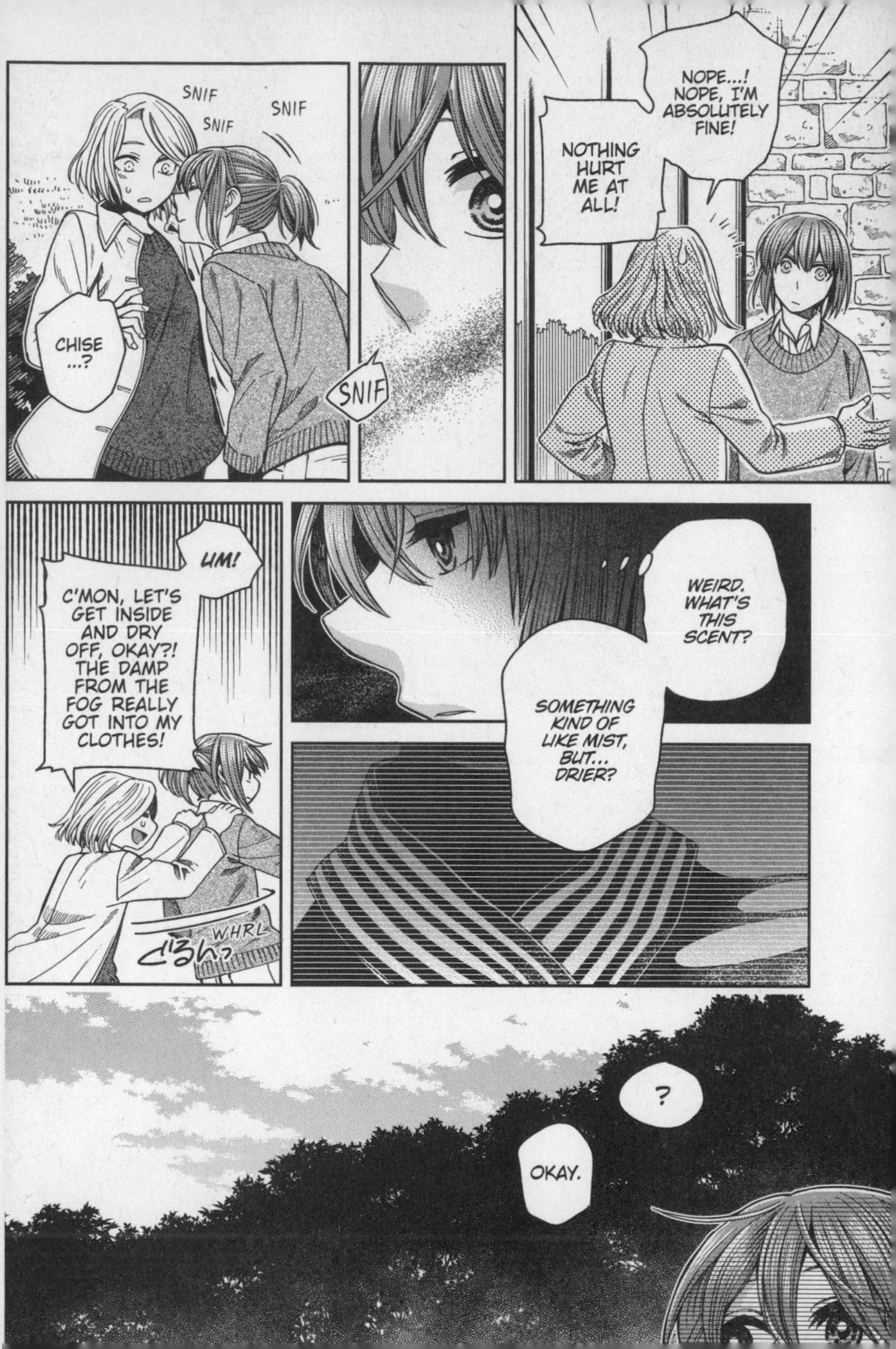
NOPE...! NOPE, I'M ABSOLUTELY FINE!
NOTHING HURT ME AT ALL!
SNIF
SNIF
SNIF
SNIF
CHISE ...?
WEIRD. WHAT'S THIS SCENT?
SOMETHING KIND OF LIKE MIST, BUT... DRIER?
UM!
C'MON, LET'S GET INSIDE AND DRY OFF, OKAY?! THE DAMP FROM THE FOG REALLY GOT INTO MY CLOTHES!
WHRL
ぐるんっ
?
OKAY.

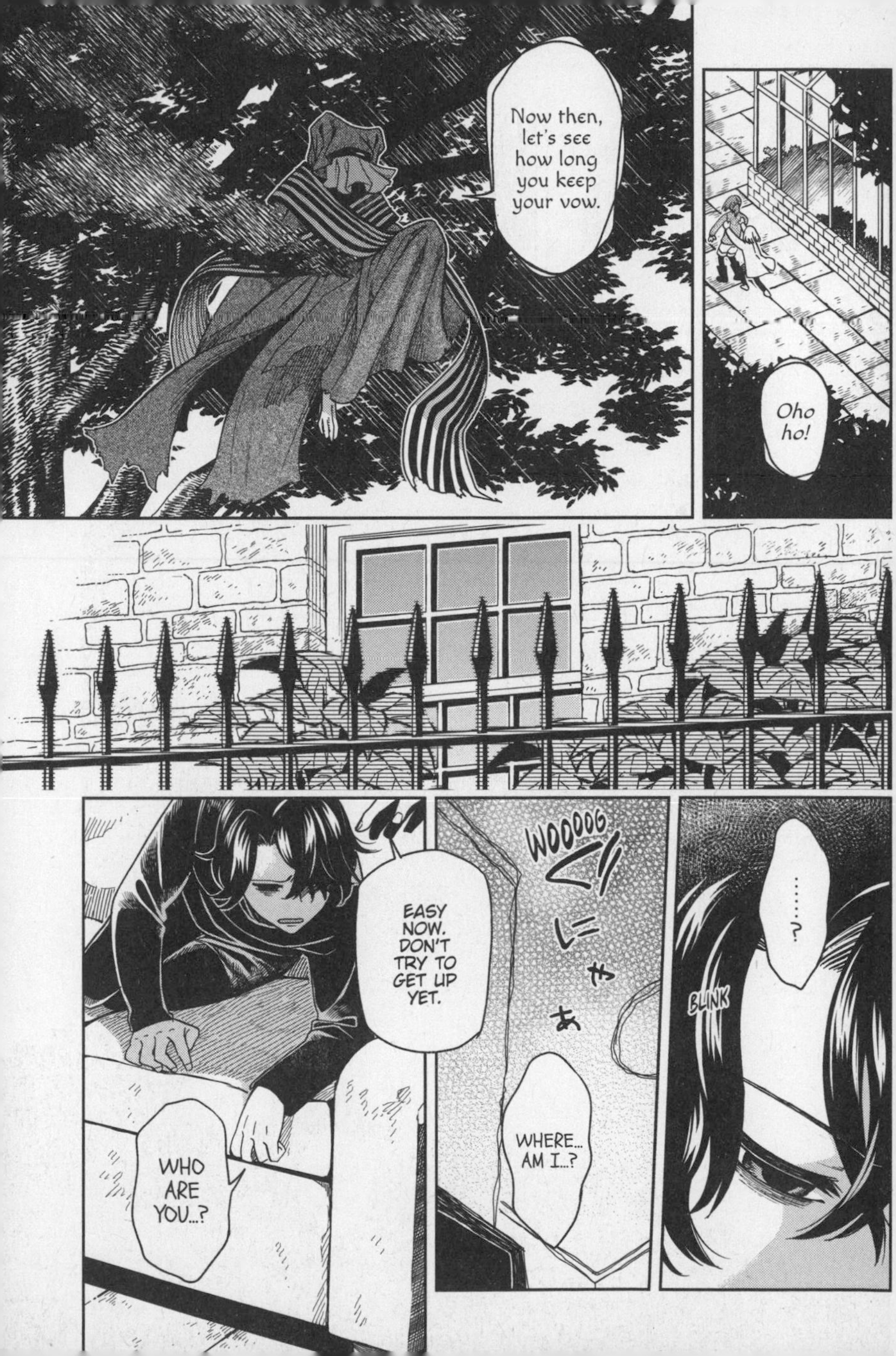
Oho ho!
Now then, let's see how long you keep your vow.
......?
BLINK
WOOOOG
WHERE... AM I...?
EASY NOW. DON'T TRY TO GET UP YET.
WHO ARE YOU...?

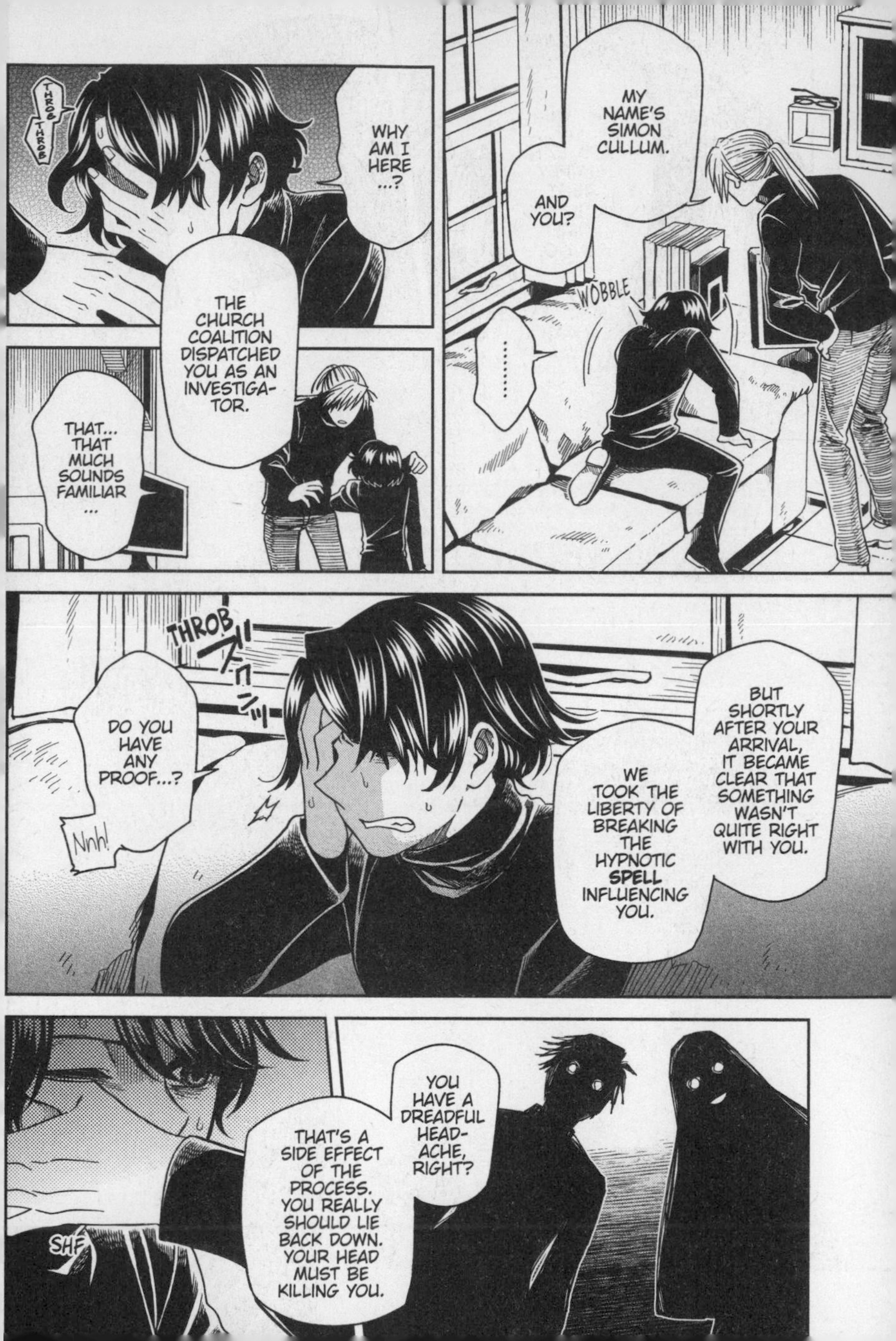
MY NAME'S SIMON CULLUM.
AND YOU?
WOBBLE
......
THROB THROB
WHY AM I HERE ...?
THE CHURCH COALITION DISPATCHED YOU AS AN INVESTIGA-TOR.
THAT... THAT MUCH SOUNDS FAMILIAR ...
BUT SHORTLY AFTER YOUR ARRIVAL, IT BECAME CLEAR THAT SOMETHING WASN'T QUITE RIGHT WITH YOU.
WE TOOK THE LIBERTY OF BREAKING THE HYPNOTIC **SPELL** INFLUENCING YOU.
THROB
DO YOU HAVE ANY PROOF...?
Nnh!
YOU HAVE A DREADFUL HEAD-ACHE, RIGHT?
THAT'S A SIDE EFFECT OF THE PROCESS. YOU REALLY SHOULD LIE BACK DOWN. YOUR HEAD MUST BE KILLING YOU.
SHF

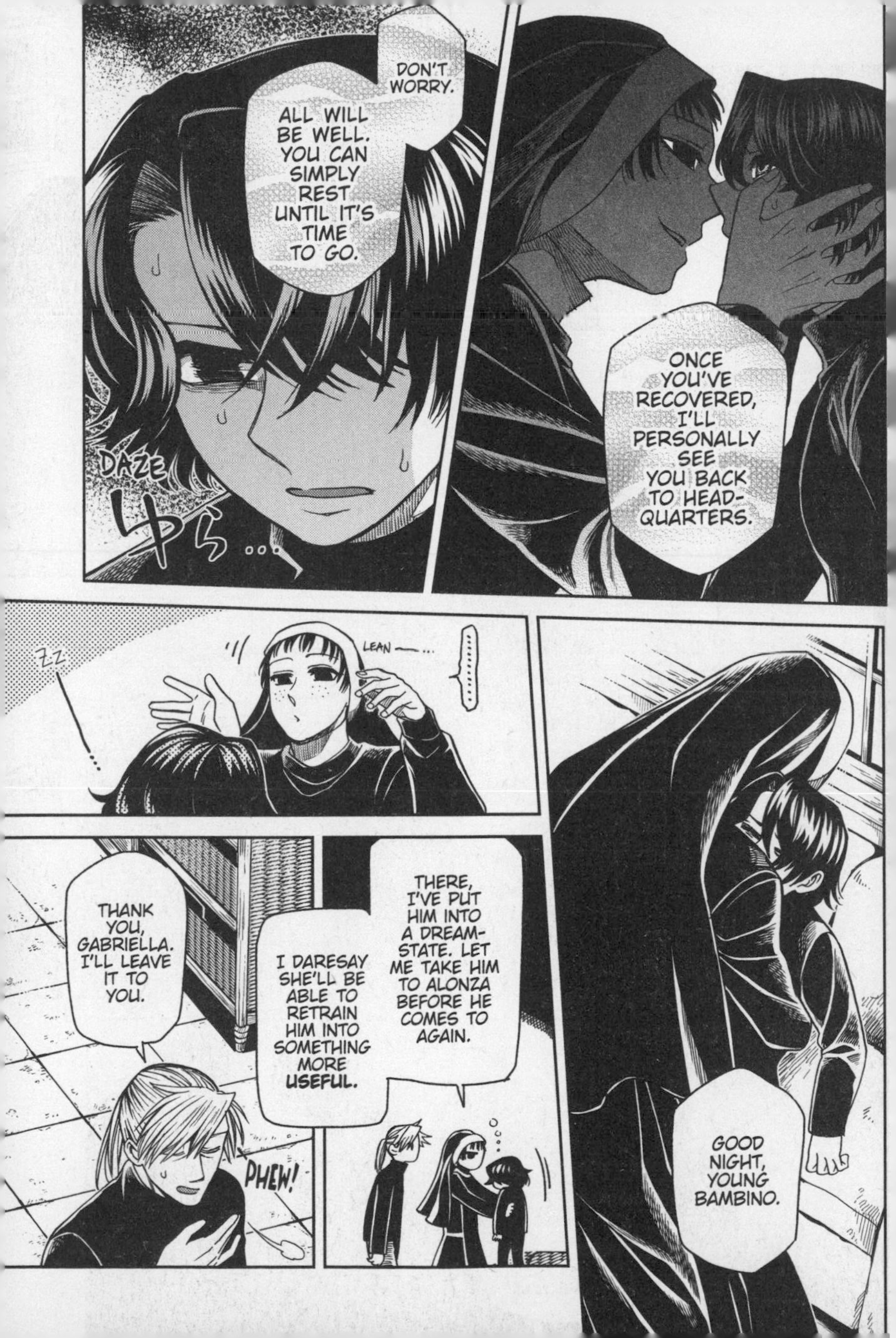
ONCE YOU'VE RECOVERED, I'LL PERSONALLY SEE YOU BACK TO HEAD-QUARTERS.
DON'T WORRY.
ALL WILL BE WELL. YOU CAN SIMPLY REST UNTIL IT'S TIME TO GO.
DAZE
ゆら…
GOOD NIGHT, YOUNG BAMBINO.
LEAN—...
......
ZZ
...
THERE, I'VE PUT HIM INTO A DREAM-STATE. LET ME TAKE HIM TO ALONZA BEFORE HE COMES TO AGAIN.
I DARESAY SHE'LL BE ABLE TO RETRAIN HIM INTO SOMETHING MORE **USEFUL**.
THANK YOU, GABRIELLA. I'LL LEAVE IT TO YOU.
PHEW!

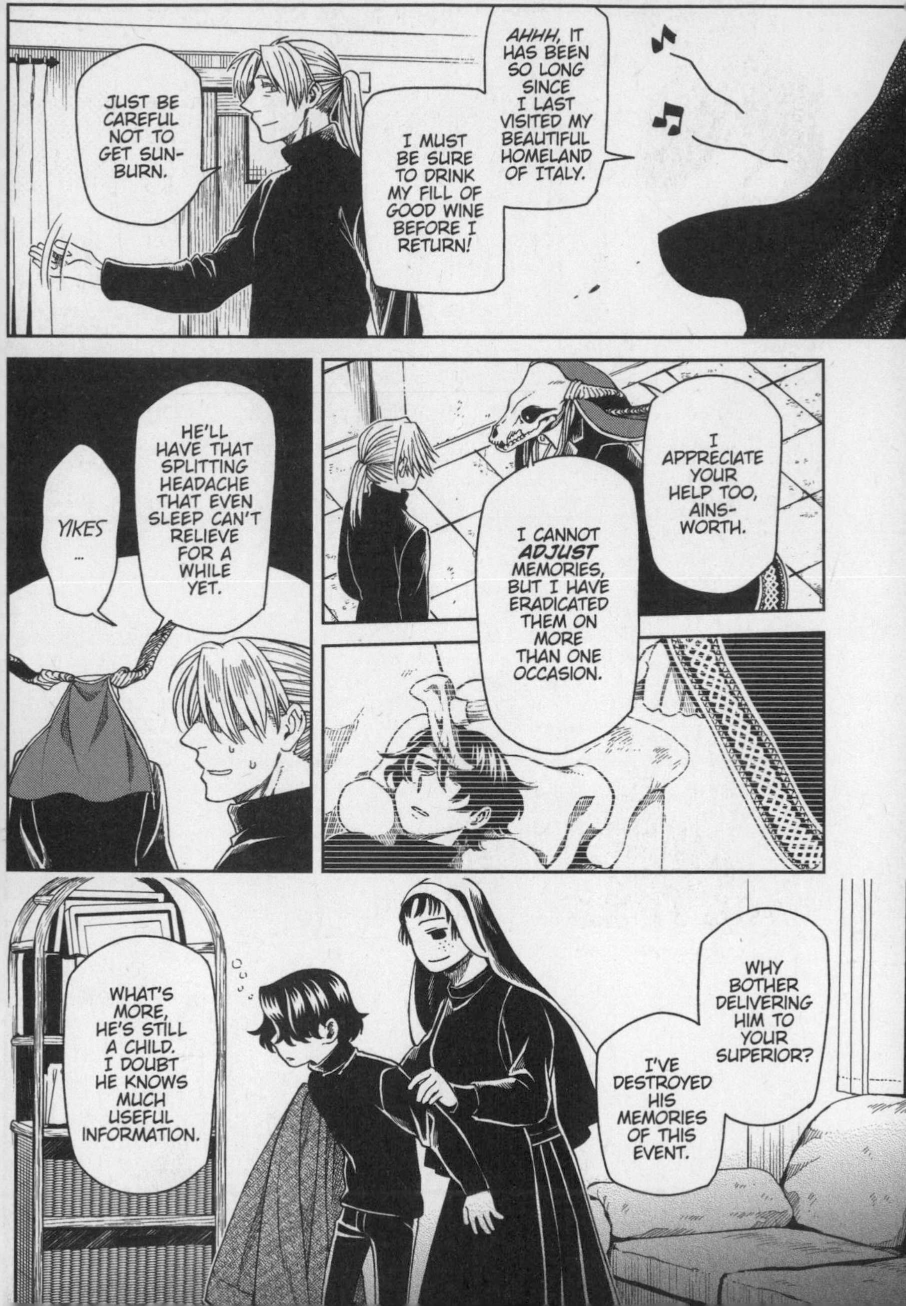
AHHH, IT HAS BEEN SO LONG SINCE I LAST VISITED MY BEAUTIFUL HOMELAND OF ITALY.
I MUST BE SURE TO DRINK MY FILL OF GOOD WINE BEFORE I RETURN!
JUST BE CAREFUL NOT TO GET SUN-BURN.
I APPRECIATE YOUR HELP TOO, AINS-WORTH.
I CANNOT ADJUST MEMORIES, BUT I HAVE ERADICATED THEM ON MORE THAN ONE OCCASION.
HE'LL HAVE THAT SPLITTING HEADACHE THAT EVEN SLEEP CAN'T RELIEVE FOR A WHILE YET.
YIKES ...
WHY BOTHER DELIVERING HIM TO YOUR SUPERIOR?
I'VE DESTROYED HIS MEMORIES OF THIS EVENT.
WHAT'S MORE, HE'S STILL A CHILD. I DOUBT HE KNOWS MUCH USEFUL INFORMATION.

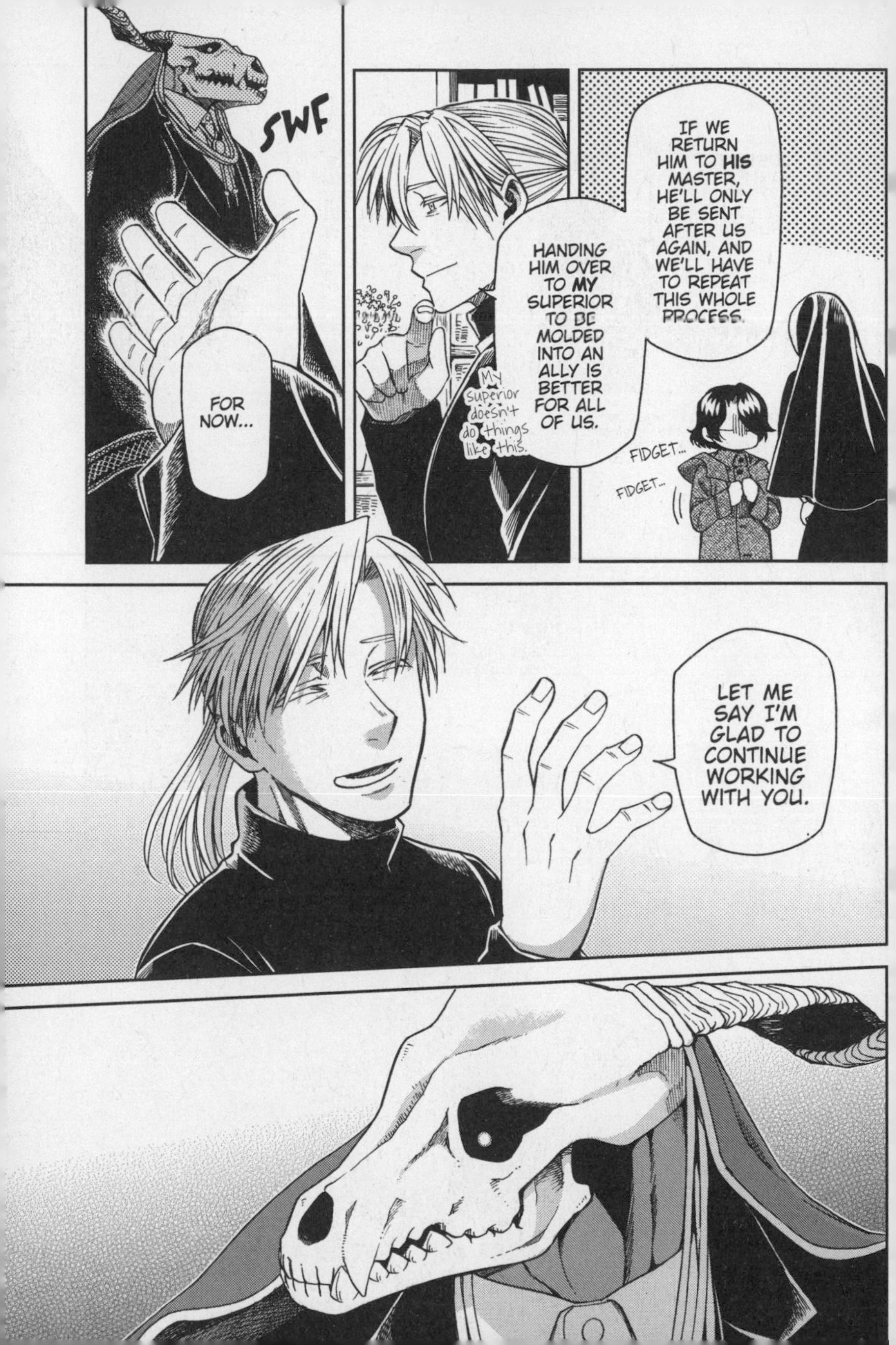
IF WE RETURN HIM TO HIS MASTER, HE'LL ONLY BE SENT AFTER US AGAIN, AND WE'LL HAVE TO REPEAT THIS WHOLE PROCESS.
FIDGET...
FIDGET...
HANDING HIM OVER TO MY SUPERIOR TO BE MOLDED INTO AN ALLY IS BETTER FOR ALL OF US.
My superior doesn't do things like this.
SWF
FOR NOW...
LET ME SAY I'M GLAD TO CONTINUE WORKING WITH YOU.

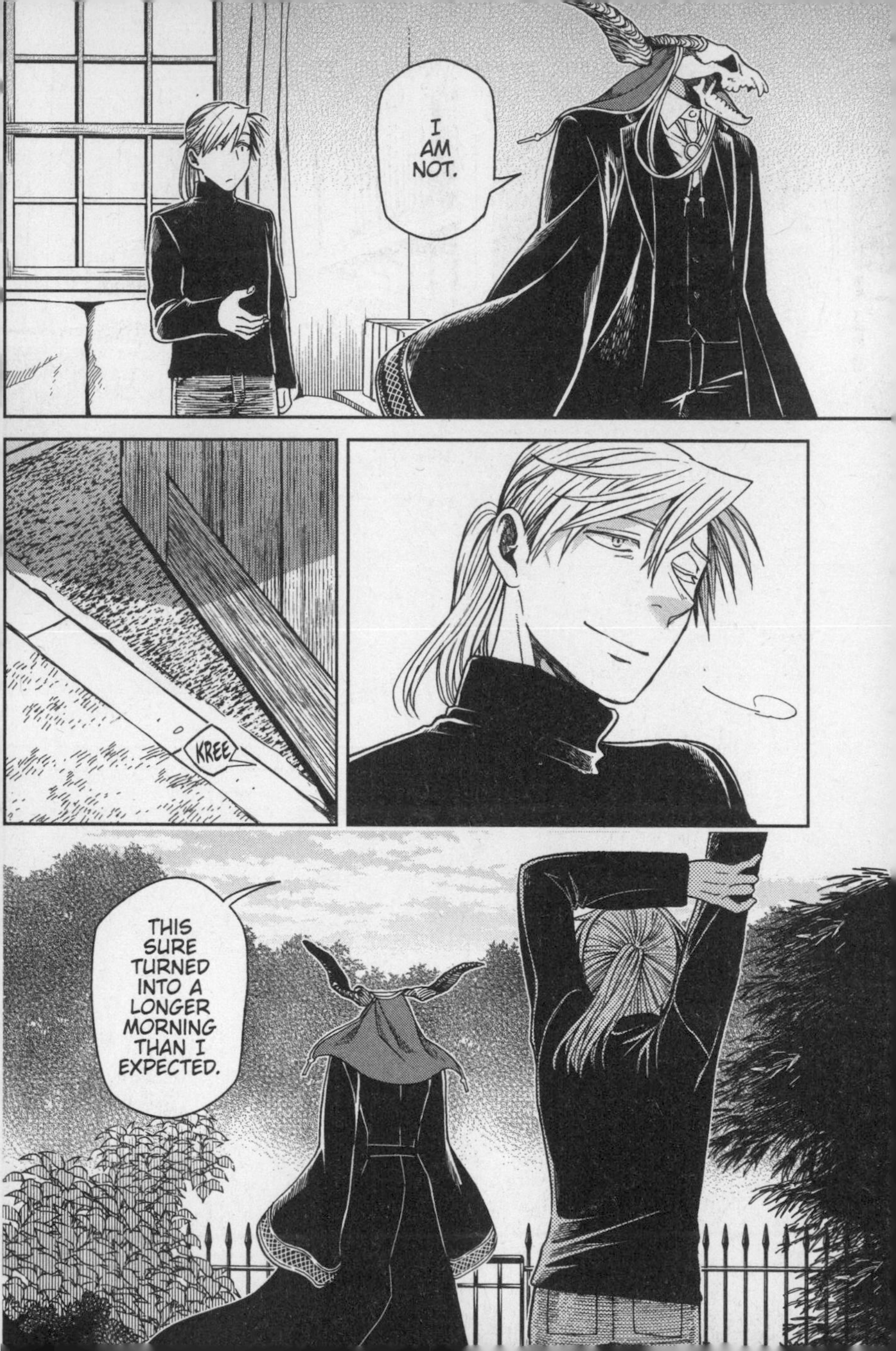
I AM NOT.
KREE
THIS SURE TURNED INTO A LONGER MORNING THAN I EXPECTED.

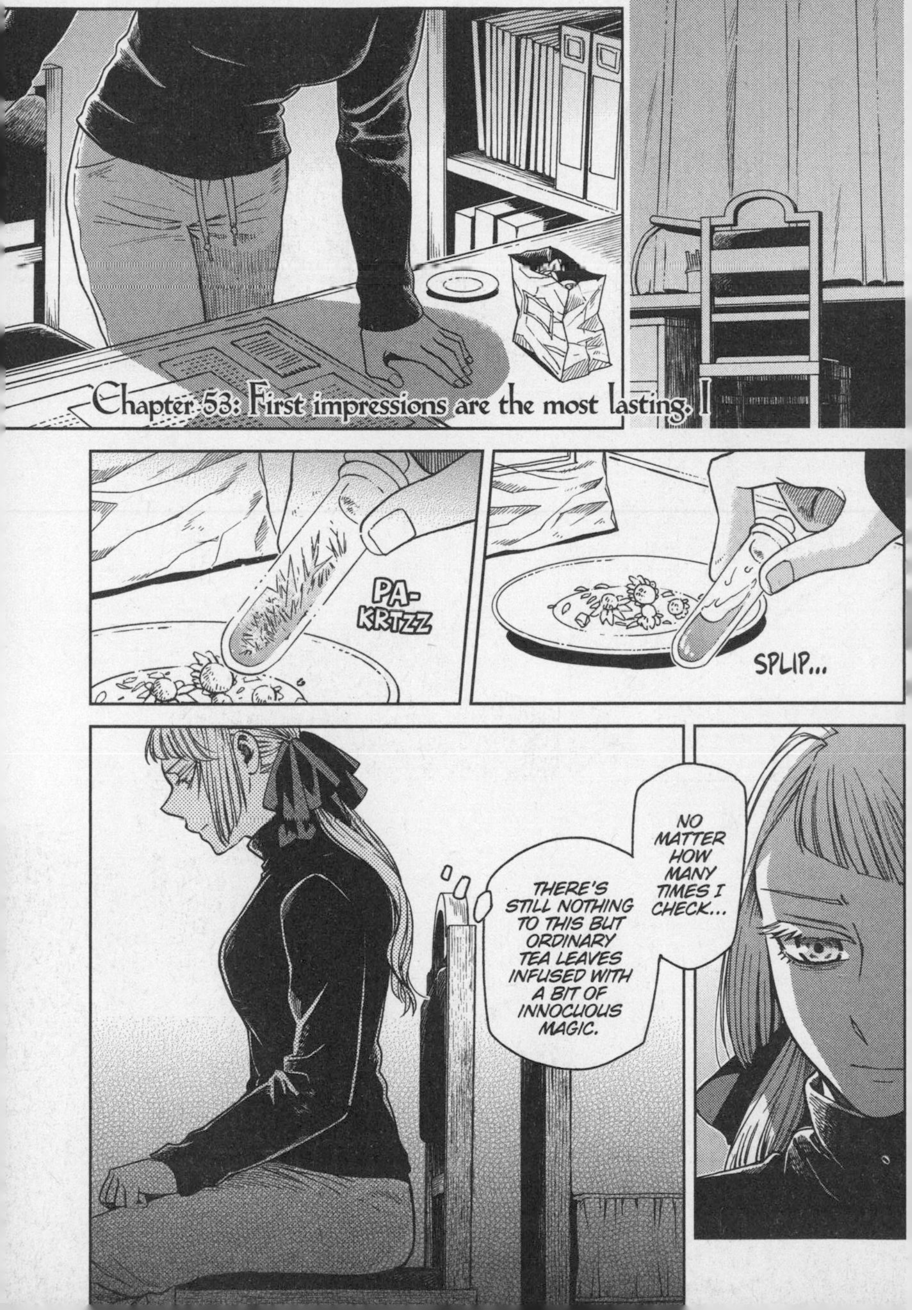
Chapter 53: First impressions are the most lasting. I
SPLIP...
PA-KRTZZ
NO MATTER HOW MANY TIMES I CHECK...
THERE'S STILL NOTHING TO THIS BUT ORDINARY TEA LEAVES INFUSED WITH A BIT OF INNOCUOUS MAGIC.

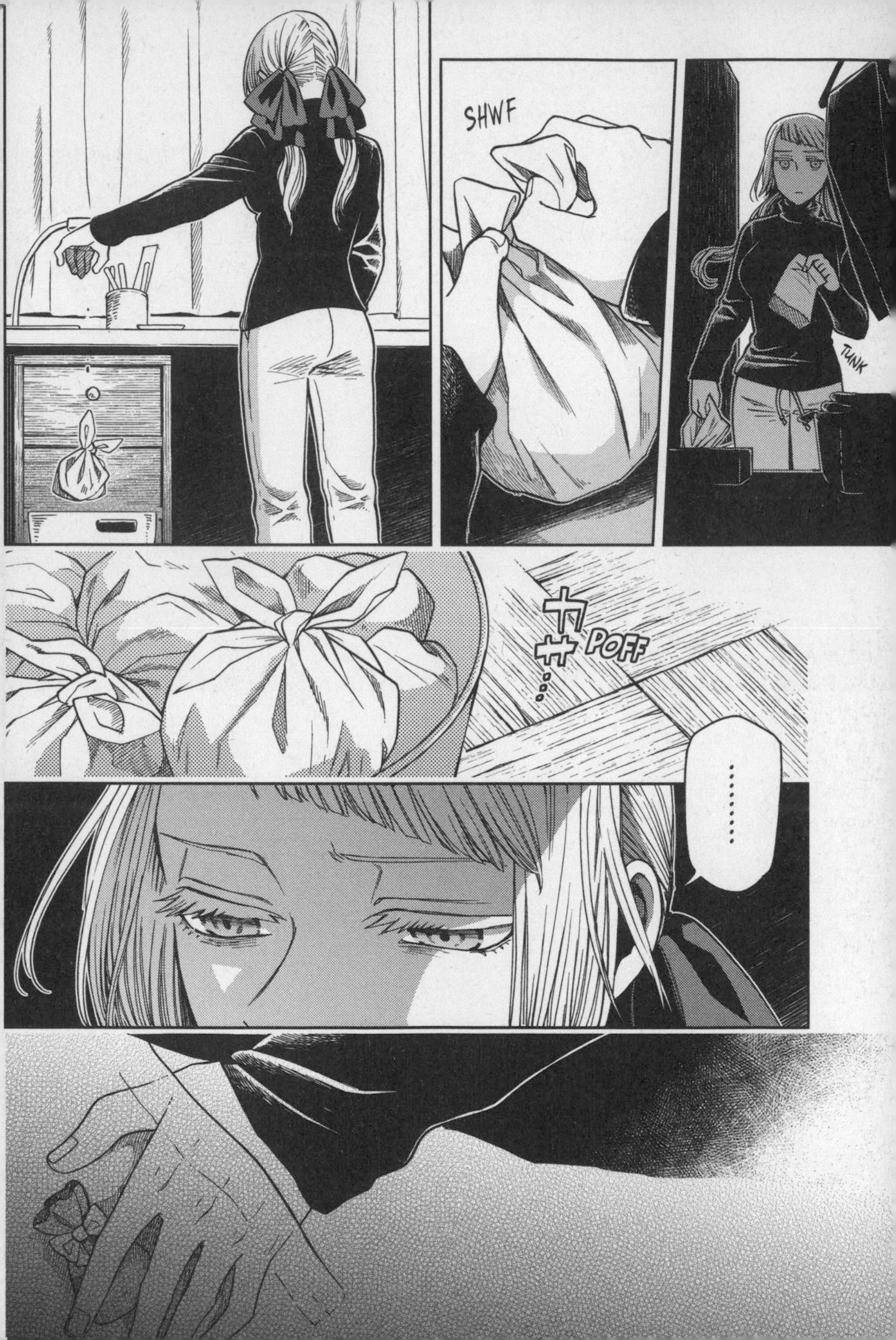
TUNK
SHWF
POFF
......

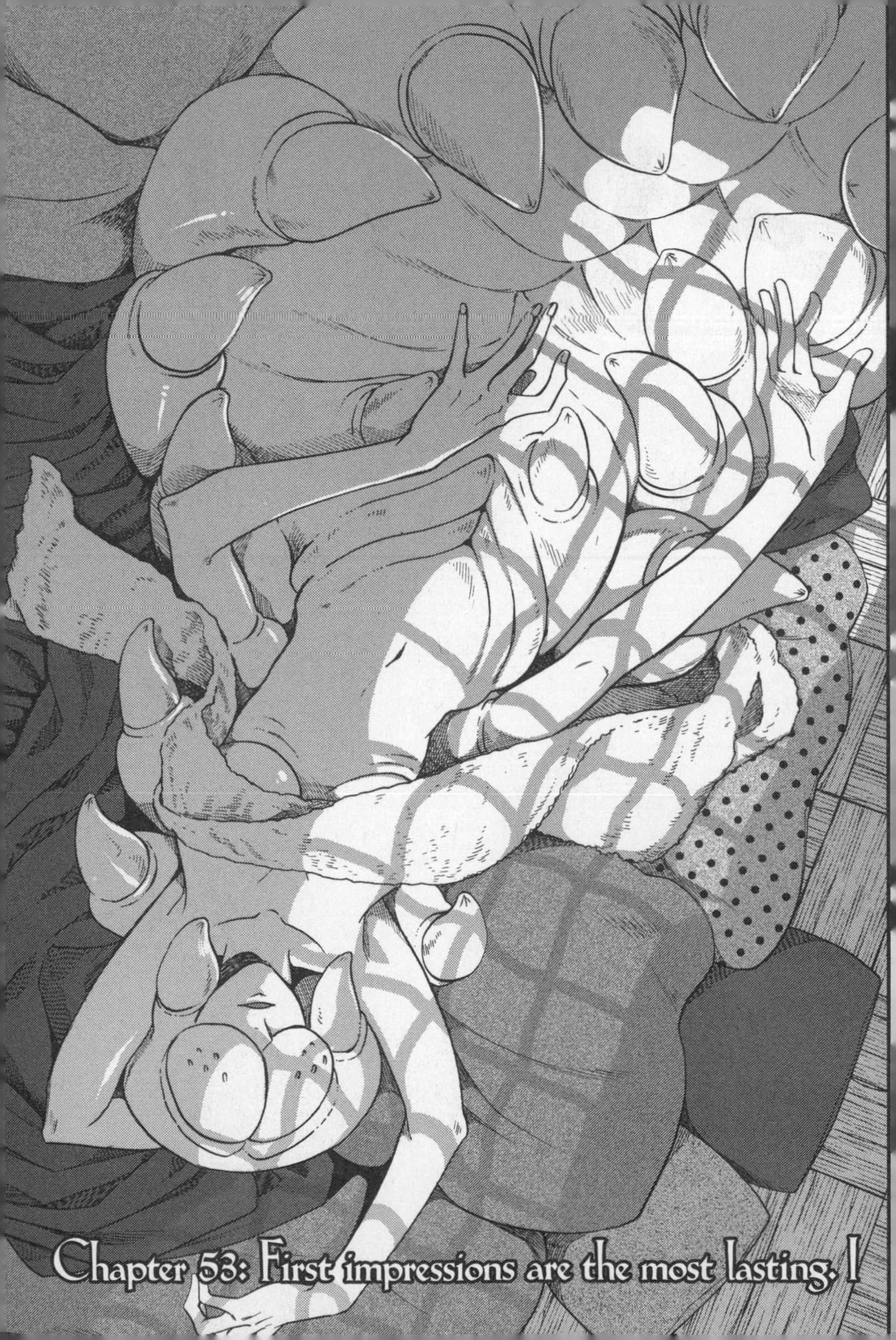
Chapter 53: First impressions are the most lasting. I

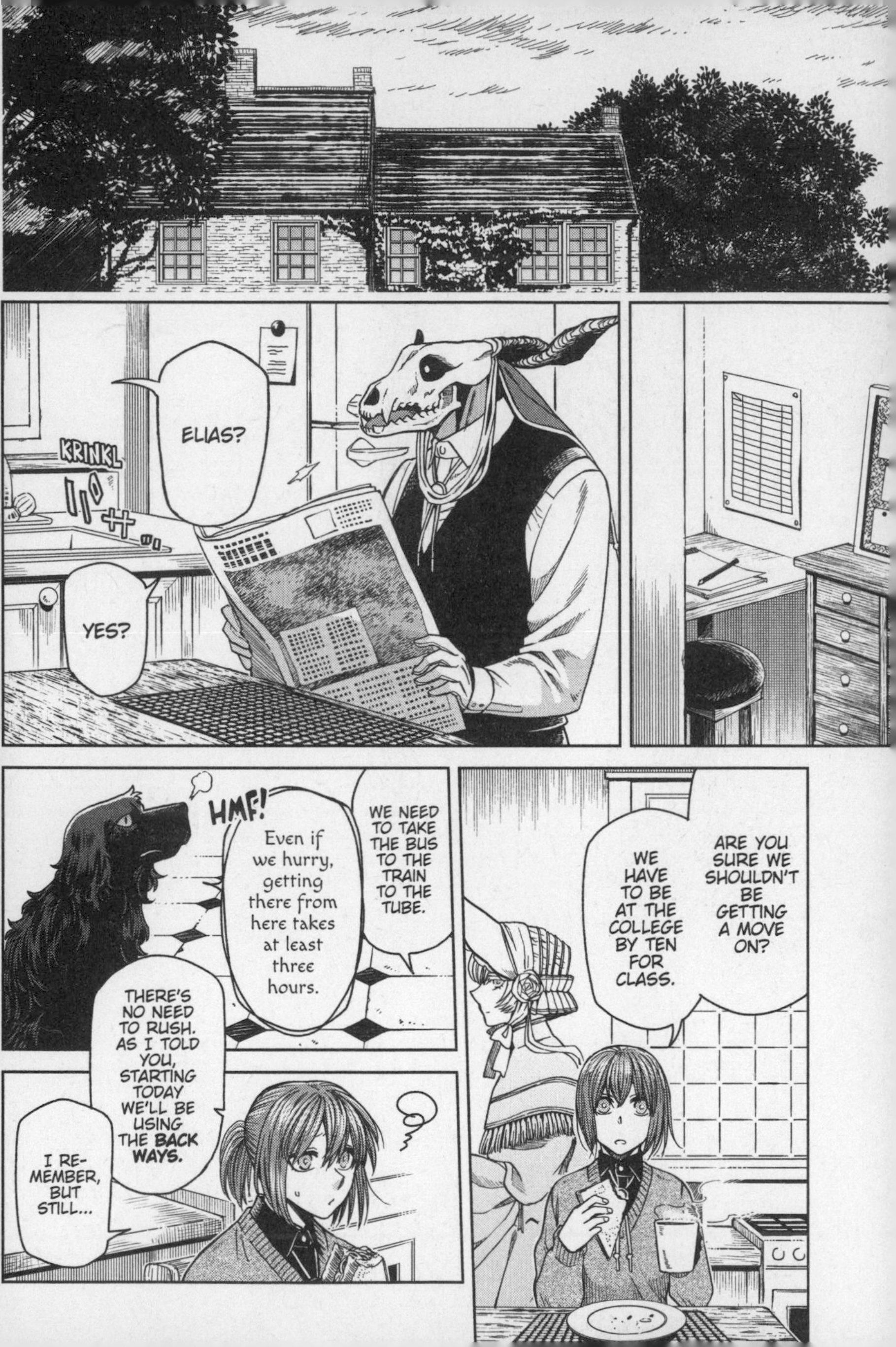
ELIAS?
KRINKL
YES?
ARE YOU SURE WE SHOULDN'T BE GETTING A MOVE ON?
WE HAVE TO BE AT THE COLLEGE BY TEN FOR CLASS.
WE NEED TO TAKE THE BUS TO THE TRAIN TO THE TUBE.
HMF!
Even if we hurry, getting there from here takes at least three hours.
THERE'S NO NEED TO RUSH. AS I TOLD YOU, STARTING TODAY WE'LL BE USING THE BACK WAYS.
I RE-MEMBER, BUT STILL...

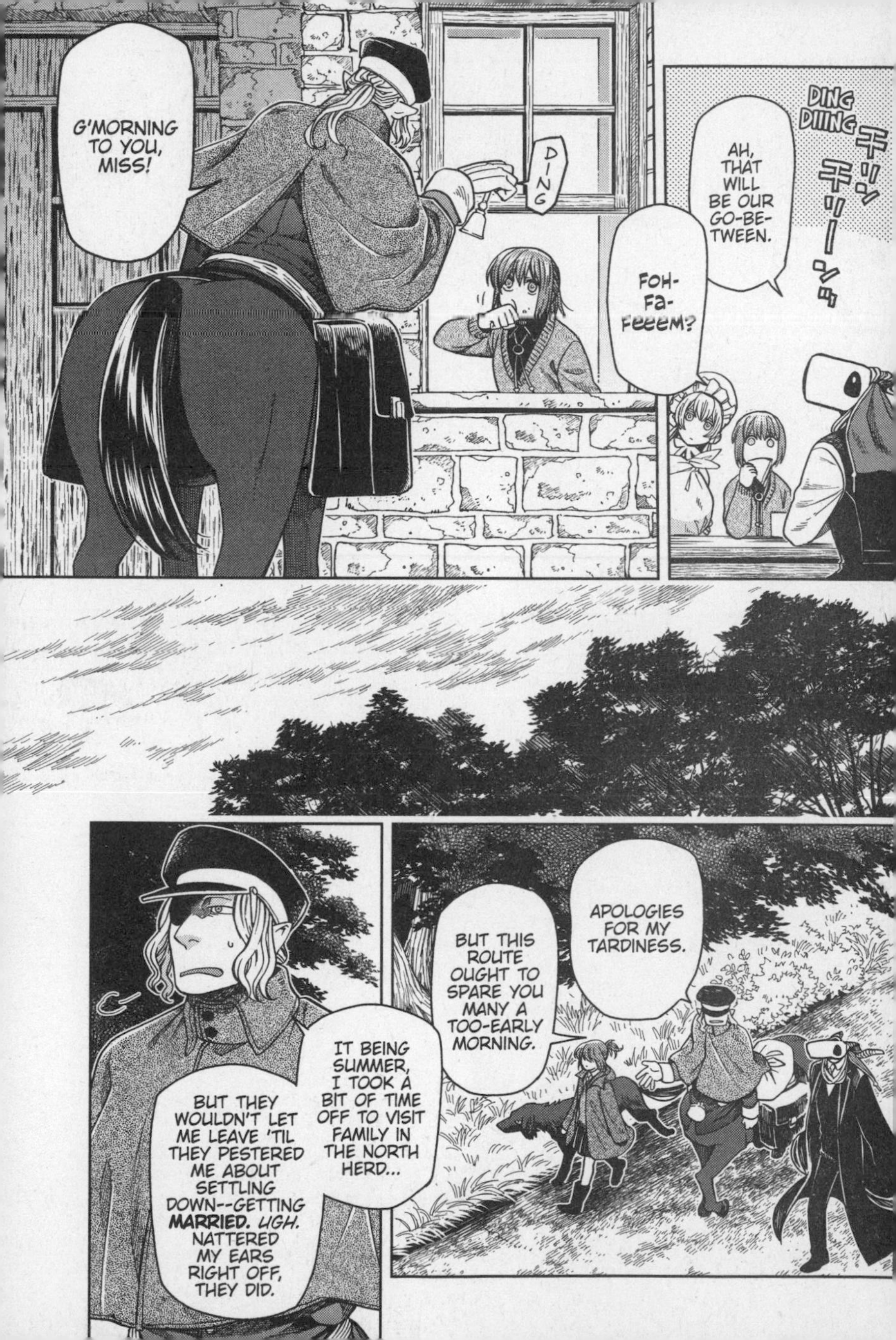
DING DIIING
チリン チリーン
AH, THAT WILL BE OUR GO-BETWEEN.
FOH-FA-FEEEM?
DING
G'MORNING TO YOU, MISS!
APOLOGIES FOR MY TARDINESS.
BUT THIS ROUTE OUGHT TO SPARE YOU MANY A TOO-EARLY MORNING.
IT BEING SUMMER, I TOOK A BIT OF TIME OFF TO VISIT FAMILY IN THE NORTH HERD...
BUT THEY WOULDN'T LET ME LEAVE 'TIL THEY PESTERED ME ABOUT SETTLING DOWN--GETTING **MARRIED.** *UGH.* NATTERED MY EARS RIGHT OFF, THEY DID.

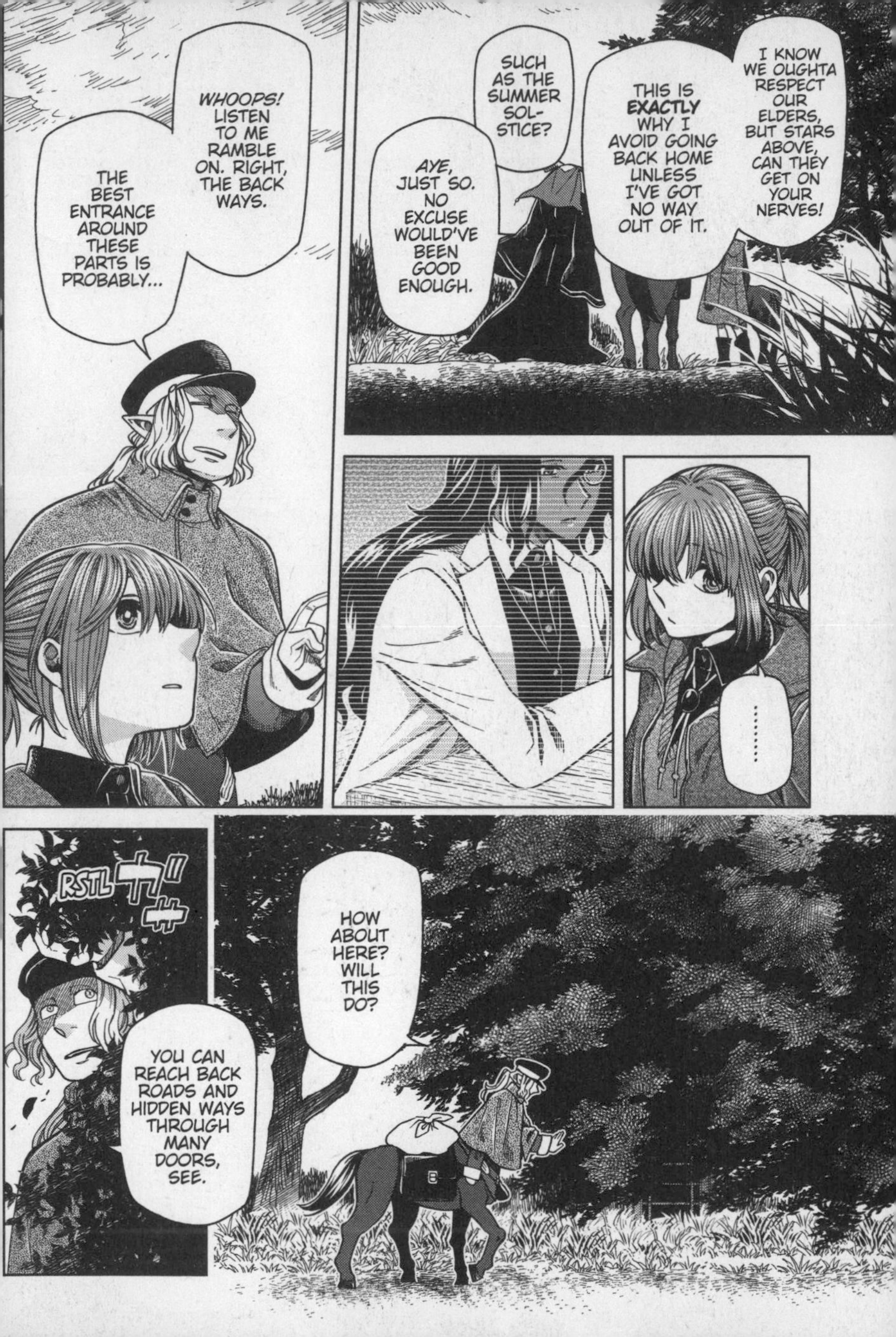
I KNOW WE OUGHTA RESPECT OUR ELDERS, BUT STARS ABOVE, CAN THEY GET ON YOUR NERVES!
THIS IS **EXACTLY** WHY I AVOID GOING BACK HOME UNLESS I'VE GOT NO WAY OUT OF IT.
SUCH AS THE SUMMER SOL-STICE?
AYE, JUST SO. NO EXCUSE WOULD'VE BEEN GOOD ENOUGH.
......
WHOOPS! LISTEN TO ME RAMBLE ON. RIGHT, THE BACK WAYS.
THE BEST ENTRANCE AROUND THESE PARTS IS PROBABLY...
HOW ABOUT HERE? WILL THIS DO?
RSTL
YOU CAN REACH BACK ROADS AND HIDDEN WAYS THROUGH MANY DOORS, SEE.

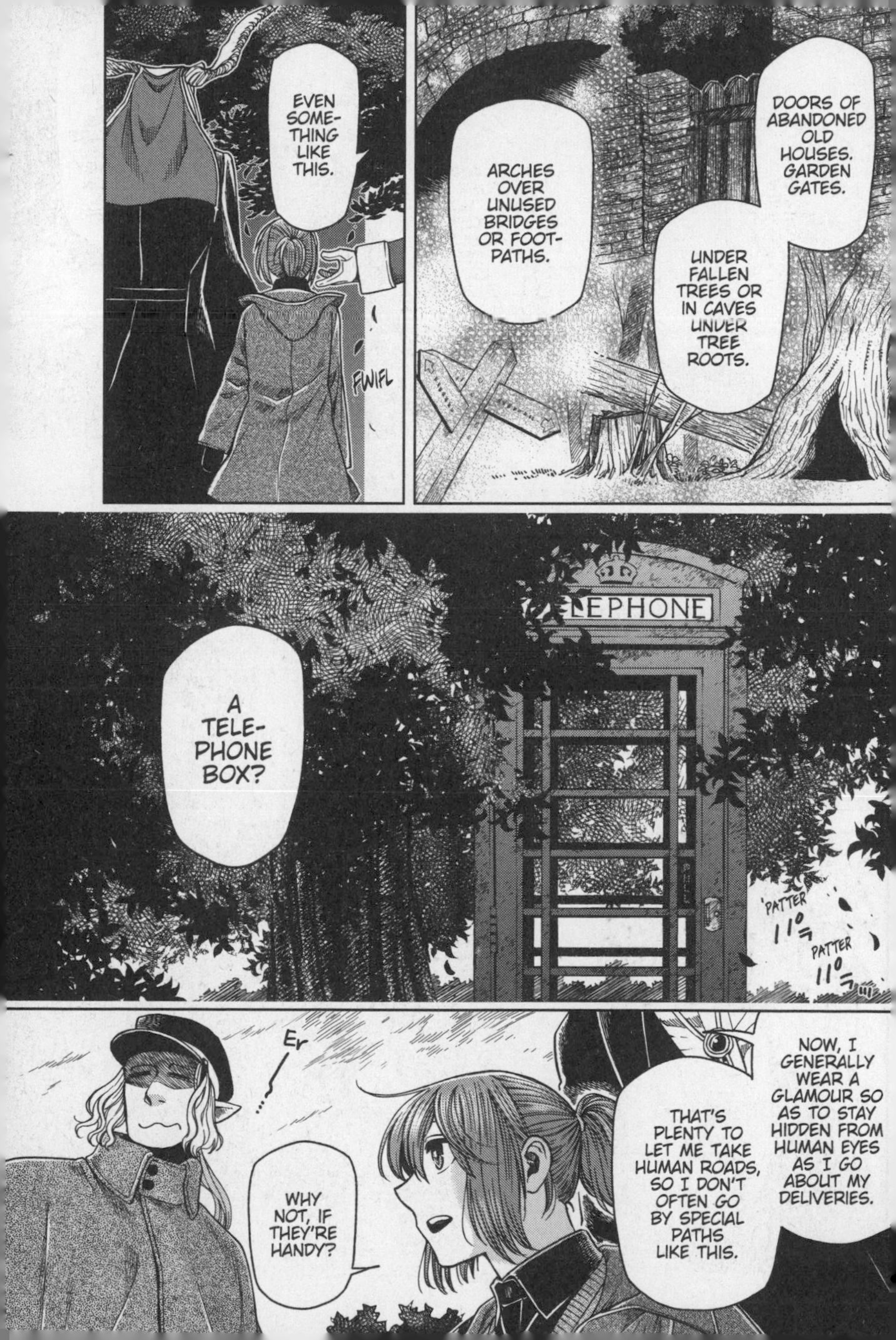
DOORS OF ABANDONED OLD HOUSES. GARDEN GATES.
UNDER FALLEN TREES OR IN CAVES UNDER TREE ROOTS.
ARCHES OVER UNUSED BRIDGES OR FOOT-PATHS.
EVEN SOME-THING LIKE THIS.
FWIFL
LEPHONE
A TELE-PHONE BOX?
PATTER
PATTER
NOW, I GENERALLY WEAR A GLAMOUR SO AS TO STAY HIDDEN FROM HUMAN EYES AS I GO ABOUT MY DELIVERIES.
THAT'S PLENTY TO LET ME TAKE HUMAN ROADS, SO I DON'T OFTEN GO BY SPECIAL PATHS LIKE THIS.
Er
WHY NOT, IF THEY'RE HANDY?

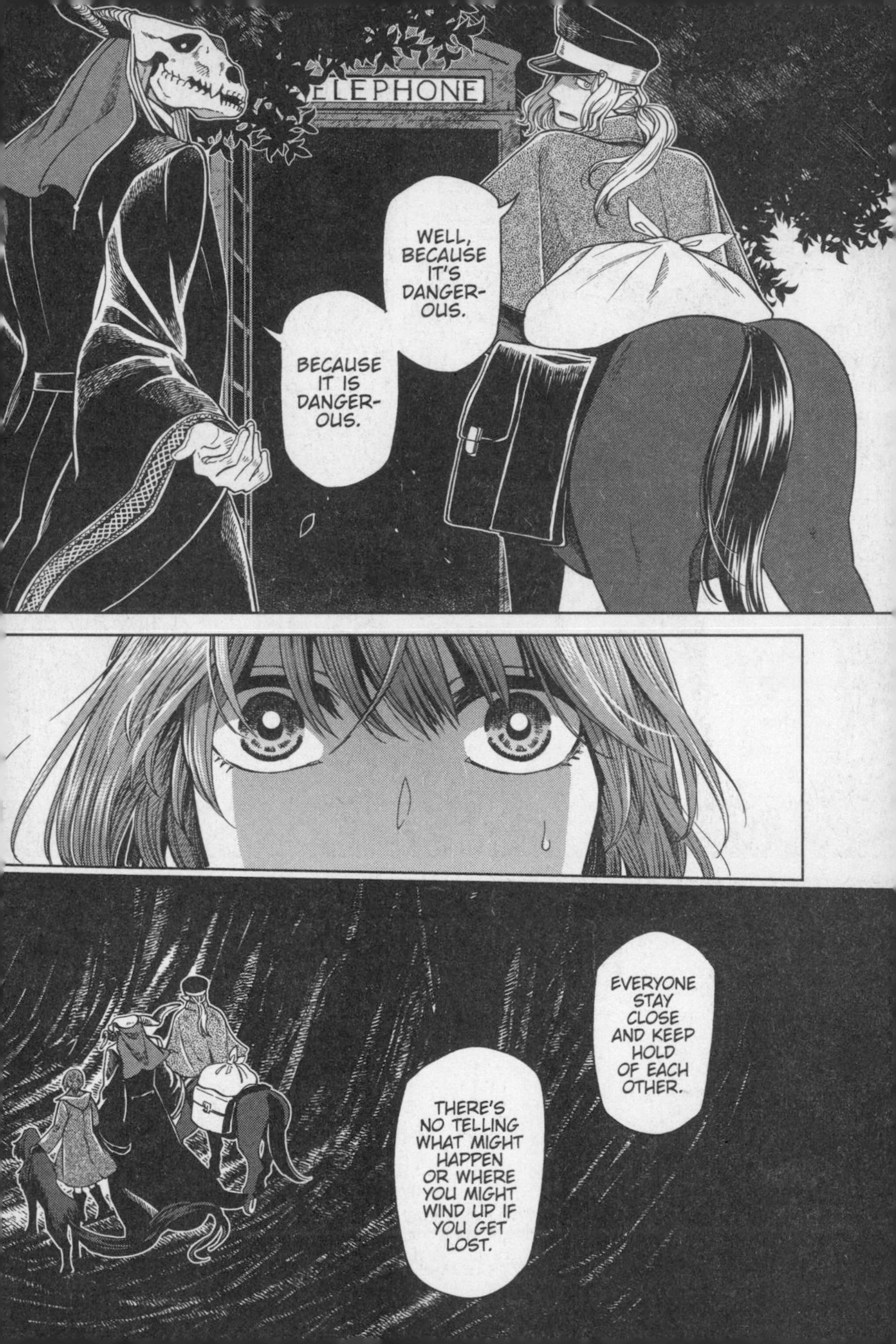
ELEPHONE
WELL, BECAUSE IT'S DANGER-OUS.
BECAUSE IT IS DANGER-OUS.
EVERYONE STAY CLOSE AND KEEP HOLD OF EACH OTHER.
THERE'S NO TELLING WHAT MIGHT HAPPEN OR WHERE YOU MIGHT WIND UP IF YOU GET LOST.

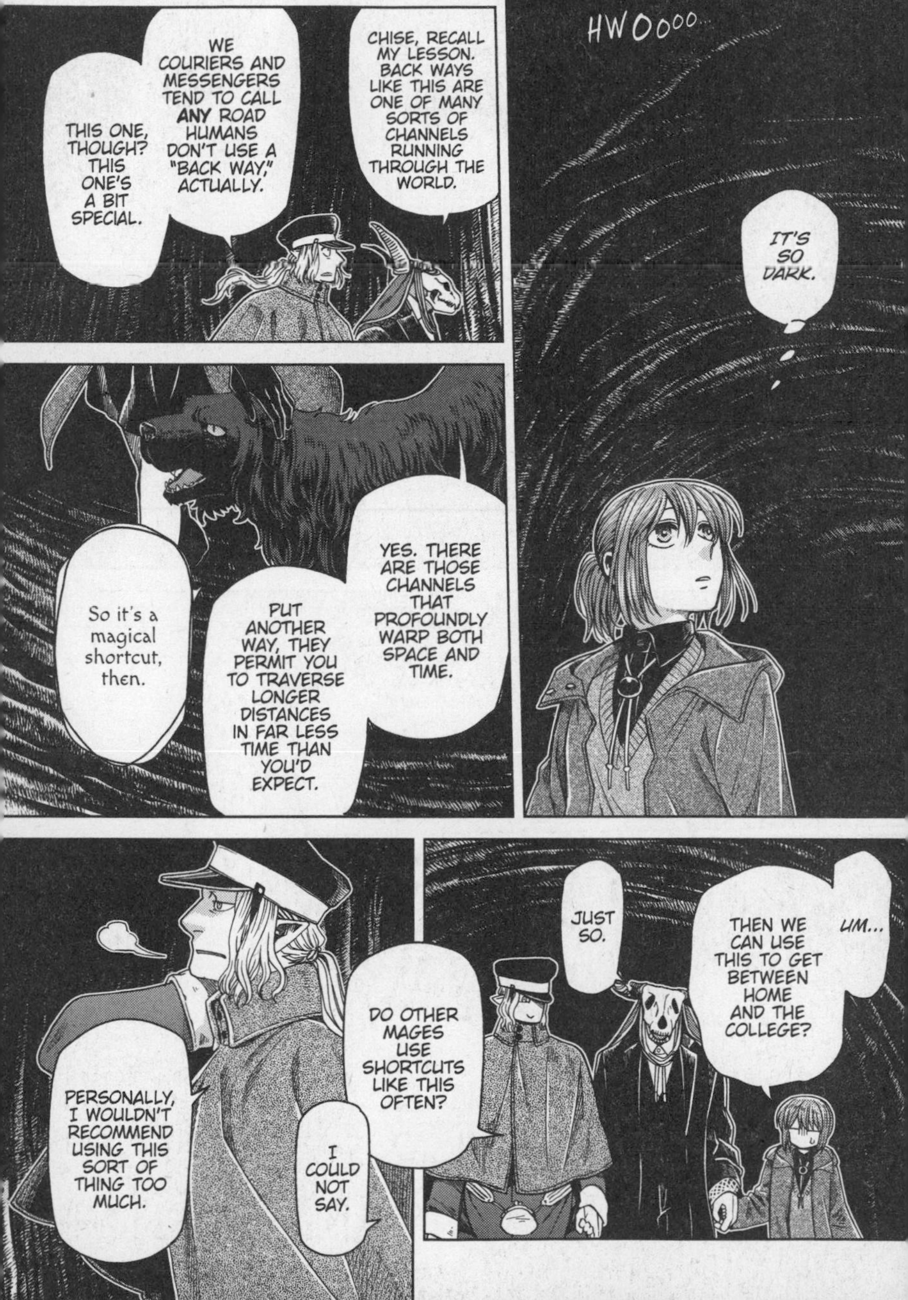
HWOooo...
IT'S SO DARK.
CHISE, RECALL MY LESSON. BACK WAYS LIKE THIS ARE ONE OF MANY SORTS OF CHANNELS RUNNING THROUGH THE WORLD.
WE COURIERS AND MESSENGERS TEND TO CALL ANY ROAD HUMANS DON'T USE A "BACK WAY," ACTUALLY.
THIS ONE, THOUGH? THIS ONE'S A BIT SPECIAL.
YES. THERE ARE THOSE CHANNELS THAT PROFOUNDLY WARP BOTH SPACE AND TIME.
PUT ANOTHER WAY, THEY PERMIT YOU TO TRAVERSE LONGER DISTANCES IN FAR LESS TIME THAN YOU'D EXPECT.
So it's a magical shortcut, then.
UM...
THEN WE CAN USE THIS TO GET BETWEEN HOME AND THE COLLEGE?
JUST SO.
DO OTHER MAGES USE SHORTCUTS LIKE THIS OFTEN?
I COULD NOT SAY.
PERSONALLY, I WOULDN'T RECOMMEND USING THIS SORT OF THING TOO MUCH.

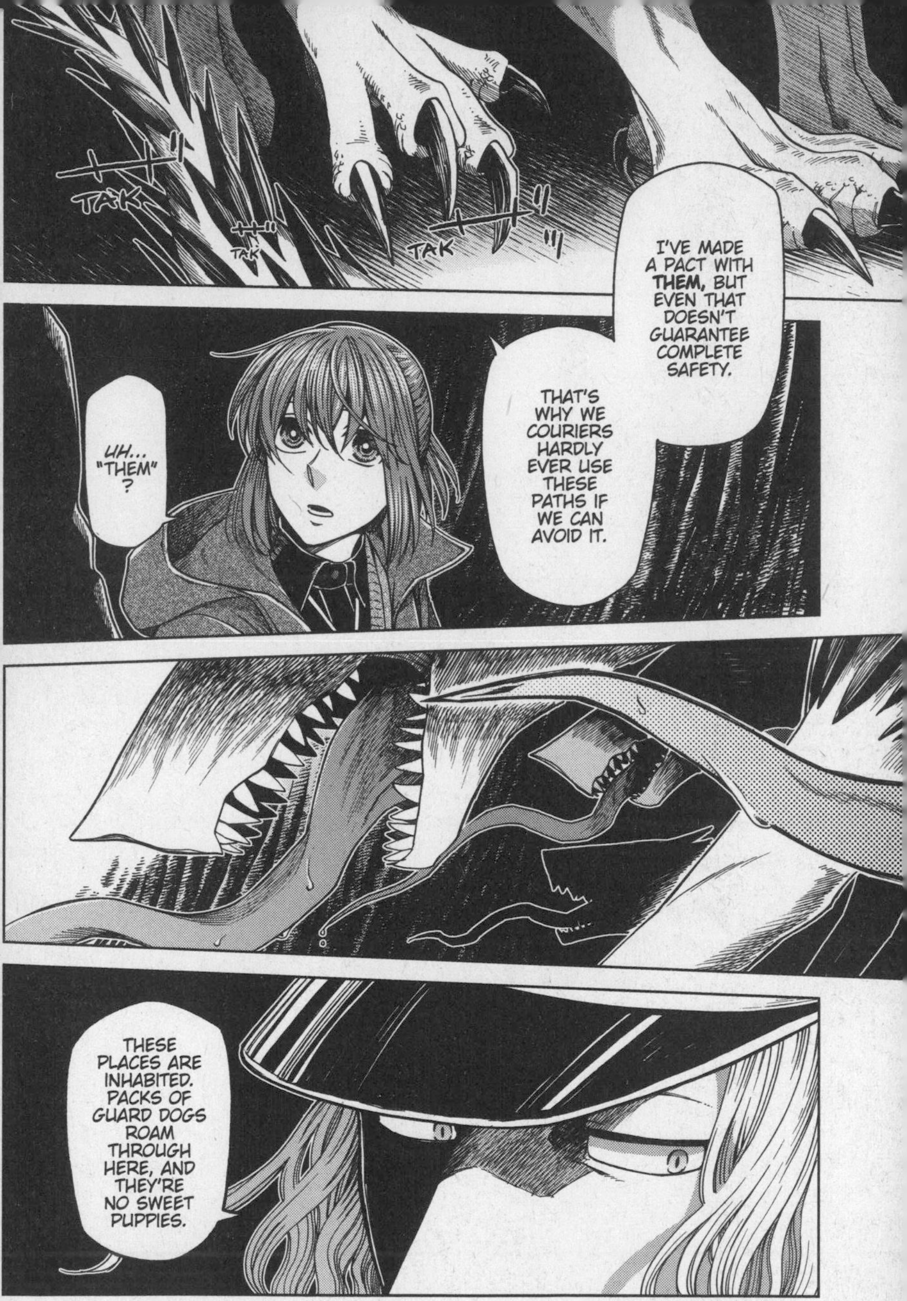
I'VE MADE A PACT WITH THEM, BUT EVEN THAT DOESN'T GUARANTEE COMPLETE SAFETY.
TAK
TAK
TAK
THAT'S WHY WE COURIERS HARDLY EVER USE THESE PATHS IF WE CAN AVOID IT.
UH... "THEM" ?
THESE PLACES ARE INHABITED. PACKS OF GUARD DOGS ROAM THROUGH HERE, AND THEY'RE NO SWEET PUPPIES.

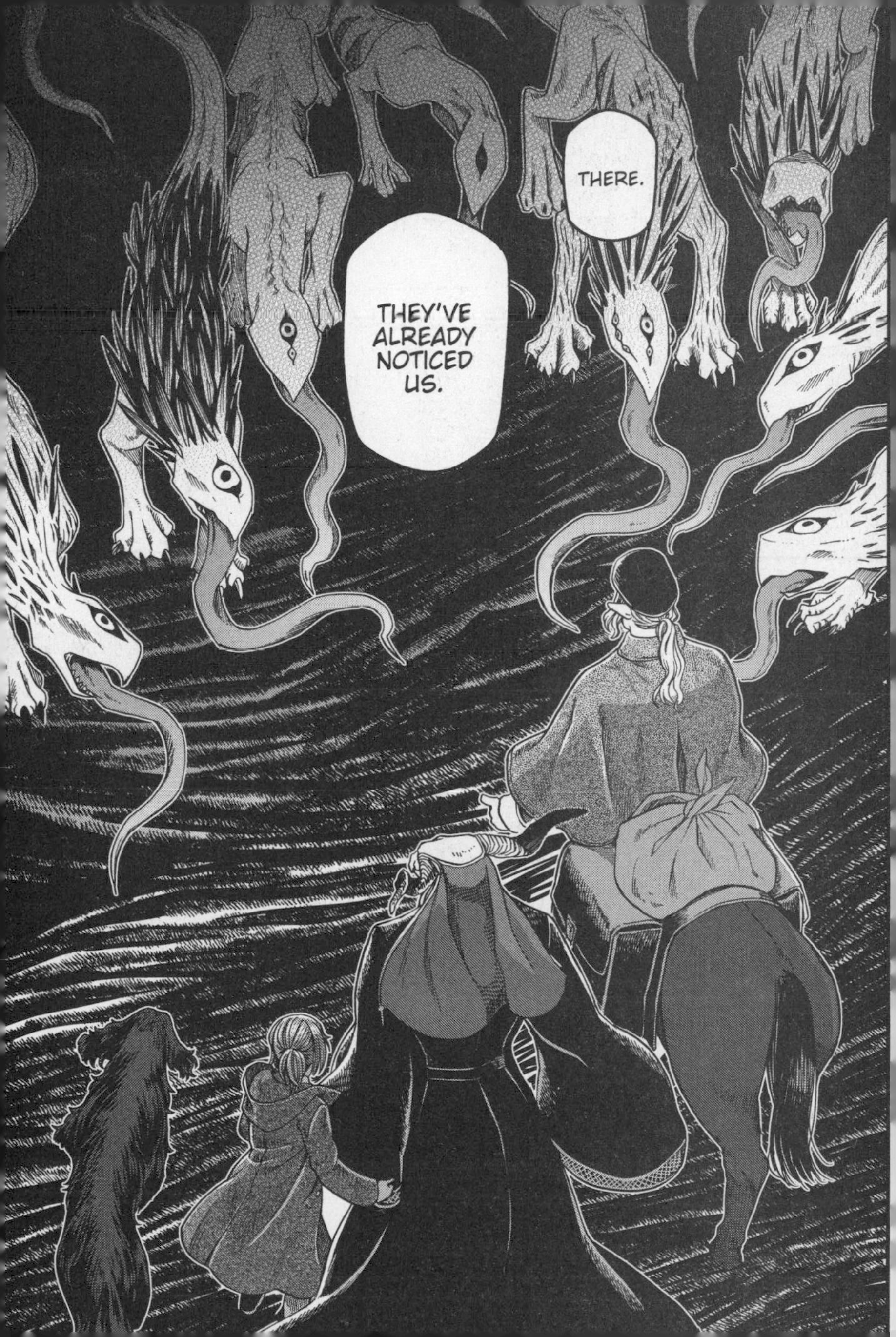
THERE.
THEY'VE ALREADY NOTICED US.

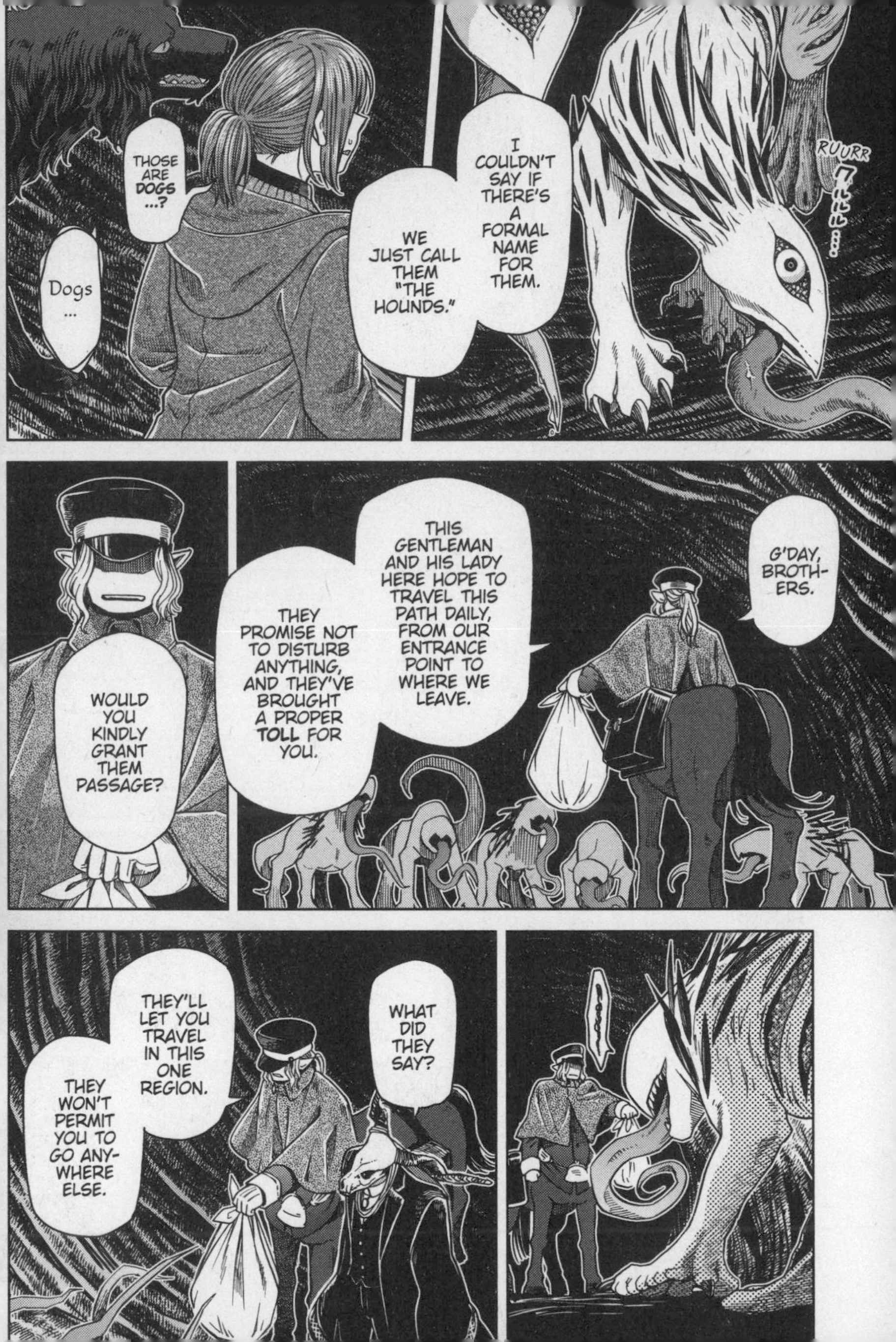
RUURR
I COULDN'T SAY IF THERE'S A FORMAL NAME FOR THEM.
WE JUST CALL THEM "THE HOUNDS."
THOSE ARE DOGS ...?
Dogs ...
G'DAY, BROTH-ERS.
THIS GENTLEMAN AND HIS LADY HERE HOPE TO TRAVEL THIS PATH DAILY, FROM OUR ENTRANCE POINT TO WHERE WE LEAVE.
THEY PROMISE NOT TO DISTURB ANYTHING, AND THEY'VE BROUGHT A PROPER TOLL FOR YOU.
WOULD YOU KINDLY GRANT THEM PASSAGE?
WHAT DID THEY SAY?
THEY'LL LET YOU TRAVEL IN THIS ONE REGION.
THEY WON'T PERMIT YOU TO GO ANY-WHERE ELSE.

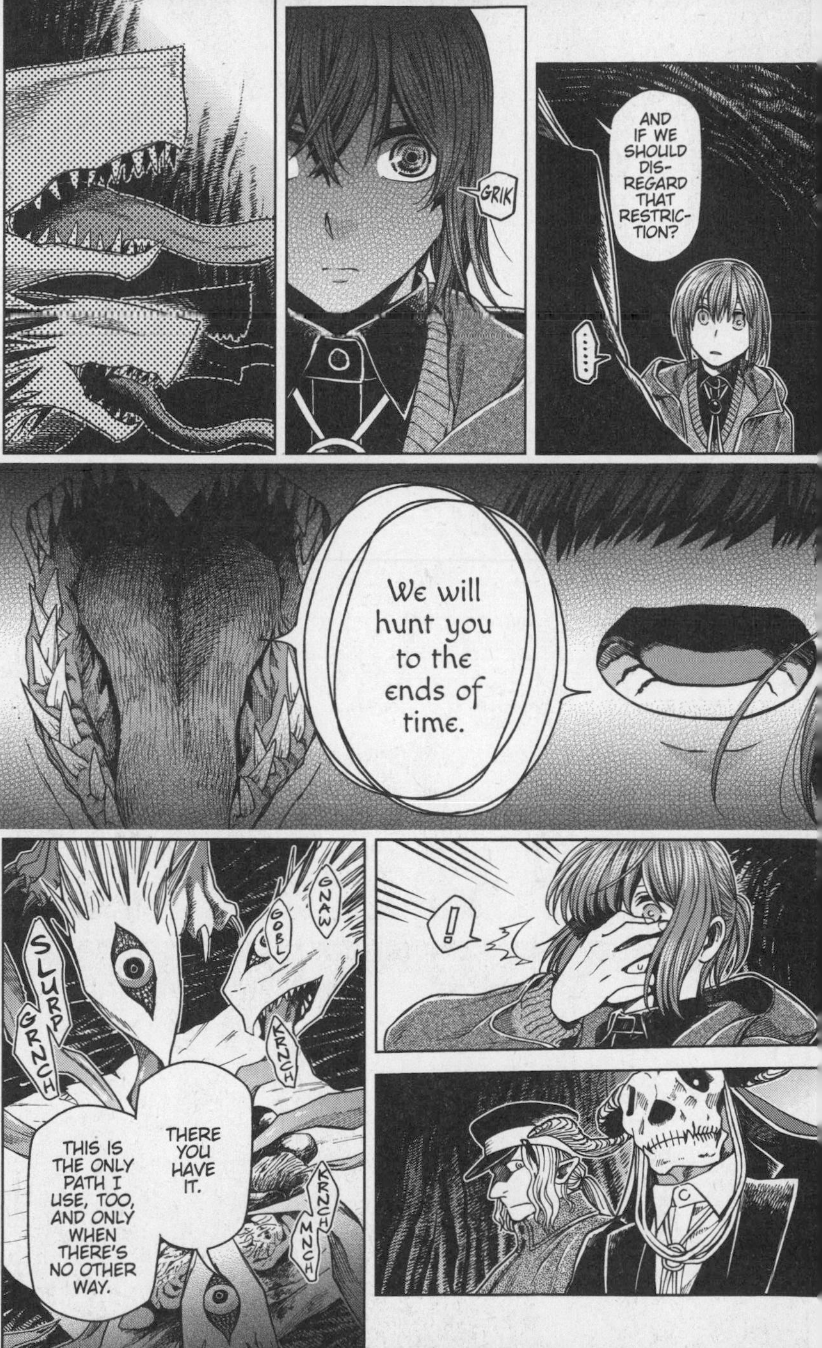
AND IF WE SHOULD DIS-REGARD THAT RESTRICTION?
......
GRIK
We will hunt you to the ends of time.
!
GNAW
GOBL
SLURP
GRNCH
KRNCH
THERE YOU HAVE IT.
THIS IS THE ONLY PATH I USE, TOO, AND ONLY WHEN THERE'S NO OTHER WAY.
KRNCH
MNCH

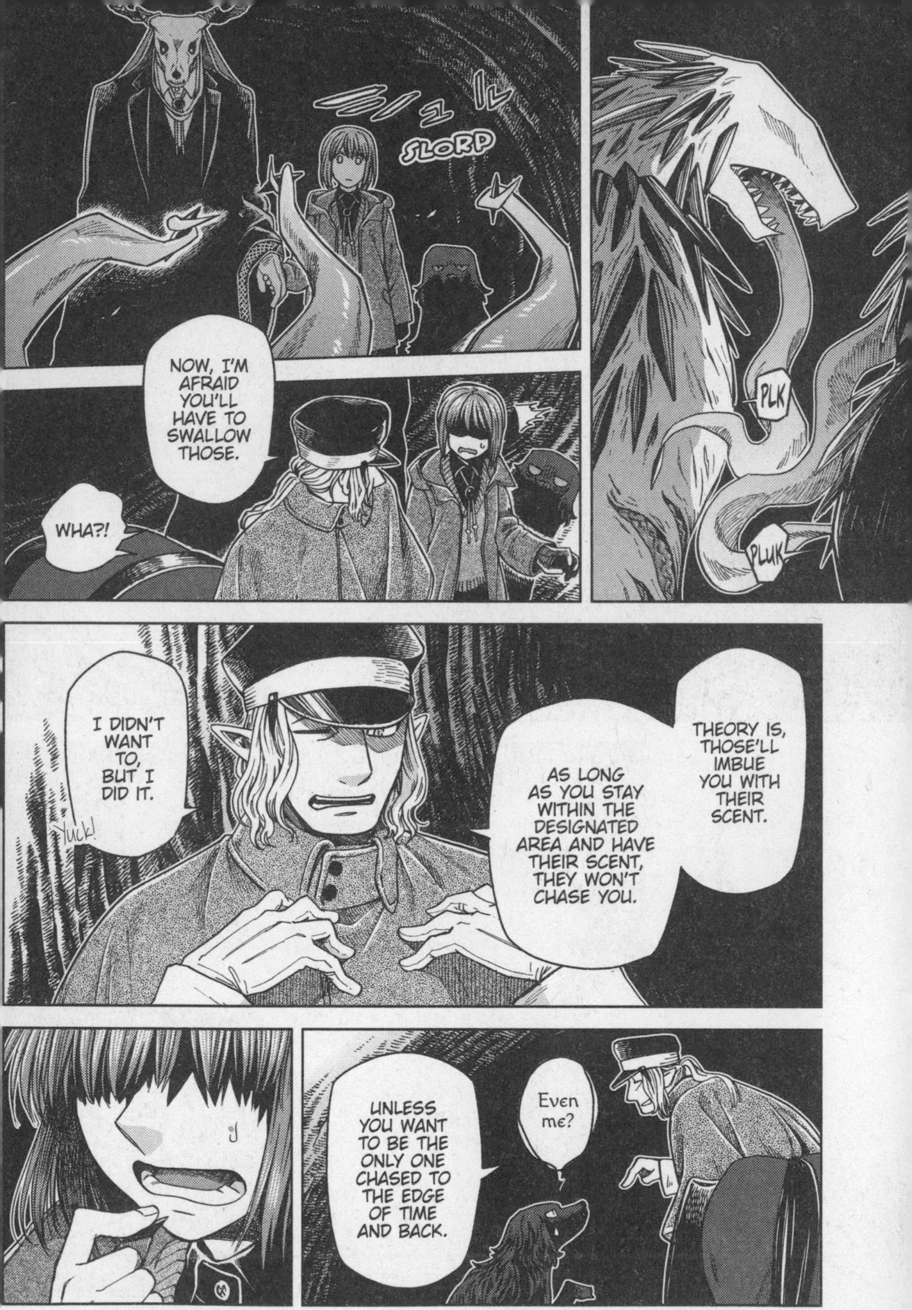
PLK
PLUK
SLORP
NOW, I'M AFRAID YOU'LL HAVE TO SWALLOW THOSE.
WHA?!
THEORY IS, THOSE'LL IMBUE YOU WITH THEIR SCENT.
AS LONG AS YOU STAY WITHIN THE DESIGNATED AREA AND HAVE THEIR SCENT, THEY WON'T CHASE YOU.
I DIDN'T WANT TO, BUT I DID IT.
Yuck!
Even me?
UNLESS YOU WANT TO BE THE ONLY ONE CHASED TO THE EDGE OF TIME AND BACK.

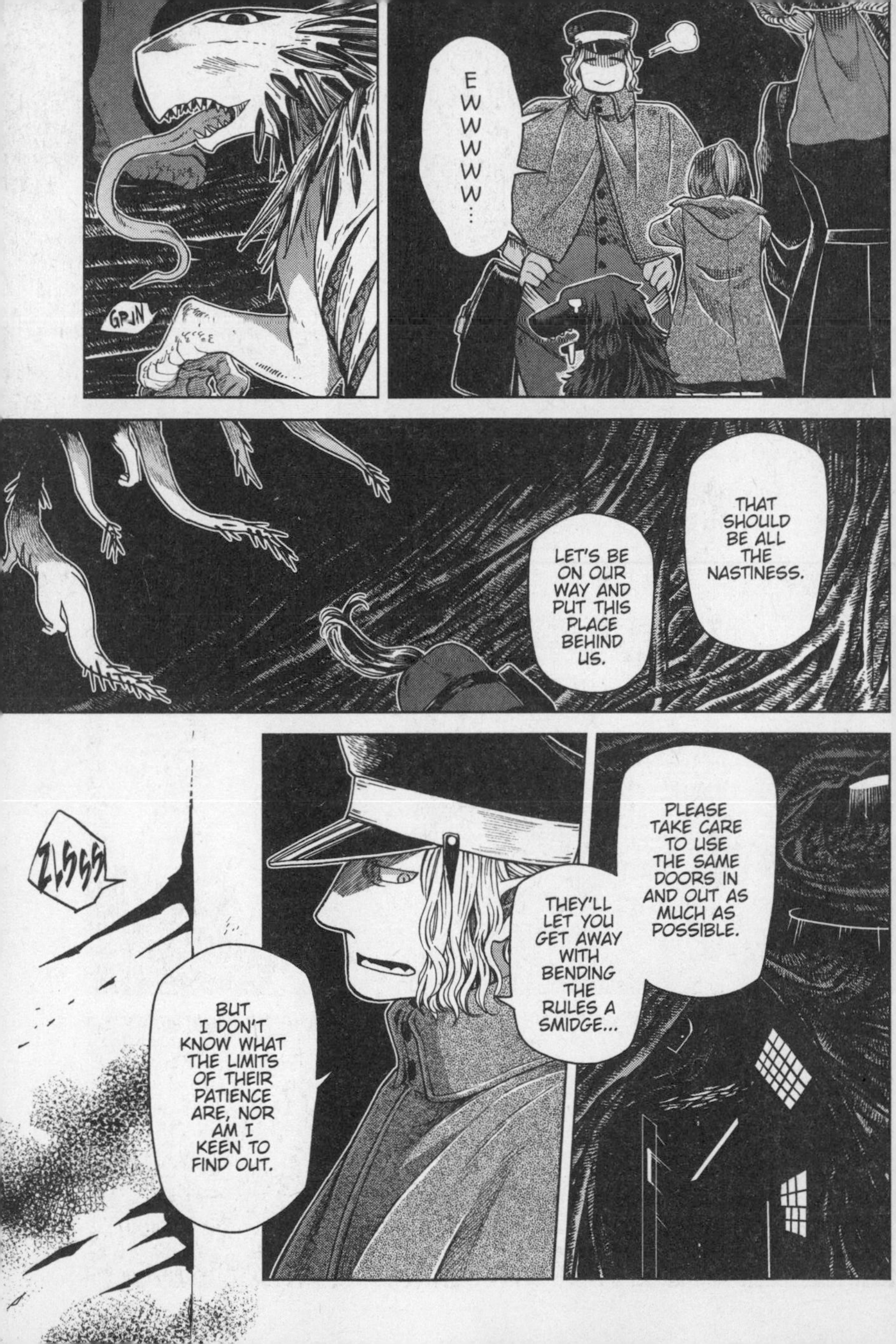
EWWWWWW...
THAT SHOULD BE ALL THE NASTINESS.
LET'S BE ON OUR WAY AND PUT THIS PLACE BEHIND US.
PLEASE TAKE CARE TO USE THE SAME DOORS IN AND OUT AS MUCH AS POSSIBLE.
THEY'LL LET YOU GET AWAY WITH BENDING THE RULES A SMIDGE...
BUT I DON'T KNOW WHAT THE LIMITS OF THEIR PATIENCE ARE, NOR AM I KEEN TO FIND OUT.
ZLSSS

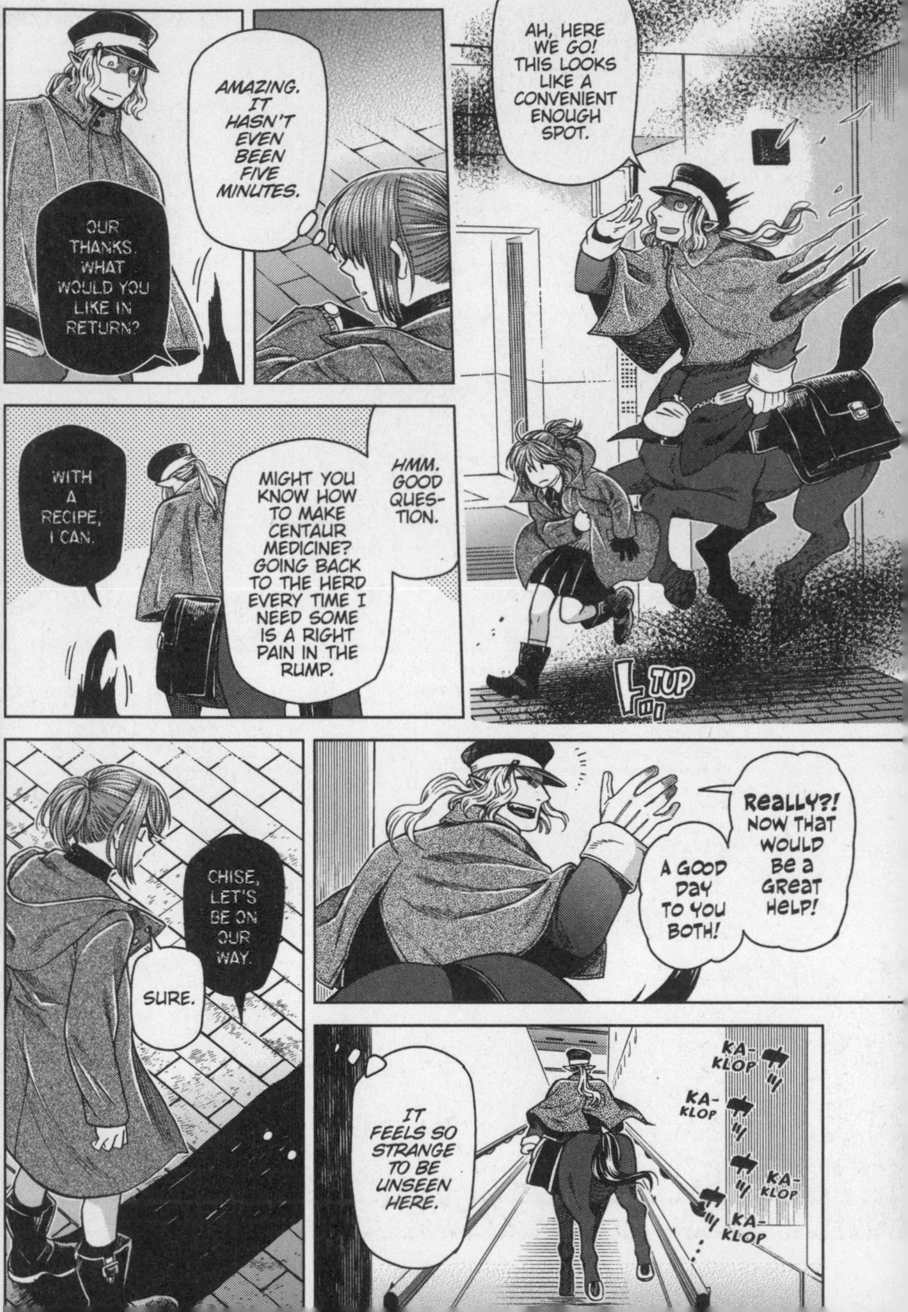
AH, HERE WE GO! THIS LOOKS LIKE A CONVENIENT ENOUGH SPOT.
TUP
AMAZING. IT HASN'T EVEN BEEN FIVE MINUTES.
OUR THANKS. WHAT WOULD YOU LIKE IN RETURN?
HMM. GOOD QUESTION.
MIGHT YOU KNOW HOW TO MAKE CENTAUR MEDICINE? GOING BACK TO THE HERD EVERY TIME I NEED SOME IS A RIGHT PAIN IN THE RUMP.
WITH A RECIPE, I CAN.
REALLY?! NOW THAT WOULD BE A GREAT HELP!
A GOOD DAY TO YOU BOTH!
KA-KLOP
KA-KLOP
KA-KLOP
KA-KLOP
IT FEELS SO STRANGE TO BE UNSEEN HERE.
CHISE, LET'S BE ON OUR WAY.
SURE.

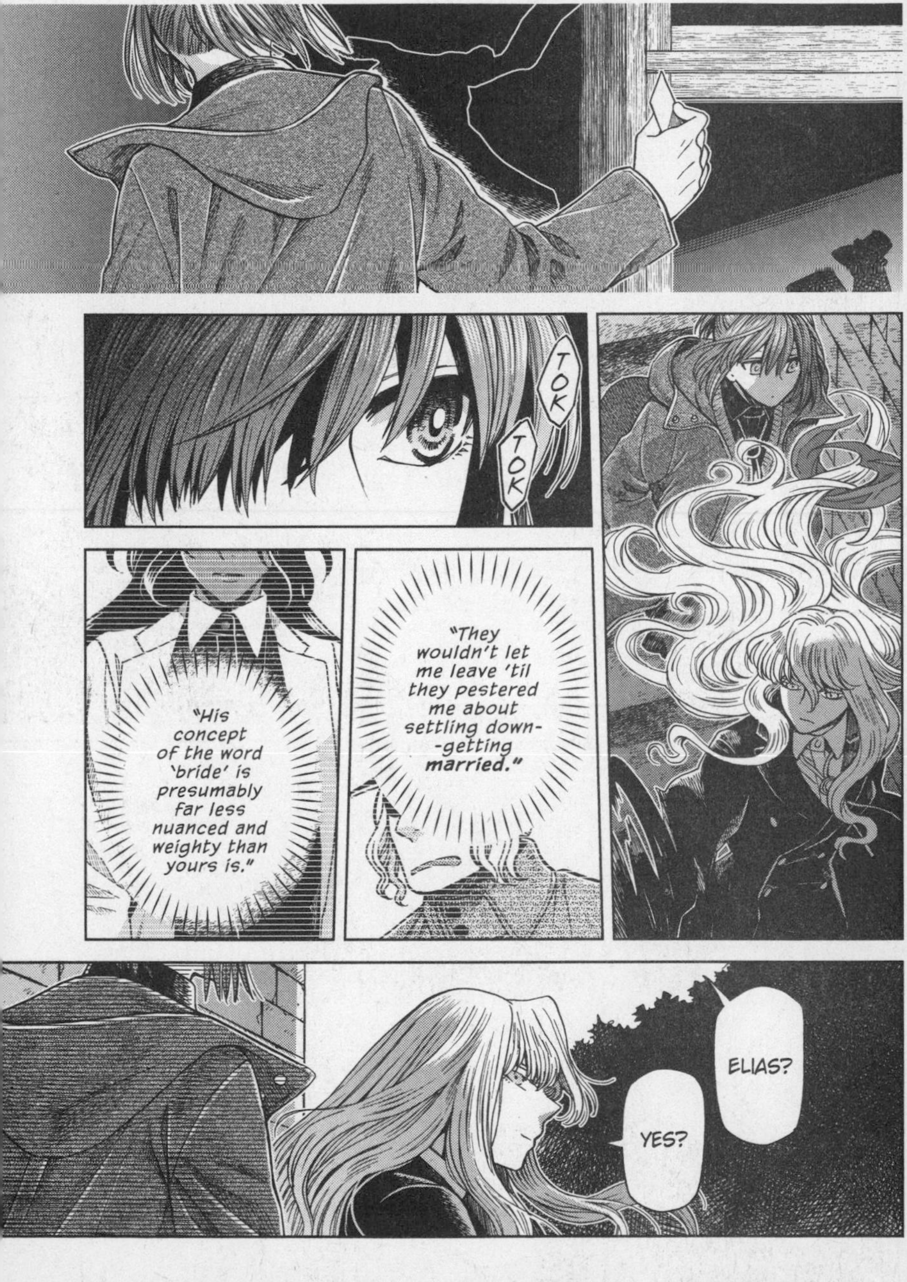
TOK TOK
"They wouldn't let me leave 'til they pestered me about settling down- -getting married."
"His concept of the word 'bride' is presumably far less nuanced and weighty than yours is."
ELIAS?
YES?

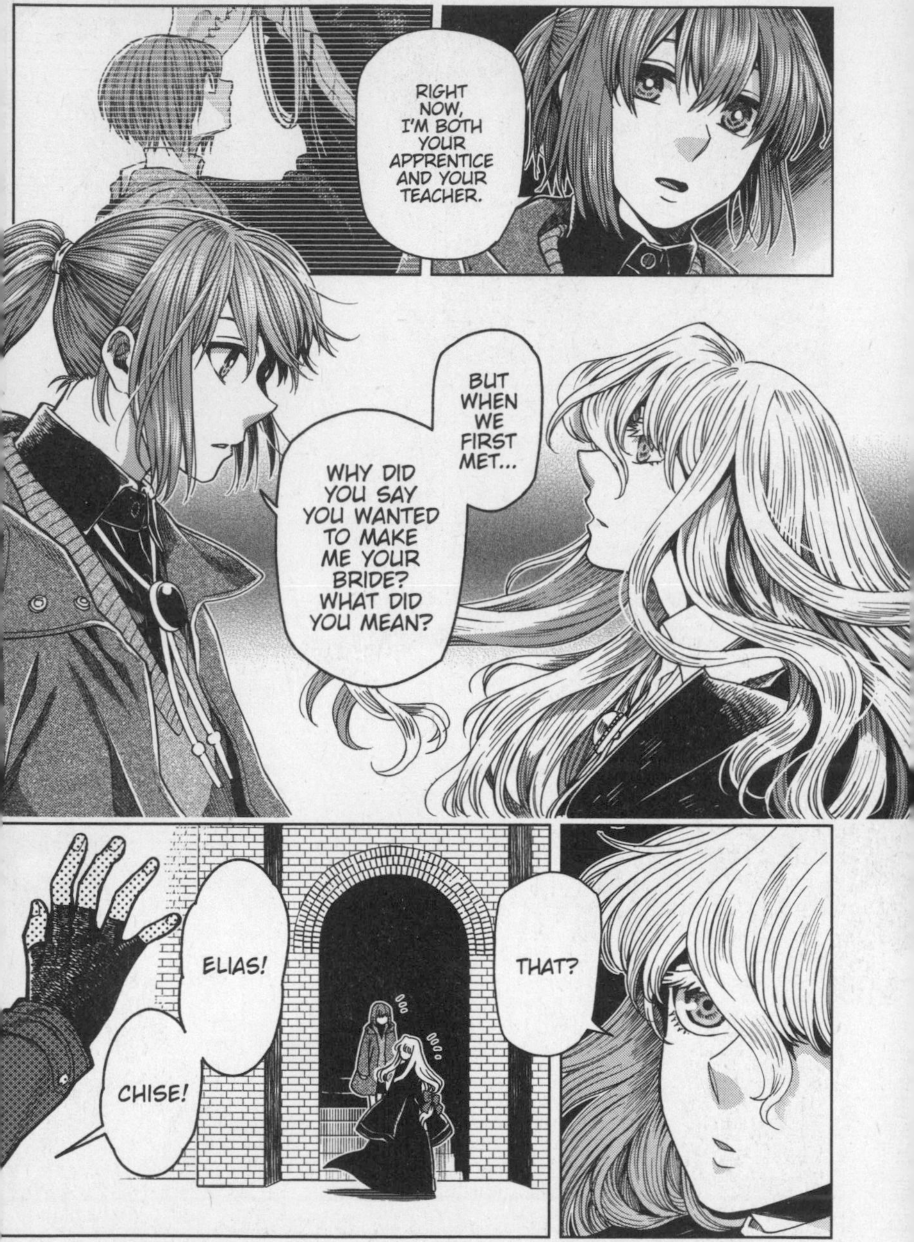
RIGHT NOW, I'M BOTH YOUR APPRENTICE AND YOUR TEACHER.
BUT WHEN WE FIRST MET...
WHY DID YOU SAY YOU WANTED TO MAKE ME YOUR BRIDE? WHAT DID YOU MEAN?
THAT?
ELIAS!
CHISE!

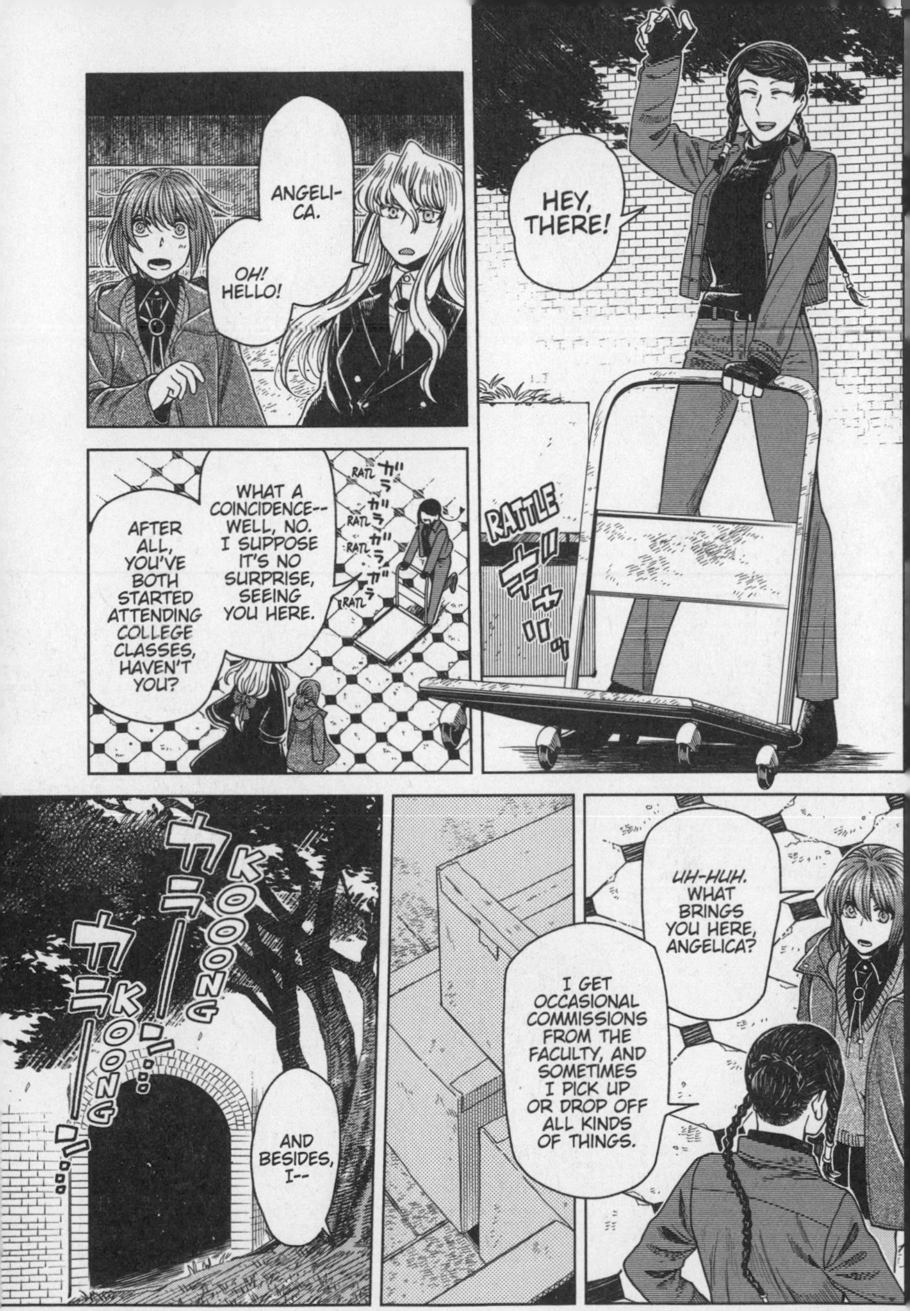

RATTLE
HEY, THERE!
ANGELI-CA.
OH! HELLO!
RATL
RATL
RATL
RATL
WHAT A COINCIDENCE--WELL, NO. I SUPPOSE IT'S NO SURPRISE, SEEING YOU HERE.
AFTER ALL, YOU'VE BOTH STARTED ATTENDING COLLEGE CLASSES, HAVEN'T YOU?
UH-HUH. WHAT BRINGS YOU HERE, ANGELICA?
I GET OCCASIONAL COMMISSIONS FROM THE FACULTY, AND SOMETIMES I PICK UP OR DROP OFF ALL KINDS OF THINGS.
KOOOONG
KOOONG
AND BESIDES, I--

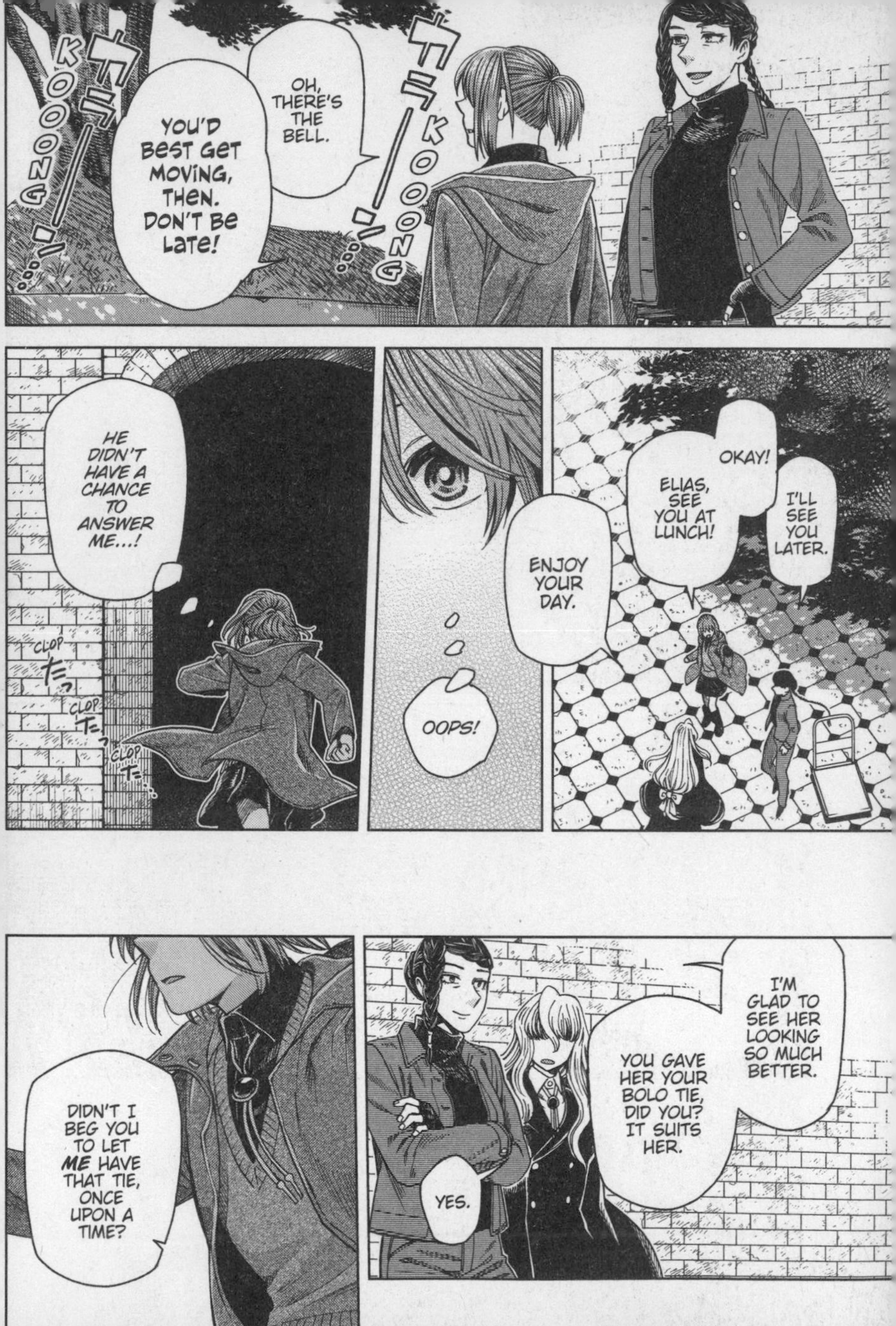
KOOOONG—!...
OH, THERE'S THE BELL.
YOU'D BEST GET MOVING, THEN. DON'T BE LATE!
KOOOONG—!...
OKAY!
I'LL SEE YOU LATER.
ELIAS, SEE YOU AT LUNCH!
ENJOY YOUR DAY.
OOPS!
HE DIDN'T HAVE A CHANCE TO ANSWER ME...!
CLOP
CLOP
CLOP
I'M GLAD TO SEE HER LOOKING SO MUCH BETTER.
YOU GAVE HER YOUR BOLO TIE, DID YOU? IT SUITS HER.
YES.
DIDN'T I BEG YOU TO LET ME HAVE THAT TIE, ONCE UPON A TIME?

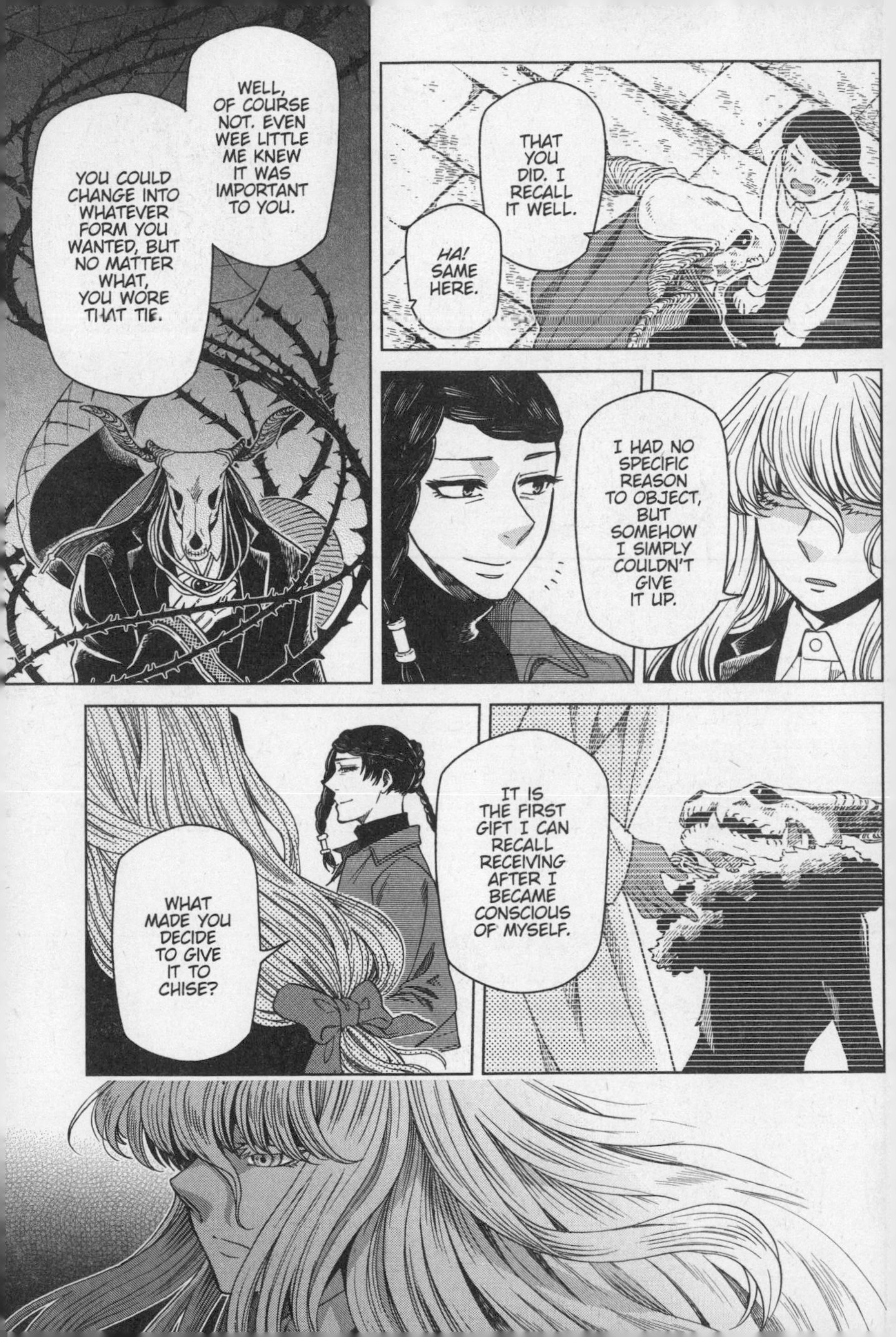
THAT YOU DID. I RECALL IT WELL.
HA! SAME HERE.
I HAD NO SPECIFIC REASON TO OBJECT, BUT SOMEHOW I SIMPLY COULDN'T GIVE IT UP.
WELL, OF COURSE NOT. EVEN WEE LITTLE ME KNEW IT WAS IMPORTANT TO YOU.
YOU COULD CHANGE INTO WHATEVER FORM YOU WANTED, BUT NO MATTER WHAT, YOU WORE THAT TIE.
IT IS THE FIRST GIFT I CAN RECALL RECEIVING AFTER I BECAME CONSCIOUS OF MYSELF.
WHAT MADE YOU DECIDE TO GIVE IT TO CHISE?

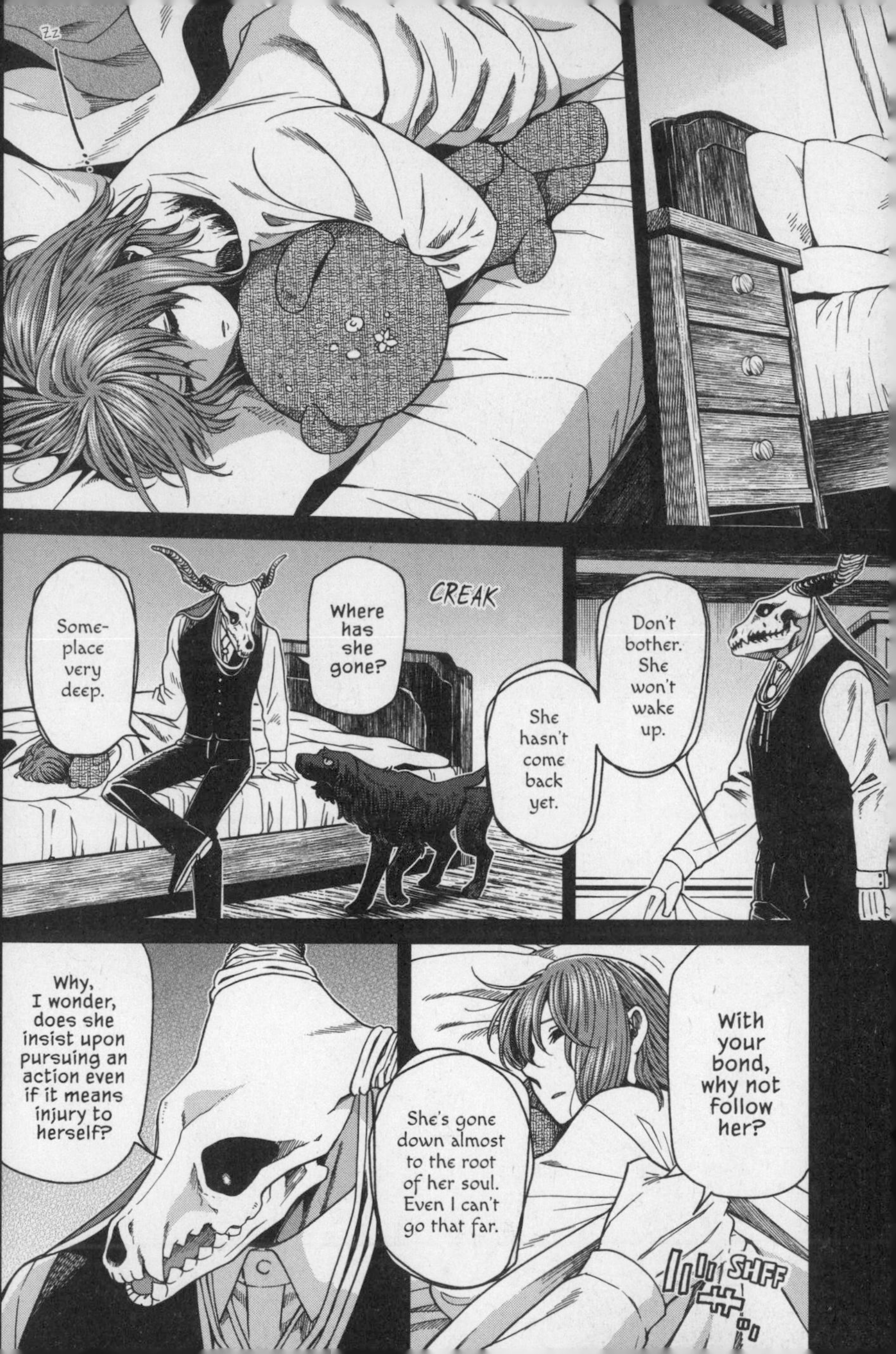
Zz
Don't bother. She won't wake up.
She hasn't come back yet.
CREAK
Where has she gone?
Some-place very deep.
With your bond, why not follow her?
She's gone down almost to the root of her soul. Even I can't go that far.
SHFF
Why, I wonder, does she insist upon pursuing an action even if it means injury to herself?

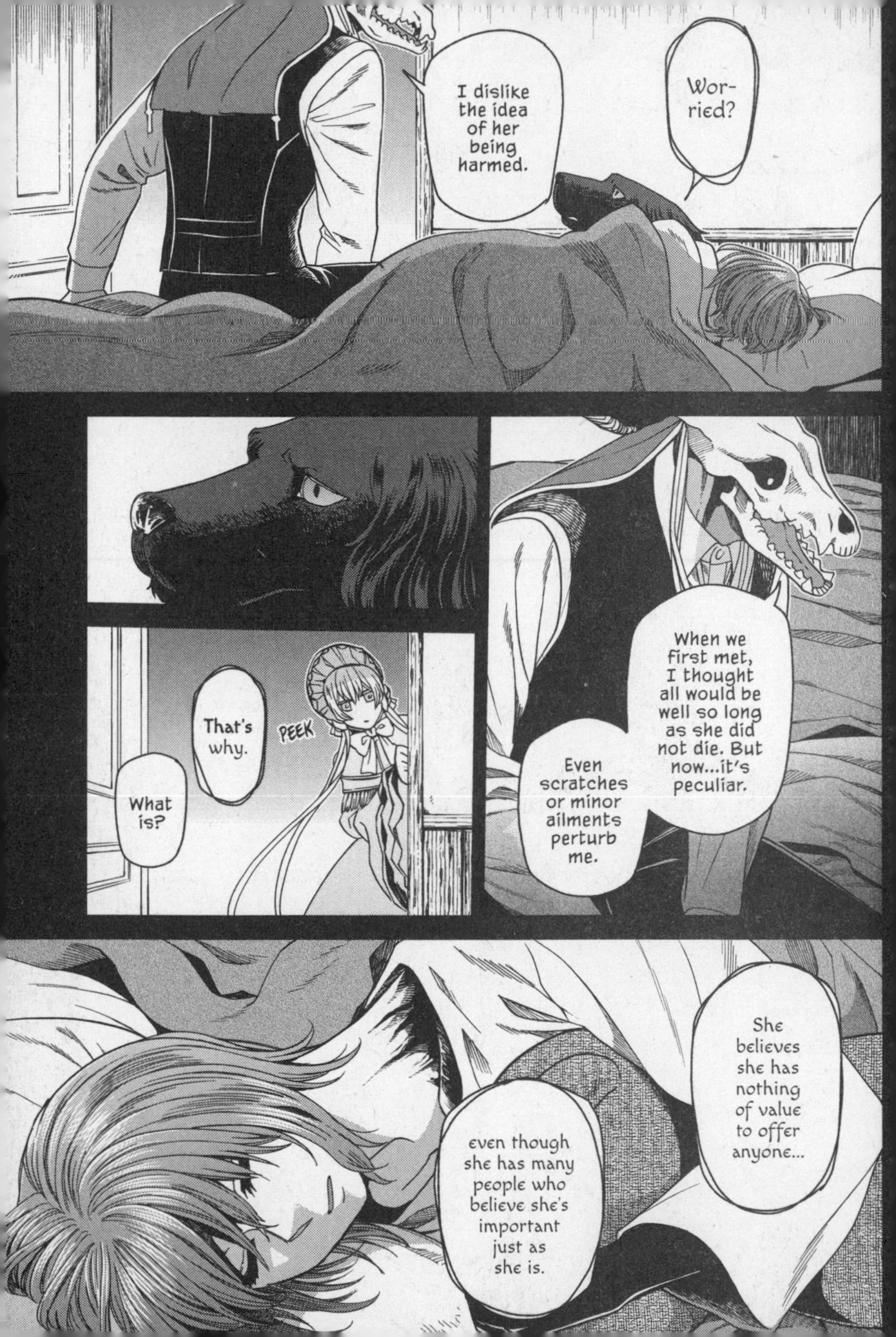
Wor-ried?
I dislike the idea of her being harmed.
When we first met, I thought all would be well so long as she did not die. But now...it's peculiar.
Even scratches or minor ailments perturb me.
PEEK
That's why.
What is?
She believes she has nothing of value to offer anyone...
even though she has many people who believe she's important just as she is.

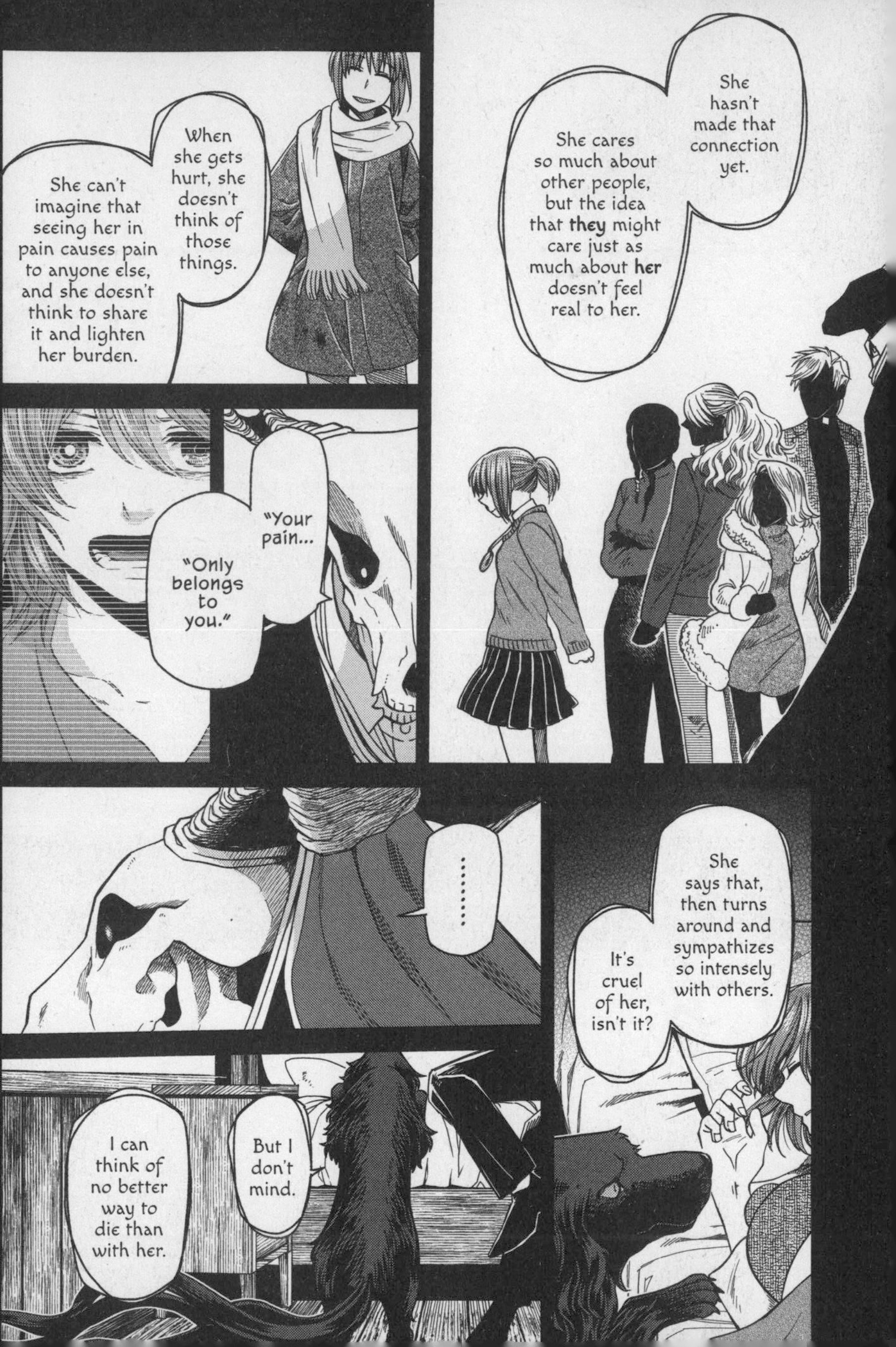
She hasn't made that connection yet.
She cares so much about other people, but the idea that **they** might care just as much about **her** doesn't feel real to her.
When she gets hurt, she doesn't think of those things.
She can't imagine that seeing her in pain causes pain to anyone else, and she doesn't think to share it and lighten her burden.
"Your pain...
"Only belongs to you."
She says that, then turns around and sympathizes so intensely with others.
It's cruel of her, isn't it?
......
But I don't mind.
I can think of no better way to die than with her.

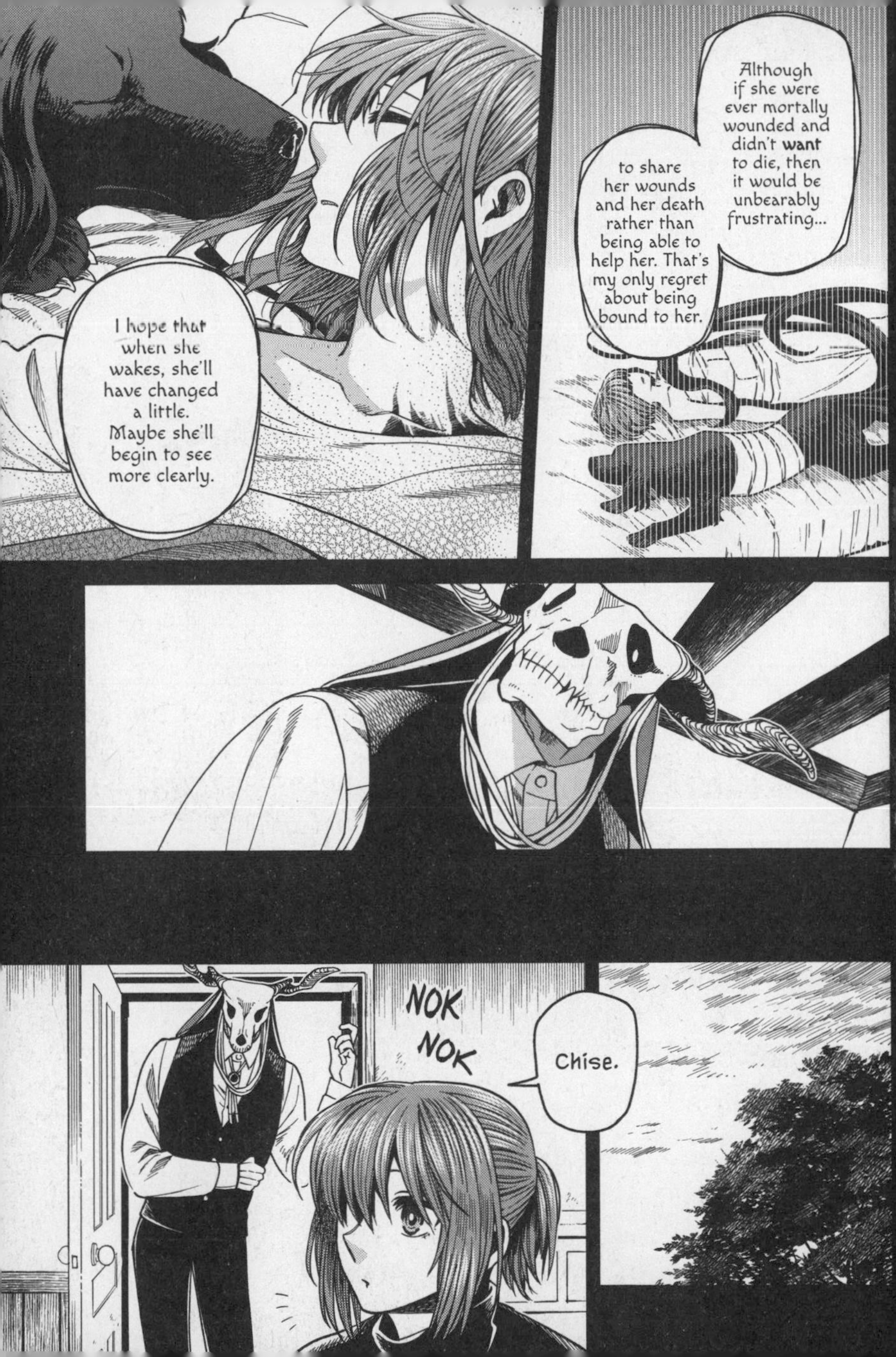
Although if she were ever mortally wounded and didn't **want** to die, then it would be unbearably frustrating...
to share her wounds and her death rather than being able to help her. That's my only regret about being bound to her.
I hope that when she wakes, she'll have changed a little. Maybe she'll begin to see more clearly.
NOK NOK
Chise.

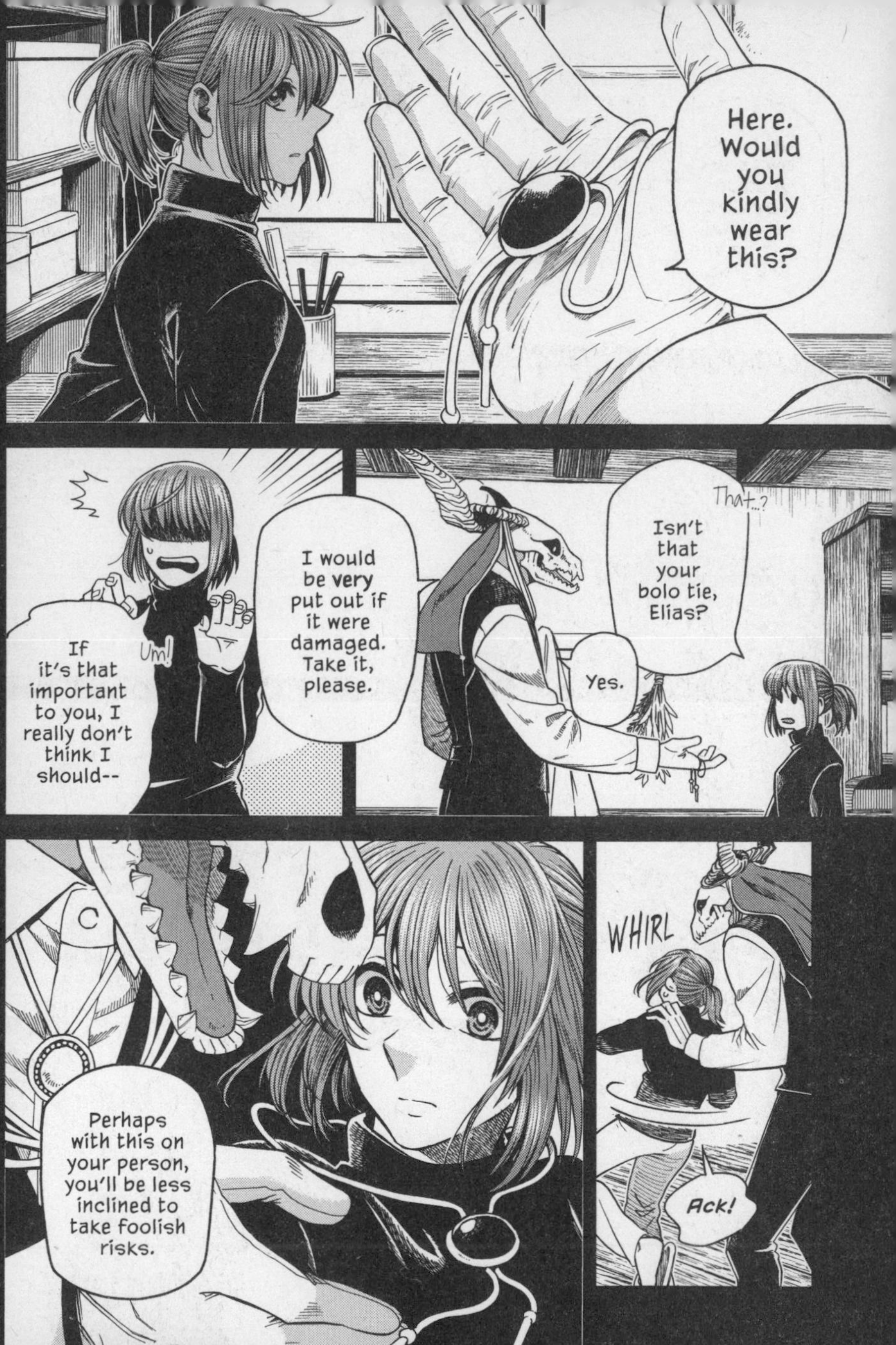
Here. Would you kindly wear this?
That...?
Isn't that your bolo tie, Elias?
Yes.
I would be very put out if it were damaged. Take it, please.
Um!
If it's that important to you, I really don't think I should--
WHIRL
Ack!
Perhaps with this on your person, you'll be less inclined to take foolish risks.

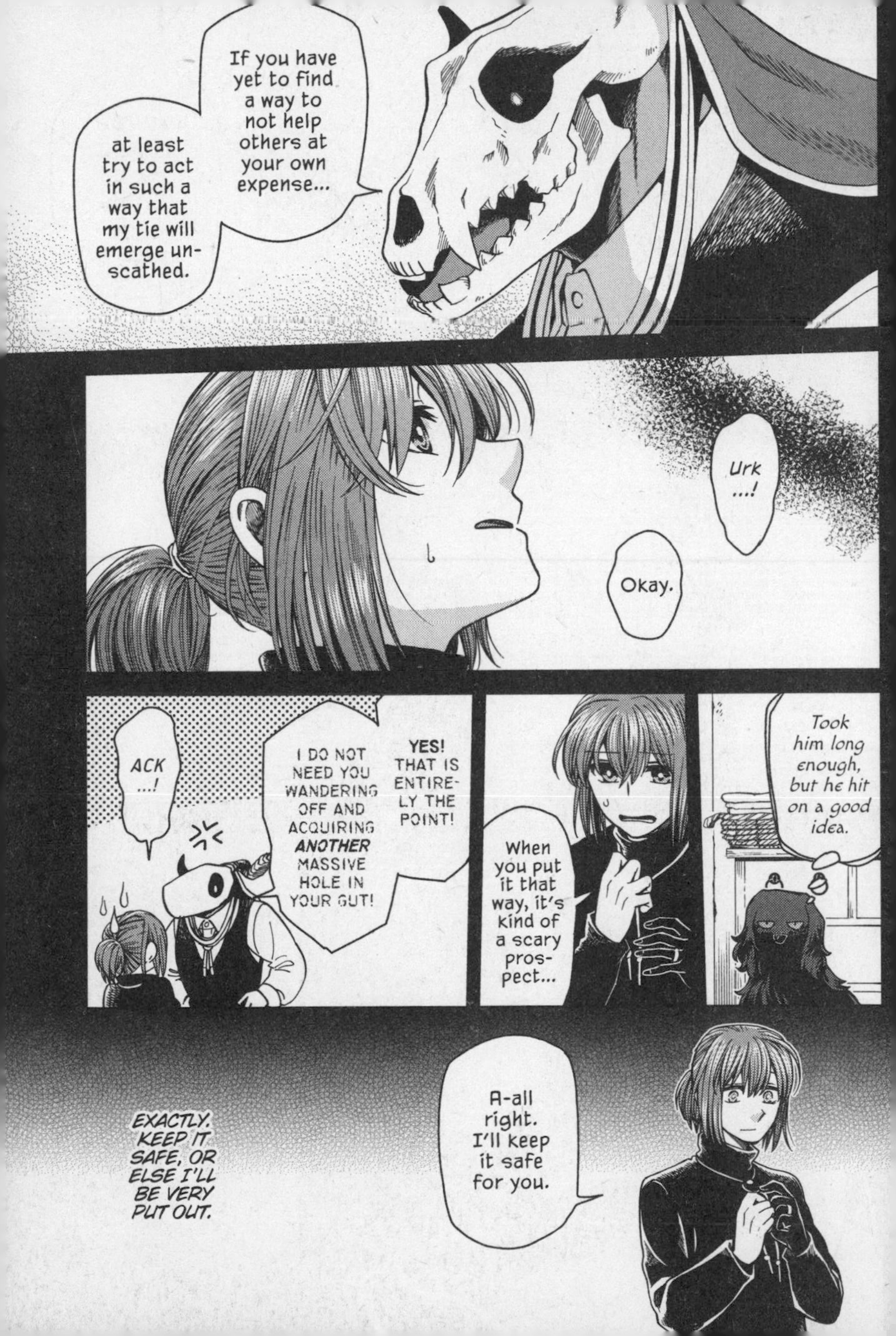

If you have yet to find a way to not help others at your own expense...
at least try to act in such a way that my tie will emerge unscathed.
Urk ...!
Okay.
Took him long enough, but he hit on a good idea.
When you put it that way, it's kind of a scary prospect...
YES! THAT IS ENTIRELY THE POINT!
I DO NOT NEED YOU WANDERING OFF AND ACQUIRING ANOTHER MASSIVE HOLE IN YOUR GUT!
ACK ...!
A-all right. I'll keep it safe for you.
EXACTLY. KEEP IT SAFE, OR ELSE I'LL BE VERY PUT OUT.

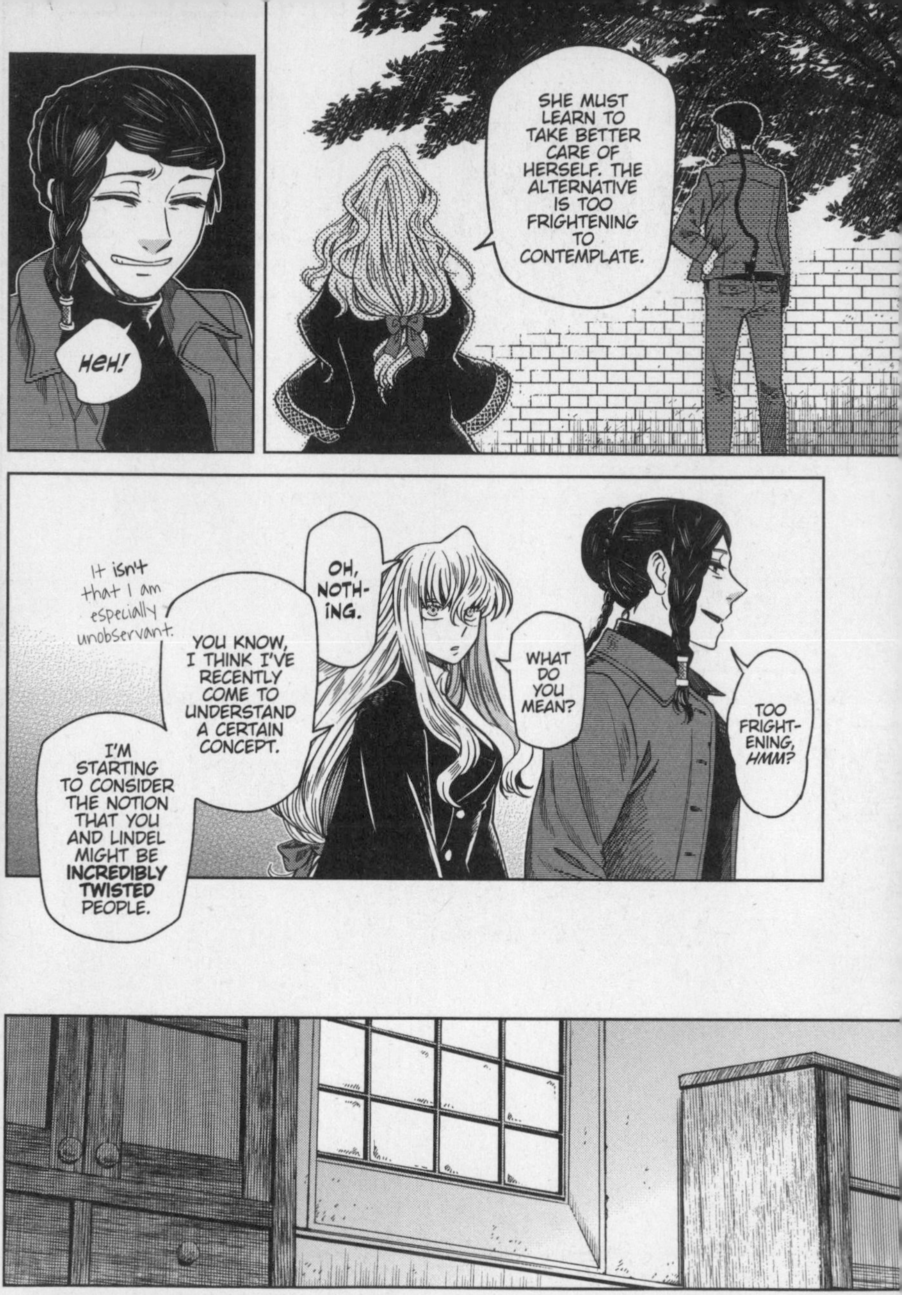
SHE MUST LEARN TO TAKE BETTER CARE OF HERSELF. THE ALTERNATIVE IS TOO FRIGHTENING TO CONTEMPLATE.
HEH!
TOO FRIGHTENING, HMM?
WHAT DO YOU MEAN?
OH, NOTHING.
It isn't that I am especially unobservant.
YOU KNOW, I THINK I'VE RECENTLY COME TO UNDERSTAND A CERTAIN CONCEPT.
I'M STARTING TO CONSIDER THE NOTION THAT YOU AND LINDEL MIGHT BE INCREDIBLY TWISTED PEOPLE.

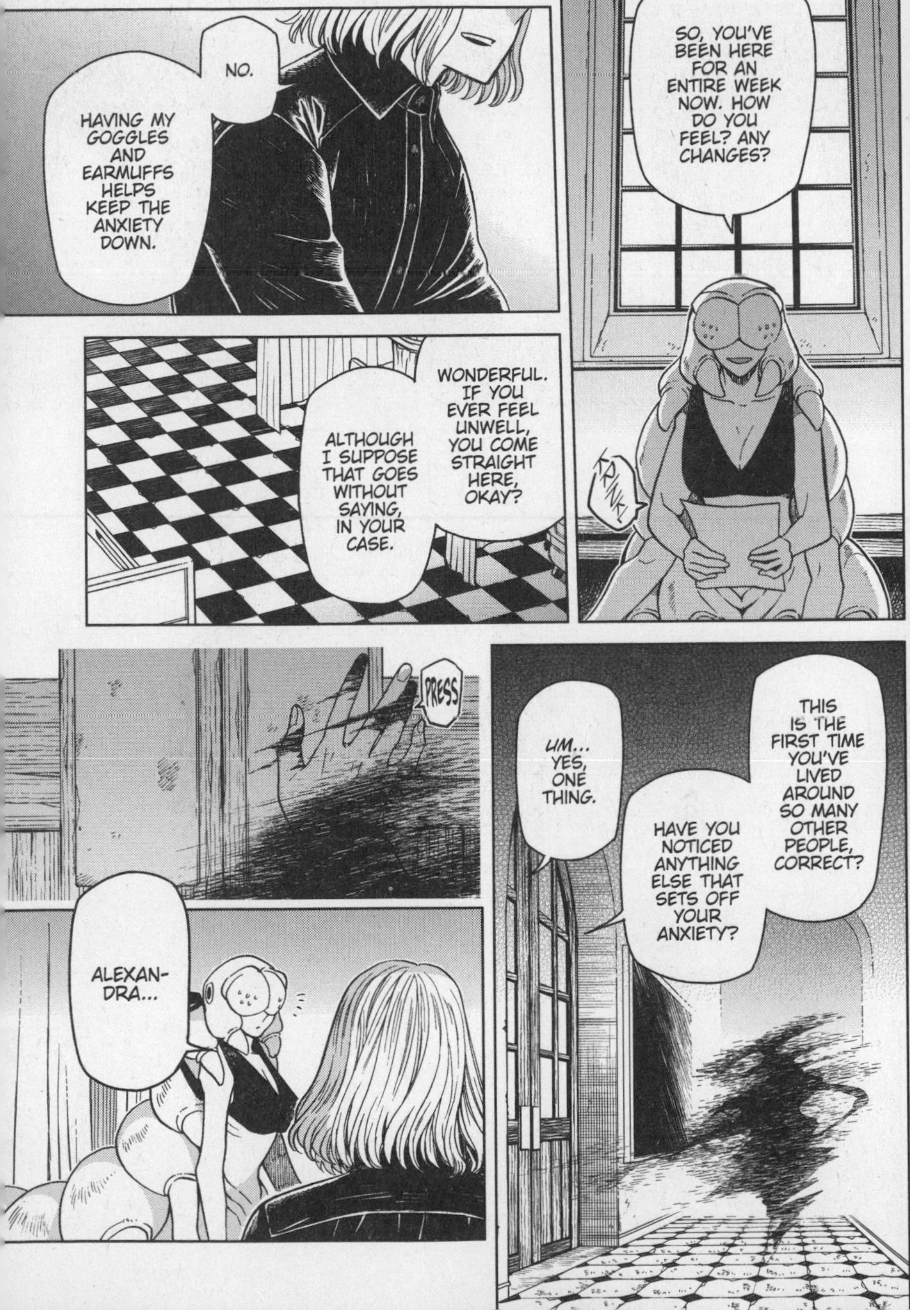
SO, YOU'VE BEEN HERE FOR AN ENTIRE WEEK NOW. HOW DO YOU FEEL? ANY CHANGES?
KRINK!
NO.
HAVING MY GOGGLES AND EARMUFFS HELPS KEEP THE ANXIETY DOWN.
WONDERFUL. IF YOU EVER FEEL UNWELL, YOU COME STRAIGHT HERE, OKAY?
ALTHOUGH I SUPPOSE THAT GOES WITHOUT SAYING, IN YOUR CASE.
THIS IS THE FIRST TIME YOU'VE LIVED AROUND SO MANY OTHER PEOPLE, CORRECT?
HAVE YOU NOTICED ANYTHING ELSE THAT SETS OFF YOUR ANXIETY?
UM... YES, ONE THING.
PRESS
ALEXAN-DRA...

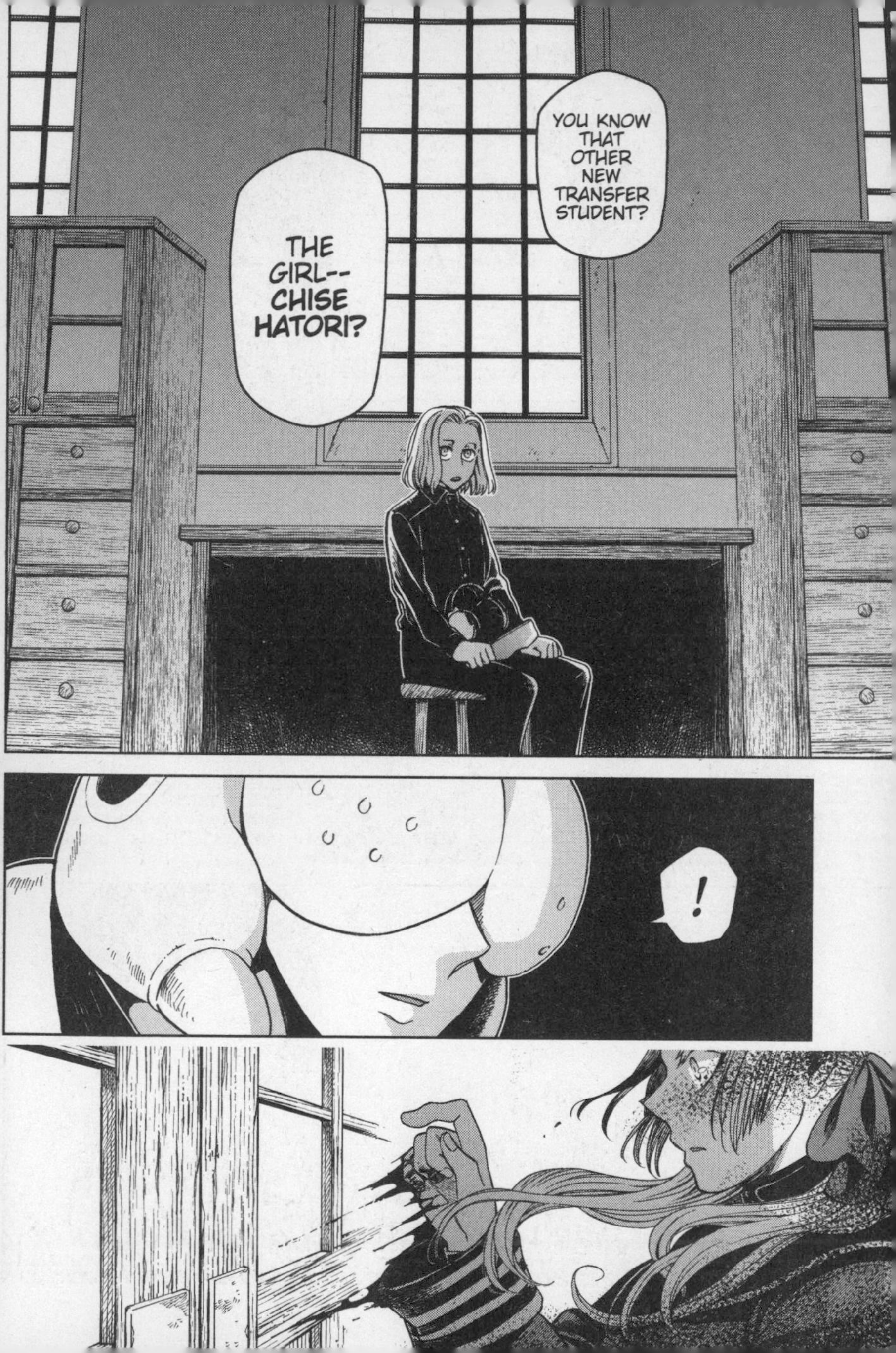
YOU KNOW THAT OTHER NEW TRANSFER STUDENT?
THE GIRL-- CHISE HATORI?
!

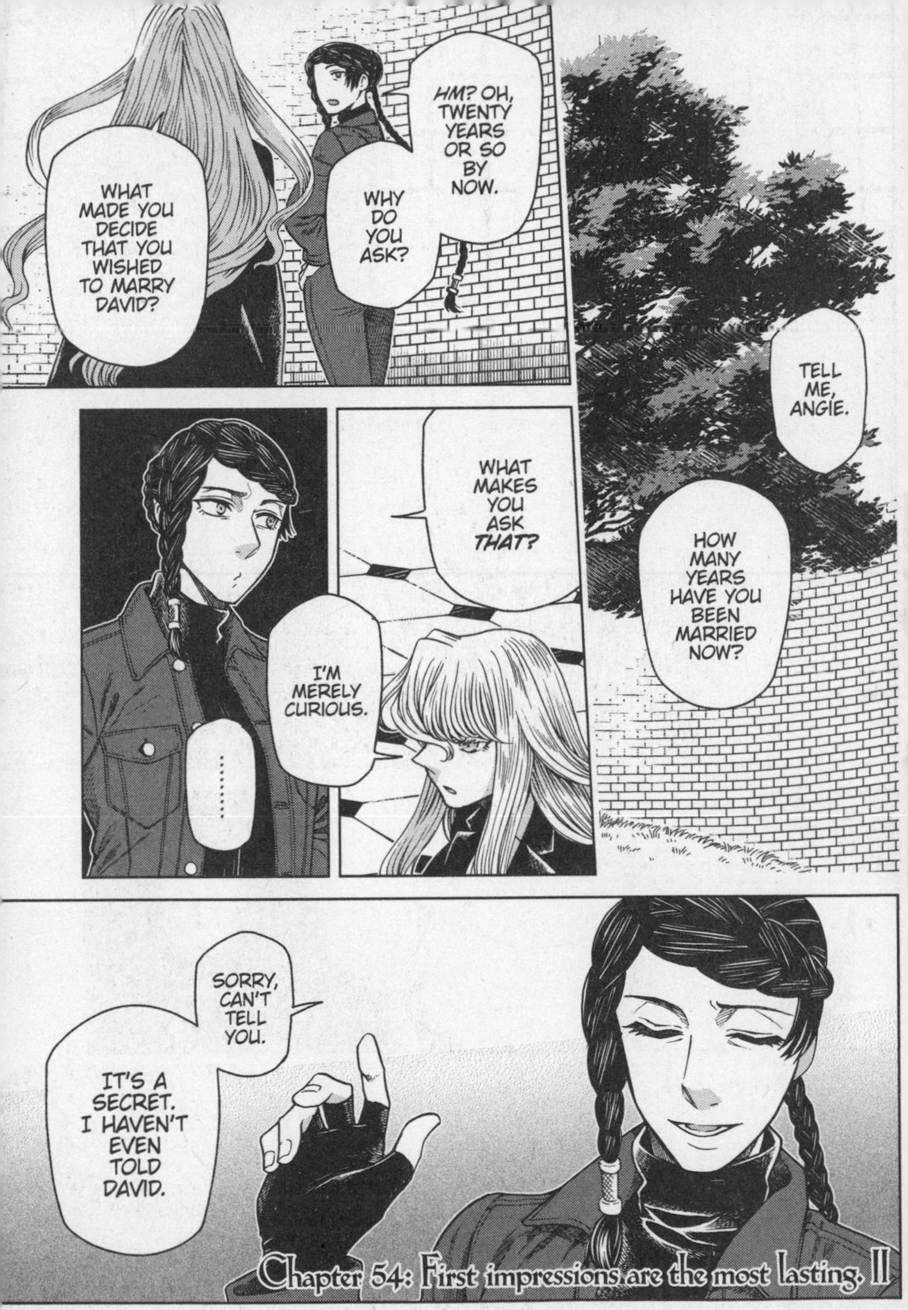
TELL ME, ANGIE.
HOW MANY YEARS HAVE YOU BEEN MARRIED NOW?
HM? OH, TWENTY YEARS OR SO BY NOW.
WHY DO YOU ASK?
WHAT MADE YOU DECIDE THAT YOU WISHED TO MARRY DAVID?
WHAT MAKES YOU ASK *THAT?*
I'M MERELY CURIOUS.
……
SORRY, CAN'T TELL YOU.
IT'S A SECRET. I HAVEN'T EVEN TOLD DAVID.
Chapter 54: First impressions are the most lasting. II

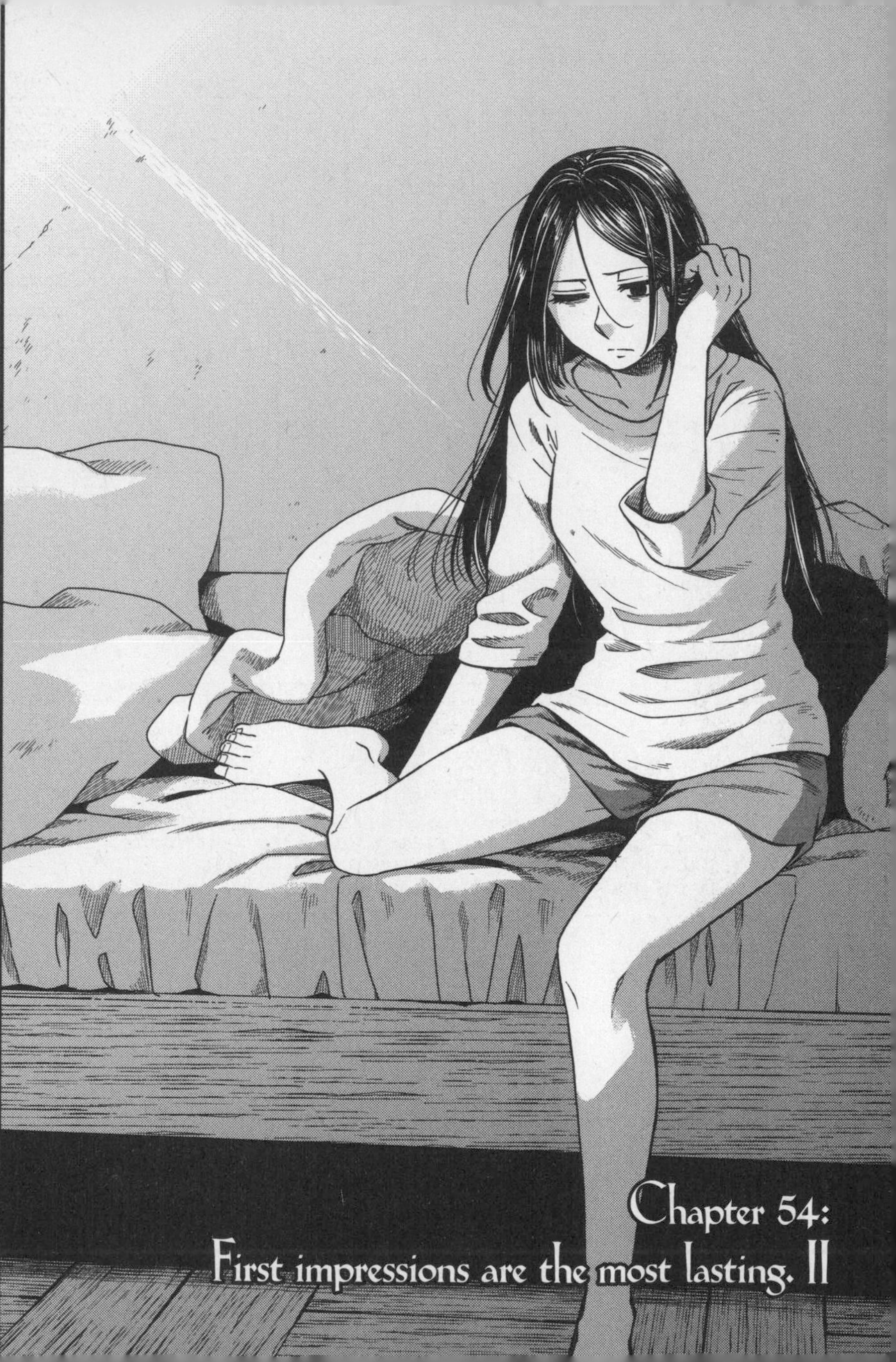
Chapter 54:
First impressions are the most lasting. II

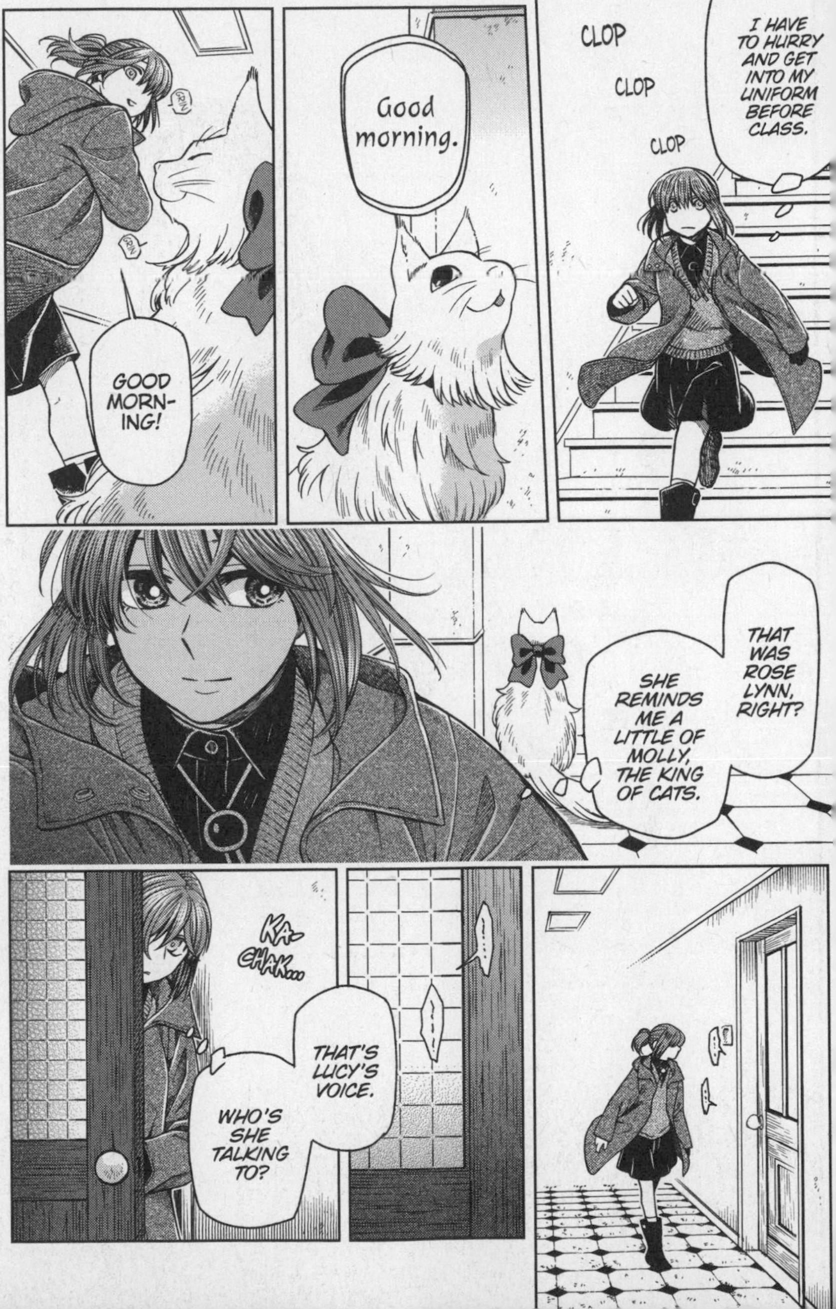
CLOP
CLOP
CLOP
I HAVE TO HURRY AND GET INTO MY UNIFORM BEFORE CLASS.
Good morning.
GOOD MORNING!
THAT WAS ROSE LYNN, RIGHT?
SHE REMINDS ME A LITTLE OF MOLLY, THE KING OF CATS.
KA-CHAK...
THAT'S LUCY'S VOICE.
WHO'S SHE TALKING TO?

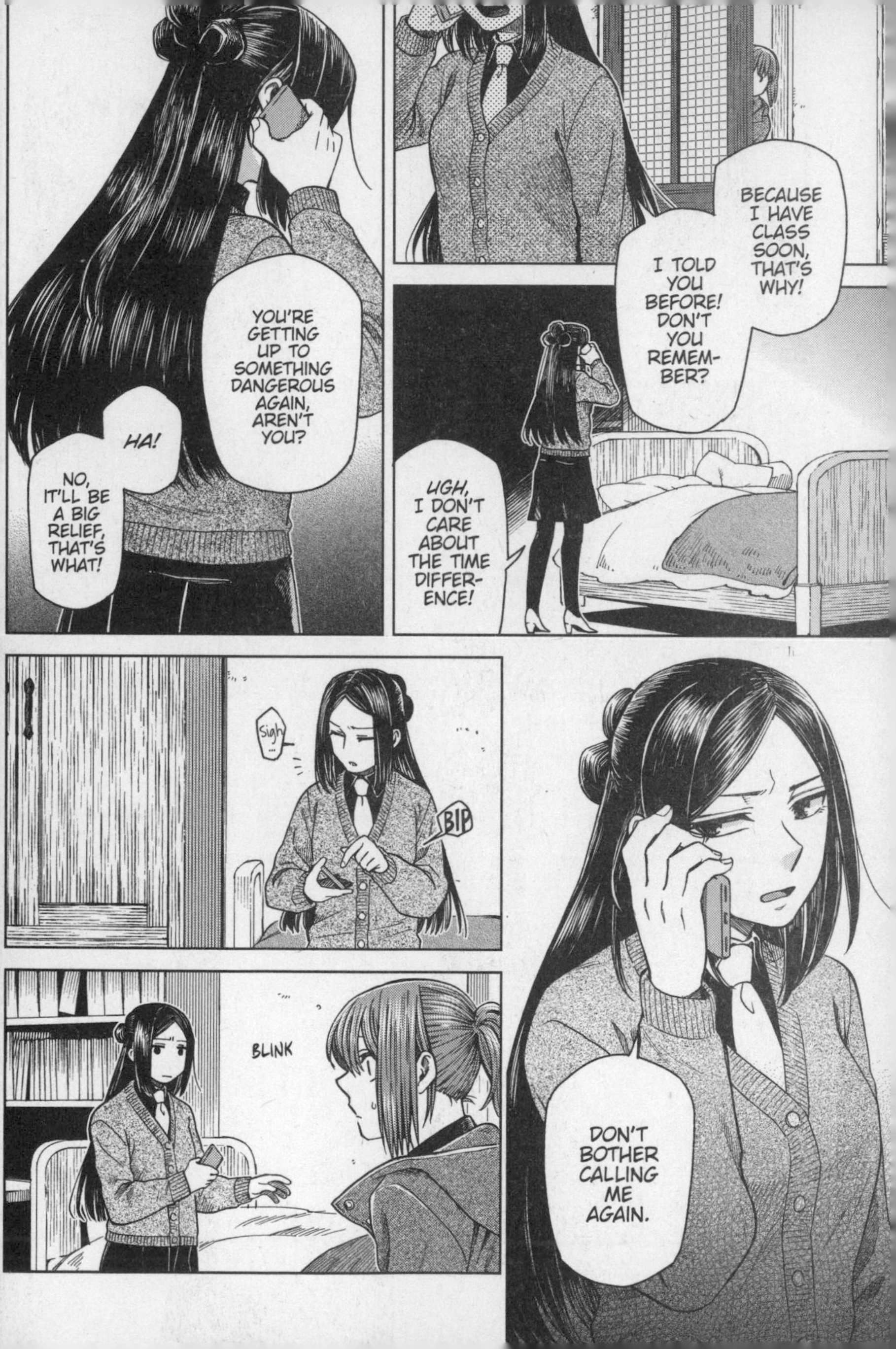
BECAUSE I HAVE CLASS SOON, THAT'S WHY!
I TOLD YOU BEFORE! DON'T YOU REMEMBER?
UGH, I DON'T CARE ABOUT THE TIME DIFFERENCE!
YOU'RE GETTING UP TO SOMETHING DANGEROUS AGAIN, AREN'T YOU?
HA!
NO, IT'LL BE A BIG RELIEF, THAT'S WHAT!
DON'T BOTHER CALLING ME AGAIN.
Sigh...
BIP
BLINK

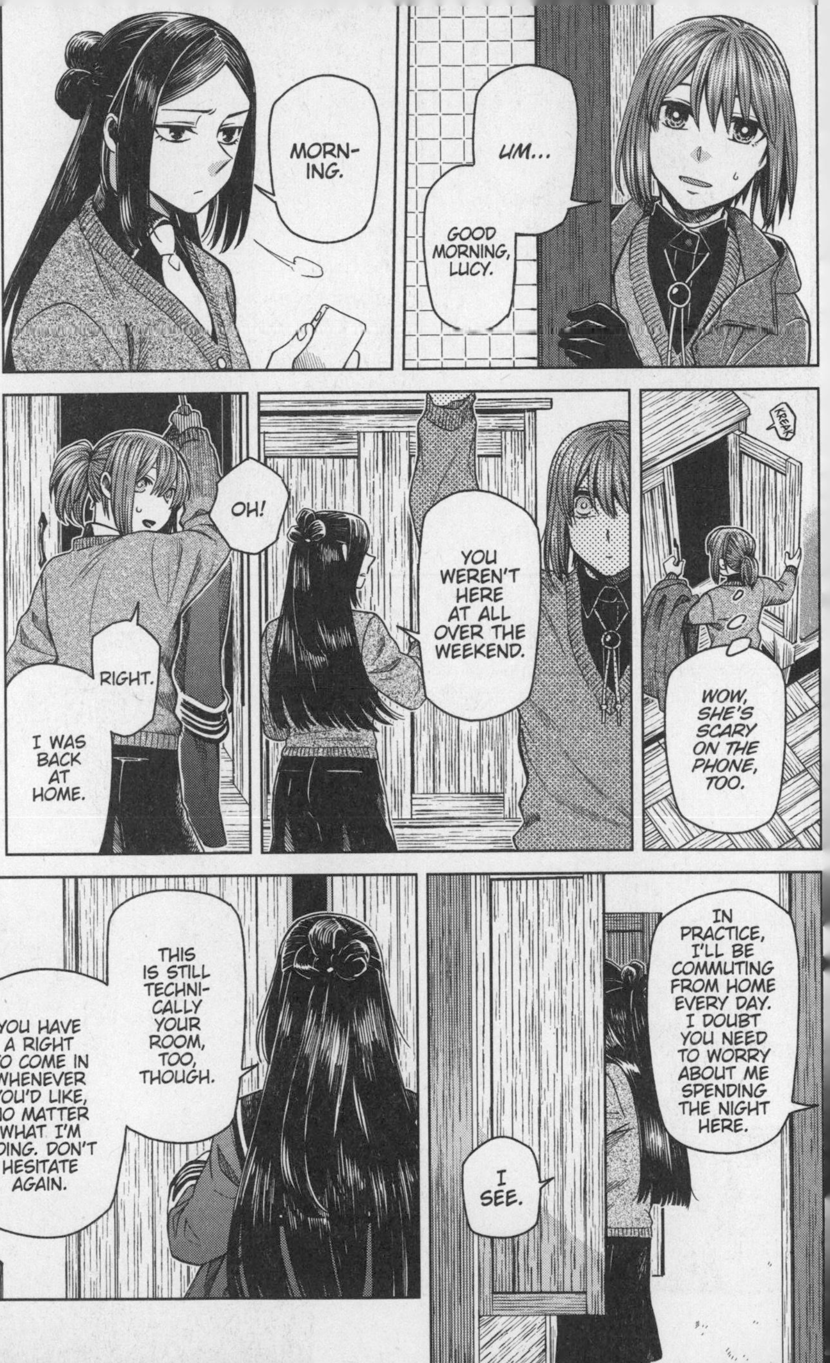
UM...
GOOD MORNING, LUCY.
MORN-ING.
KREAK
WOW, SHE'S SCARY ON THE PHONE, TOO.
YOU WEREN'T HERE AT ALL OVER THE WEEKEND.
OH!
RIGHT.
I WAS BACK AT HOME.
IN PRACTICE, I'LL BE COMMUTING FROM HOME EVERY DAY. I DOUBT YOU NEED TO WORRY ABOUT ME SPENDING THE NIGHT HERE.
I SEE.
THIS IS STILL TECHNICALLY YOUR ROOM, TOO, THOUGH.
YOU HAVE A RIGHT TO COME IN WHENEVER YOU'D LIKE, NO MATTER WHAT I'M DOING. DON'T HESITATE AGAIN.

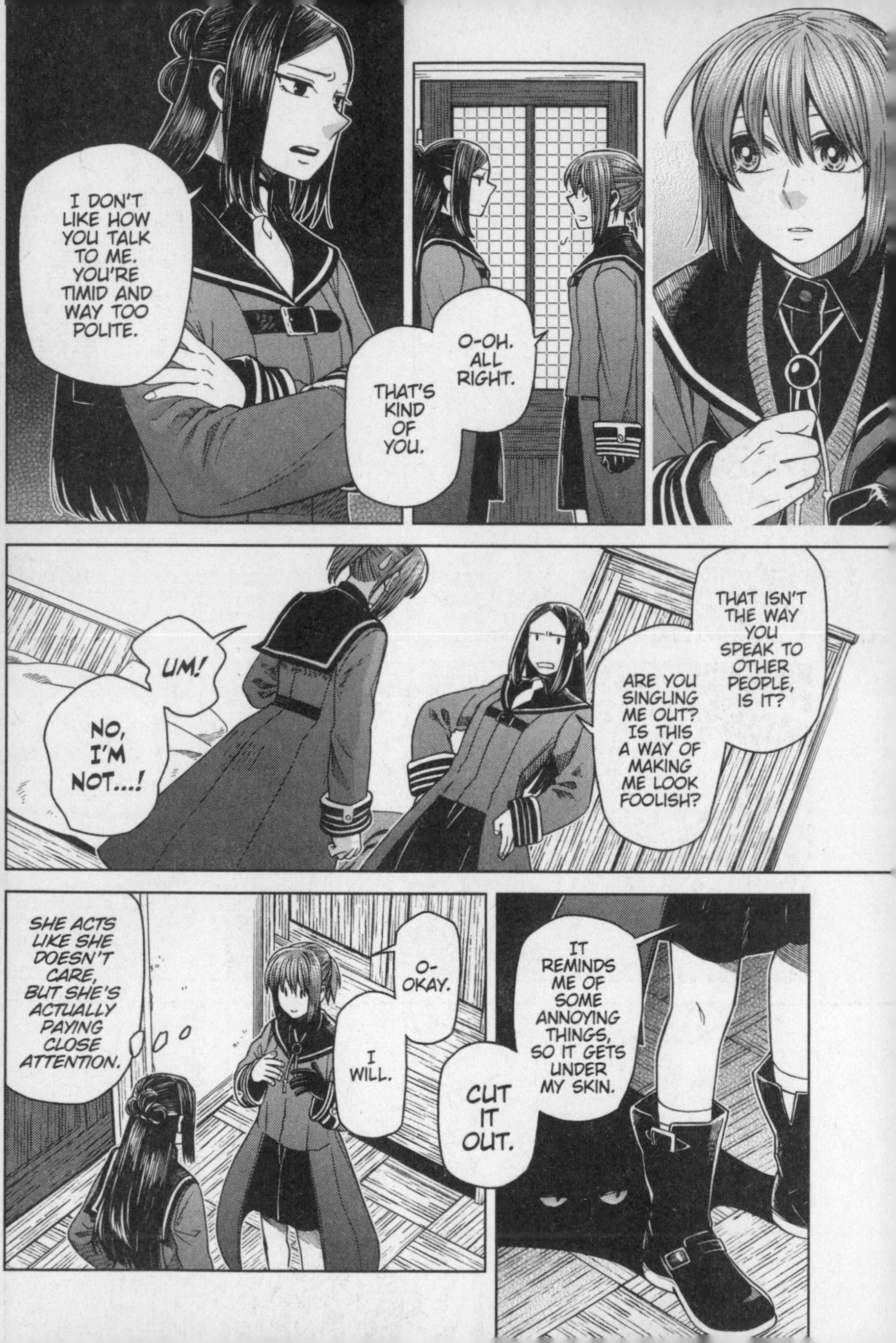
O-OH. ALL RIGHT.
THAT'S KIND OF YOU.
I DON'T LIKE HOW YOU TALK TO ME. YOU'RE TIMID AND WAY TOO POLITE.
THAT ISN'T THE WAY YOU SPEAK TO OTHER PEOPLE, IS IT?
ARE YOU SINGLING ME OUT? IS THIS A WAY OF MAKING ME LOOK FOOLISH?
UM!
NO, I'M NOT...!
IT REMINDS ME OF SOME ANNOYING THINGS, SO IT GETS UNDER MY SKIN.
CUT IT OUT.
O-OKAY.
I WILL.
SHE ACTS LIKE SHE DOESN'T CARE, BUT SHE'S ACTUALLY PAYING CLOSE ATTENTION.

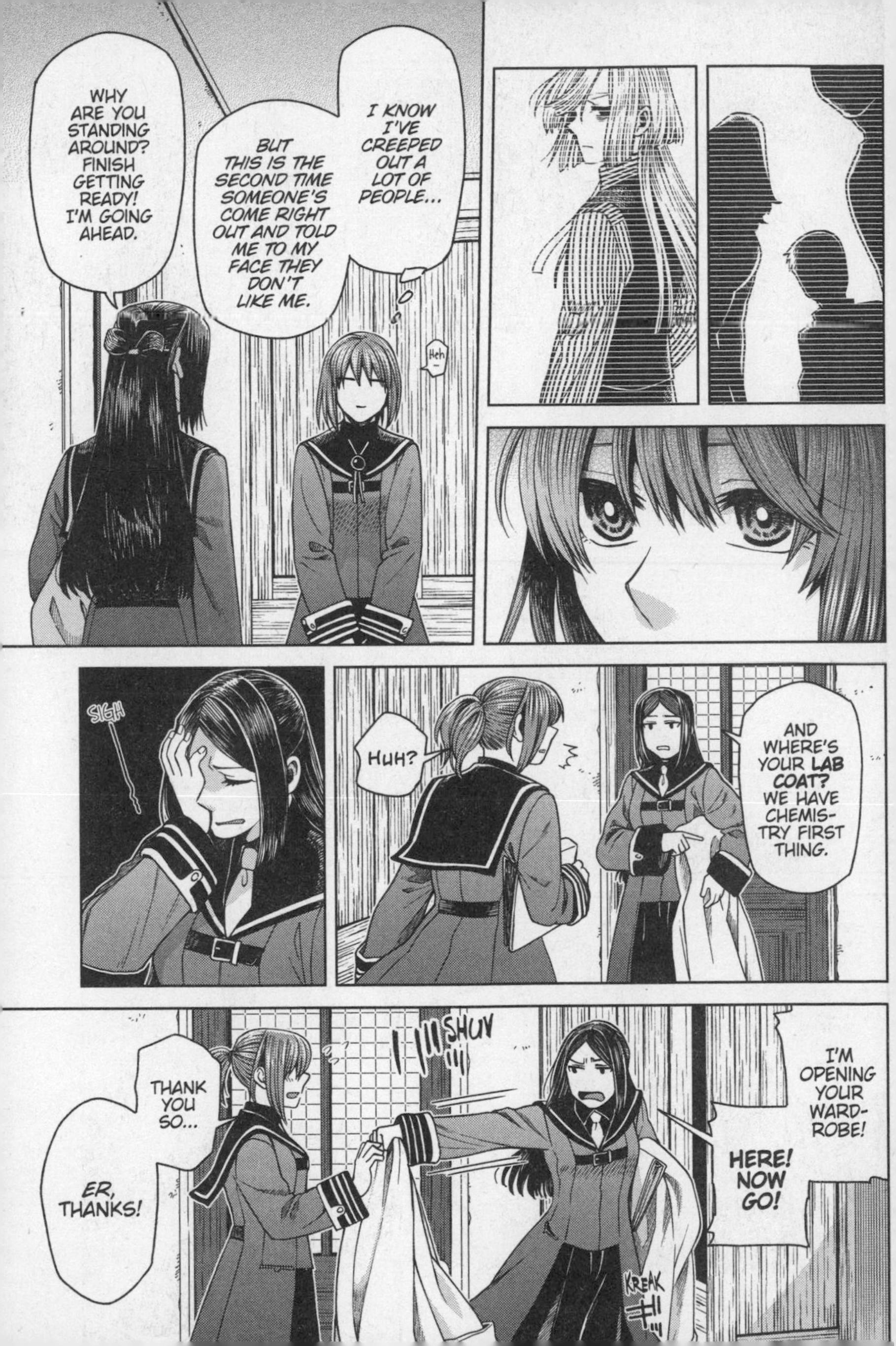
I KNOW I'VE CREEPED OUT A LOT OF PEOPLE...
BUT THIS IS THE SECOND TIME SOMEONE'S COME RIGHT OUT AND TOLD ME TO MY FACE THEY DON'T LIKE ME.
WHY ARE YOU STANDING AROUND? FINISH GETTING READY! I'M GOING AHEAD.
Heh
AND WHERE'S YOUR LAB COAT? WE HAVE CHEMISTRY FIRST THING.
HUH?
SIGH
I'M OPENING YOUR WARDROBE!
SHUV
HERE! NOW GO!
KREAK
THANK YOU SO...
ER, THANKS!

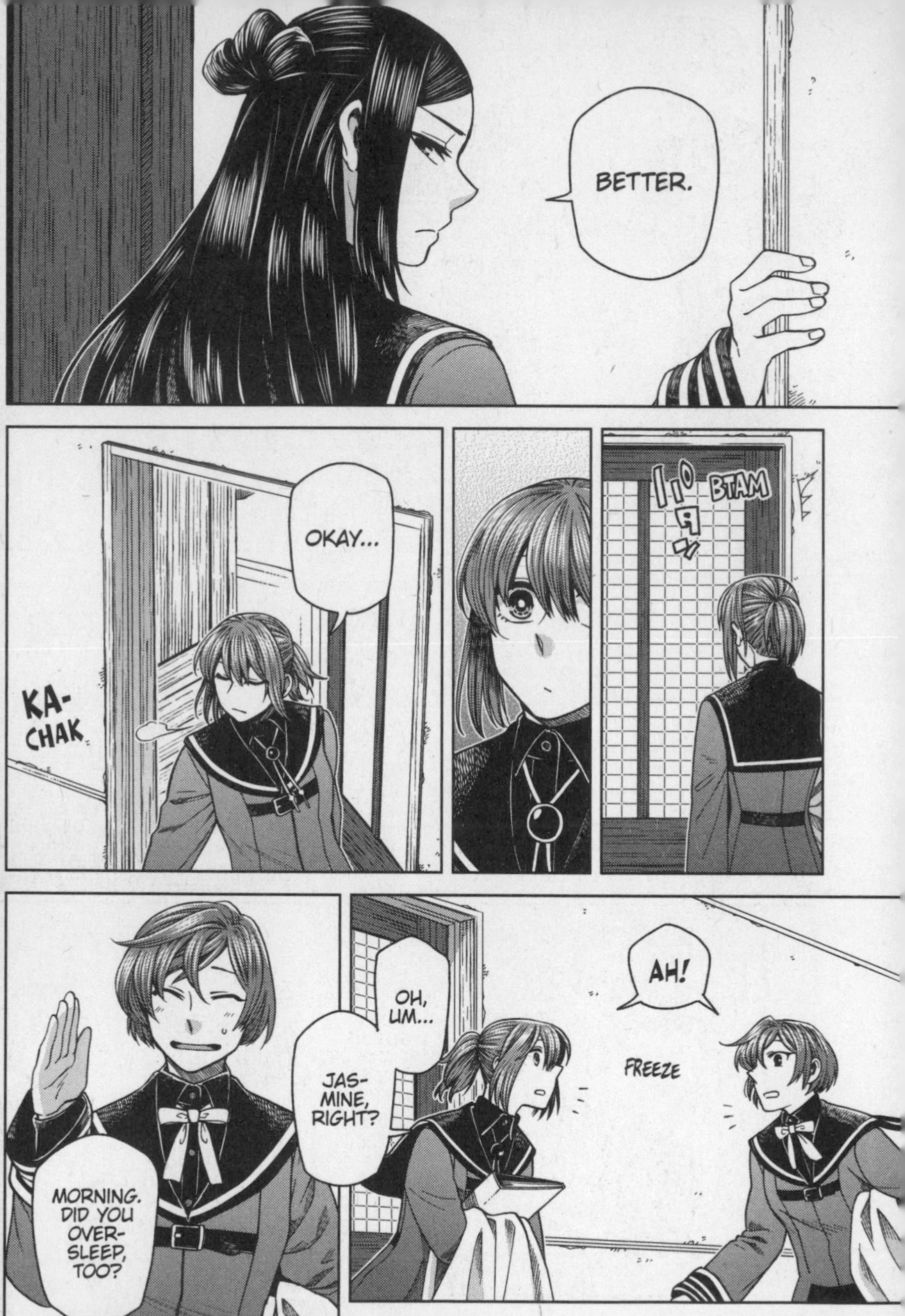
BETTER.
BTAM
OKAY...
KA-CHAK
AH!
FREEZE
OH, UM...
JAS-MINE, RIGHT?
MORNING. DID YOU OVER-SLEEP, TOO?

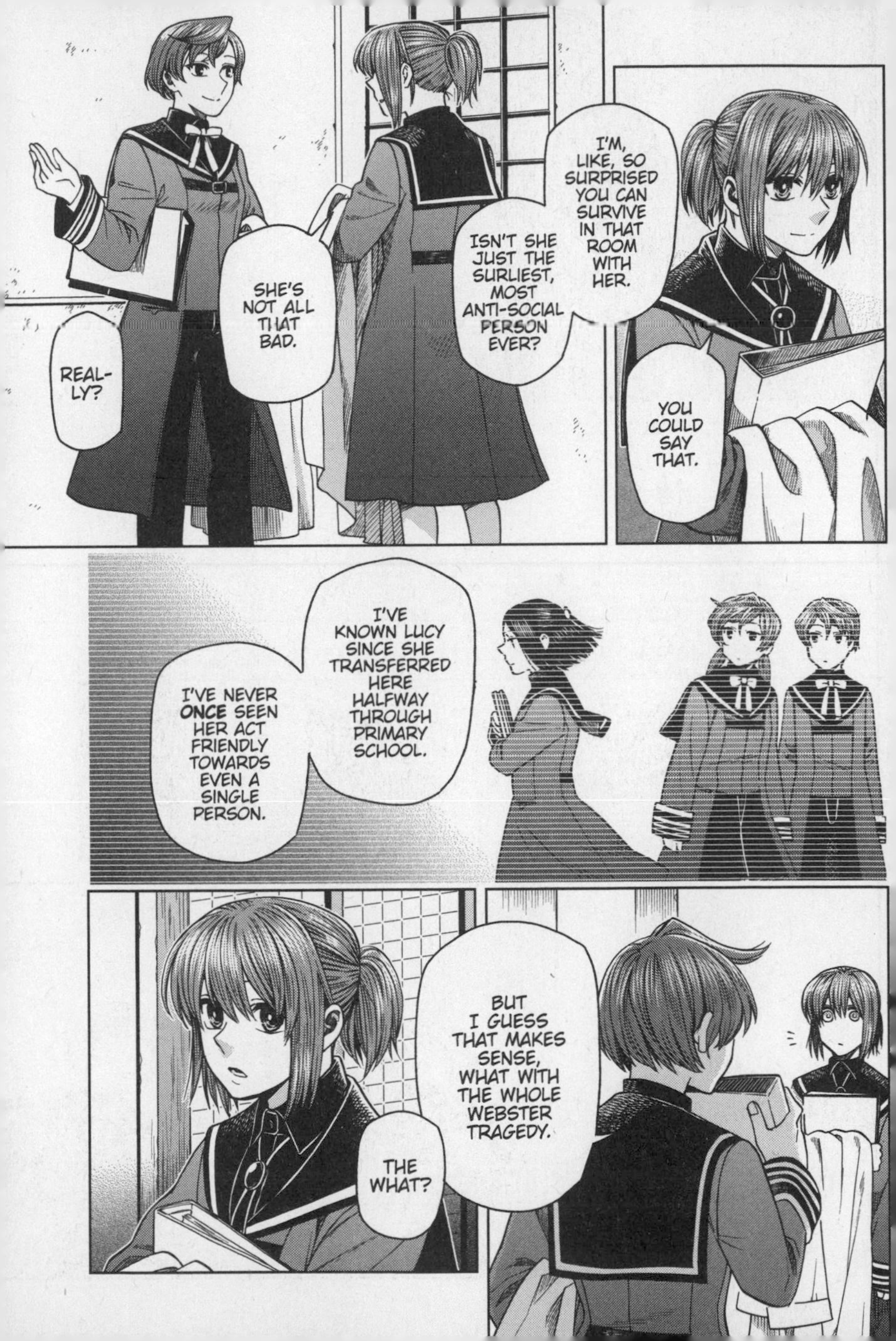
I'M, LIKE, SO SURPRISED YOU CAN SURVIVE IN THAT ROOM WITH HER.
YOU COULD SAY THAT.
ISN'T SHE JUST THE SURLIEST, MOST ANTI-SOCIAL PERSON EVER?
SHE'S NOT ALL THAT BAD.
REAL-LY?
I'VE KNOWN LUCY SINCE SHE TRANSFERRED HERE HALFWAY THROUGH PRIMARY SCHOOL.
I'VE NEVER ONCE SEEN HER ACT FRIENDLY TOWARDS EVEN A SINGLE PERSON.
BUT I GUESS THAT MAKES SENSE, WHAT WITH THE WHOLE WEBSTER TRAGEDY.
THE WHAT?

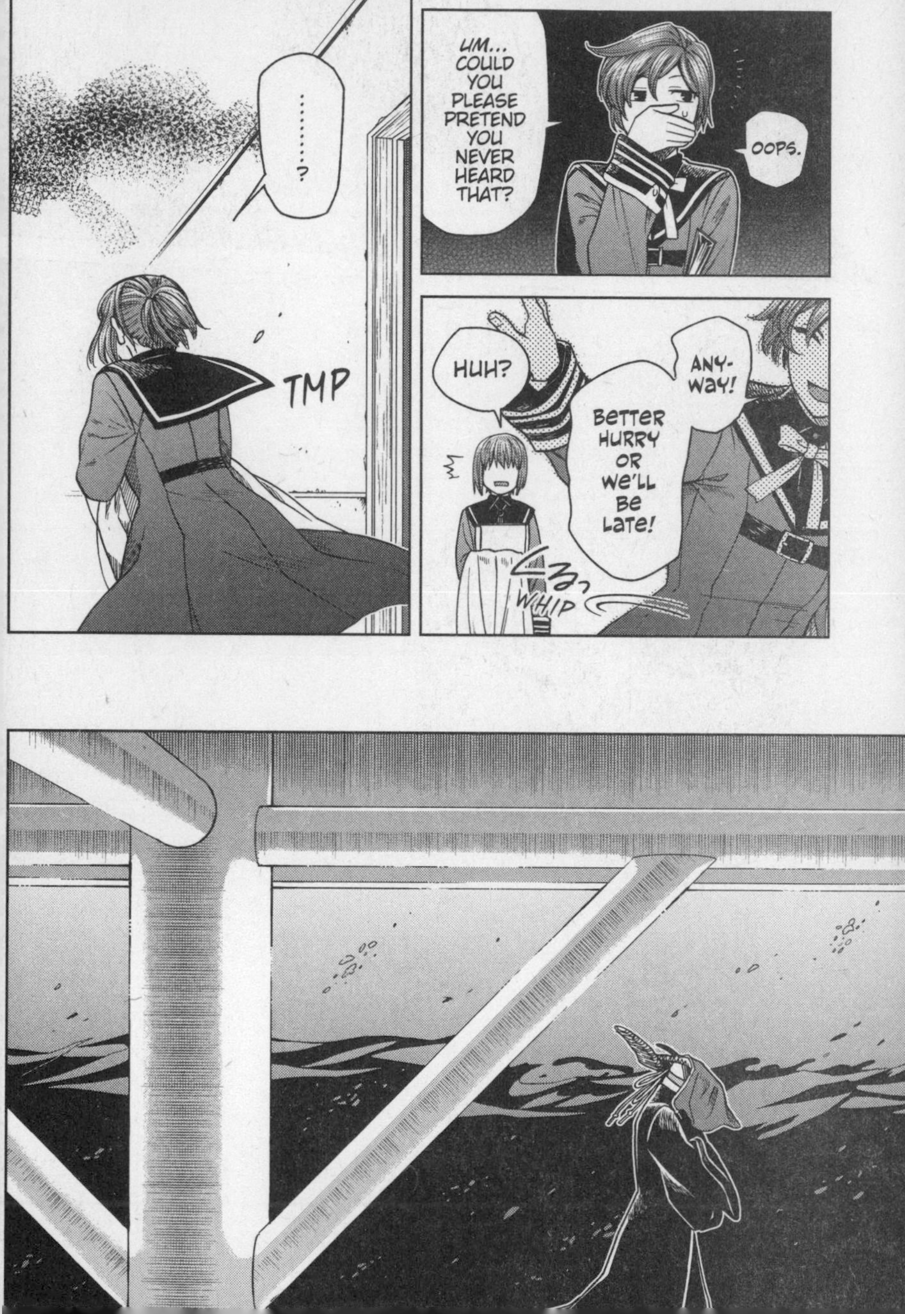
OOPS.
UM... COULD YOU PLEASE PRETEND YOU NEVER HEARD THAT?
ANY-WAY!
BETTER HURRY OR WE'LL BE LATE!
HUH?
くるっ
WHIP
......?
TMP

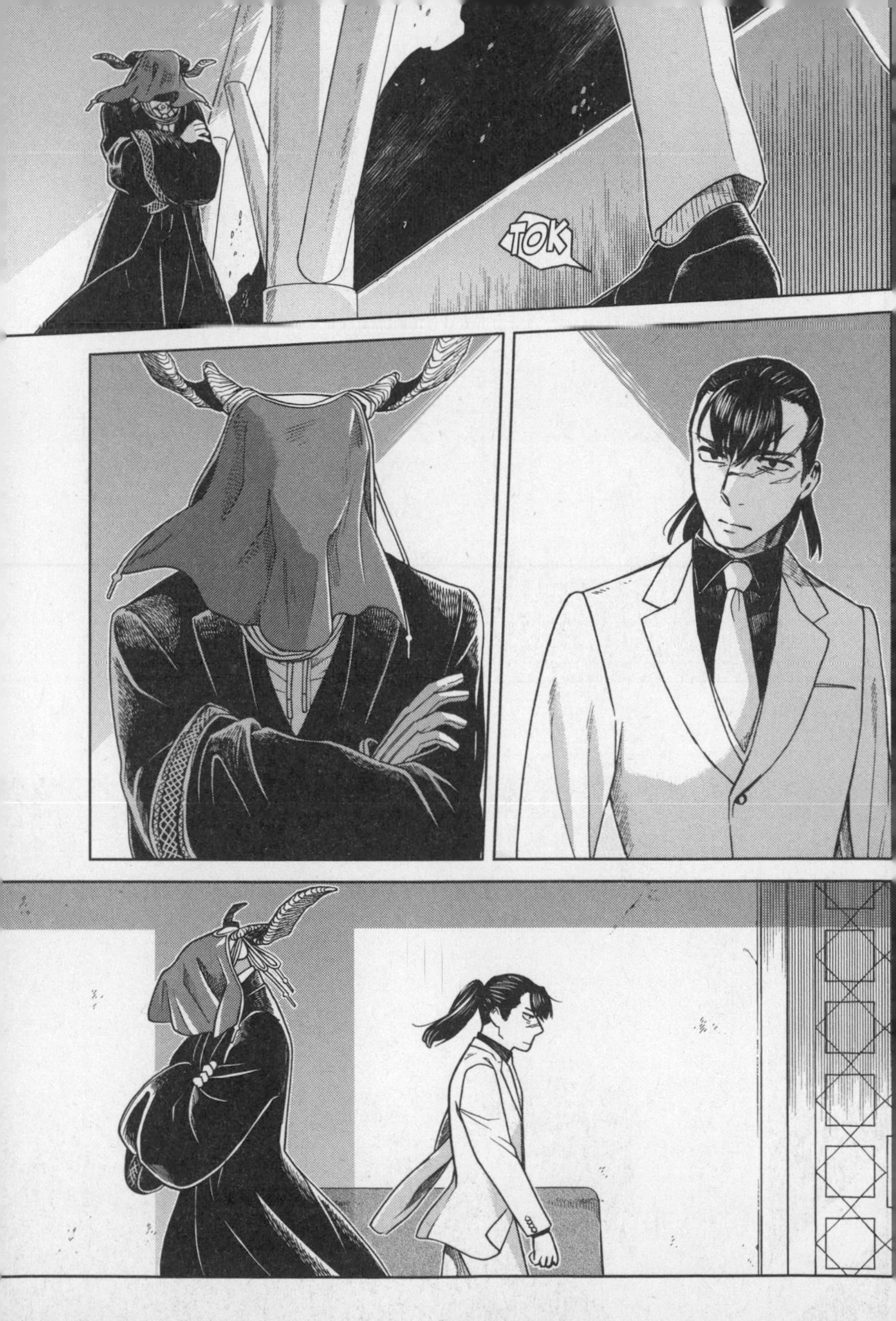
TOK

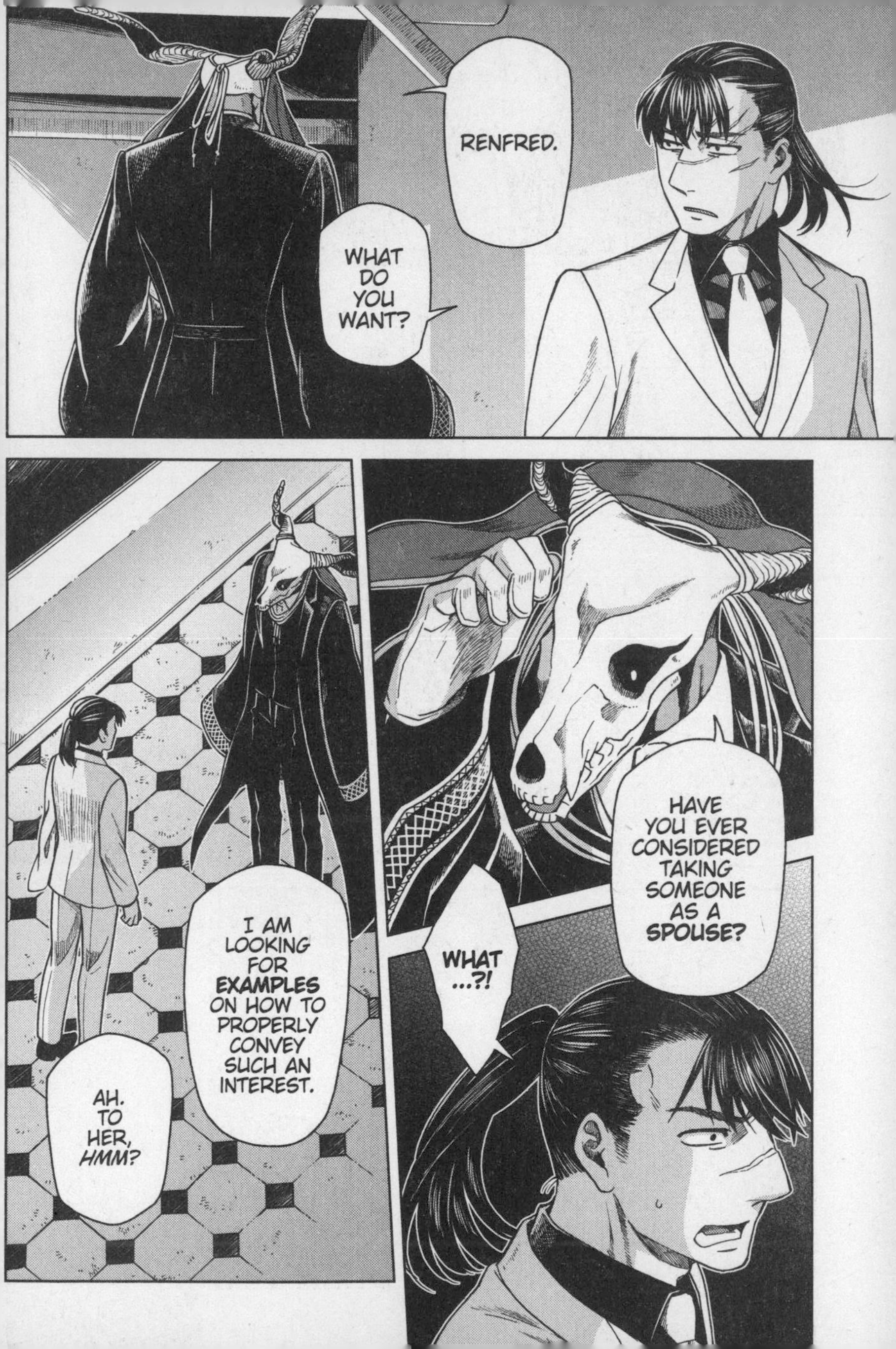
RENFRED.
WHAT DO YOU WANT?
HAVE YOU EVER CONSIDERED TAKING SOMEONE AS A SPOUSE?
WHAT ...?!
I AM LOOKING FOR **EXAMPLES** ON HOW TO PROPERLY CONVEY SUCH AN INTEREST.
AH. TO HER, *HMM?*

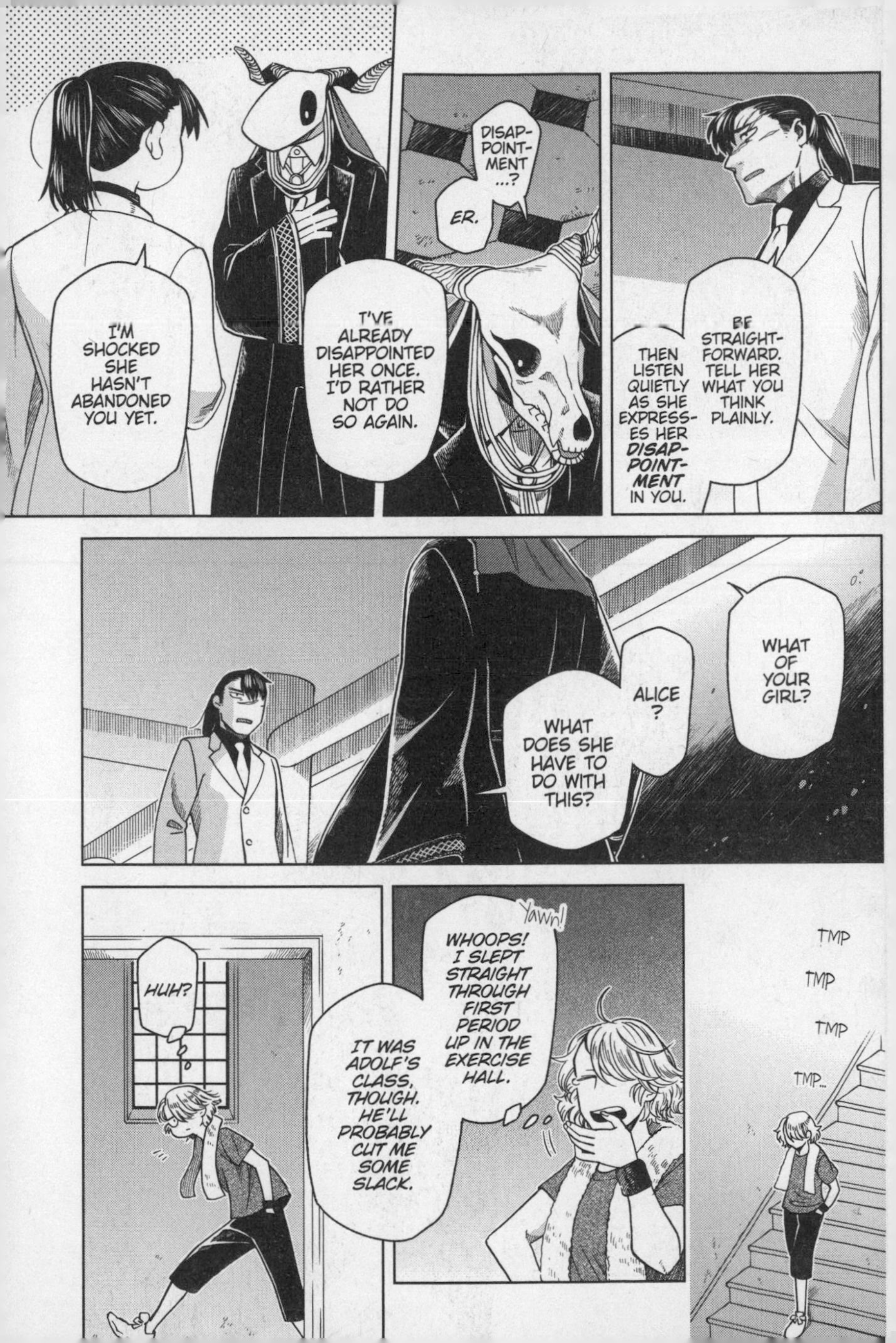
BE STRAIGHTFORWARD. TELL HER WHAT YOU THINK PLAINLY.
THEN LISTEN QUIETLY AS SHE EXPRESSES HER *DISAPPOINTMENT* IN YOU.
DISAPPOINTMENT...?
ER.
I'VE ALREADY DISAPPOINTED HER ONCE. I'D RATHER NOT DO SO AGAIN.
I'M SHOCKED SHE HASN'T ABANDONED YOU YET.
WHAT OF YOUR GIRL?
ALICE?
WHAT DOES SHE HAVE TO DO WITH THIS?
TMP
TMP
TMP
TMP...
Yawn!
WHOOPS! I SLEPT STRAIGHT THROUGH FIRST PERIOD UP IN THE EXERCISE HALL.
IT WAS ADOLF'S CLASS, THOUGH. HE'LL PROBABLY CUT ME SOME SLACK.
HUH?

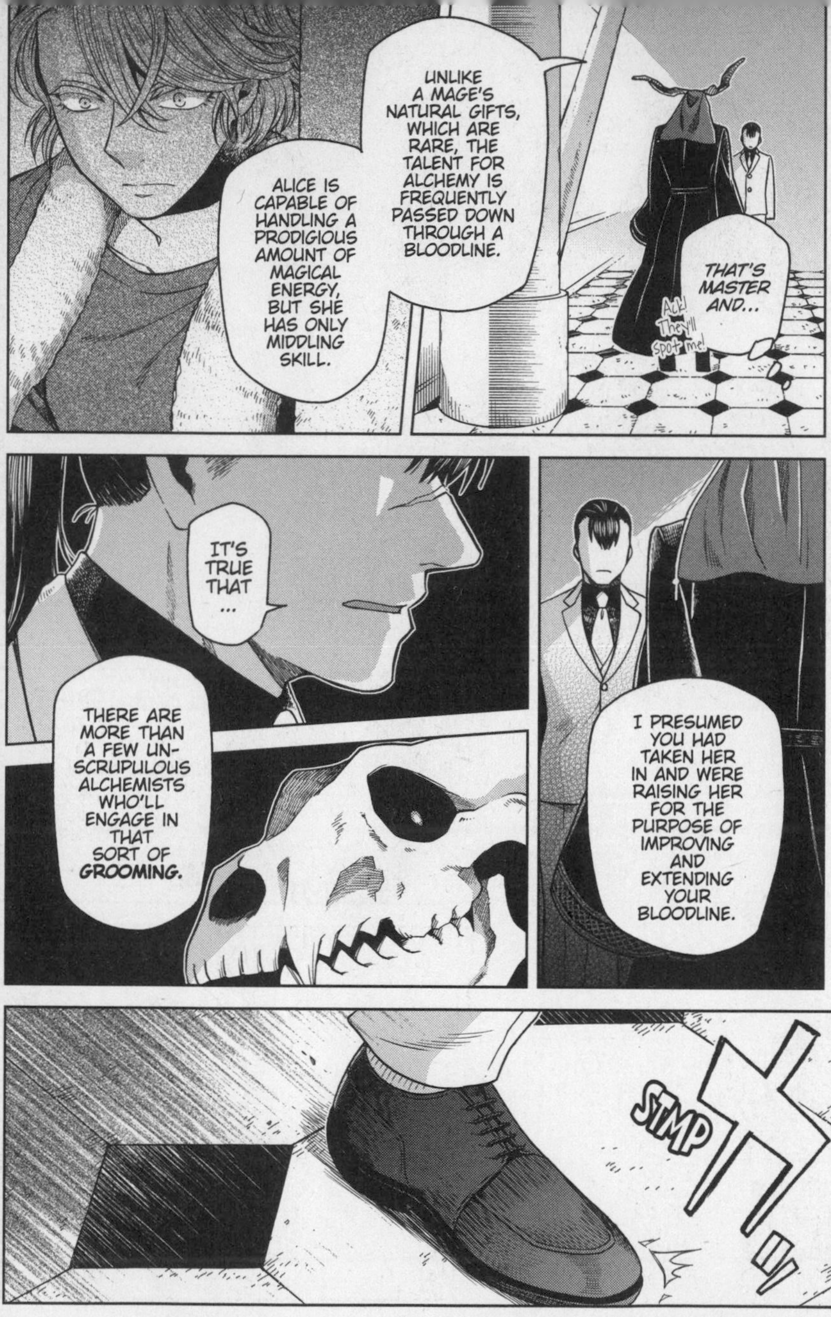
THAT'S MASTER AND...
Ack! They'll spot me!
UNLIKE A MAGE'S NATURAL GIFTS, WHICH ARE RARE, THE TALENT FOR ALCHEMY IS FREQUENTLY PASSED DOWN THROUGH A BLOODLINE.
ALICE IS CAPABLE OF HANDLING A PRODIGIOUS AMOUNT OF MAGICAL ENERGY, BUT SHE HAS ONLY MIDDLING SKILL.
I PRESUMED YOU HAD TAKEN HER IN AND WERE RAISING HER FOR THE PURPOSE OF IMPROVING AND EXTENDING YOUR BLOODLINE.
IT'S TRUE THAT ...
THERE ARE MORE THAN A FEW UN-SCRUPULOUS ALCHEMISTS WHO'LL ENGAGE IN THAT SORT OF GROOMING.
STMP

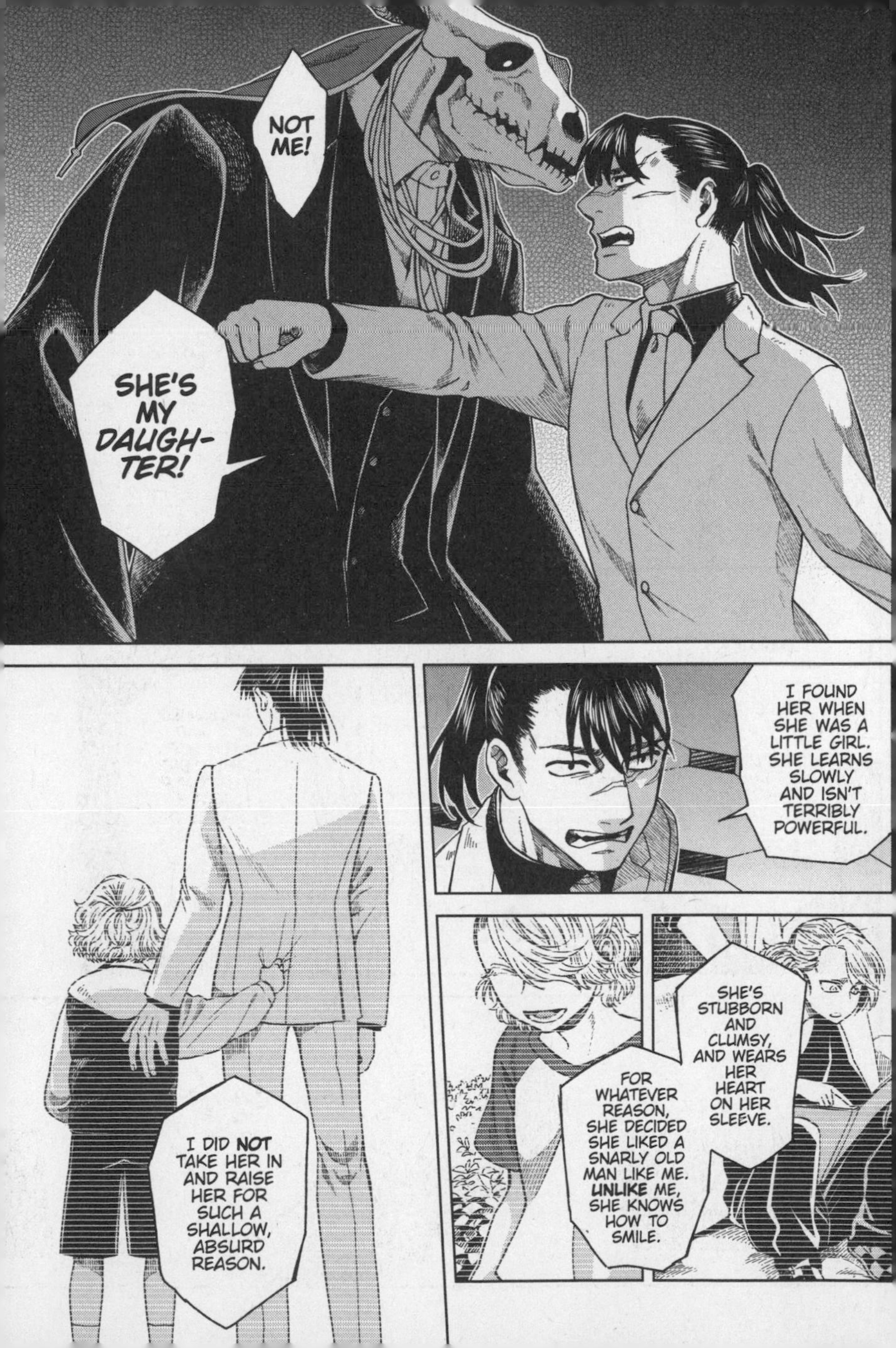
NOT ME!
SHE'S MY DAUGHTER!
I FOUND HER WHEN SHE WAS A LITTLE GIRL. SHE LEARNS SLOWLY AND ISN'T TERRIBLY POWERFUL.
SHE'S STUBBORN AND CLUMSY, AND WEARS HER HEART ON HER SLEEVE.
FOR WHATEVER REASON, SHE DECIDED SHE LIKED A SNARLY OLD MAN LIKE ME. UNLIKE ME, SHE KNOWS HOW TO SMILE.
I DID NOT TAKE HER IN AND RAISE HER FOR SUCH A SHALLOW, ABSURD REASON.

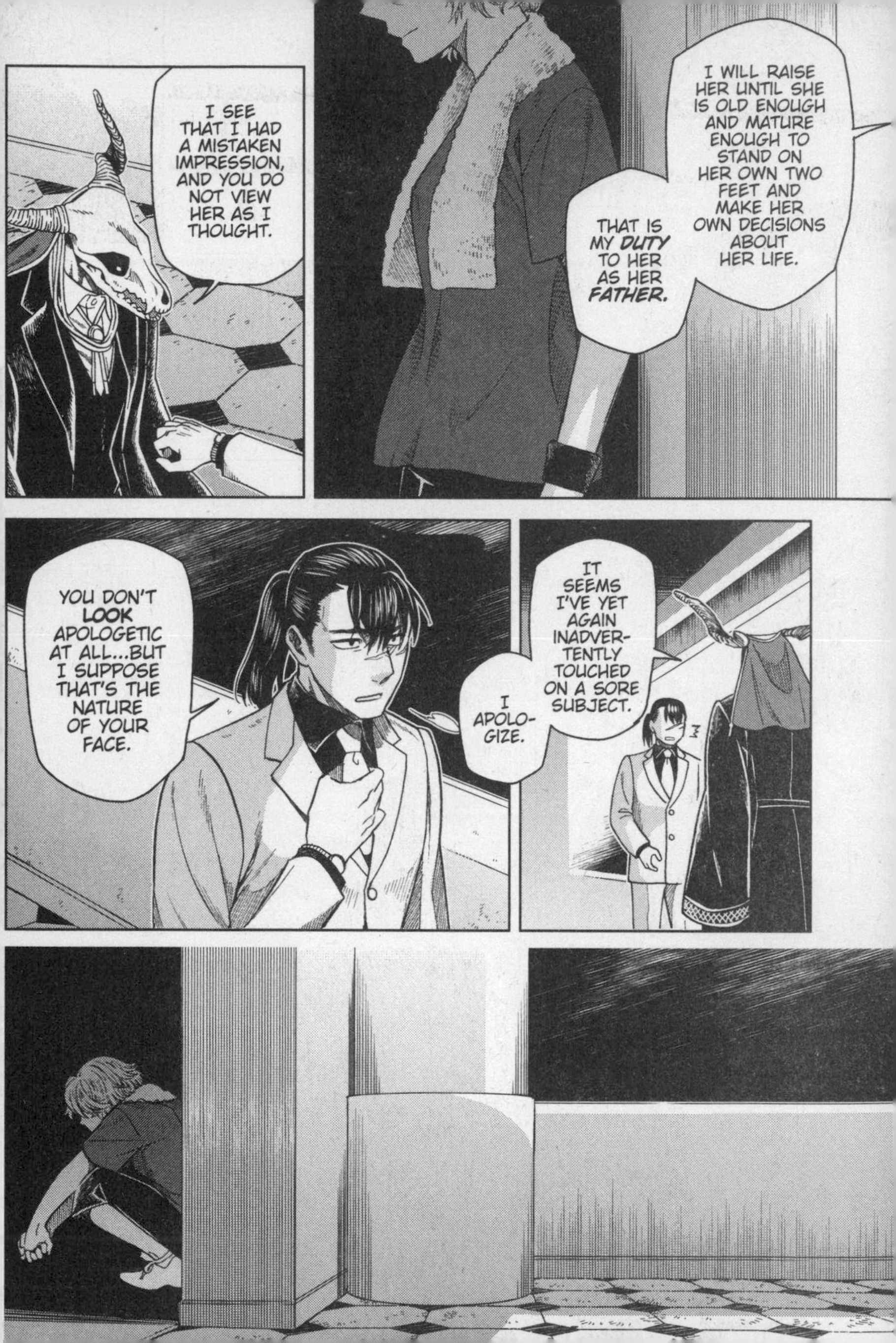
I WILL RAISE HER UNTIL SHE IS OLD ENOUGH AND MATURE ENOUGH TO STAND ON HER OWN TWO FEET AND MAKE HER OWN DECISIONS ABOUT HER LIFE.
THAT IS MY ***DUTY*** TO HER AS HER ***FATHER.***
I SEE THAT I HAD A MISTAKEN IMPRESSION, AND YOU DO NOT VIEW HER AS I THOUGHT.
IT SEEMS I'VE YET AGAIN INADVERTENTLY TOUCHED ON A SORE SUBJECT.
I APOLOGIZE.
YOU DON'T **LOOK** APOLOGETIC AT ALL...BUT I SUPPOSE THAT'S THE NATURE OF YOUR FACE.

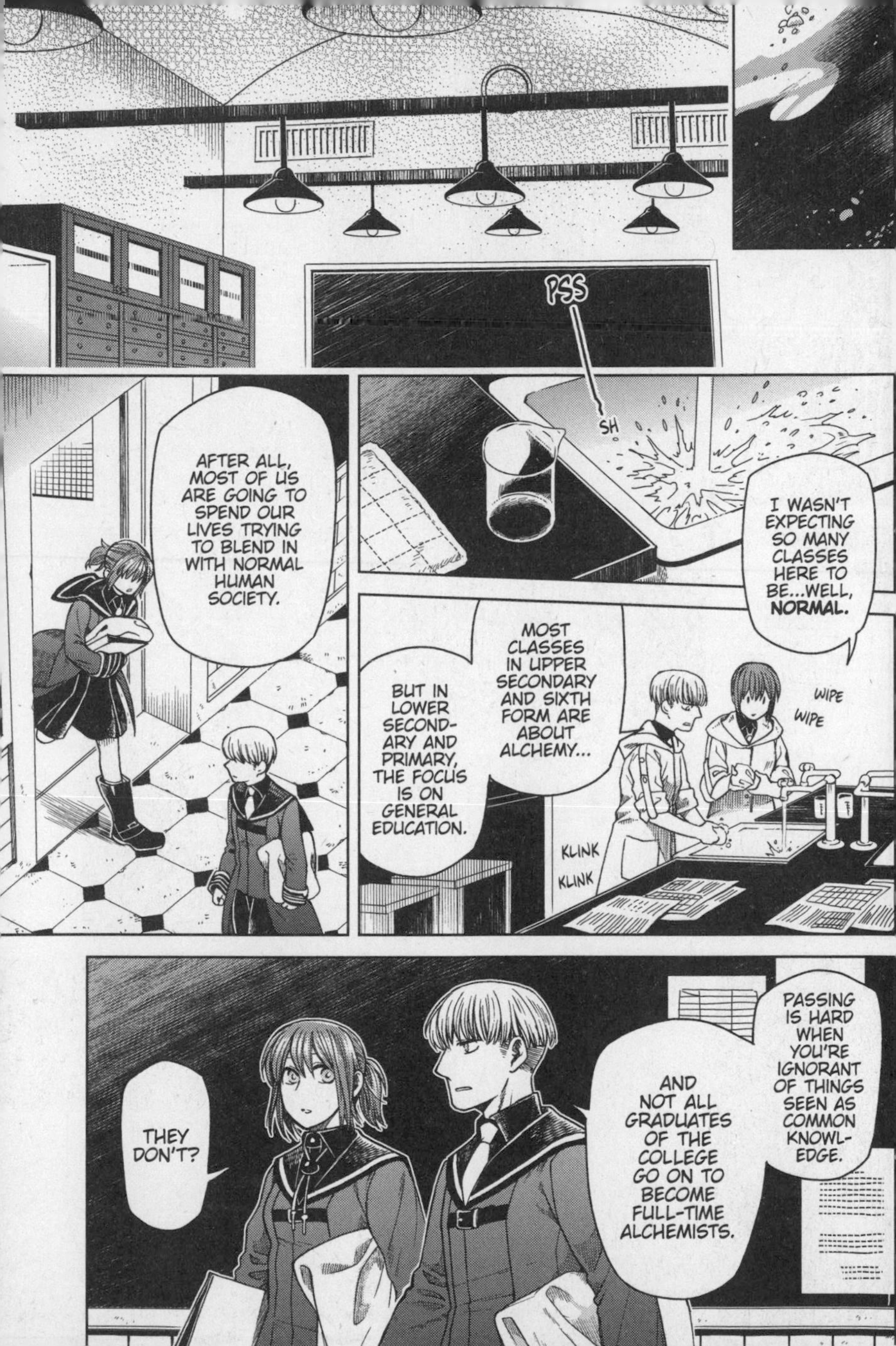
PSS
SH
I WASN'T EXPECTING SO MANY CLASSES HERE TO BE...WELL, **NORMAL.**
WIPE
WIPE
MOST CLASSES IN UPPER SECONDARY AND SIXTH FORM ARE ABOUT ALCHEMY...
BUT IN LOWER SECOND-ARY AND PRIMARY, THE FOCUS IS ON GENERAL EDUCATION.
KLINK
KLINK
AFTER ALL, MOST OF US ARE GOING TO SPEND OUR LIVES TRYING TO BLEND IN WITH NORMAL HUMAN SOCIETY.
PASSING IS HARD WHEN YOU'RE IGNORANT OF THINGS SEEN AS COMMON KNOWL-EDGE.
AND NOT ALL GRADUATES OF THE COLLEGE GO ON TO BECOME FULL-TIME ALCHEMISTS.
THEY DON'T?

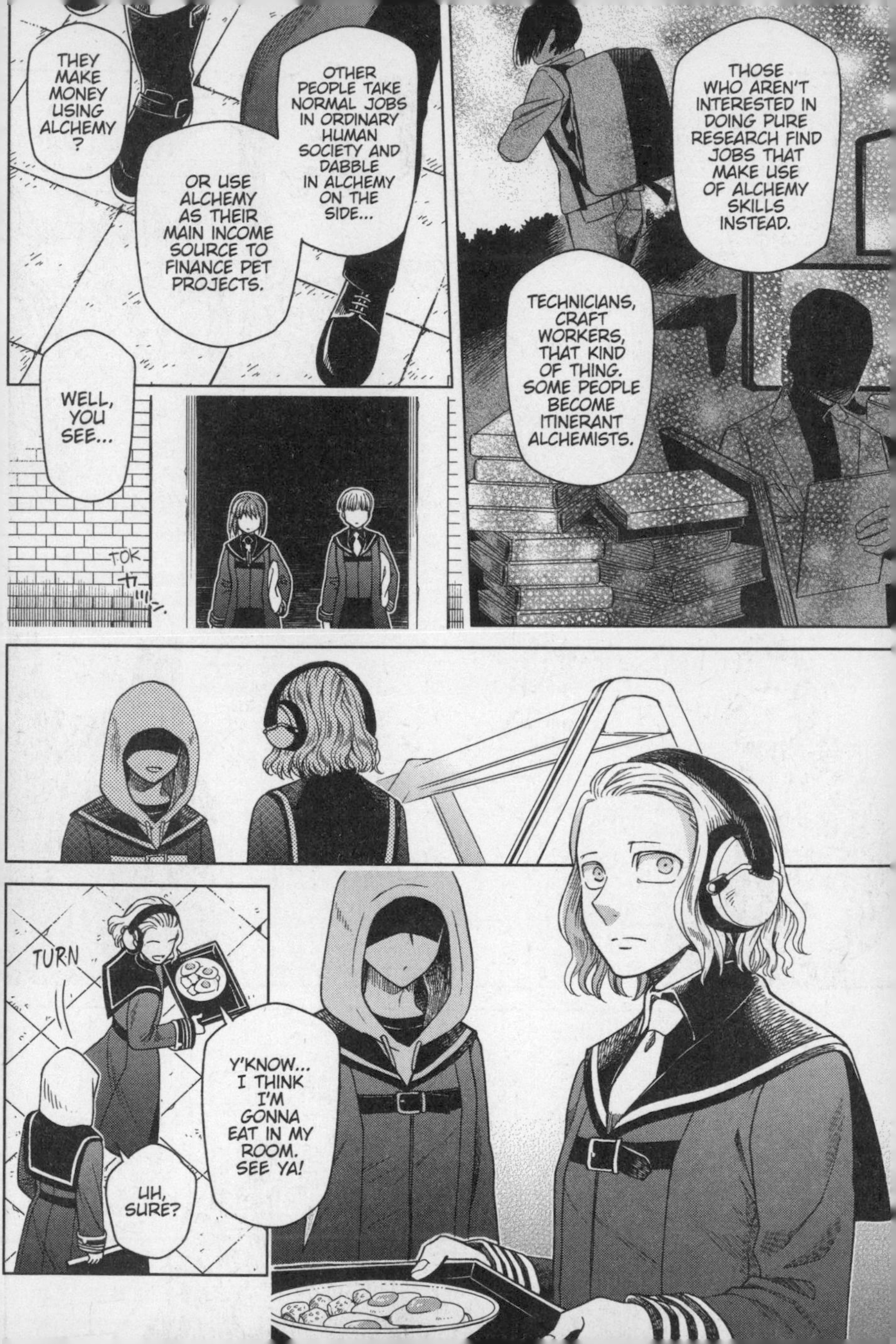
THOSE WHO AREN'T INTERESTED IN DOING PURE RESEARCH FIND JOBS THAT MAKE USE OF ALCHEMY SKILLS INSTEAD.
TECHNICIANS, CRAFT WORKERS, THAT KIND OF THING. SOME PEOPLE BECOME ITINERANT ALCHEMISTS.
OTHER PEOPLE TAKE NORMAL JOBS IN ORDINARY HUMAN SOCIETY AND DABBLE IN ALCHEMY ON THE SIDE...
THEY MAKE MONEY USING ALCHEMY?
OR USE ALCHEMY AS THEIR MAIN INCOME SOURCE TO FINANCE PET PROJECTS.
WELL, YOU SEE...
TOK
TURN
Y'KNOW... I THINK I'M GONNA EAT IN MY ROOM. SEE YA!
UH, SURE?

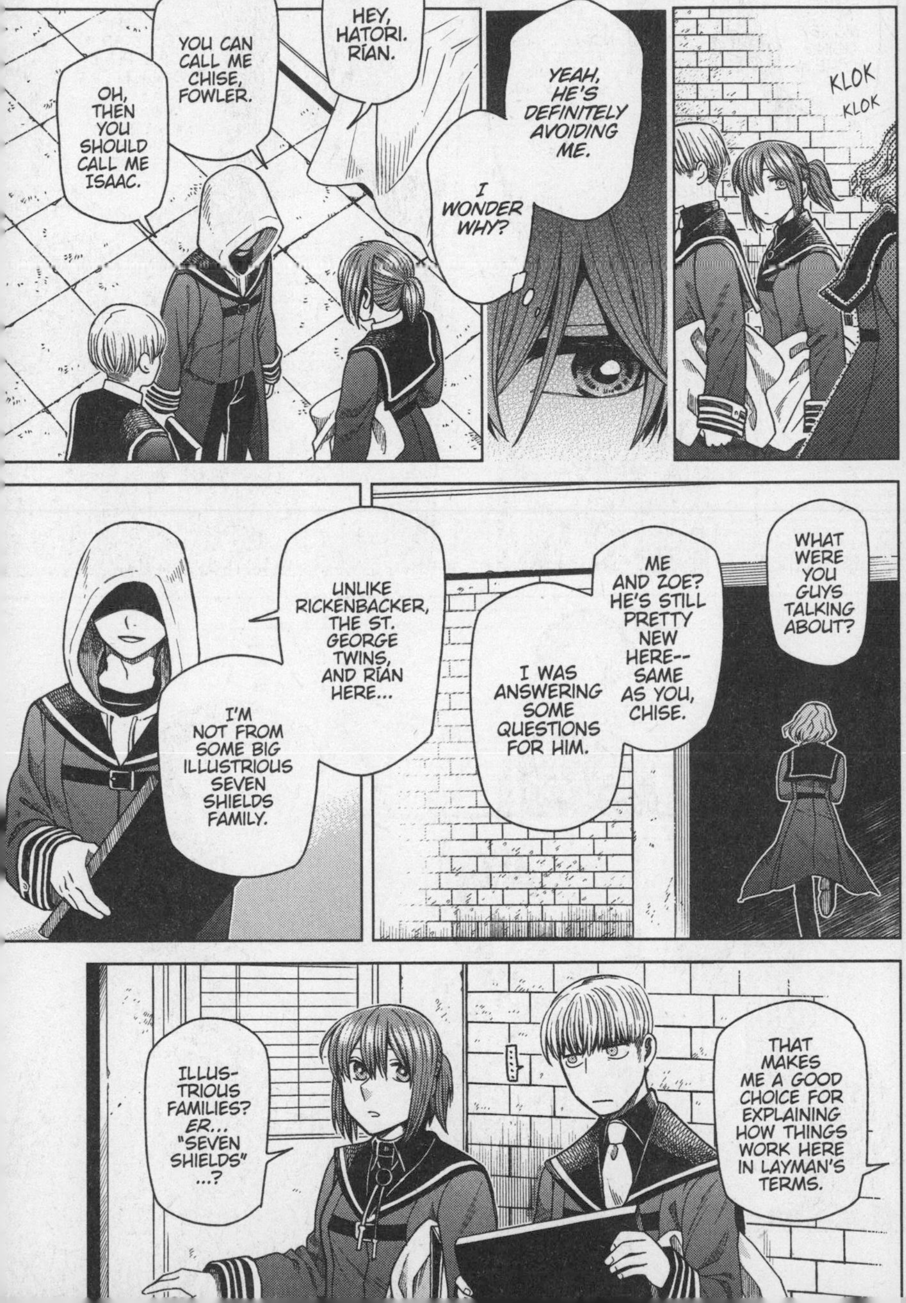
KLOK KLOK
YEAH, HE'S DEFINITELY AVOIDING ME.
I WONDER WHY?
HEY, HATORI. RÍAN.
YOU CAN CALL ME CHISE, FOWLER.
OH, THEN YOU SHOULD CALL ME ISAAC.
WHAT WERE YOU GUYS TALKING ABOUT?
ME AND ZOE? HE'S STILL PRETTY NEW HERE-- SAME AS YOU, CHISE.
I WAS ANSWERING SOME QUESTIONS FOR HIM.
UNLIKE RICKENBACKER, THE ST. GEORGE TWINS, AND RÍAN HERE...
I'M NOT FROM SOME BIG ILLUSTRIOUS SEVEN SHIELDS FAMILY.
THAT MAKES ME A GOOD CHOICE FOR EXPLAINING HOW THINGS WORK HERE IN LAYMAN'S TERMS.
...
ILLUS-TRIOUS FAMILIES? ER... "SEVEN SHIELDS" ...?

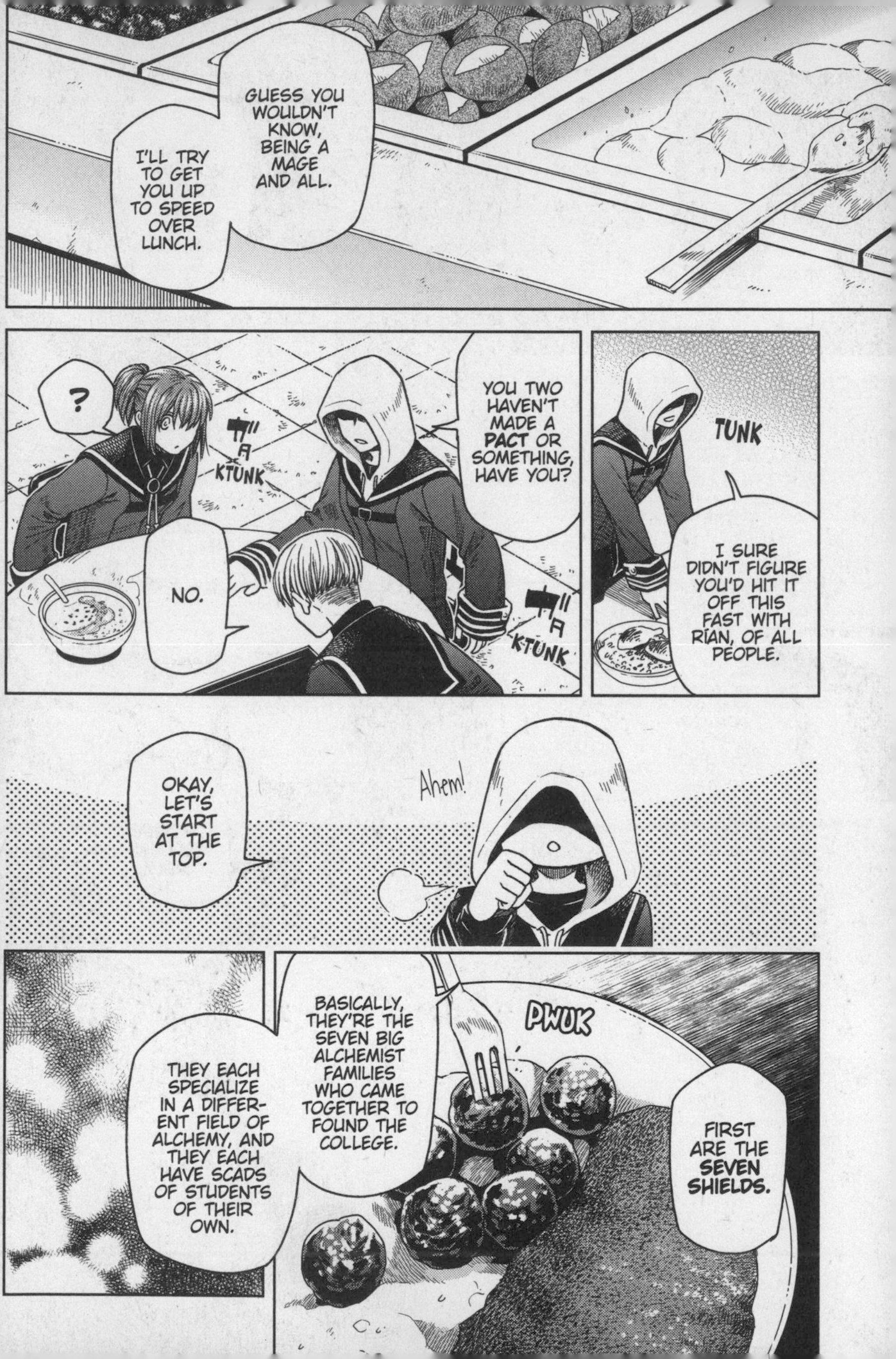
GUESS YOU WOULDN'T KNOW, BEING A MAGE AND ALL.
I'LL TRY TO GET YOU UP TO SPEED OVER LUNCH.
TUNK
I SURE DIDN'T FIGURE YOU'D HIT IT OFF THIS FAST WITH RÍAN, OF ALL PEOPLE.
YOU TWO HAVEN'T MADE A **PACT** OR SOMETHING, HAVE YOU?
?
KTUNK
NO.
KTUNK
Ahem!
OKAY, LET'S START AT THE TOP.
FIRST ARE THE **SEVEN SHIELDS.**
PWUK
BASICALLY, THEY'RE THE SEVEN BIG ALCHEMIST FAMILIES WHO CAME TOGETHER TO FOUND THE COLLEGE.
THEY EACH SPECIALIZE IN A DIFFERENT FIELD OF ALCHEMY, AND THEY EACH HAVE SCADS OF STUDENTS OF THEIR OWN.

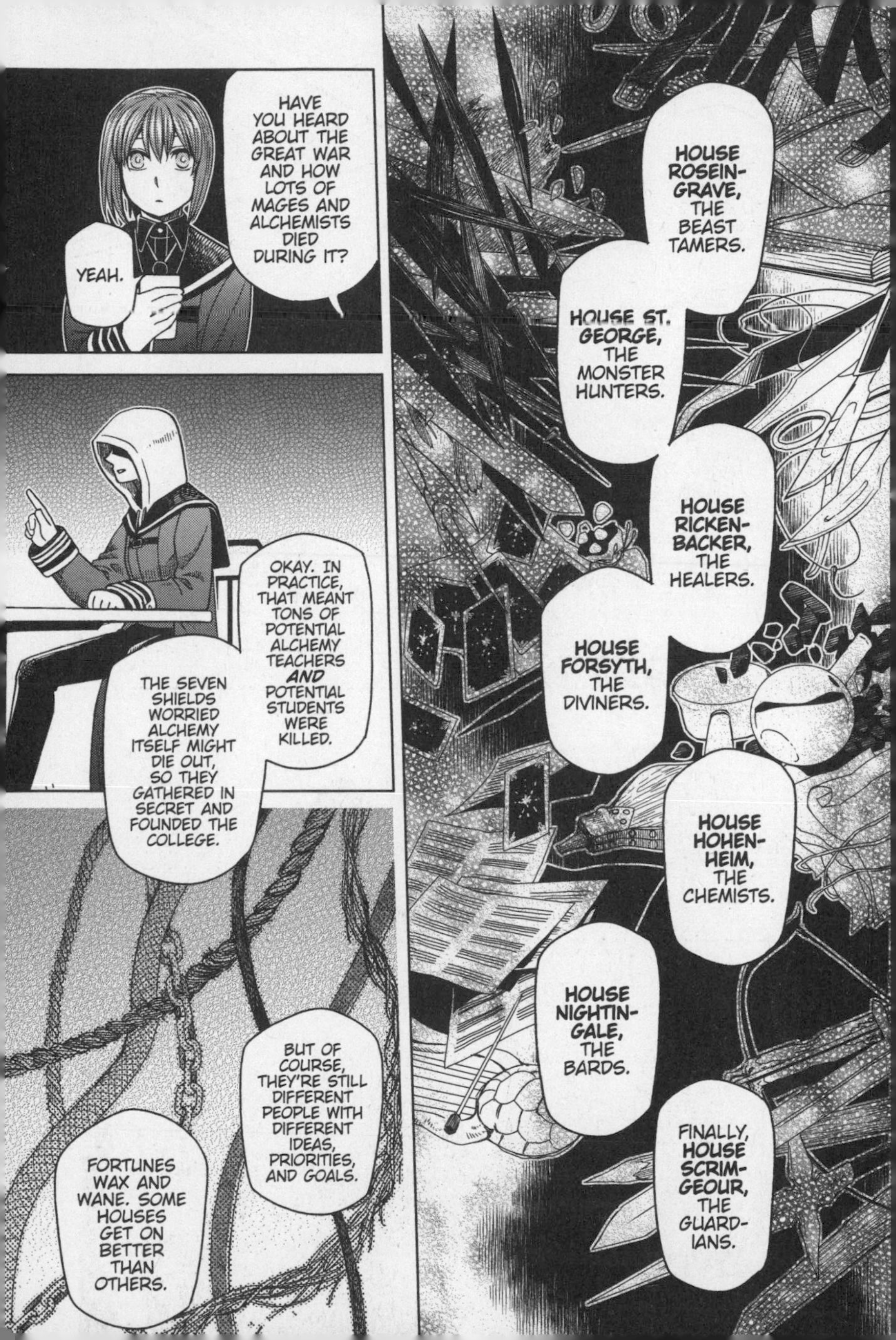
HOUSE ROSEIN-GRAVE, THE BEAST TAMERS.
HOUSE ST. GEORGE, THE MONSTER HUNTERS.
HOUSE RICKEN-BACKER, THE HEALERS.
HOUSE FORSYTH, THE DIVINERS.
HOUSE HOHEN-HEIM, THE CHEMISTS.
HOUSE NIGHTIN-GALE, THE BARDS.
FINALLY, HOUSE SCRIM-GEOUR, THE GUARD-IANS.
HAVE YOU HEARD ABOUT THE GREAT WAR AND HOW LOTS OF MAGES AND ALCHEMISTS DIED DURING IT?
YEAH.
OKAY. IN PRACTICE, THAT MEANT TONS OF POTENTIAL ALCHEMY TEACHERS AND POTENTIAL STUDENTS WERE KILLED.
THE SEVEN SHIELDS WORRIED ALCHEMY ITSELF MIGHT DIE OUT, SO THEY GATHERED IN SECRET AND FOUNDED THE COLLEGE.
BUT OF COURSE, THEY'RE STILL DIFFERENT PEOPLE WITH DIFFERENT IDEAS, PRIORITIES, AND GOALS.
FORTUNES WAX AND WANE. SOME HOUSES GET ON BETTER THAN OTHERS.

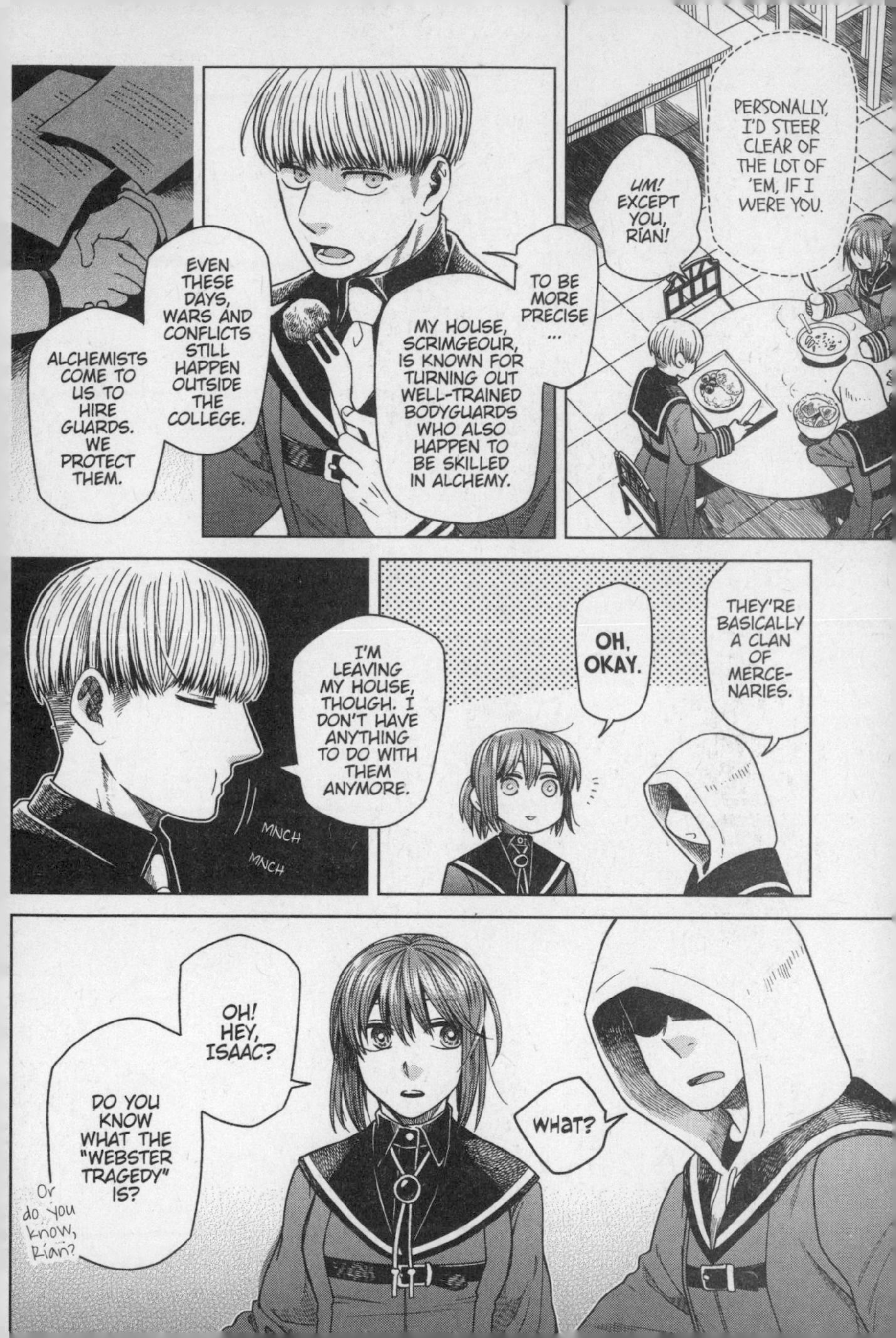
PERSONALLY, I'D STEER CLEAR OF THE LOT OF 'EM, IF I WERE YOU.
UM! EXCEPT YOU, RÍAN!
TO BE MORE PRECISE...
MY HOUSE, SCRIMGEOUR, IS KNOWN FOR TURNING OUT WELL-TRAINED BODYGUARDS WHO ALSO HAPPEN TO BE SKILLED IN ALCHEMY.
EVEN THESE DAYS, WARS AND CONFLICTS STILL HAPPEN OUTSIDE THE COLLEGE.
ALCHEMISTS COME TO US TO HIRE GUARDS. WE PROTECT THEM.
THEY'RE BASICALLY A CLAN OF MERCE-NARIES.
OH, OKAY.
I'M LEAVING MY HOUSE, THOUGH. I DON'T HAVE ANYTHING TO DO WITH THEM ANYMORE.
MNCH
MNCH
OH! HEY, ISAAC?
WHAT?
DO YOU KNOW WHAT THE "WEBSTER TRAGEDY" IS?
Or do you know, Rían?

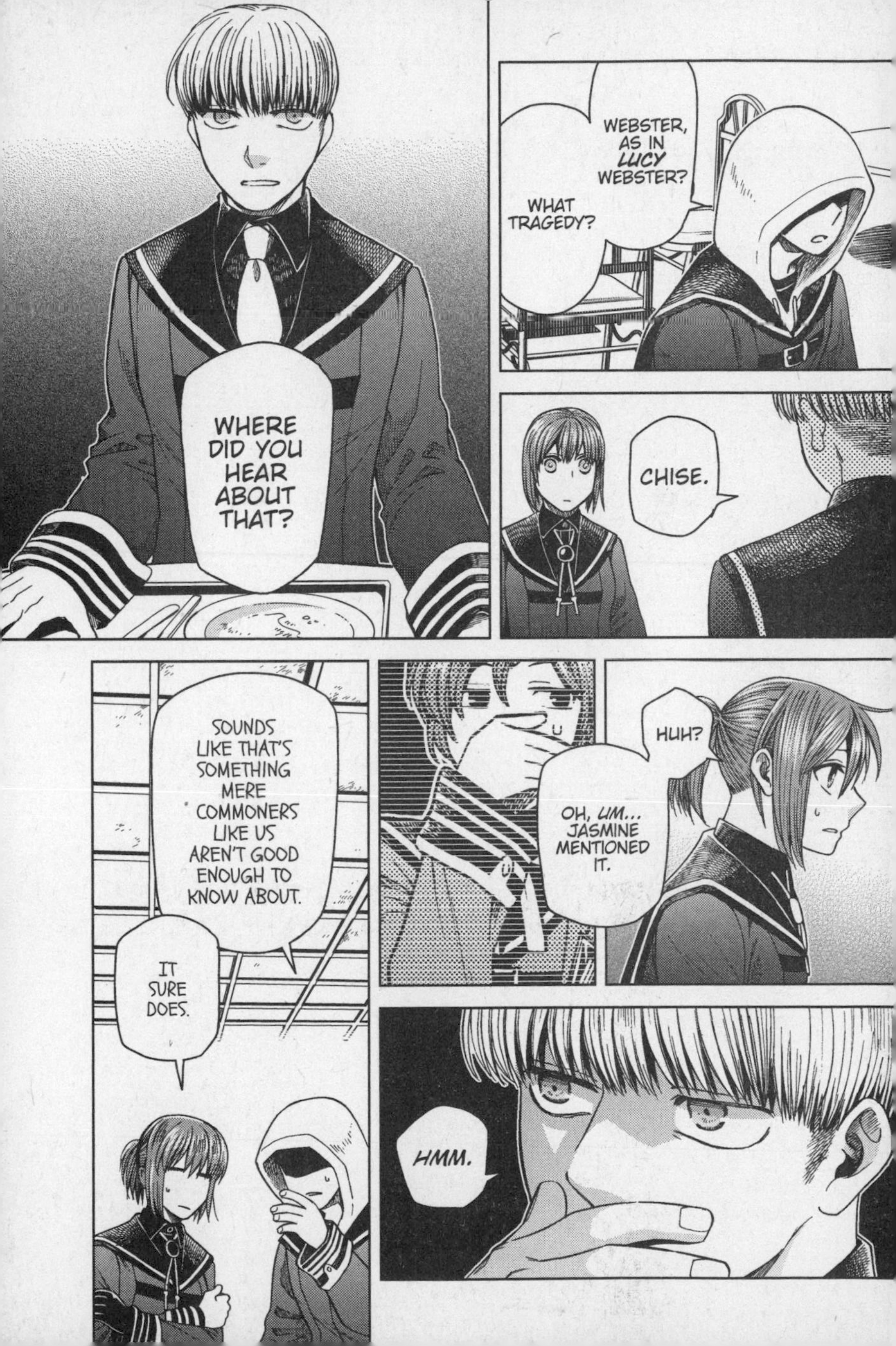
WEBSTER, AS IN *LUCY* WEBSTER?
WHAT TRAGEDY?
CHISE.
WHERE DID YOU HEAR ABOUT THAT?
HUH?
OH, *UM*... JASMINE MENTIONED IT.
HMM.
SOUNDS LIKE THAT'S SOMETHING MERE COMMONERS LIKE US AREN'T GOOD ENOUGH TO KNOW ABOUT.
IT SURE DOES.

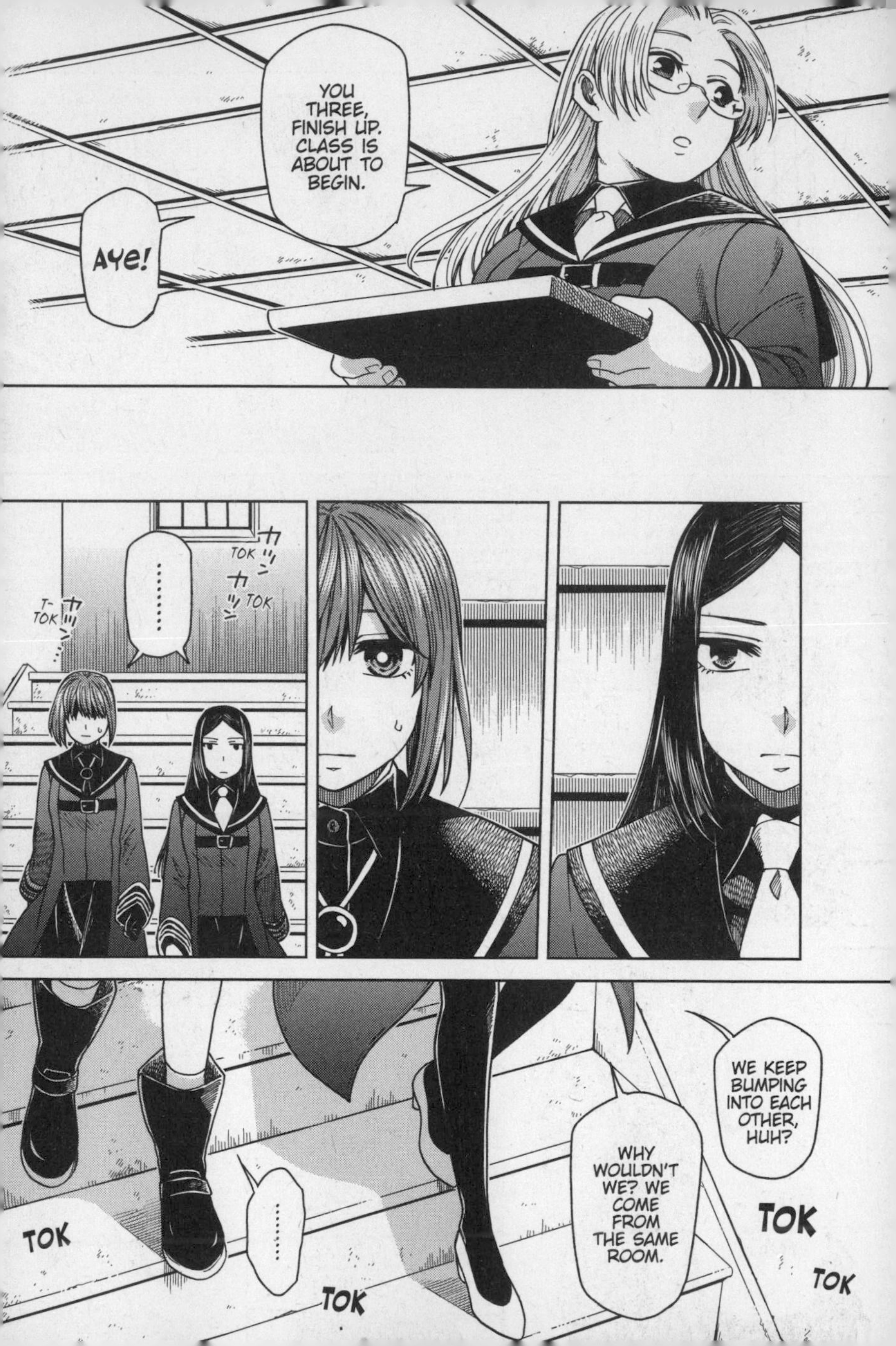
YOU THREE, FINISH UP. CLASS IS ABOUT TO BEGIN.
AYE!
TOK
TOK
T-TOK
......
TOK
TOK
WE KEEP BUMPING INTO EACH OTHER, HUH?
WHY WOULDN'T WE? WE COME FROM THE SAME ROOM.
......
TOK
TOK

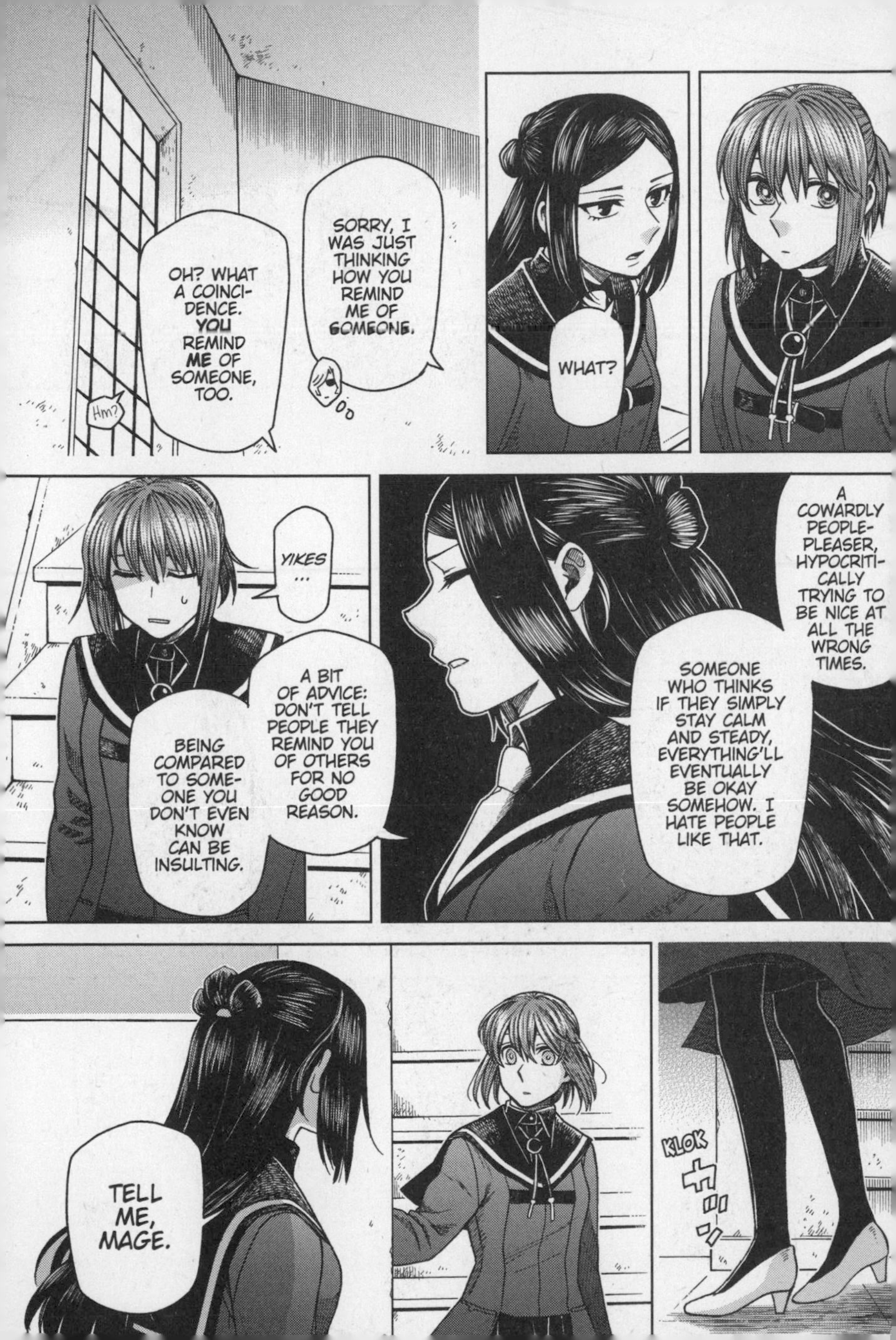
WHAT?
SORRY, I WAS JUST THINKING HOW YOU REMIND ME OF SOMEONE.
OH? WHAT A COINCIDENCE. YOU REMIND ME OF SOMEONE, TOO.
Hm?
A COWARDLY PEOPLE-PLEASER, HYPOCRITICALLY TRYING TO BE NICE AT ALL THE WRONG TIMES.
SOMEONE WHO THINKS IF THEY SIMPLY STAY CALM AND STEADY, EVERYTHING'LL EVENTUALLY BE OKAY SOMEHOW. I HATE PEOPLE LIKE THAT.
YIKES...
A BIT OF ADVICE: DON'T TELL PEOPLE THEY REMIND YOU OF OTHERS FOR NO GOOD REASON.
BEING COMPARED TO SOMEONE YOU DON'T EVEN KNOW CAN BE INSULTING.
KLOK
TELL ME, MAGE.

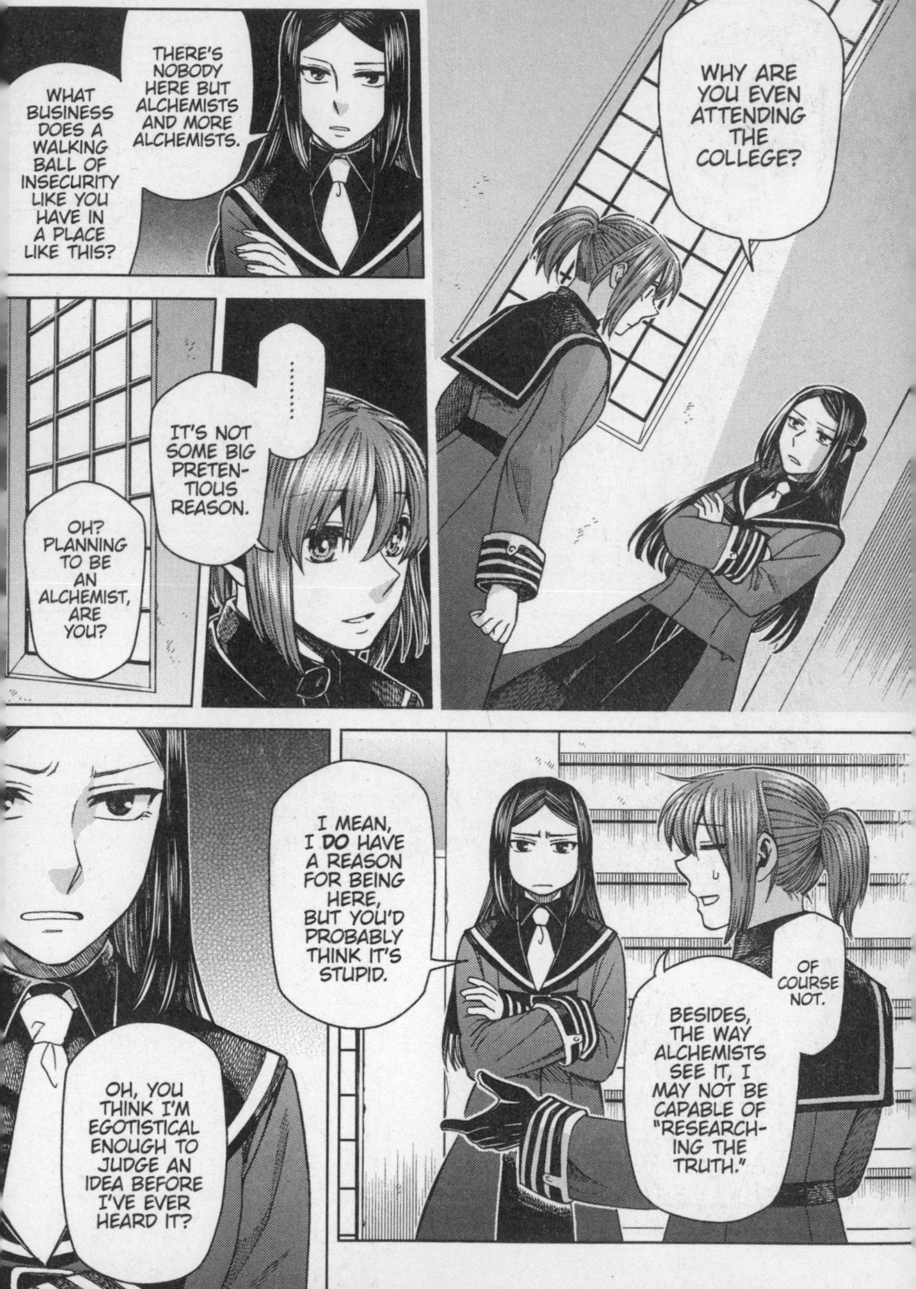
WHY ARE YOU EVEN ATTENDING THE COLLEGE?
THERE'S NOBODY HERE BUT ALCHEMISTS AND MORE ALCHEMISTS.
WHAT BUSINESS DOES A WALKING BALL OF INSECURITY LIKE YOU HAVE IN A PLACE LIKE THIS?
......
IT'S NOT SOME BIG PRETEN-TIOUS REASON.
OH? PLANNING TO BE AN ALCHEMIST, ARE YOU?
I MEAN, I **DO** HAVE A REASON FOR BEING HERE, BUT YOU'D PROBABLY THINK IT'S STUPID.
OF COURSE NOT.
BESIDES, THE WAY ALCHEMISTS SEE IT, I MAY NOT BE CAPABLE OF "RESEARCH-ING THE TRUTH."
OH, YOU THINK I'M EGOTISTICAL ENOUGH TO JUDGE AN IDEA BEFORE I'VE EVER HEARD IT?

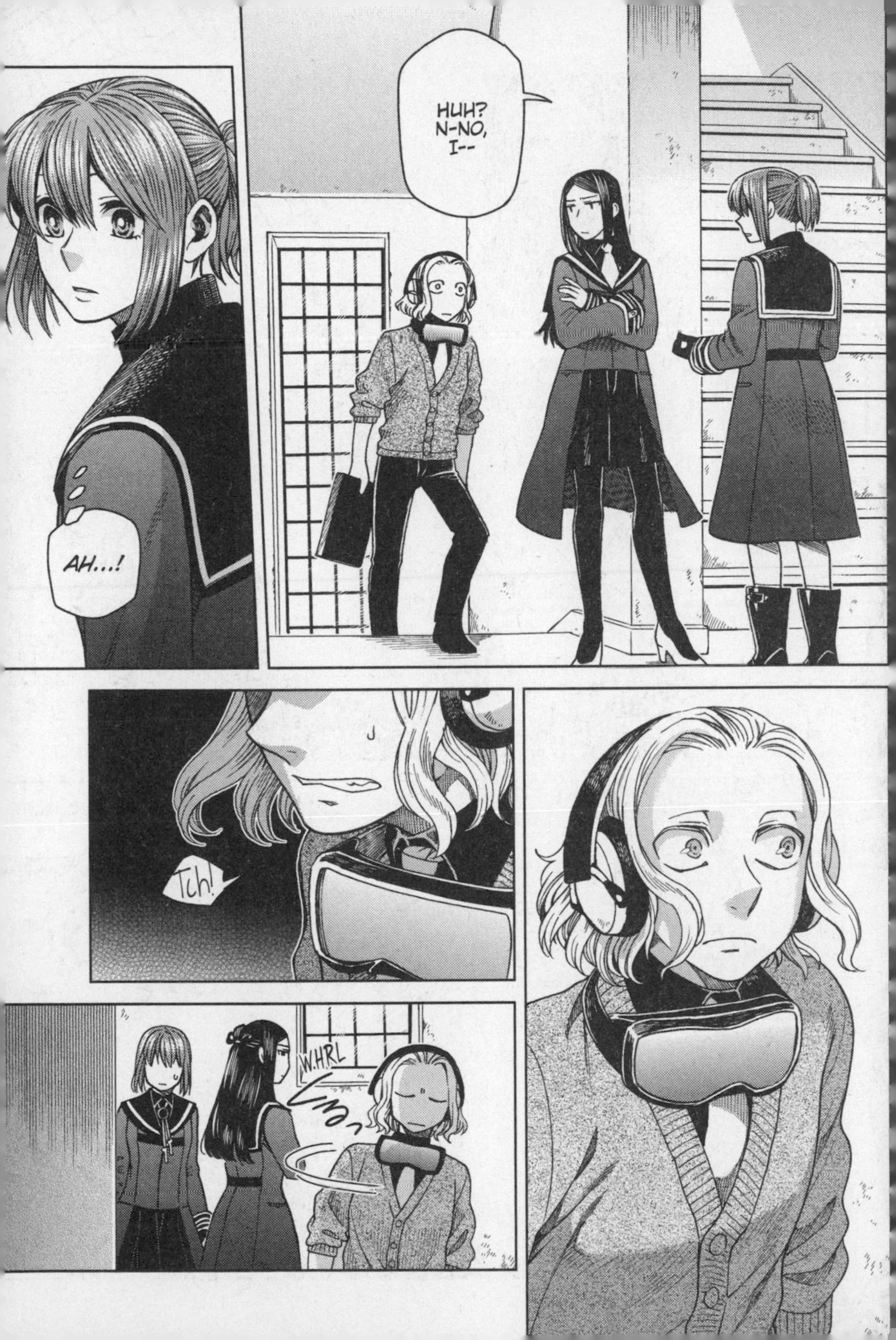
HUH? N-NO, I--
AH...!
Tch!
WHIRL
くるっ

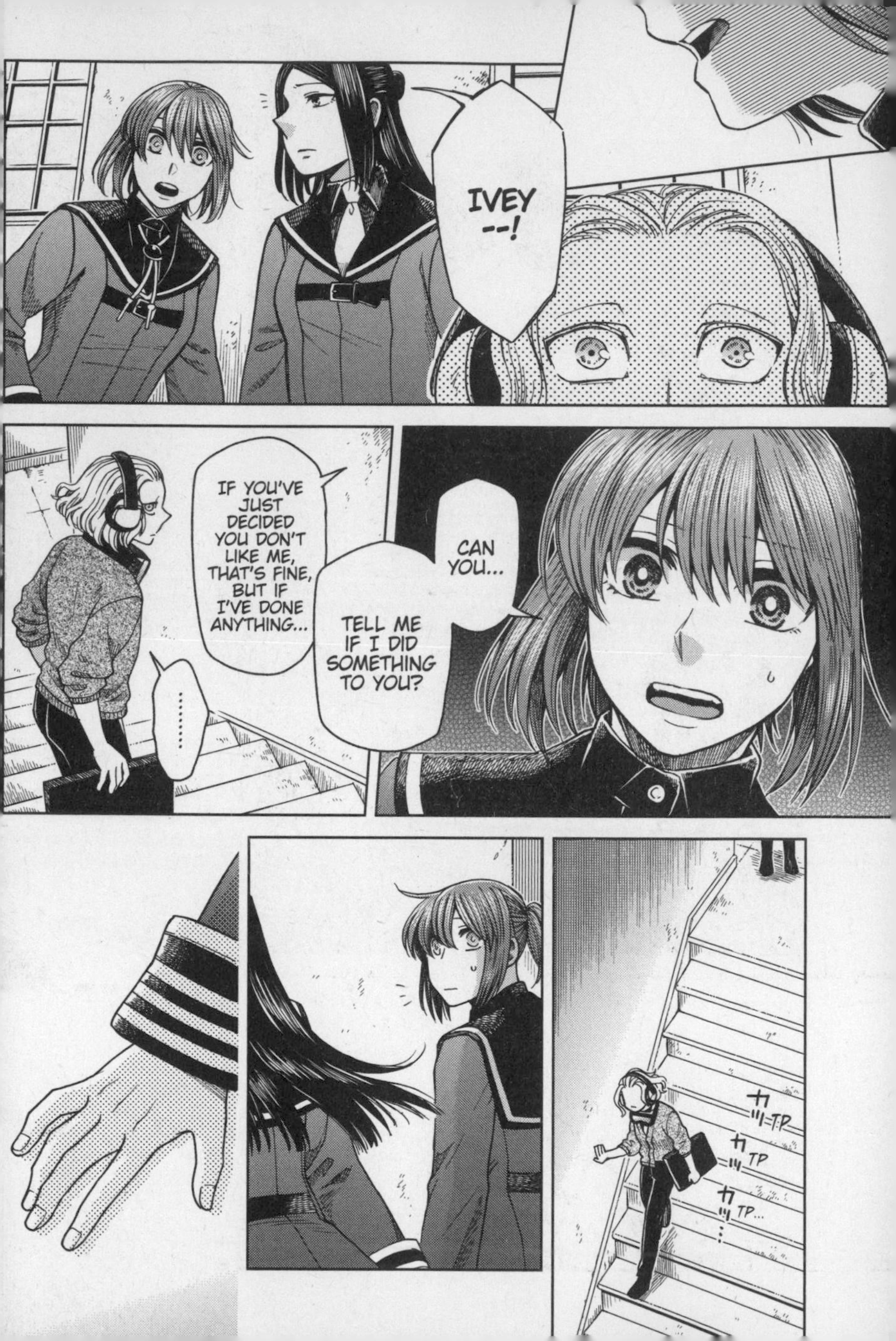
IVEY --!
CAN YOU...
TELL ME IF I DID SOMETHING TO YOU?
IF YOU'VE JUST DECIDED YOU DON'T LIKE ME, THAT'S FINE, BUT IF I'VE DONE ANYTHING...
......
TP
TP
TP...

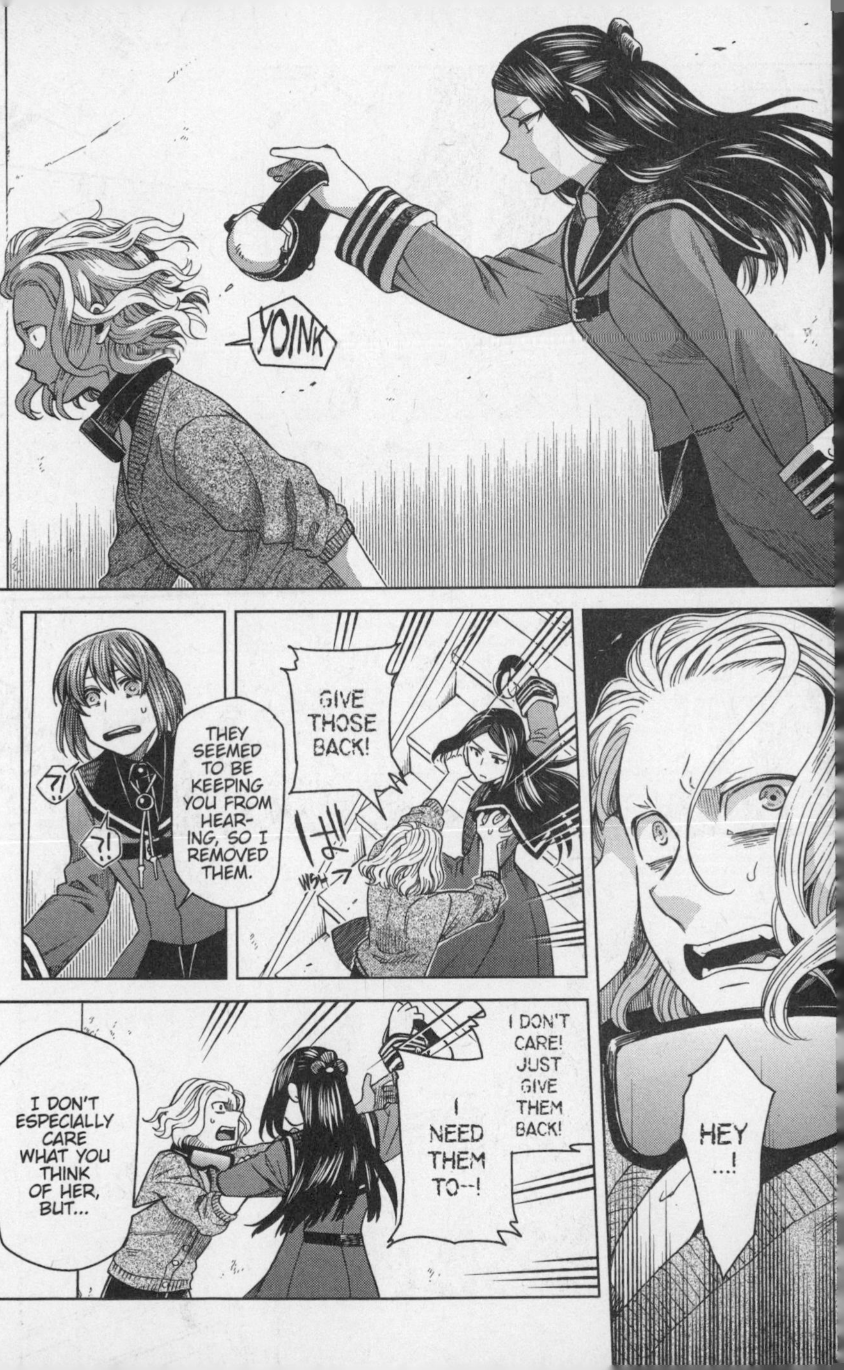
YOINK
HEY ...!
GIVE THOSE BACK!
WSH
THEY SEEMED TO BE KEEPING YOU FROM HEAR-ING, SO I REMOVED THEM.
?!
?!
I DON'T CARE! JUST GIVE THEM BACK!
I NEED THEM TO--!
I DON'T ESPECIALLY CARE WHAT YOU THINK OF HER, BUT...

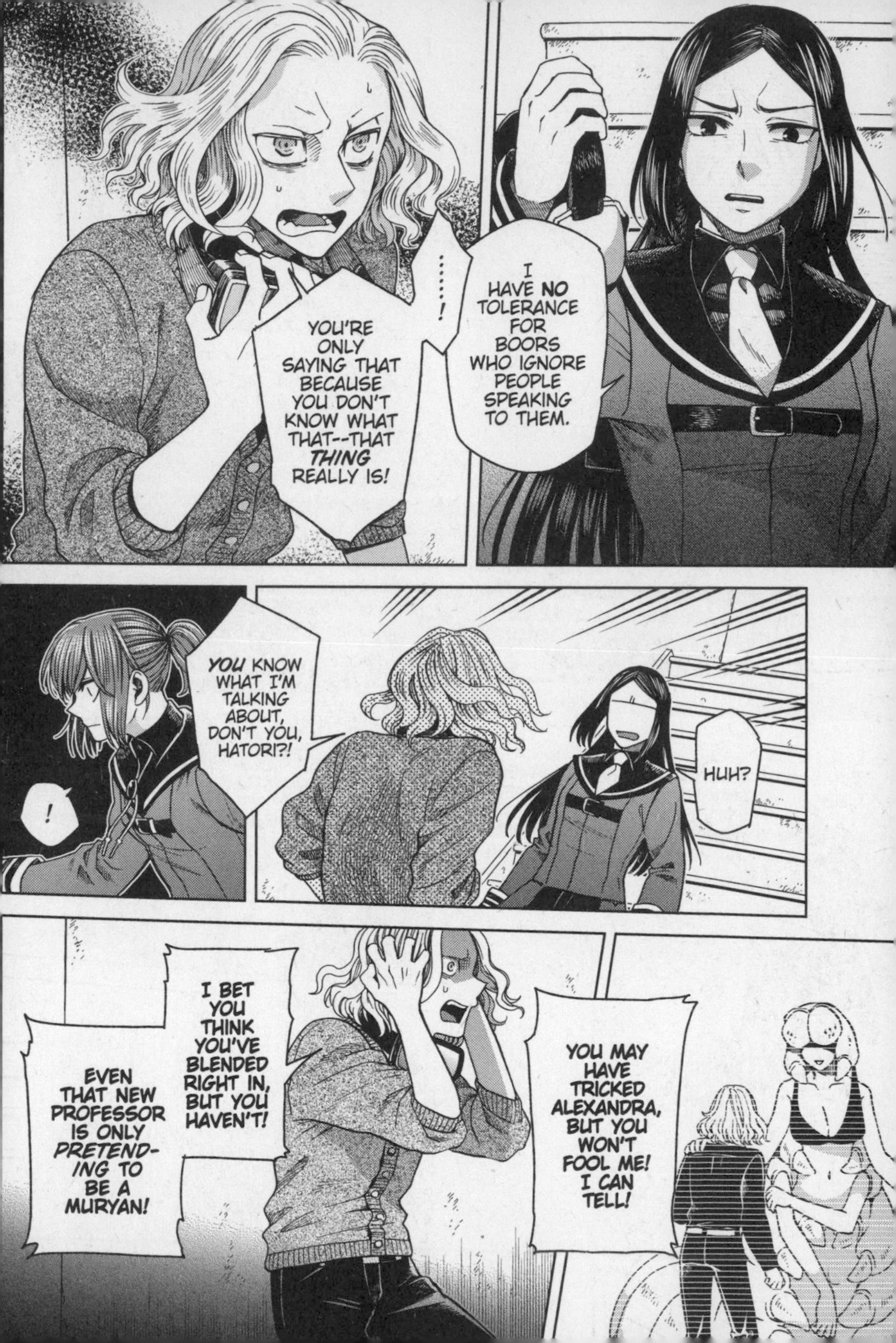
I HAVE NO TOLERANCE FOR BOORS WHO IGNORE PEOPLE SPEAKING TO THEM.
......!
YOU'RE ONLY SAYING THAT BECAUSE YOU DON'T KNOW WHAT THAT--THAT *THING* REALLY IS!
YOU KNOW WHAT I'M TALKING ABOUT, DON'T YOU, HATORI?!
HUH?
!
YOU MAY HAVE TRICKED ALEXANDRA, BUT YOU WON'T FOOL ME! I CAN TELL!
I BET YOU THINK YOU'VE BLENDED RIGHT IN, BUT YOU HAVEN'T!
EVEN THAT NEW PROFESSOR IS ONLY *PRETEND-ING* TO BE A MURYAN!

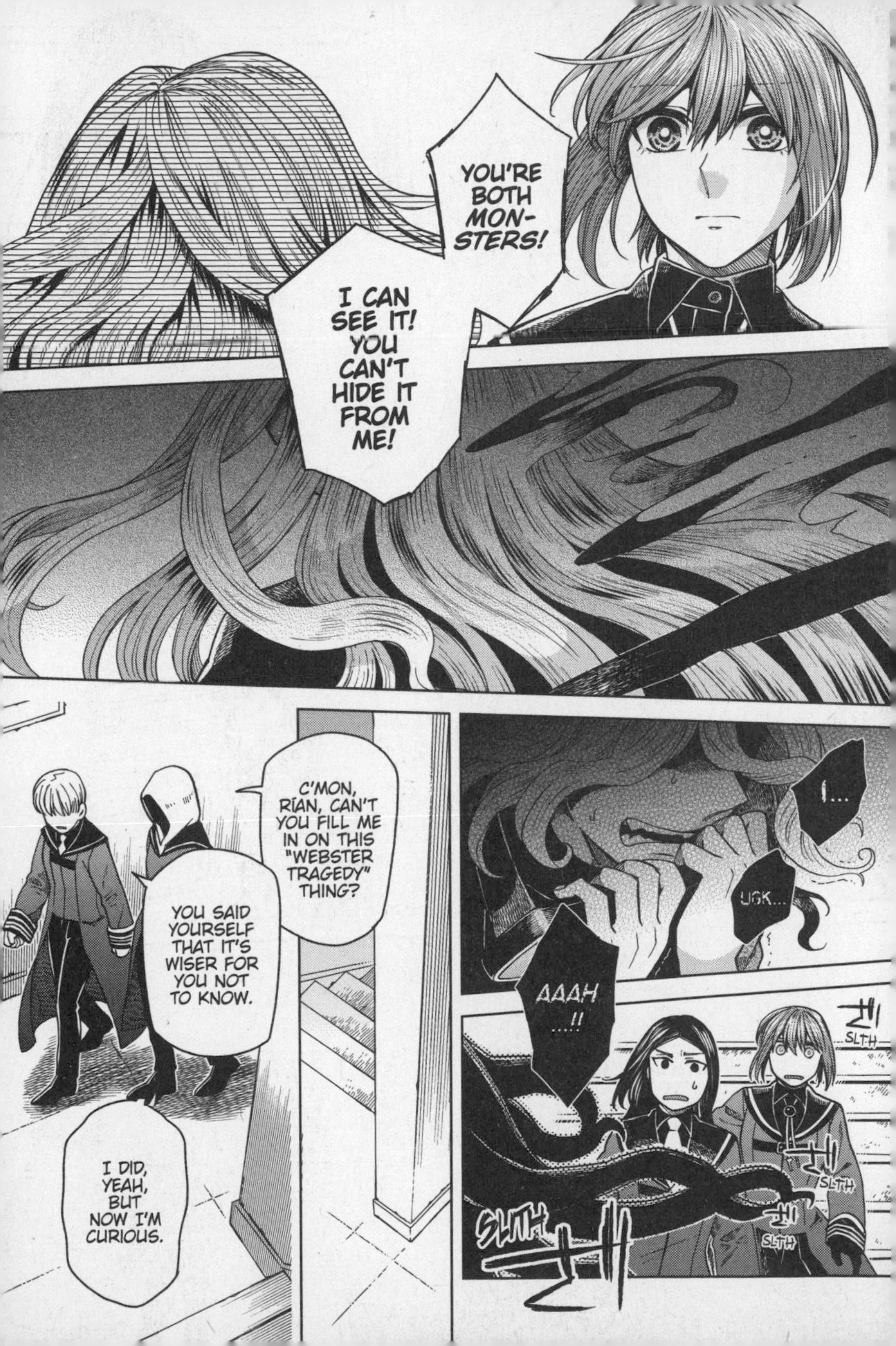
YOU'RE BOTH MON-STERS!
I CAN SEE IT! YOU CAN'T HIDE IT FROM ME!
I...
UGK...
AAAH ....!!
SLTH
SLTH
SLTH
SLTH
C'MON, RÍAN, CAN'T YOU FILL ME IN ON THIS "WEBSTER TRAGEDY" THING?
YOU SAID YOURSELF THAT IT'S WISER FOR YOU NOT TO KNOW.
I DID, YEAH, BUT NOW I'M CURIOUS.

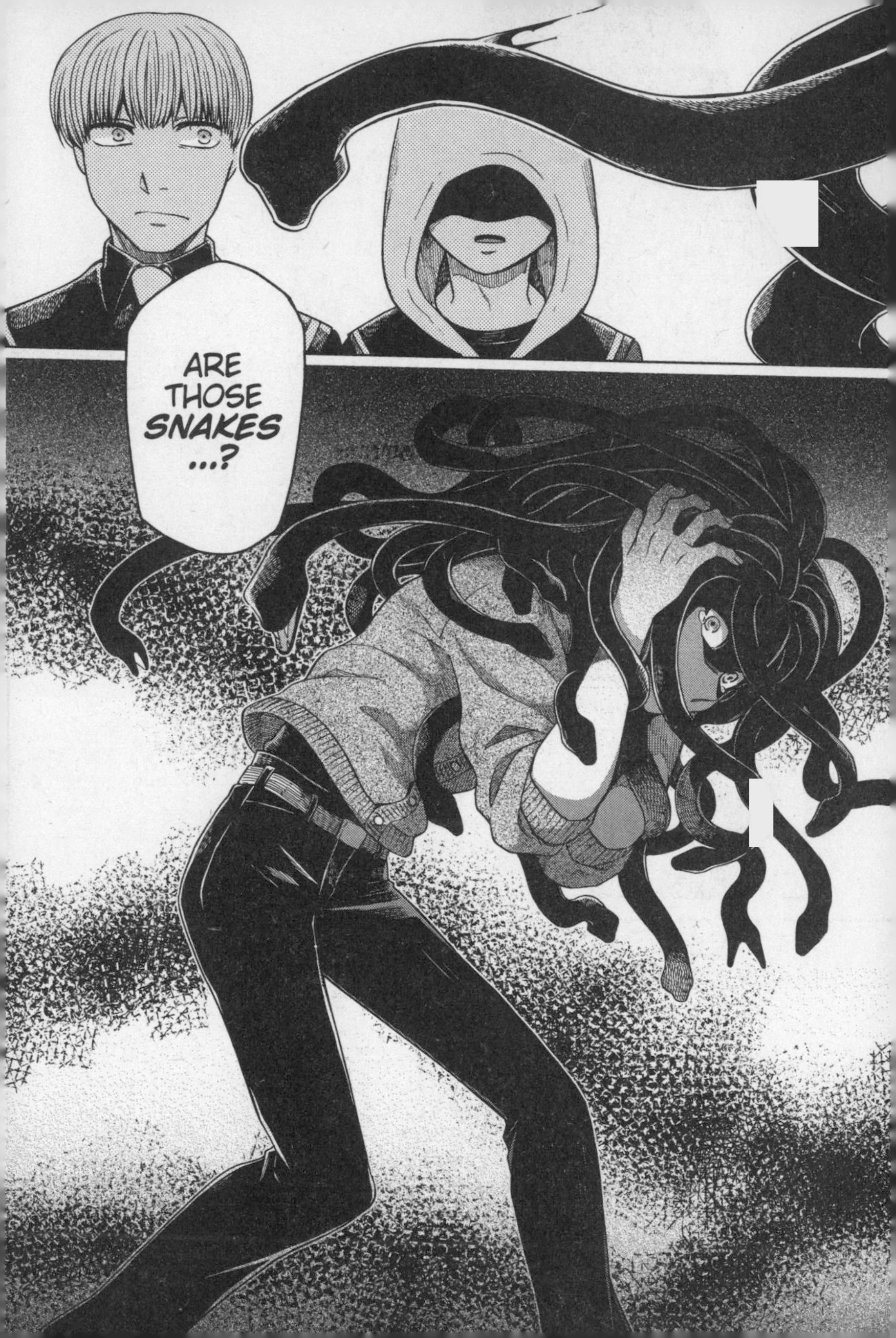
ARE THOSE SNAKES ...?

Chapter 55: First impressions are the most lasting. III

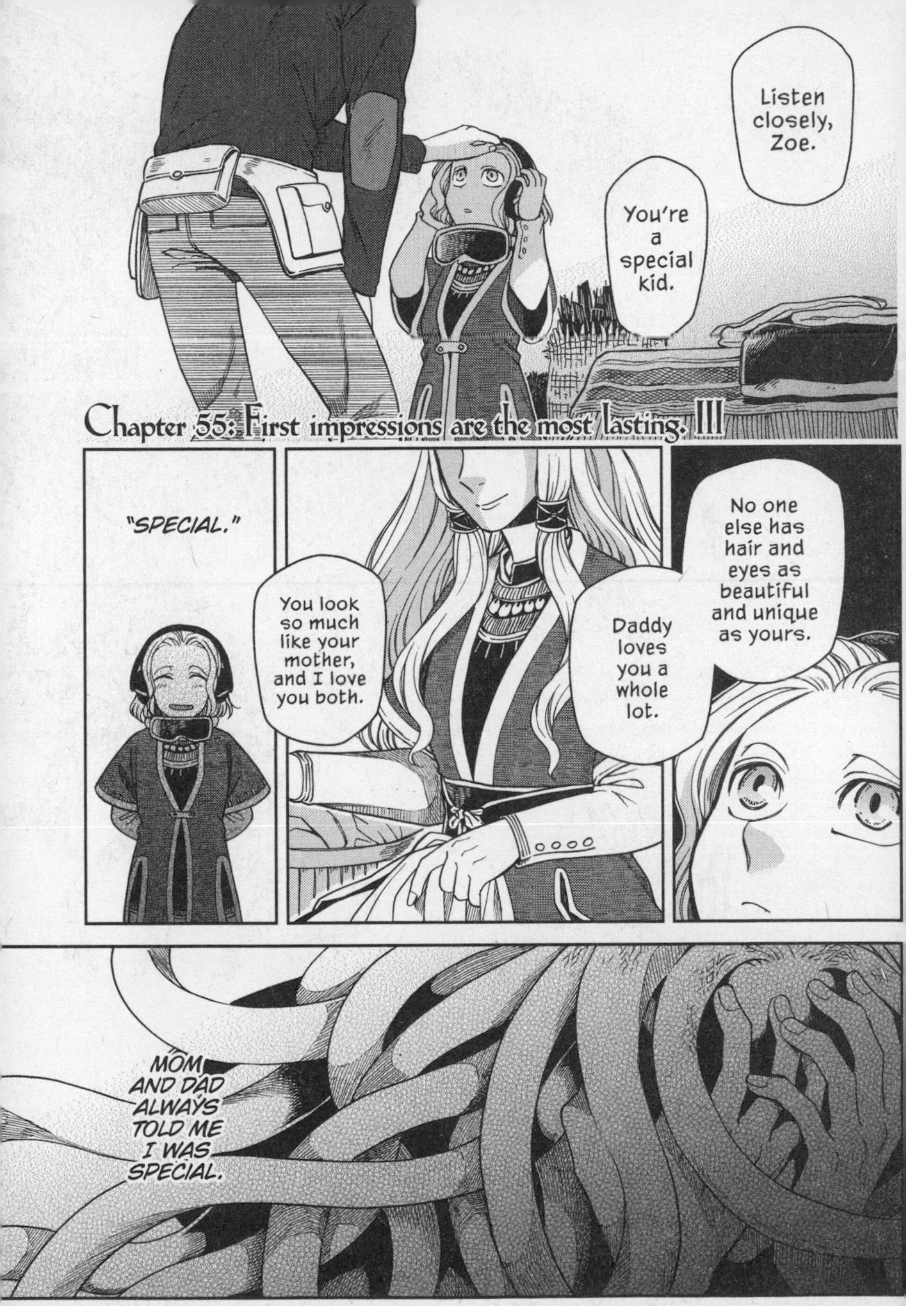
Listen closely, Zoe.
You're a special kid.
No one else has hair and eyes as beautiful and unique as yours.
Daddy loves you a whole lot.
You look so much like your mother, and I love you both.
"SPECIAL."
MOM AND DAD ALWAYS TOLD ME I WAS SPECIAL.

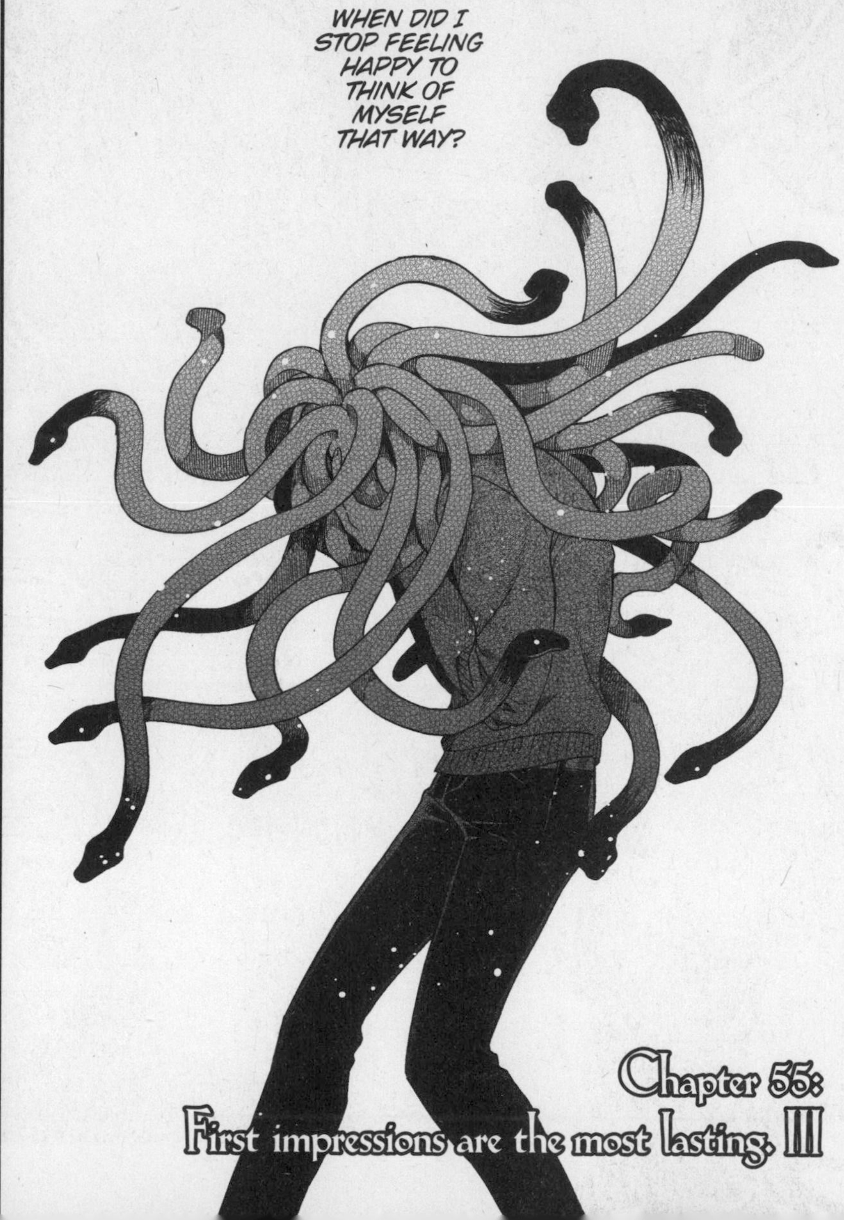
WHEN DID I STOP FEELING HAPPY TO THINK OF MYSELF THAT WAY?

Chapter 55: First impressions are the most lasting. III

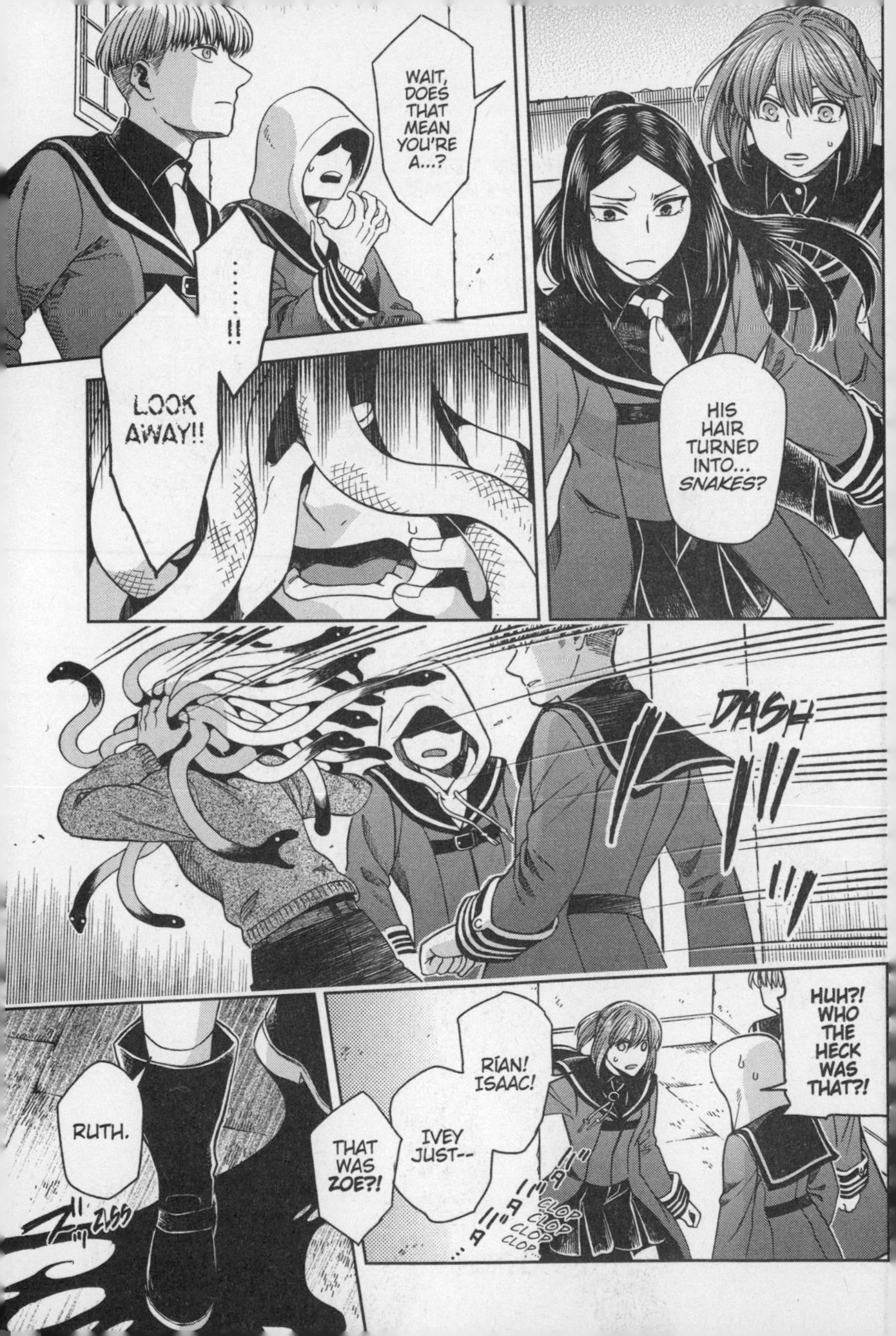
HIS HAIR TURNED INTO... SNAKES?
WAIT, DOES THAT MEAN YOU'RE A...?
......!!
LOOK AWAY!!
DASH
HUH?! WHO THE HECK WAS THAT?!
RÍAN! ISAAC!
IVEY JUST--
THAT WAS ZOE?!
CLOP CLOP CLOP CLOP...
RUTH.
ZASS

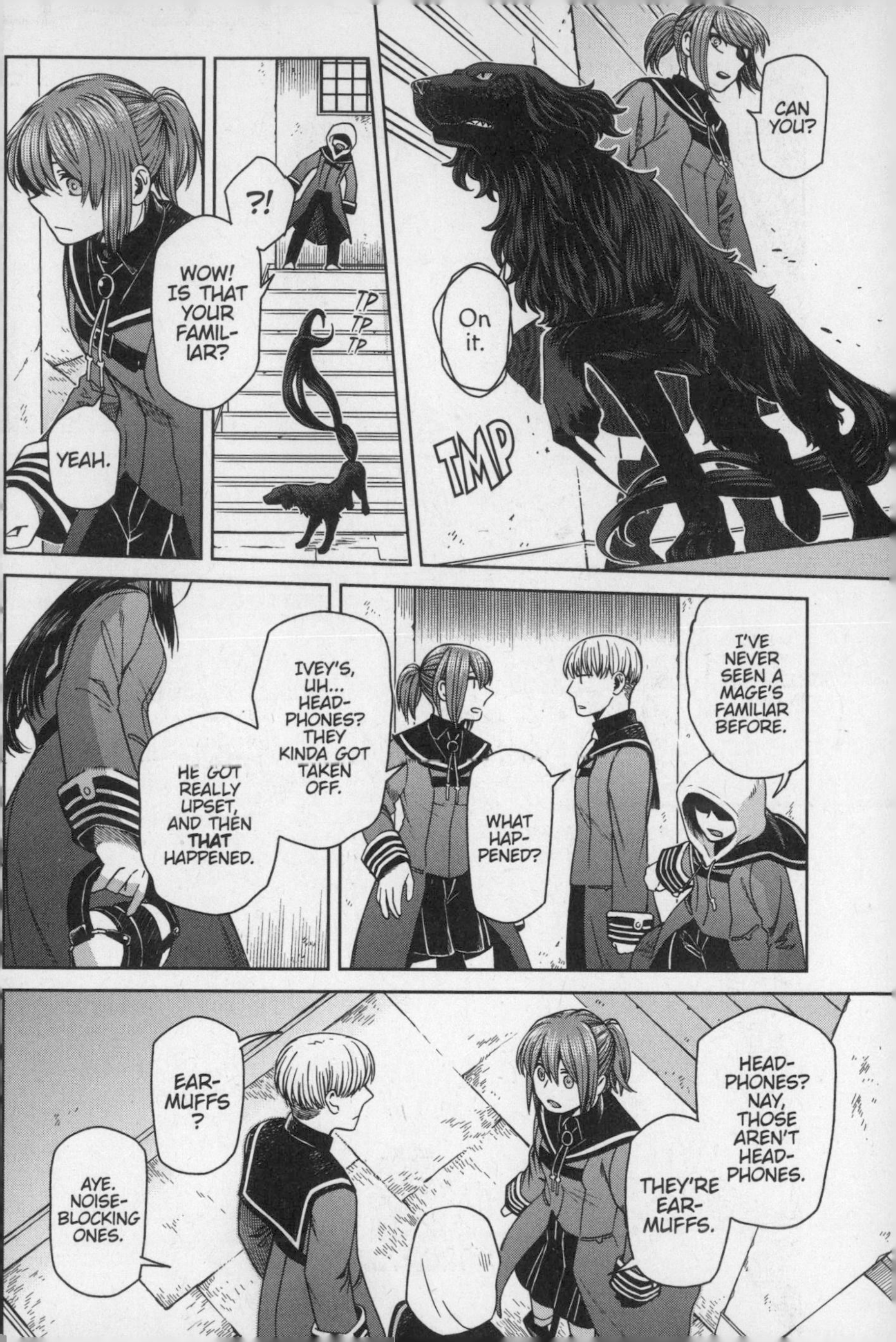
CAN YOU?
On it.
TMP
?!
TP TP TP
WOW! IS THAT YOUR FAMILIAR?
YEAH.
I'VE NEVER SEEN A MAGE'S FAMILIAR BEFORE.
WHAT HAPPENED?
IVEY'S, UH... HEADPHONES? THEY KINDA GOT TAKEN OFF.
HE GOT REALLY UPSET, AND THEN THAT HAPPENED.
HEADPHONES? NAY, THOSE AREN'T HEADPHONES.
THEY'RE EARMUFFS.
EARMUFFS?
AYE. NOISE-BLOCKING ONES.

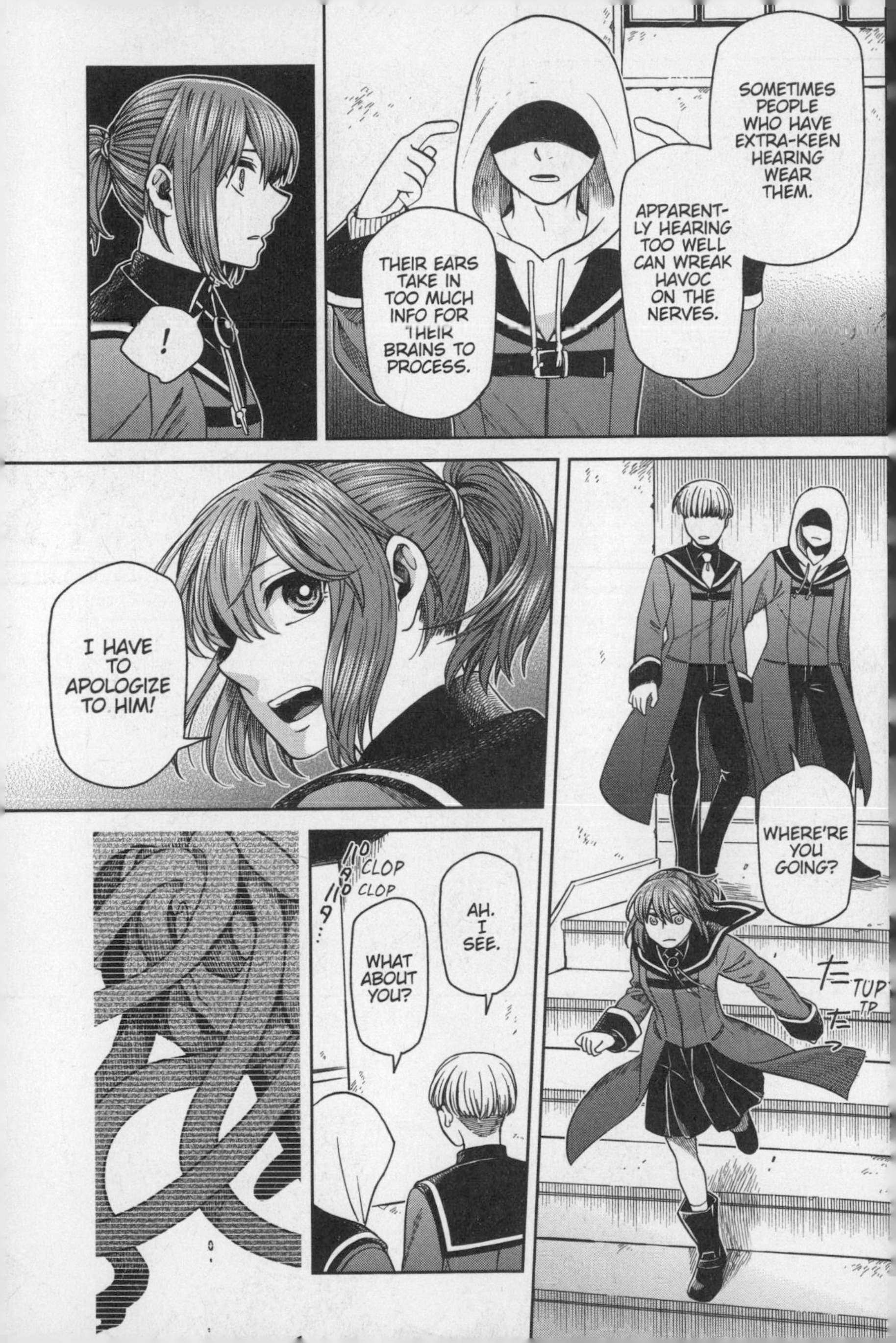
SOMETIMES PEOPLE WHO HAVE EXTRA-KEEN HEARING WEAR THEM.
APPARENT-LY HEARING TOO WELL CAN WREAK HAVOC ON THE NERVES.
THEIR EARS TAKE IN TOO MUCH INFO FOR THEIR BRAINS TO PROCESS.
!
WHERE'RE YOU GOING?
TUP TP
I HAVE TO APOLOGIZE TO HIM!
AH. I SEE.
CLOP CLOP
WHAT ABOUT YOU?

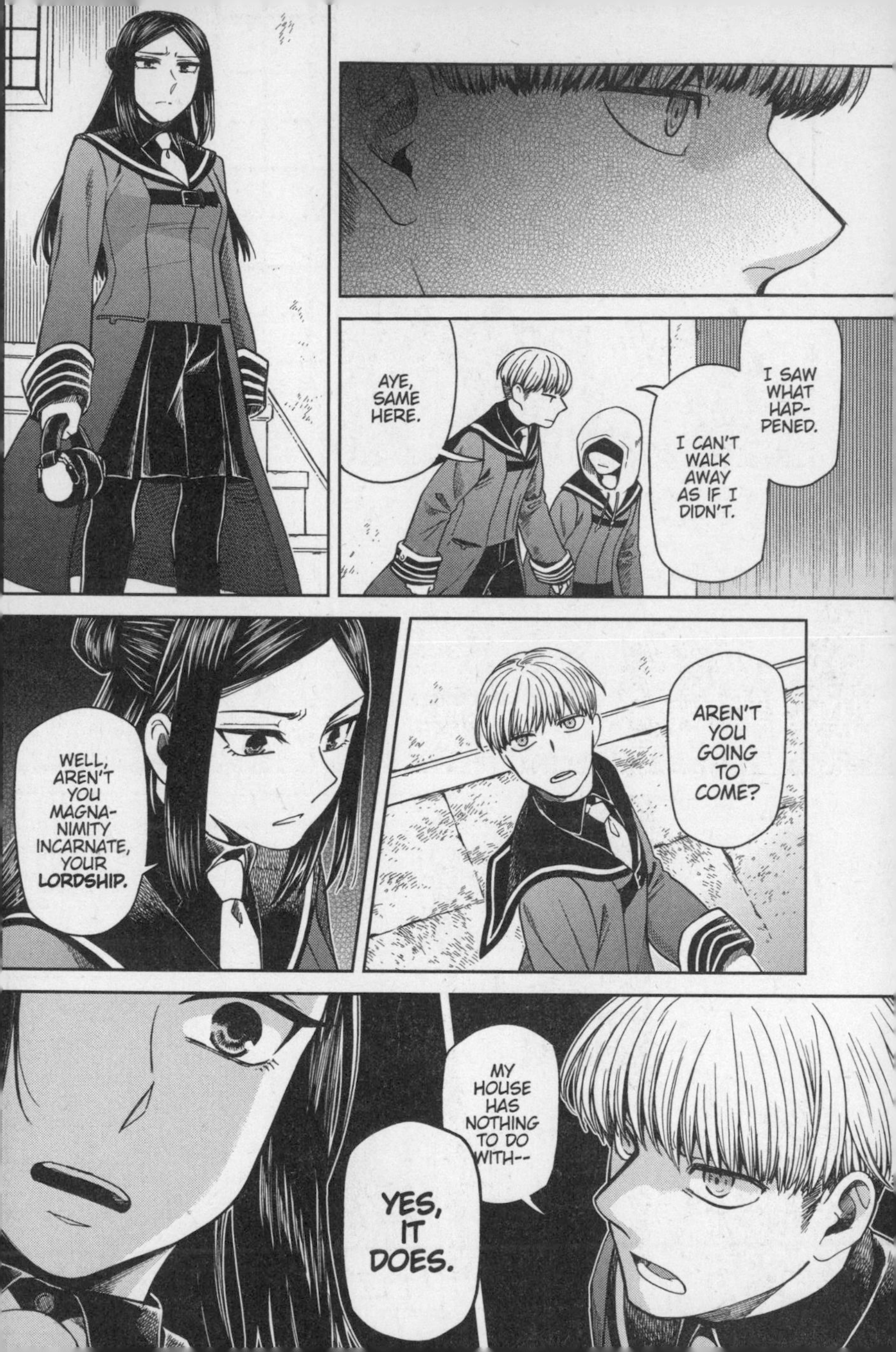
I SAW WHAT HAP-PENED.
I CAN'T WALK AWAY AS IF I DIDN'T.
AYE, SAME HERE.
AREN'T YOU GOING TO COME?
WELL, AREN'T YOU MAGNA-NIMITY INCARNATE, YOUR LORDSHIP.
MY HOUSE HAS NOTHING TO DO WITH--
YES, IT DOES.

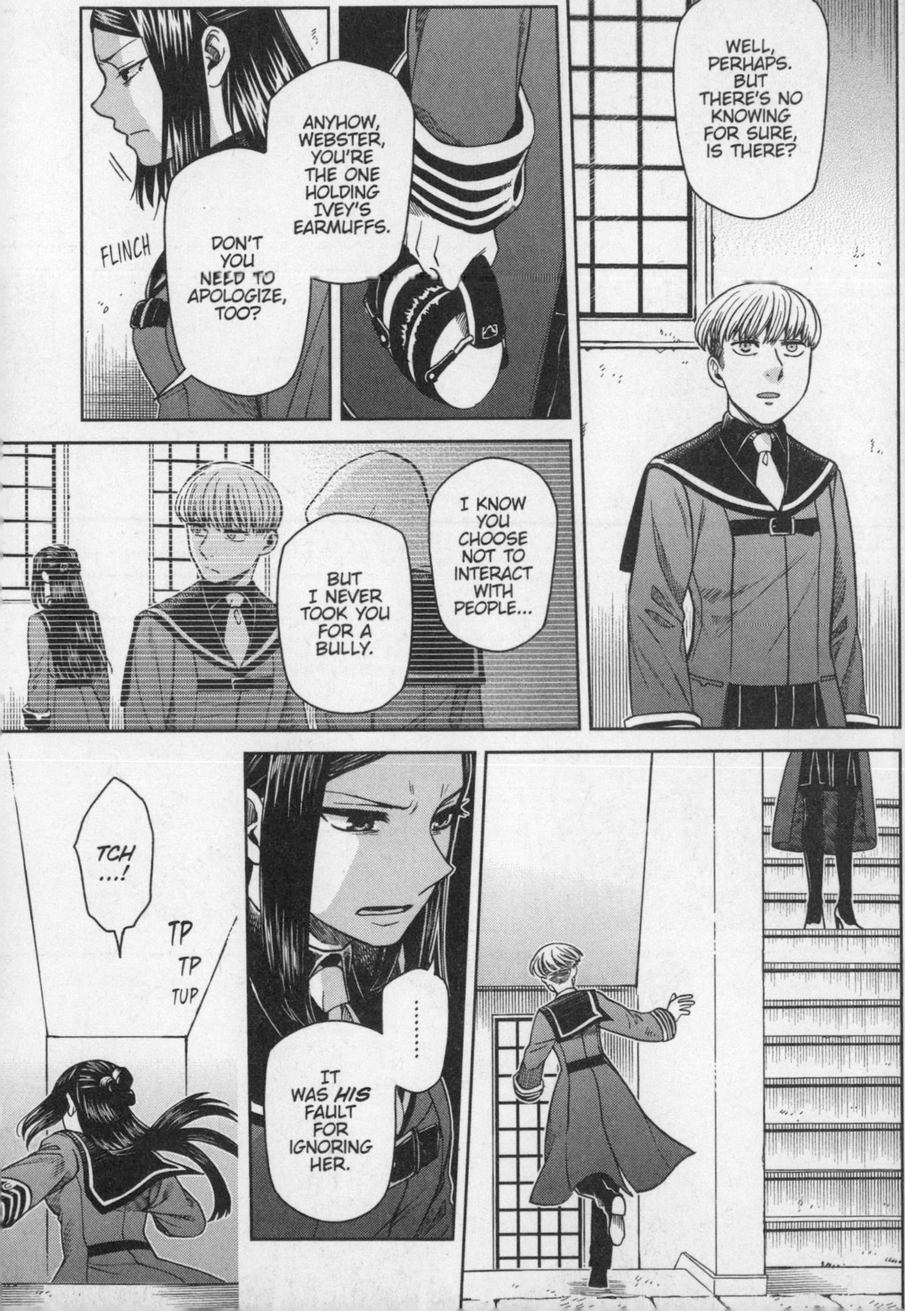
WELL, PERHAPS. BUT THERE'S NO KNOWING FOR SURE, IS THERE?
ANYHOW, WEBSTER, YOU'RE THE ONE HOLDING IVEY'S EARMUFFS.
DON'T YOU NEED TO APOLOGIZE, TOO?
FLINCH
I KNOW YOU CHOOSE NOT TO INTERACT WITH PEOPLE...
BUT I NEVER TOOK YOU FOR A BULLY.
......
IT WAS *HIS* FAULT FOR IGNORING HER.
TCH ...!
TP
TP
TUP

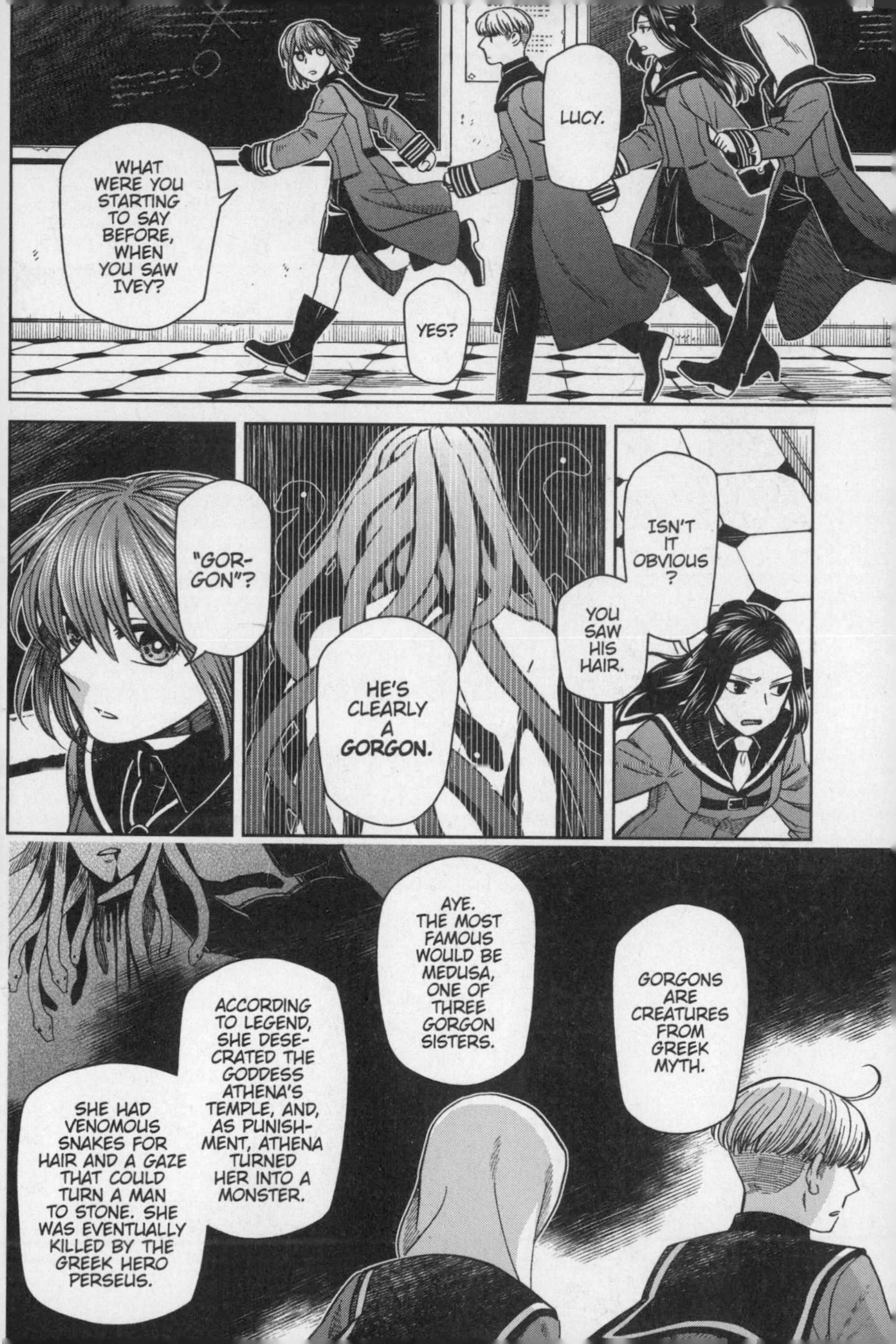
LUCY.
YES?
WHAT WERE YOU STARTING TO SAY BEFORE, WHEN YOU SAW IVEY?
ISN'T IT OBVIOUS?
YOU SAW HIS HAIR.
HE'S CLEARLY A GORGON.
"GOR-GON"?
GORGONS ARE CREATURES FROM GREEK MYTH.
AYE. THE MOST FAMOUS WOULD BE MEDUSA, ONE OF THREE GORGON SISTERS.
ACCORDING TO LEGEND, SHE DESE-CRATED THE GODDESS ATHENA'S TEMPLE, AND, AS PUNISH-MENT, ATHENA TURNED HER INTO A MONSTER.
SHE HAD VENOMOUS SNAKES FOR HAIR AND A GAZE THAT COULD TURN A MAN TO STONE. SHE WAS EVENTUALLY KILLED BY THE GREEK HERO PERSEUS.

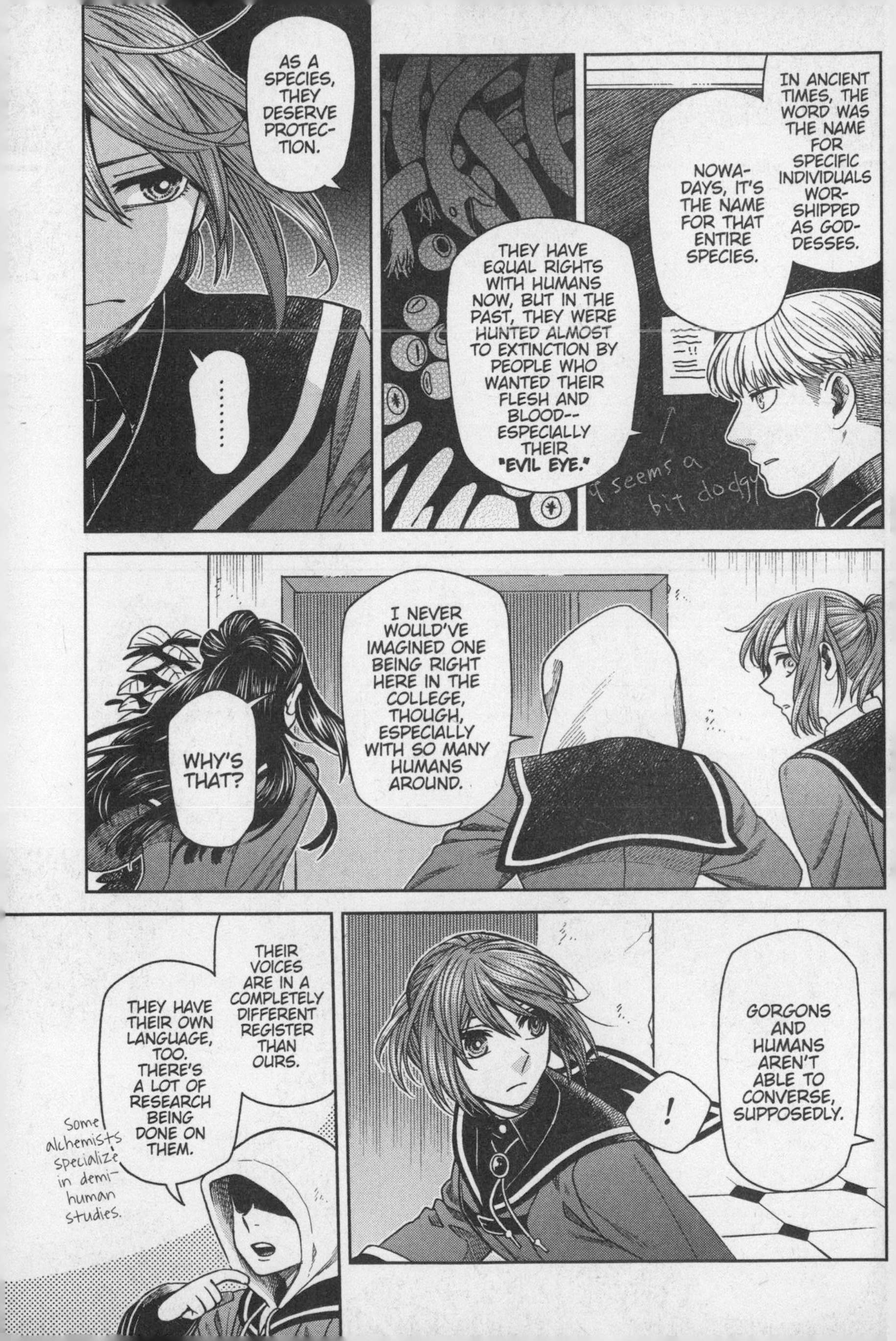

IN ANCIENT TIMES, THE WORD WAS THE NAME FOR SPECIFIC INDIVIDUALS WORSHIPPED AS GODDESSES.
NOWADAYS, IT'S THE NAME FOR THAT ENTIRE SPECIES.
seems a bit dodgy
THEY HAVE EQUAL RIGHTS WITH HUMANS NOW, BUT IN THE PAST, THEY WERE HUNTED ALMOST TO EXTINCTION BY PEOPLE WHO WANTED THEIR FLESH AND BLOOD--ESPECIALLY THEIR **"EVIL EYE."**
AS A SPECIES, THEY DESERVE PROTECTION.
......
I NEVER WOULD'VE IMAGINED ONE BEING RIGHT HERE IN THE COLLEGE, THOUGH, ESPECIALLY WITH SO MANY HUMANS AROUND.
WHY'S THAT?
GORGONS AND HUMANS AREN'T ABLE TO CONVERSE, SUPPOSEDLY.
!
THEIR VOICES ARE IN A COMPLETELY DIFFERENT REGISTER THAN OURS.
THEY HAVE THEIR OWN LANGUAGE, TOO. THERE'S A LOT OF RESEARCH BEING DONE ON THEM.
Some alchemists specialize in demi-human studies.

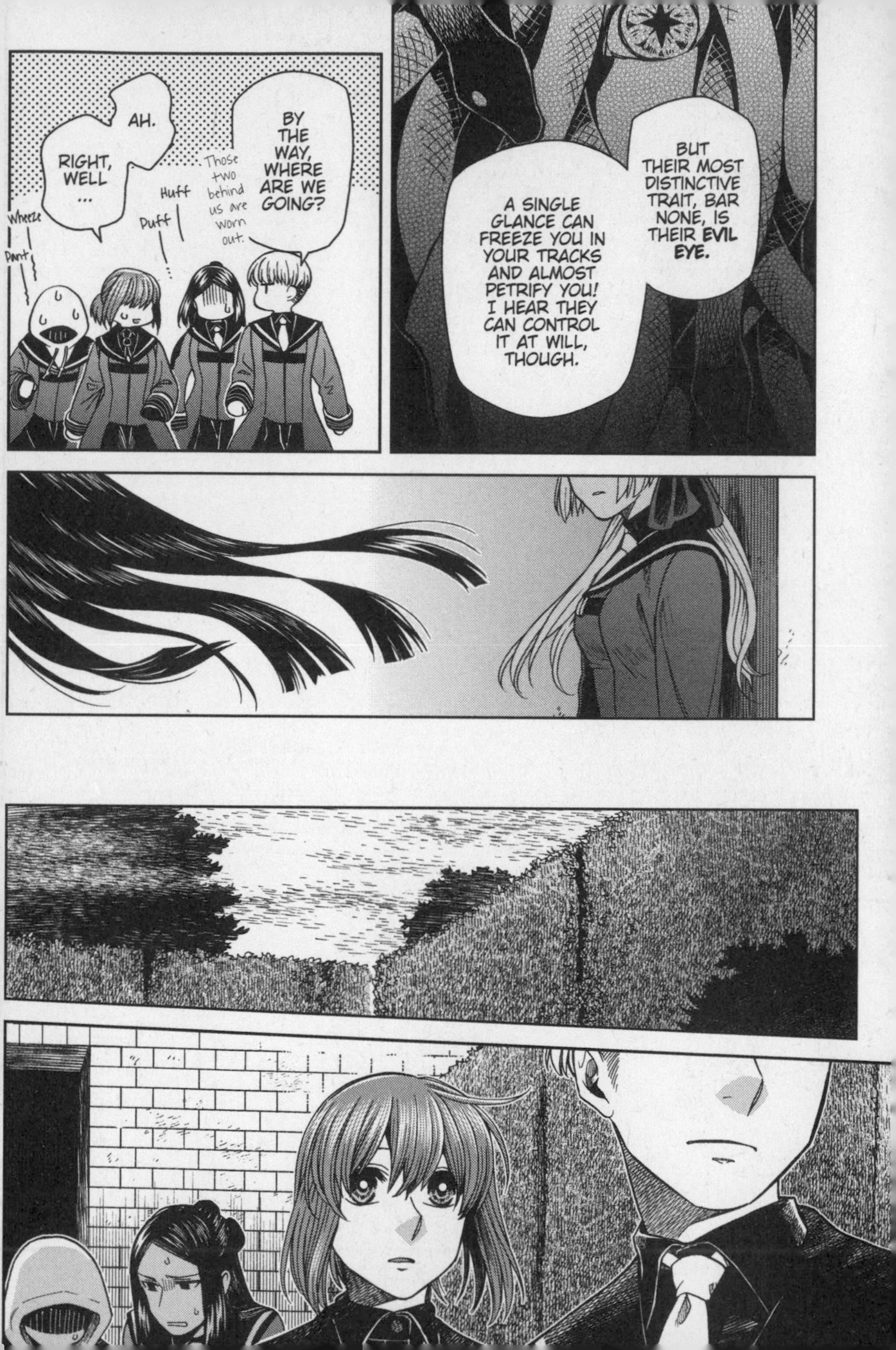

BUT THEIR MOST DISTINCTIVE TRAIT, BAR NONE, IS THEIR EVIL EYE.
A SINGLE GLANCE CAN FREEZE YOU IN YOUR TRACKS AND ALMOST PETRIFY YOU! I HEAR THEY CAN CONTROL IT AT WILL, THOUGH.
BY THE WAY, WHERE ARE WE GOING?
Those two behind us are worn out.
AH.
RIGHT, WELL ...
Huff
Puff
Wheeze
Pant

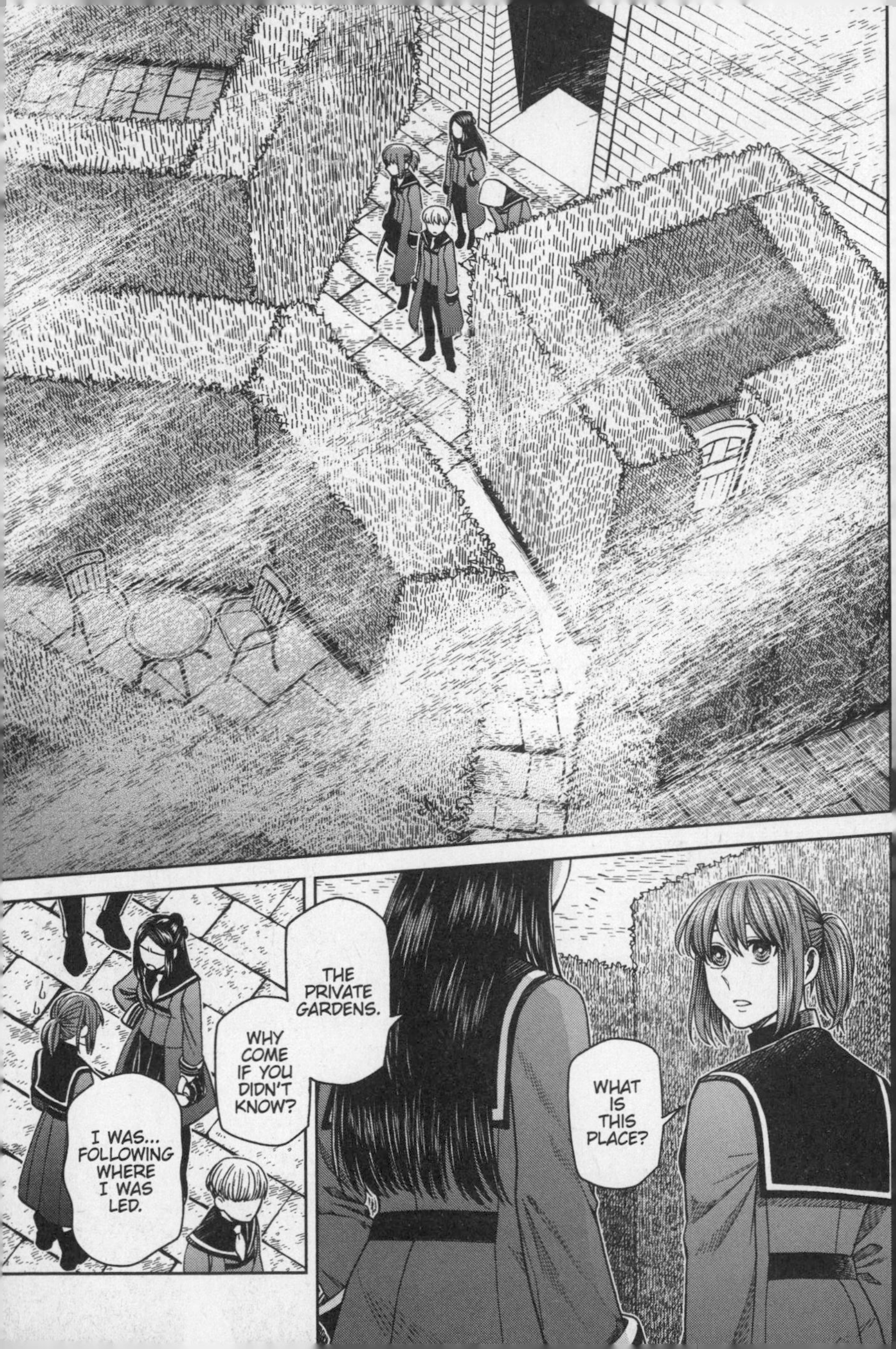
WHAT IS THIS PLACE?
THE PRIVATE GARDENS.
WHY COME IF YOU DIDN'T KNOW?
I WAS... FOLLOWING WHERE I WAS LED.

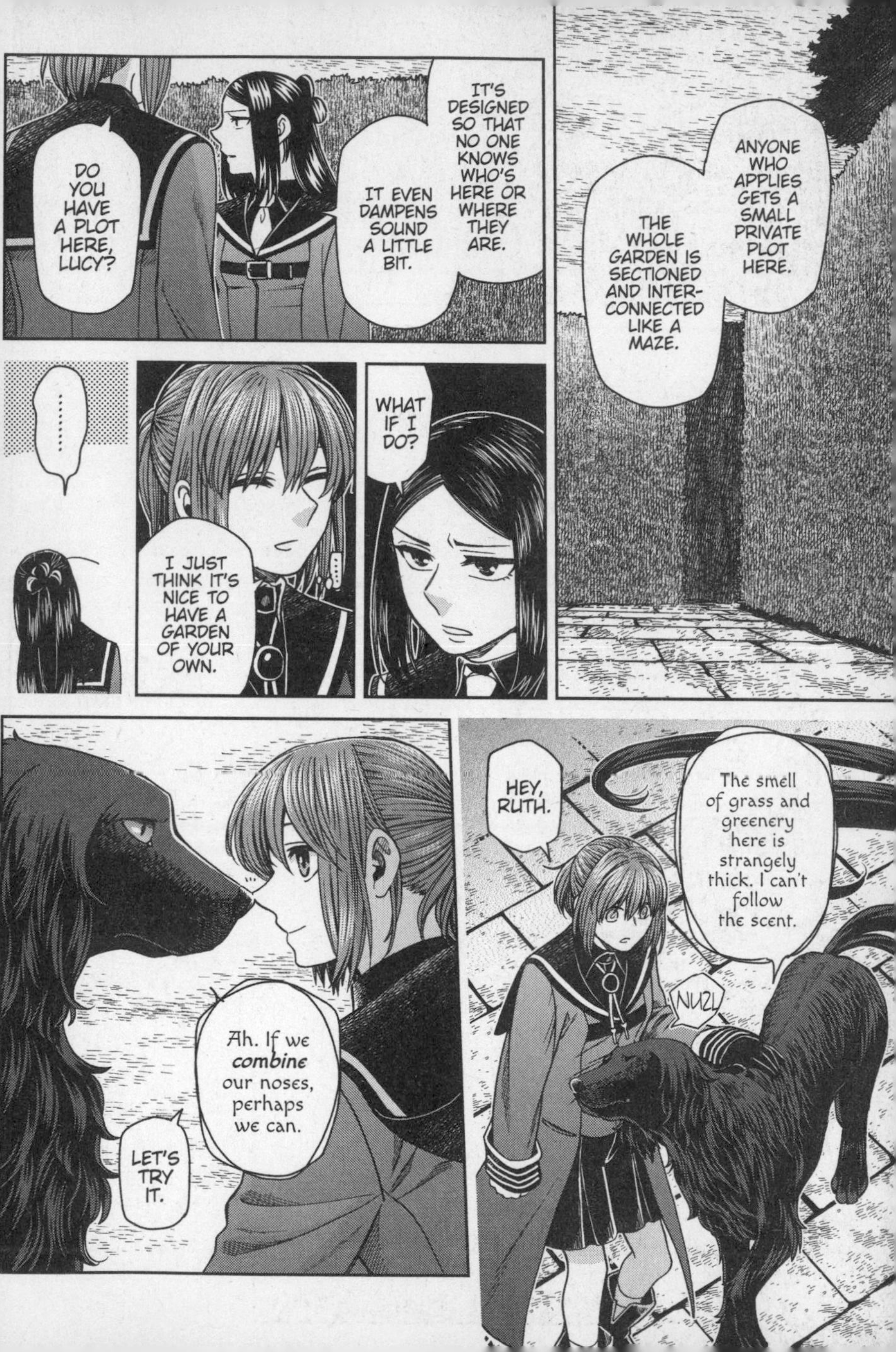
ANYONE WHO APPLIES GETS A SMALL PRIVATE PLOT HERE.
THE WHOLE GARDEN IS SECTIONED AND INTER-CONNECTED LIKE A MAZE.
IT'S DESIGNED SO THAT NO ONE KNOWS WHO'S HERE OR WHERE THEY ARE.
IT EVEN DAMPENS SOUND A LITTLE BIT.
DO YOU HAVE A PLOT HERE, LUCY?
WHAT IF I DO?
I JUST THINK IT'S NICE TO HAVE A GARDEN OF YOUR OWN.
......
The smell of grass and greenery here is strangely thick. I can't follow the scent.
HEY, RUTH.
NUZL
Ah. If we *combine* our noses, perhaps we can.
LET'S TRY IT.

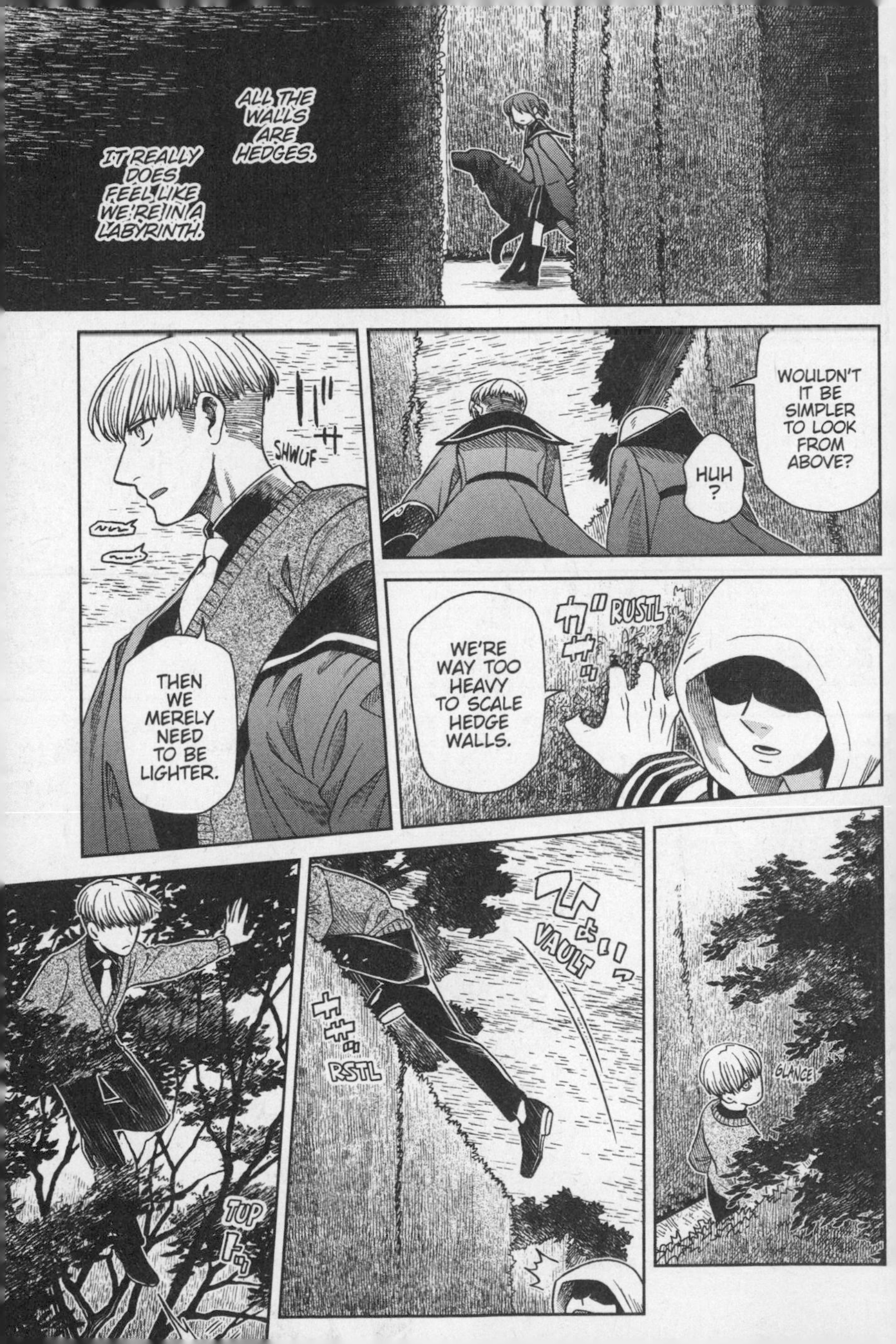
ALL THE WALLS ARE HEDGES.
IT REALLY DOES FEEL LIKE WE'RE IN A LABYRINTH.
WOULDN'T IT BE SIMPLER TO LOOK FROM ABOVE?
HUH?
RUSTL
WE'RE WAY TOO HEAVY TO SCALE HEDGE WALLS.
SHWUF
THEN WE MERELY NEED TO BE LIGHTER.
GLANCE
VAULT
RSTL
TUP

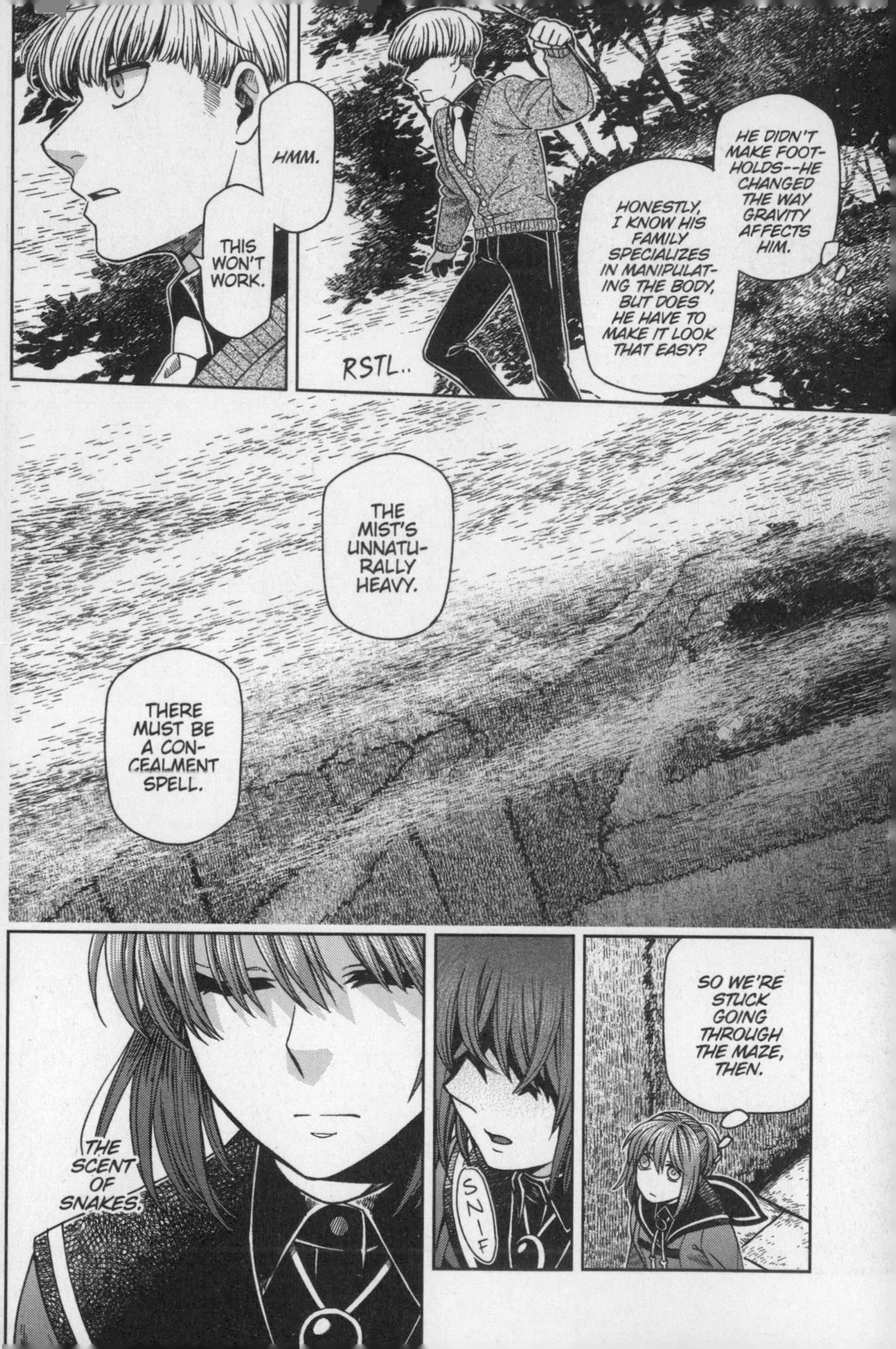
HE DIDN'T MAKE FOOT-HOLDS--HE CHANGED THE WAY GRAVITY AFFECTS HIM.
HONESTLY, I KNOW HIS FAMILY SPECIALIZES IN MANIPULAT-ING THE BODY, BUT DOES HE HAVE TO MAKE IT LOOK THAT EASY?
RSTL..
HMM.
THIS WON'T WORK.
THE MIST'S UNNATU-RALLY HEAVY.
THERE MUST BE A CON-CEALMENT SPELL.
SO WE'RE STUCK GOING THROUGH THE MAZE, THEN.
SNIF
THE SCENT OF SNAKES.

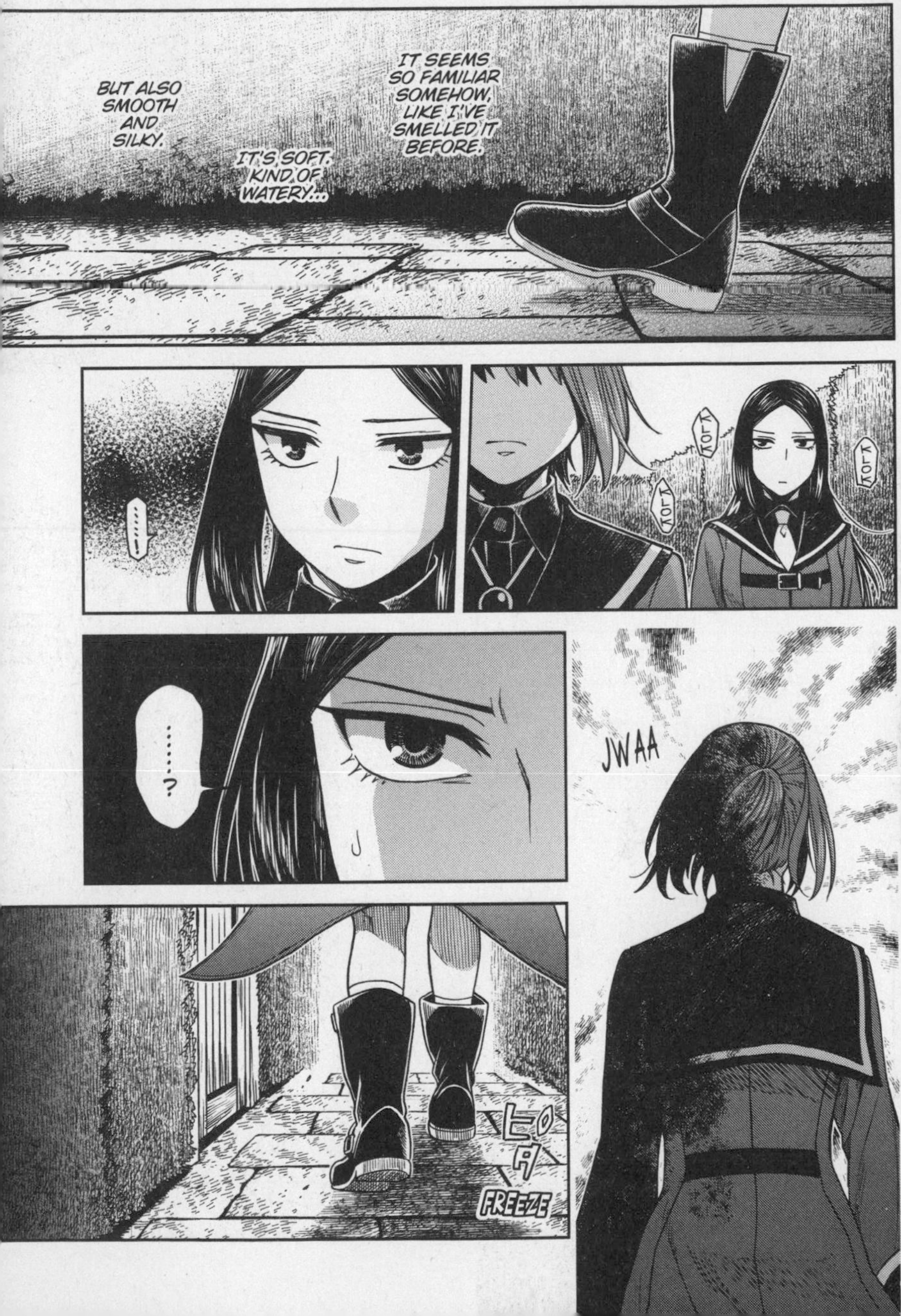
IT SEEMS SO FAMILIAR SOMEHOW, LIKE I'VE SMELLED IT BEFORE.
IT'S SOFT, KIND OF WATERY...
BUT ALSO SMOOTH AND SILKY.
KLOK
KLOK
KLOK
......!
JWAA
......?
ヒタ
FREEZE

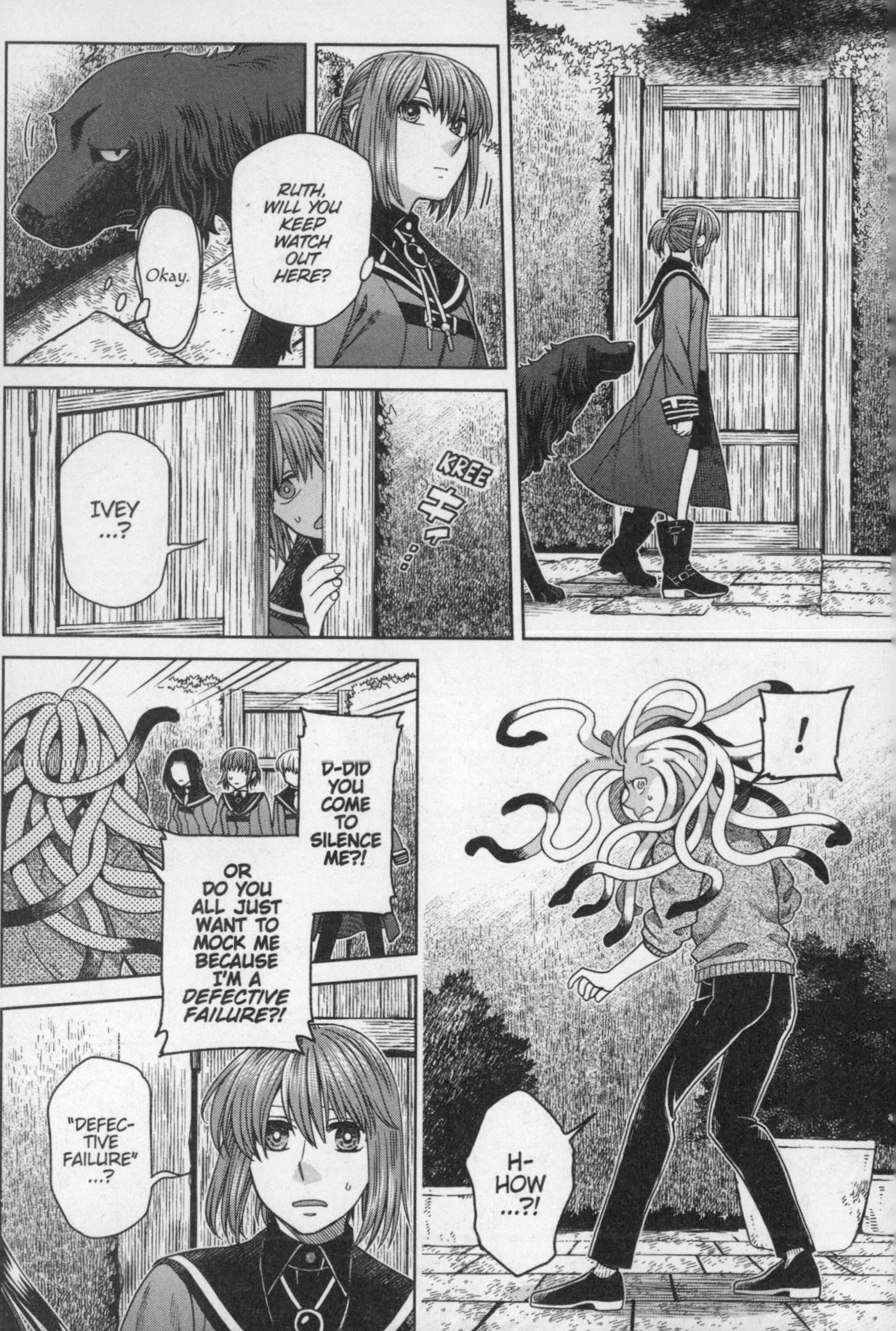
RUTH, WILL YOU KEEP WATCH OUT HERE?
Okay.
KREE
IVEY ...?
!
H-HOW ...?!
D-DID YOU COME TO SILENCE ME?!
OR DO YOU ALL JUST WANT TO MOCK ME BECAUSE I'M A DEFECTIVE FAILURE?!
"DEFEC-TIVE FAILURE" ...?

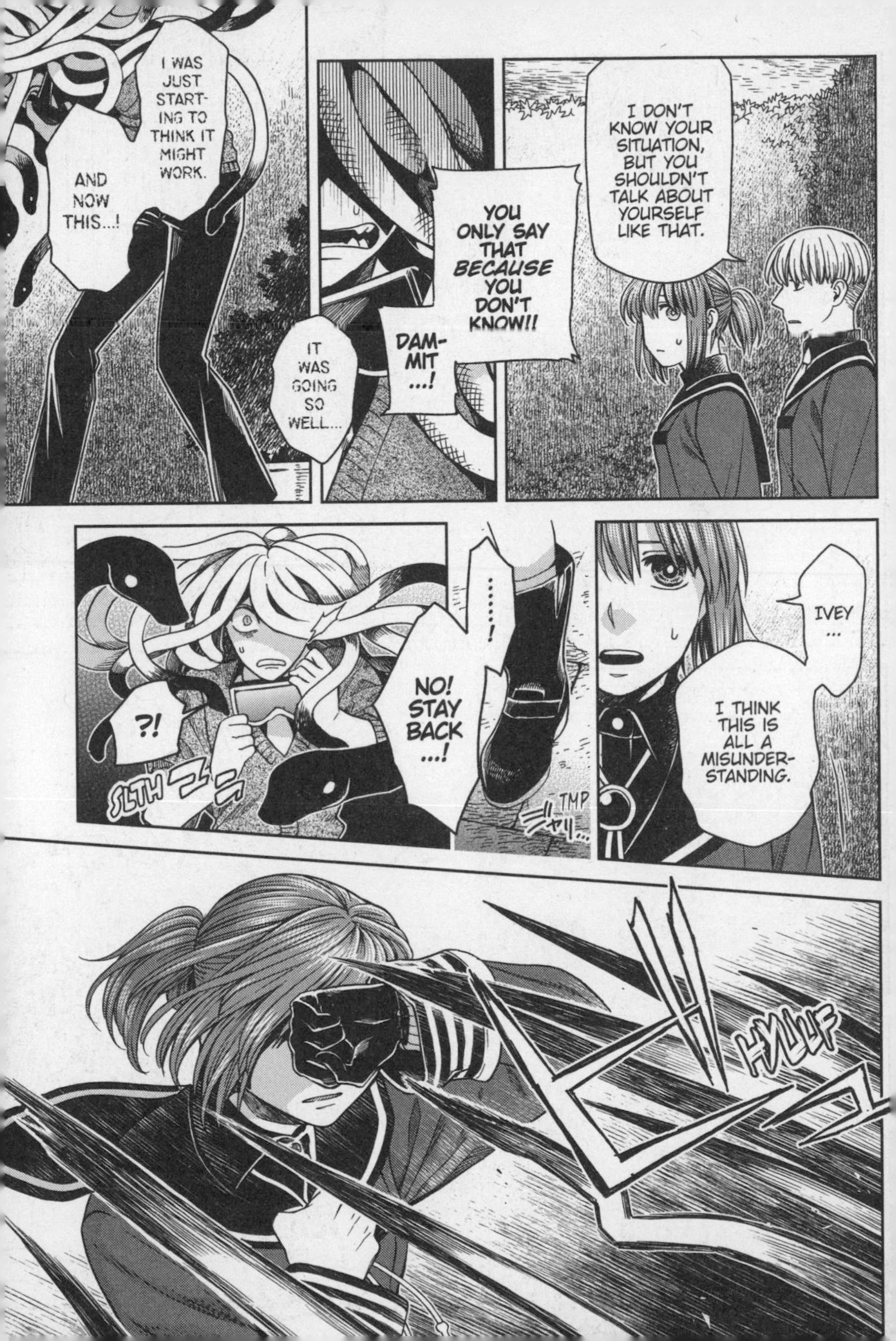

I DON'T KNOW YOUR SITUATION, BUT YOU SHOULDN'T TALK ABOUT YOURSELF LIKE THAT.
YOU ONLY SAY THAT *BECAUSE* YOU DON'T KNOW!!
DAM-MIT ...!
IT WAS GOING SO WELL...
I WAS JUST START-ING TO THINK IT MIGHT WORK.
AND NOW THIS...!
IVEY ...
I THINK THIS IS ALL A MISUNDER-STANDING.
......!
NO! STAY BACK ...!
TMP
?!
SLTH
HWUF

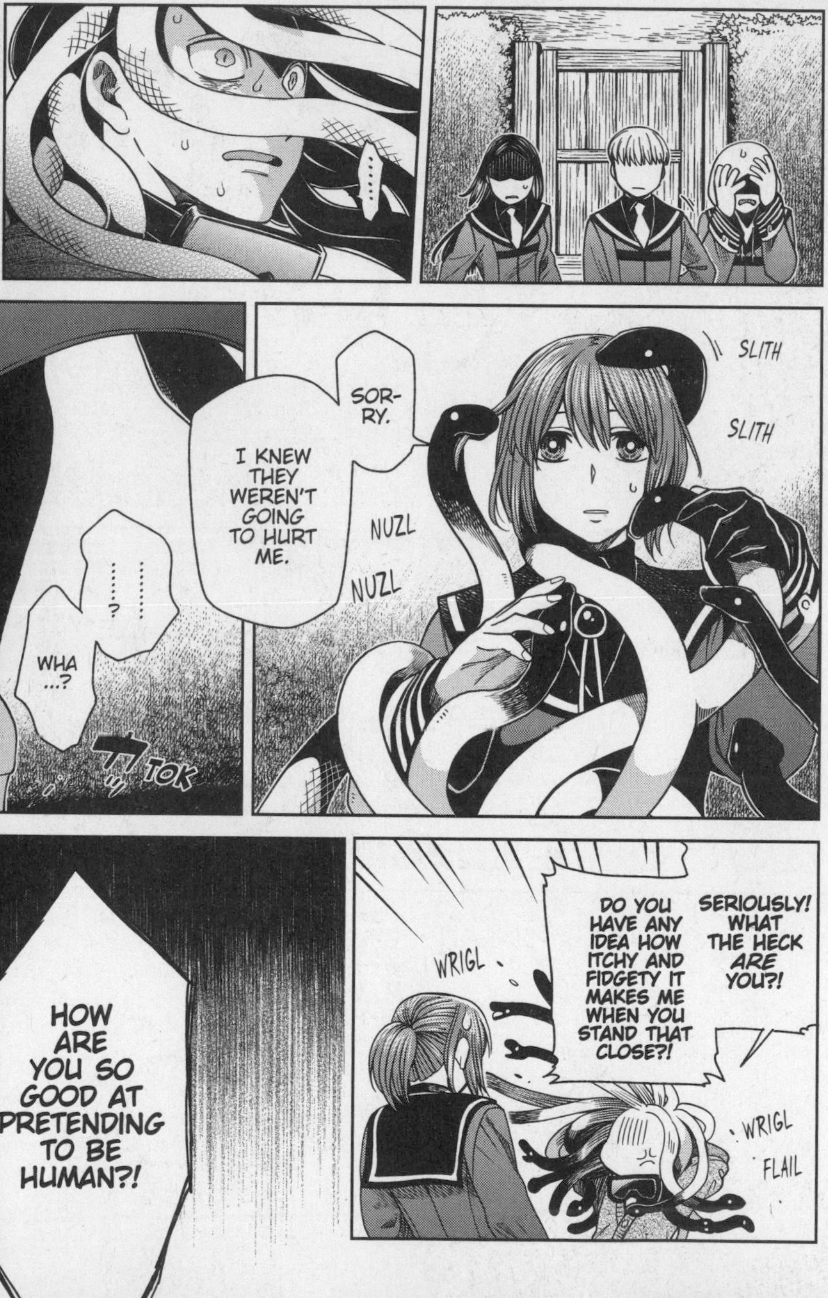
…
SLITH
SLITH
SOR-RY.
I KNEW THEY WEREN'T GOING TO HURT ME.
NUZL
NUZL
……
……?
WHA ...?
TOK
SERIOUSLY! WHAT THE HECK *ARE* YOU?!
DO YOU HAVE ANY IDEA HOW ITCHY AND FIDGETY IT MAKES ME WHEN YOU STAND THAT CLOSE?!
WRIGL
WRIGL
FLAIL
HOW ARE YOU SO GOOD AT PRETENDING TO BE HUMAN?!

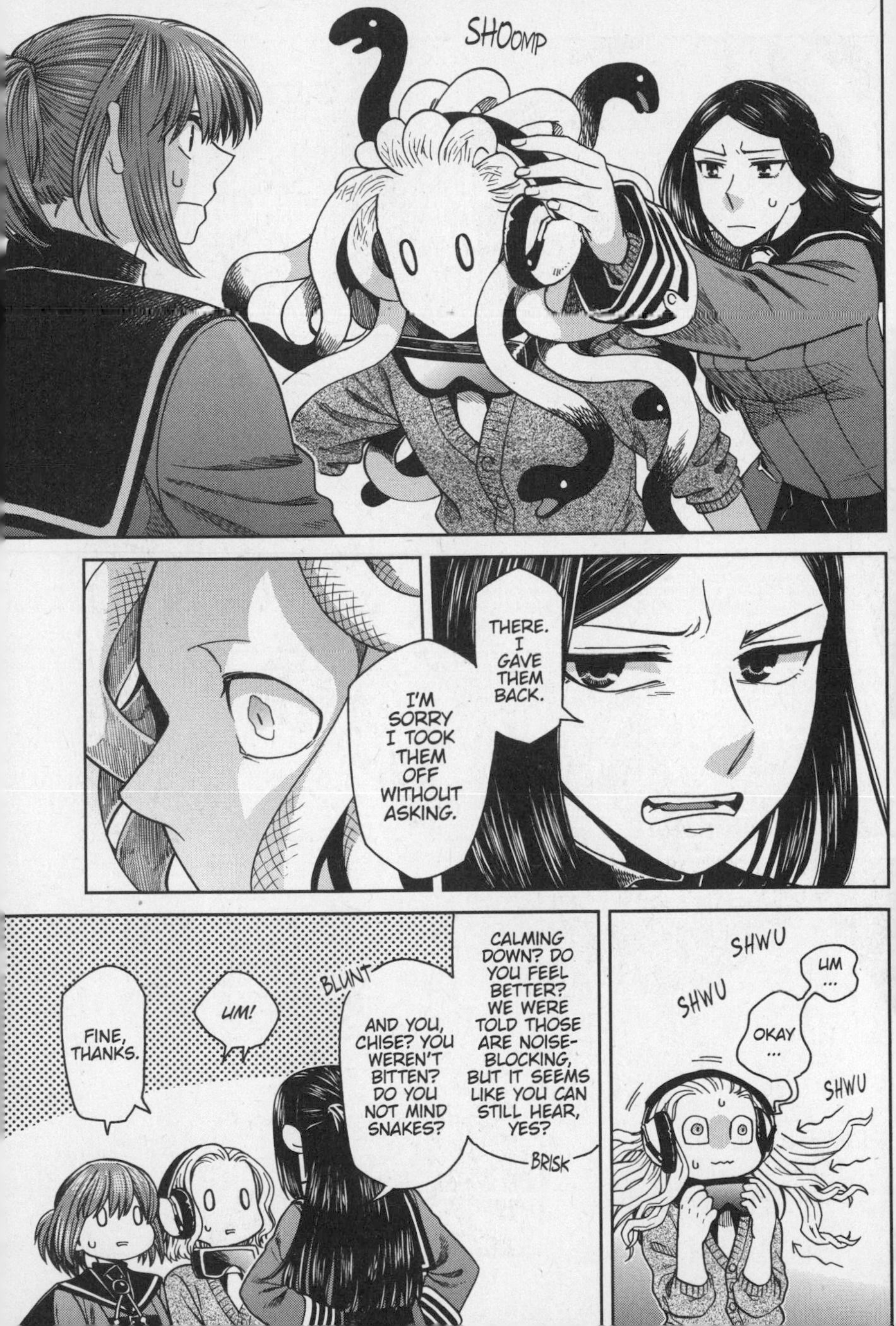
SHOOMP
THERE. I GAVE THEM BACK.
I'M SORRY I TOOK THEM OFF WITHOUT ASKING.
SHWU
UM ...
SHWU
OKAY ...
SHWU
CALMING DOWN? DO YOU FEEL BETTER? WE WERE TOLD THOSE ARE NOISE-BLOCKING, BUT IT SEEMS LIKE YOU CAN STILL HEAR, YES?
BRISK
BLUNT
AND YOU, CHISE? YOU WEREN'T BITTEN? DO YOU NOT MIND SNAKES?
UM!
FINE, THANKS.

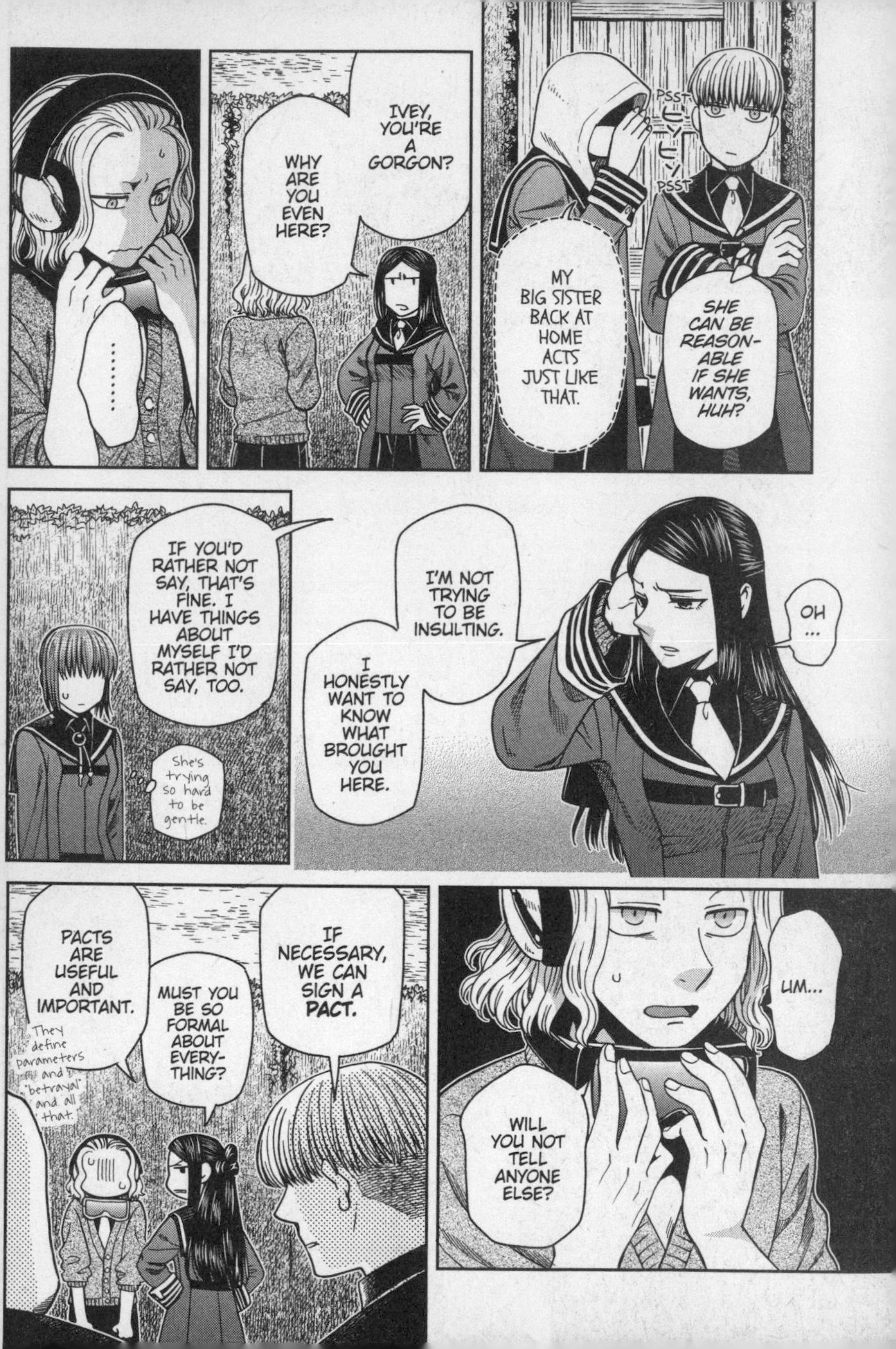
PSST
ヒソ
ヒソ
PSST
SHE CAN BE REASON-ABLE IF SHE WANTS, HUH?
MY BIG SISTER BACK AT HOME ACTS JUST LIKE THAT.
IVEY, YOU'RE A GORGON?
WHY ARE YOU EVEN HERE?
......
OH ...
I'M NOT TRYING TO BE INSULTING.
I HONESTLY WANT TO KNOW WHAT BROUGHT YOU HERE.
IF YOU'D RATHER NOT SAY, THAT'S FINE. I HAVE THINGS ABOUT MYSELF I'D RATHER NOT SAY, TOO.
She's trying so hard to be gentle.
UM...
WILL YOU NOT TELL ANYONE ELSE?
IF NECESSARY, WE CAN SIGN A PACT.
MUST YOU BE SO FORMAL ABOUT EVERYTHING?
PACTS ARE USEFUL AND IMPORTANT.
They define parameters and "betrayal" and all that.

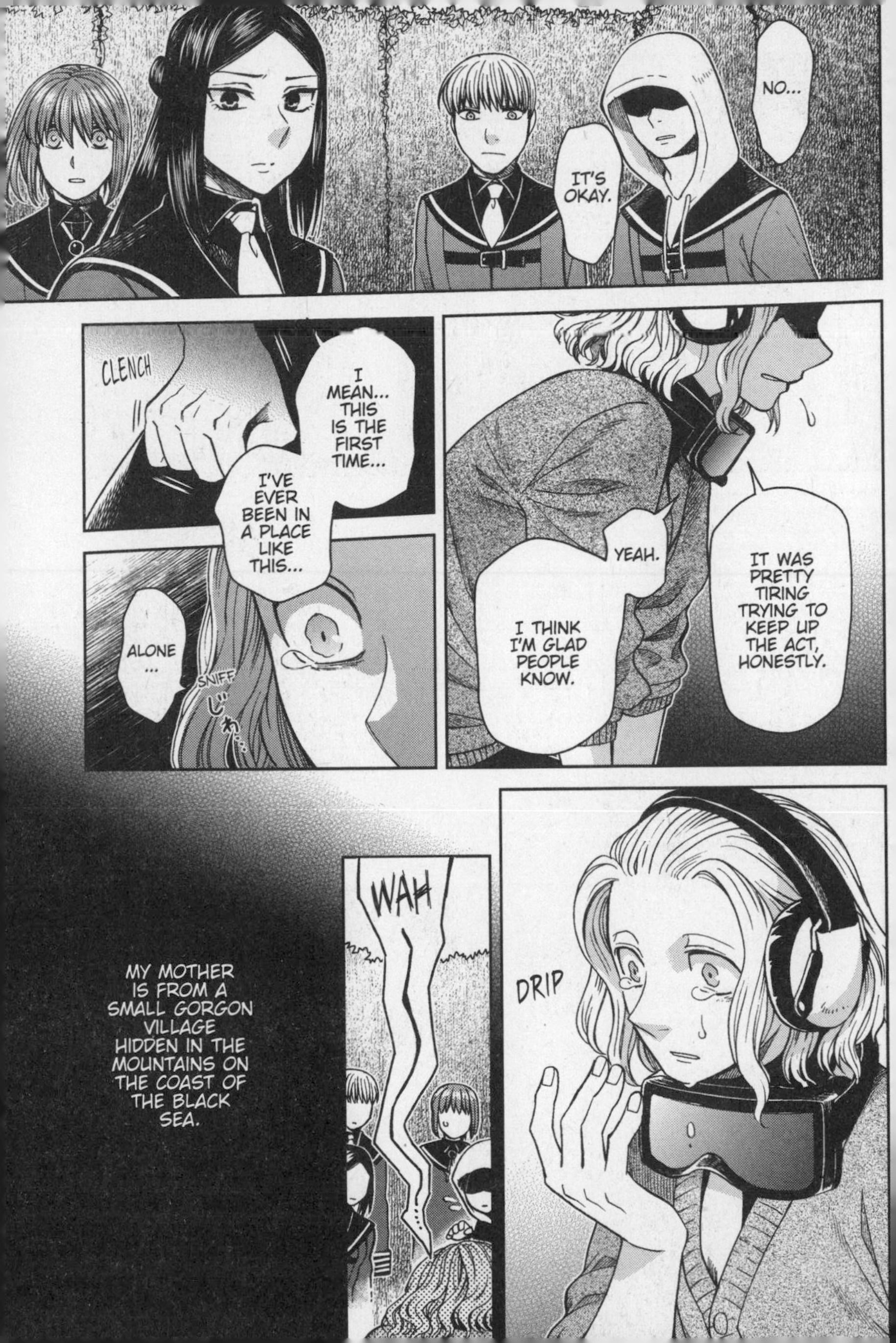
NO...
IT'S OKAY.
IT WAS PRETTY TIRING TRYING TO KEEP UP THE ACT, HONESTLY.
YEAH.
I THINK I'M GLAD PEOPLE KNOW.
CLENCH
I MEAN... THIS IS THE FIRST TIME...
I'VE EVER BEEN IN A PLACE LIKE THIS...
SNIFF
じわ...
ALONE ...
DRIP
WAH
MY MOTHER IS FROM A SMALL GORGON VILLAGE HIDDEN IN THE MOUNTAINS ON THE COAST OF THE BLACK SEA.

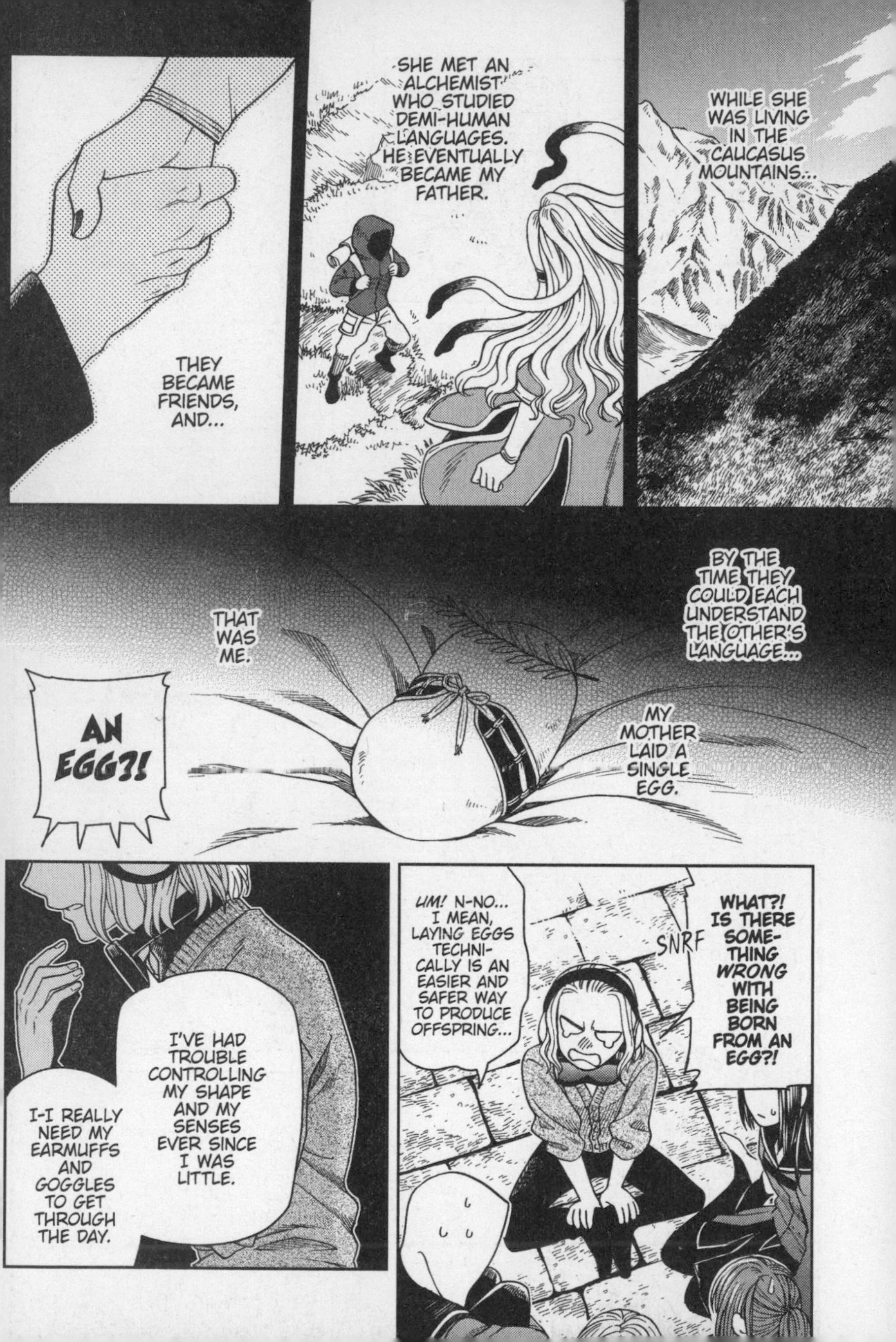
WHILE SHE WAS LIVING IN THE CAUCASUS MOUNTAINS...
SHE MET AN ALCHEMIST WHO STUDIED DEMI-HUMAN LANGUAGES. HE EVENTUALLY BECAME MY FATHER.
THEY BECAME FRIENDS, AND...
BY THE TIME THEY COULD EACH UNDERSTAND THE OTHER'S LANGUAGE...
MY MOTHER LAID A SINGLE EGG.
THAT WAS ME.
AN EGG?!
WHAT?! IS THERE SOME-THING WRONG WITH BEING BORN FROM AN EGG?!
SNRF
UM! N-NO... I MEAN, LAYING EGGS TECHNI-CALLY IS AN EASIER AND SAFER WAY TO PRODUCE OFFSPRING...
I'VE HAD TROUBLE CONTROLLING MY SHAPE AND MY SENSES EVER SINCE I WAS LITTLE.
I-I REALLY NEED MY EARMUFFS AND GOGGLES TO GET THROUGH THE DAY.

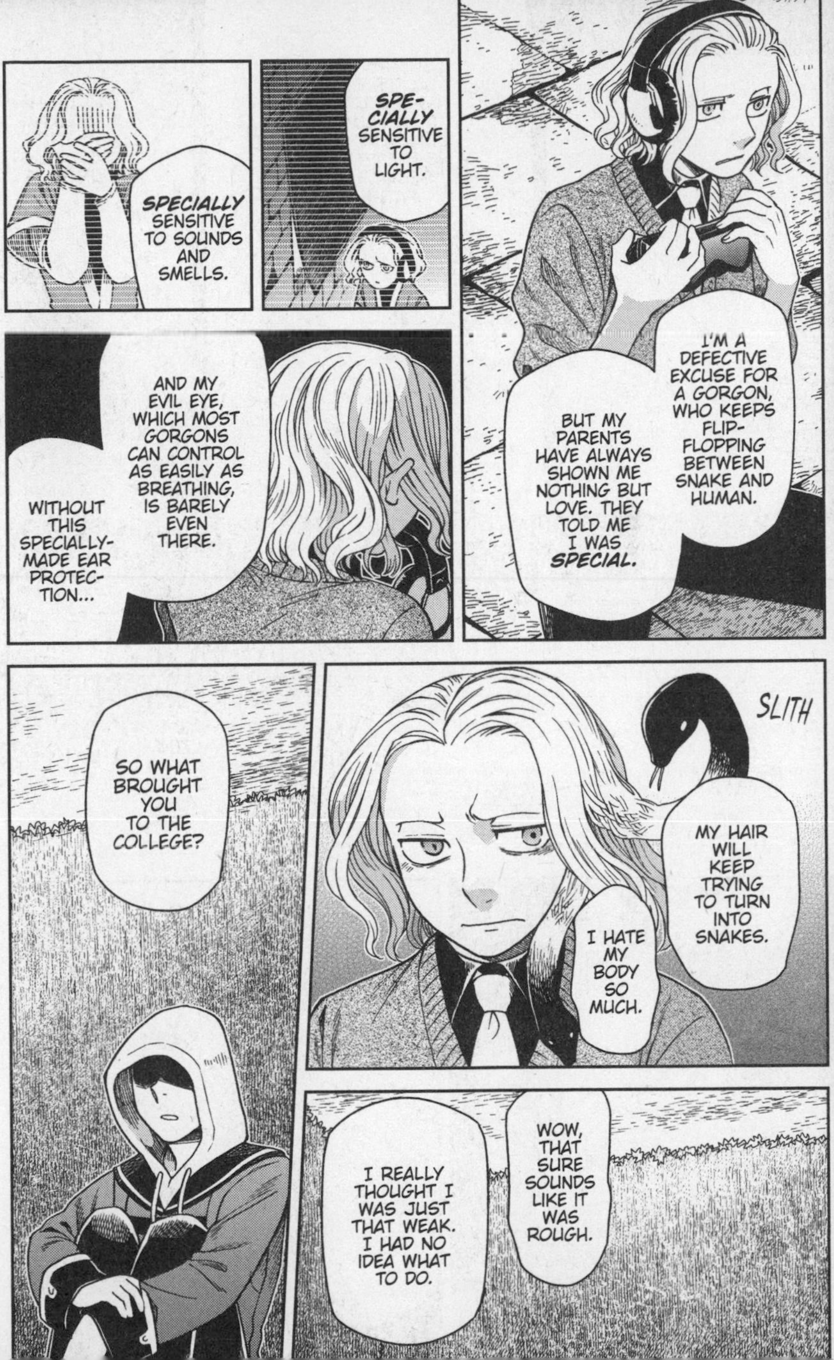
I'M A DEFECTIVE EXCUSE FOR A GORGON, WHO KEEPS FLIP-FLOPPING BETWEEN SNAKE AND HUMAN.
BUT MY PARENTS HAVE ALWAYS SHOWN ME NOTHING BUT LOVE. THEY TOLD ME I WAS *SPECIAL.*
SPE-CIALLY SENSITIVE TO LIGHT.
SPECIALLY SENSITIVE TO SOUNDS AND SMELLS.
AND MY EVIL EYE, WHICH MOST GORGONS CAN CONTROL AS EASILY AS BREATHING, IS BARELY EVEN THERE.
WITHOUT THIS SPECIALLY-MADE EAR PROTEC-TION...
SLITH
MY HAIR WILL KEEP TRYING TO TURN INTO SNAKES.
I HATE MY BODY SO MUCH.
WOW, THAT SURE SOUNDS LIKE IT WAS ROUGH.
I REALLY THOUGHT I WAS JUST THAT WEAK. I HAD NO IDEA WHAT TO DO.
SO WHAT BROUGHT YOU TO THE COLLEGE?

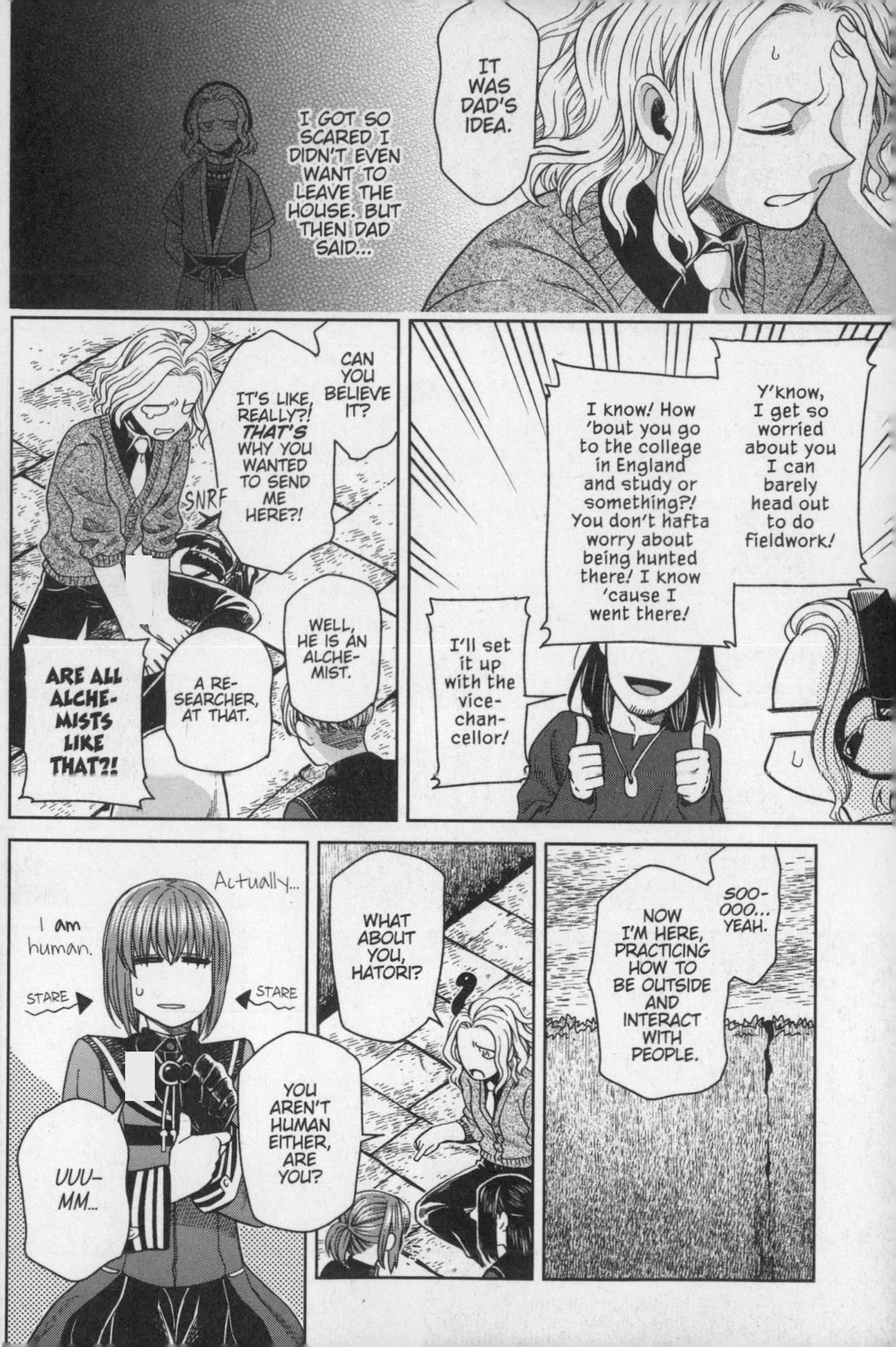
IT WAS DAD'S IDEA.
I GOT SO SCARED I DIDN'T EVEN WANT TO LEAVE THE HOUSE. BUT THEN DAD SAID...
Y'know, I get so worried about you I can barely head out to do fieldwork!
I know! How 'bout you go to the college in England and study or something?! You don't hafta worry about being hunted there! I know 'cause I went there!
I'll set it up with the vice-chancellor!
CAN YOU BELIEVE IT?
IT'S LIKE, REALLY?! *THAT'S* WHY YOU WANTED TO SEND ME HERE?!
SNRF
WELL, HE IS AN ALCHEMIST.
A RESEARCHER, AT THAT.
ARE ALL ALCHEMISTS LIKE THAT?!
SOOOOO... YEAH.
NOW I'M HERE, PRACTICING HOW TO BE OUTSIDE AND INTERACT WITH PEOPLE.
WHAT ABOUT YOU, HATORI?
YOU AREN'T HUMAN EITHER, ARE YOU?
Actually...
I am human.
STARE
STARE
UUU-MM...

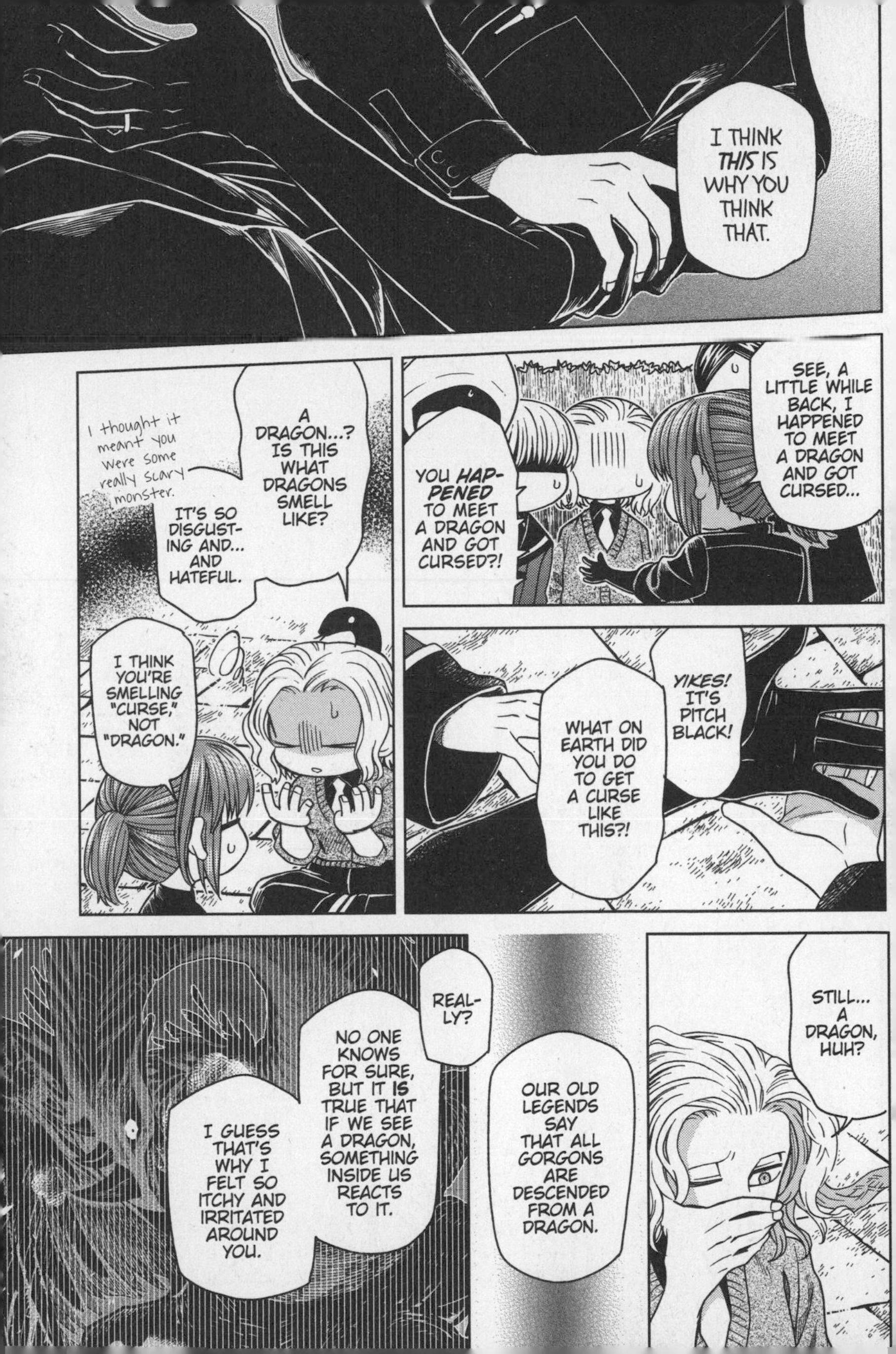
I THINK THIS IS WHY YOU THINK THAT.
SEE, A LITTLE WHILE BACK, I HAPPENED TO MEET A DRAGON AND GOT CURSED...
YOU HAPPENED TO MEET A DRAGON AND GOT CURSED?!
YIKES! IT'S PITCH BLACK!
WHAT ON EARTH DID YOU DO TO GET A CURSE LIKE THIS?!
A DRAGON...? IS THIS WHAT DRAGONS SMELL LIKE?
IT'S SO DISGUSTING AND... AND HATEFUL.
I thought it meant you were some really scary monster.
I THINK YOU'RE SMELLING "CURSE," NOT "DRAGON."
STILL... A DRAGON, HUH?
OUR OLD LEGENDS SAY THAT ALL GORGONS ARE DESCENDED FROM A DRAGON.
NO ONE KNOWS FOR SURE, BUT IT IS TRUE THAT IF WE SEE A DRAGON, SOMETHING INSIDE US REACTS TO IT.
REALLY?
I GUESS THAT'S WHY I FELT SO ITCHY AND IRRITATED AROUND YOU.

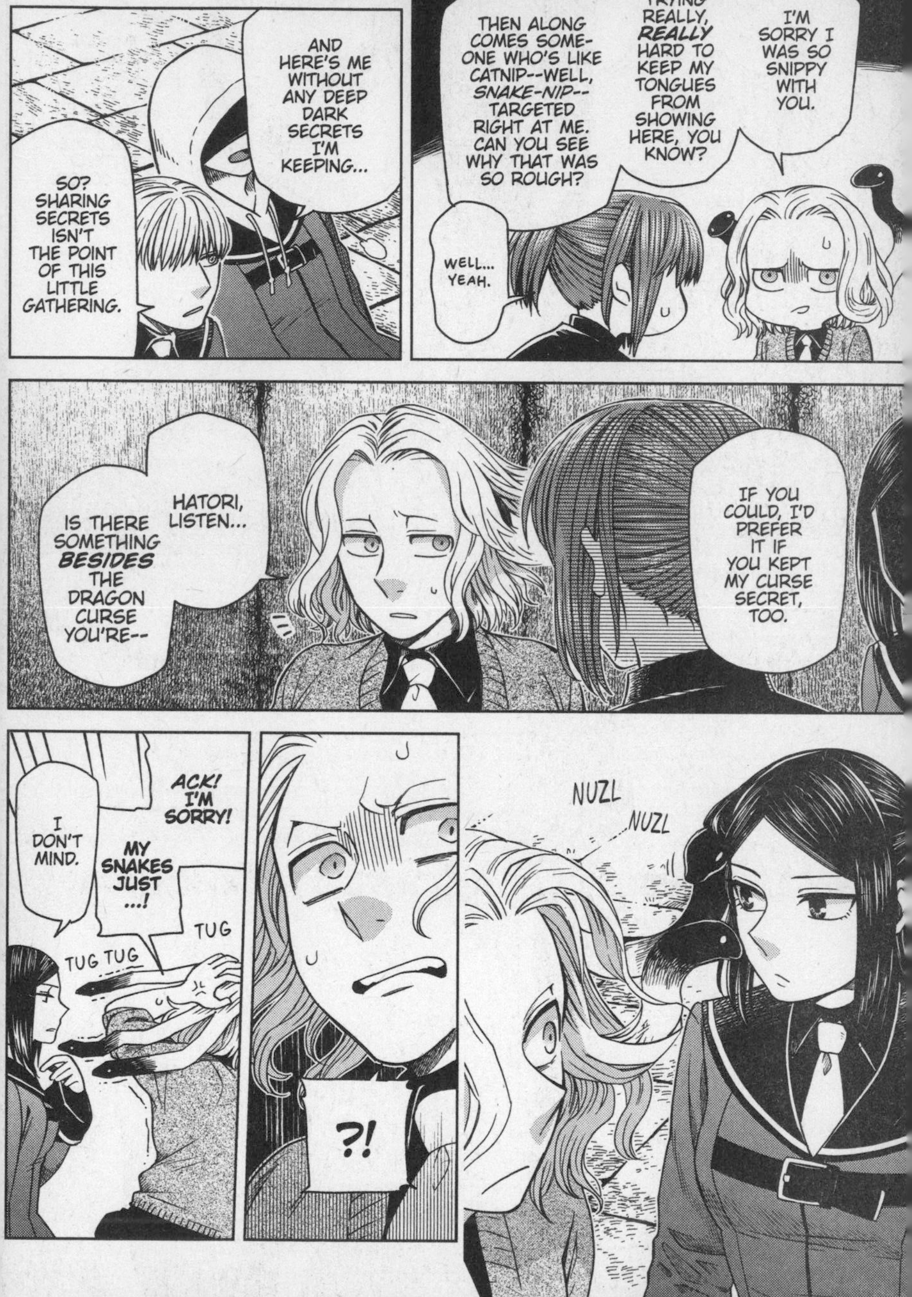
I'M SORRY I WAS SO SNIPPY WITH YOU.
I'M TRYING REALLY, REALLY HARD TO KEEP MY TONGUES FROM SHOWING HERE, YOU KNOW?
THEN ALONG COMES SOME-ONE WHO'S LIKE CATNIP--WELL, SNAKE-NIP--TARGETED RIGHT AT ME. CAN YOU SEE WHY THAT WAS SO ROUGH?
WELL... YEAH.
AND HERE'S ME WITHOUT ANY DEEP DARK SECRETS I'M KEEPING...
SO? SHARING SECRETS ISN'T THE POINT OF THIS LITTLE GATHERING.
IF YOU COULD, I'D PREFER IT IF YOU KEPT MY CURSE SECRET, TOO.
HATORI, LISTEN...
IS THERE SOMETHING BESIDES THE DRAGON CURSE YOU'RE--
NUZL
NUZL
?!
ACK! I'M SORRY!
MY SNAKES JUST ...!
I DON'T MIND.
TUG
TUG TUG

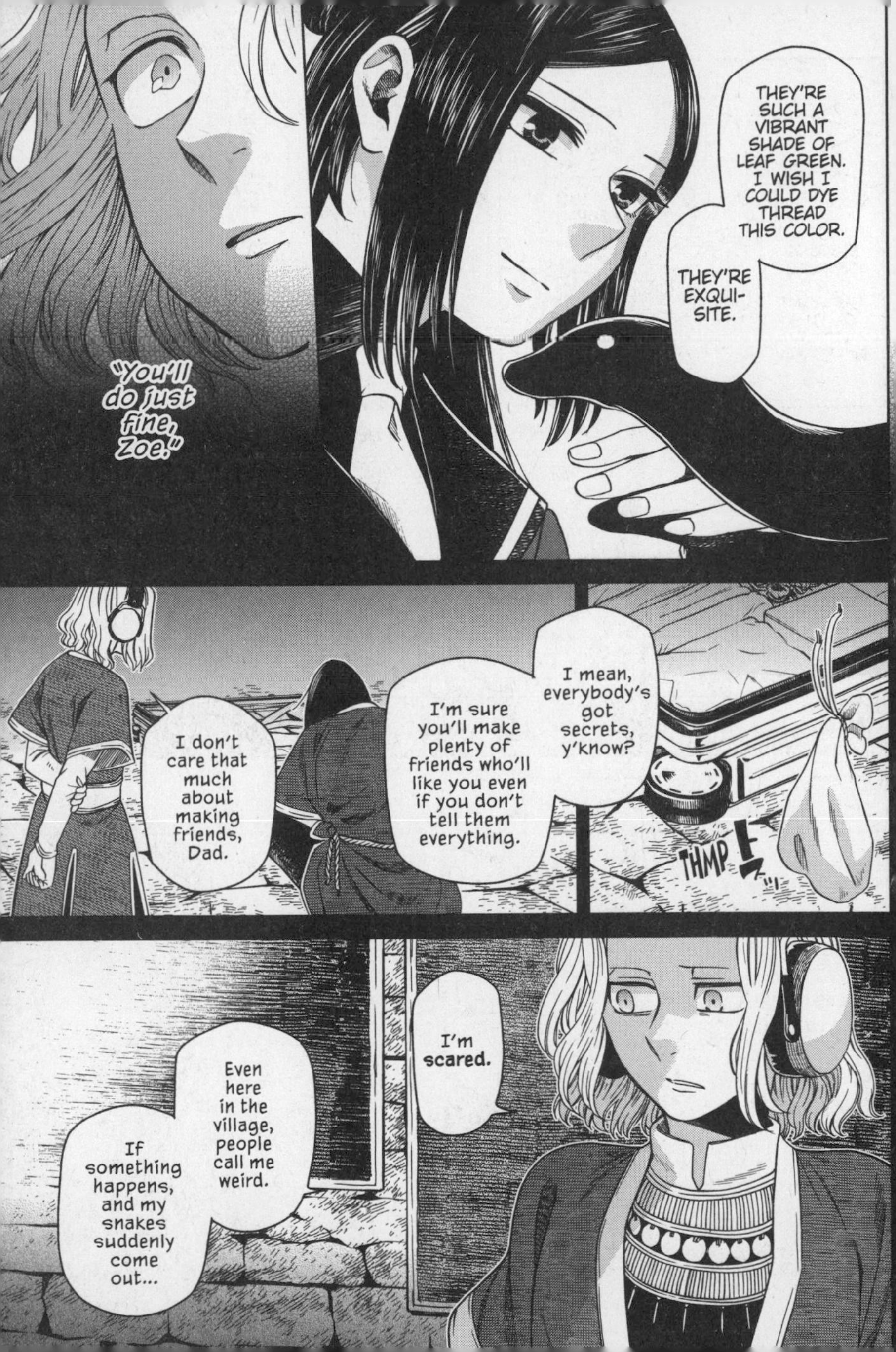
THEY'RE SUCH A VIBRANT SHADE OF LEAF GREEN. I WISH I COULD DYE THREAD THIS COLOR.
THEY'RE EXQUI-SITE.
"You'll do just fine, Zoe."
THMP
I mean, everybody's got secrets, y'know?
I'm sure you'll make plenty of friends who'll like you even if you don't tell them everything.
I don't care that much about making friends, Dad.
I'm scared.
Even here in the village, people call me weird.
If something happens, and my snakes suddenly come out...

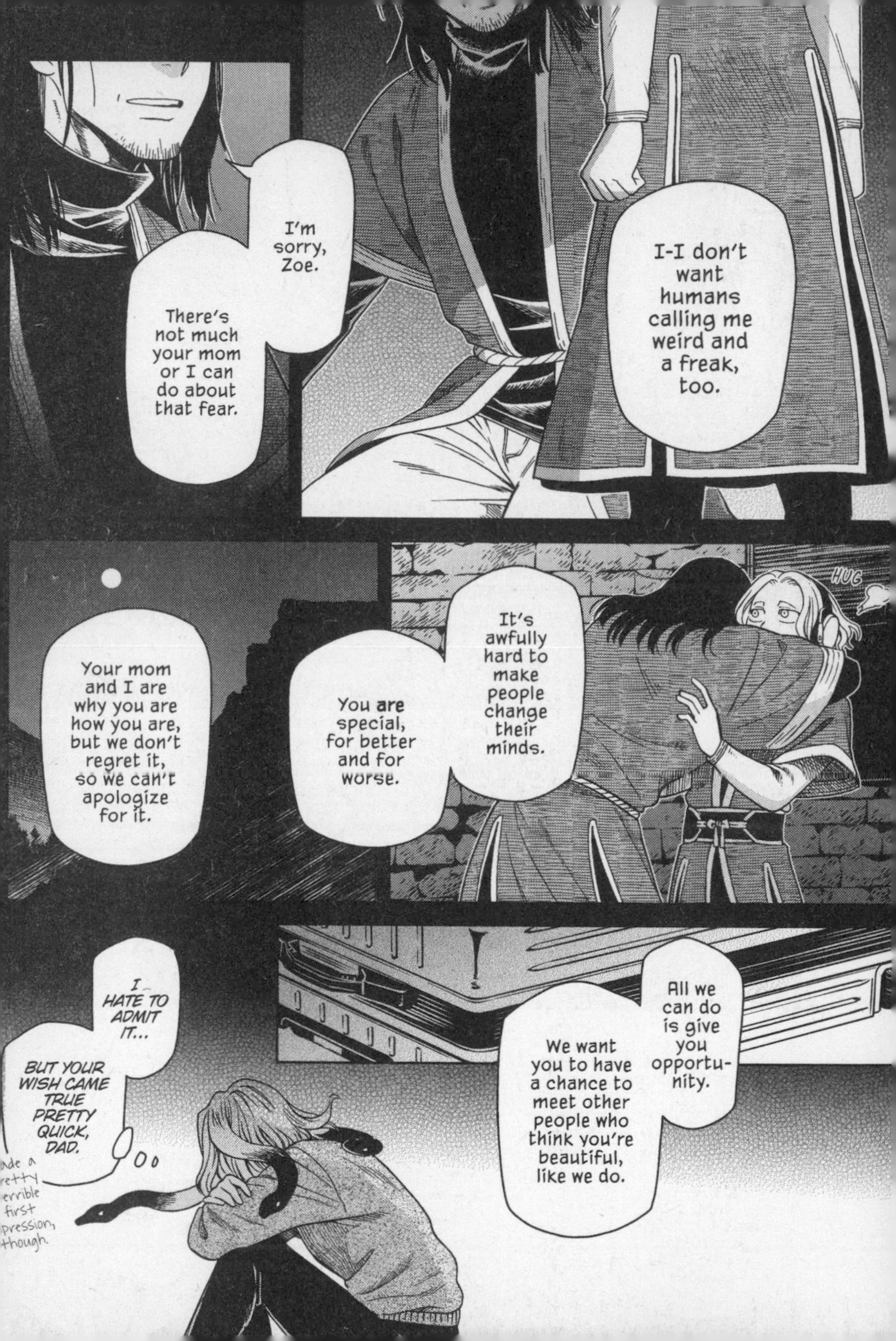

I-I don't want humans calling me weird and a freak, too.
I'm sorry, Zoe.
There's not much your mom or I can do about that fear.
HUG
It's awfully hard to make people change their minds.
You **are** special, for better and for worse.
Your mom and I are why you are how you are, but we don't regret it, so we can't apologize for it.
All we can do is give you opportunity.
We want you to have a chance to meet other people who think you're beautiful, like we do.
I HATE TO ADMIT IT...
BUT YOUR WISH CAME TRUE PRETTY QUICK, DAD.
ade a retty errible first pression, though.

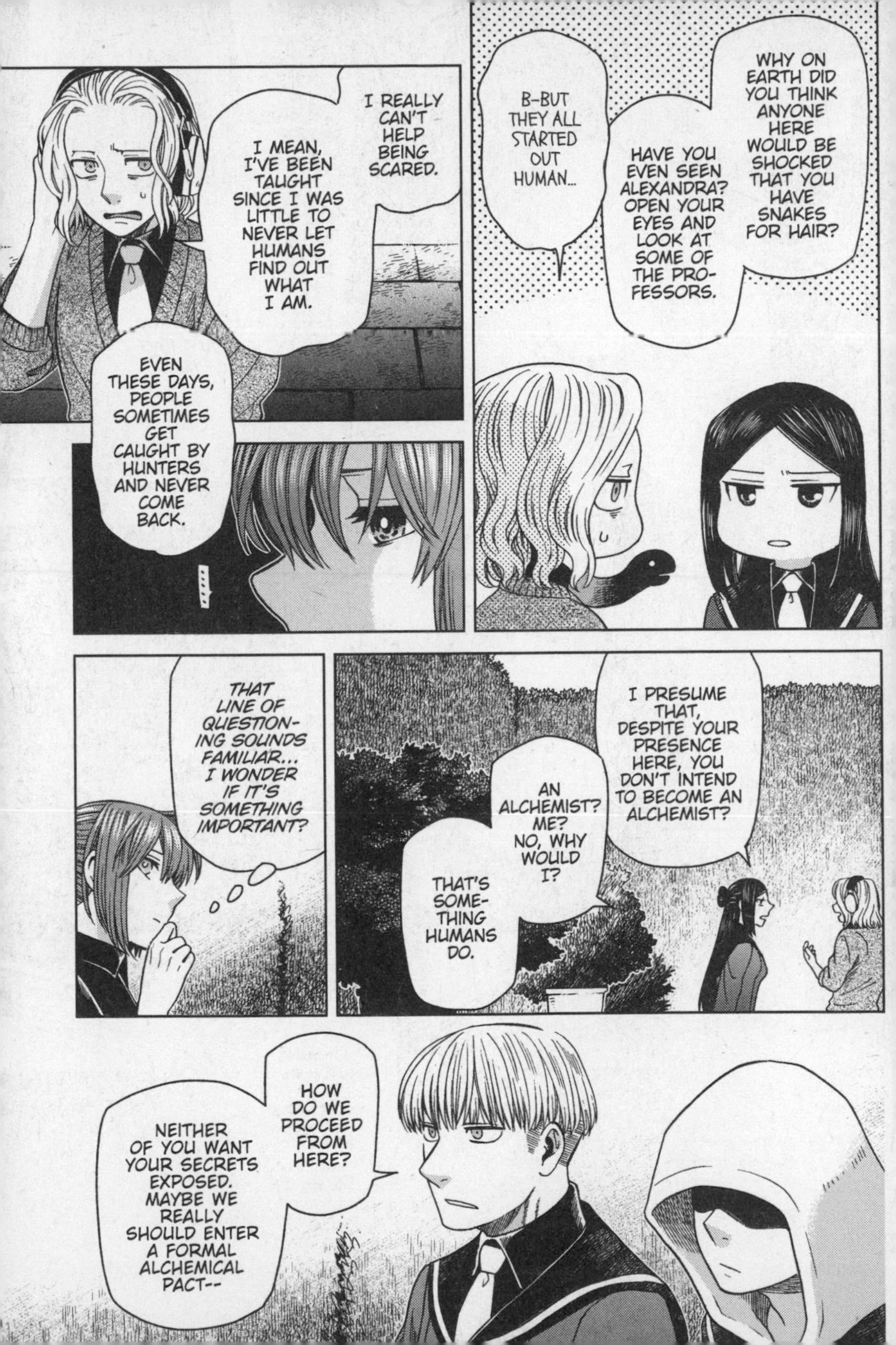
WHY ON EARTH DID YOU THINK ANYONE HERE WOULD BE SHOCKED THAT YOU HAVE SNAKES FOR HAIR?
HAVE YOU EVEN SEEN ALEXANDRA? OPEN YOUR EYES AND LOOK AT SOME OF THE PRO-FESSORS.
B-BUT THEY ALL STARTED OUT HUMAN...
I REALLY CAN'T HELP BEING SCARED.
I MEAN, I'VE BEEN TAUGHT SINCE I WAS LITTLE TO NEVER LET HUMANS FIND OUT WHAT I AM.
EVEN THESE DAYS, PEOPLE SOMETIMES GET CAUGHT BY HUNTERS AND NEVER COME BACK.
.....
I PRESUME THAT, DESPITE YOUR PRESENCE HERE, YOU DON'T INTEND TO BECOME AN ALCHEMIST?
AN ALCHEMIST? ME? NO, WHY WOULD I?
THAT'S SOME-THING HUMANS DO.
THAT LINE OF QUESTION-ING SOUNDS FAMILIAR... I WONDER IF IT'S SOMETHING IMPORTANT?
HOW DO WE PROCEED FROM HERE?
NEITHER OF YOU WANT YOUR SECRETS EXPOSED. MAYBE WE REALLY SHOULD ENTER A FORMAL ALCHEMICAL PACT--

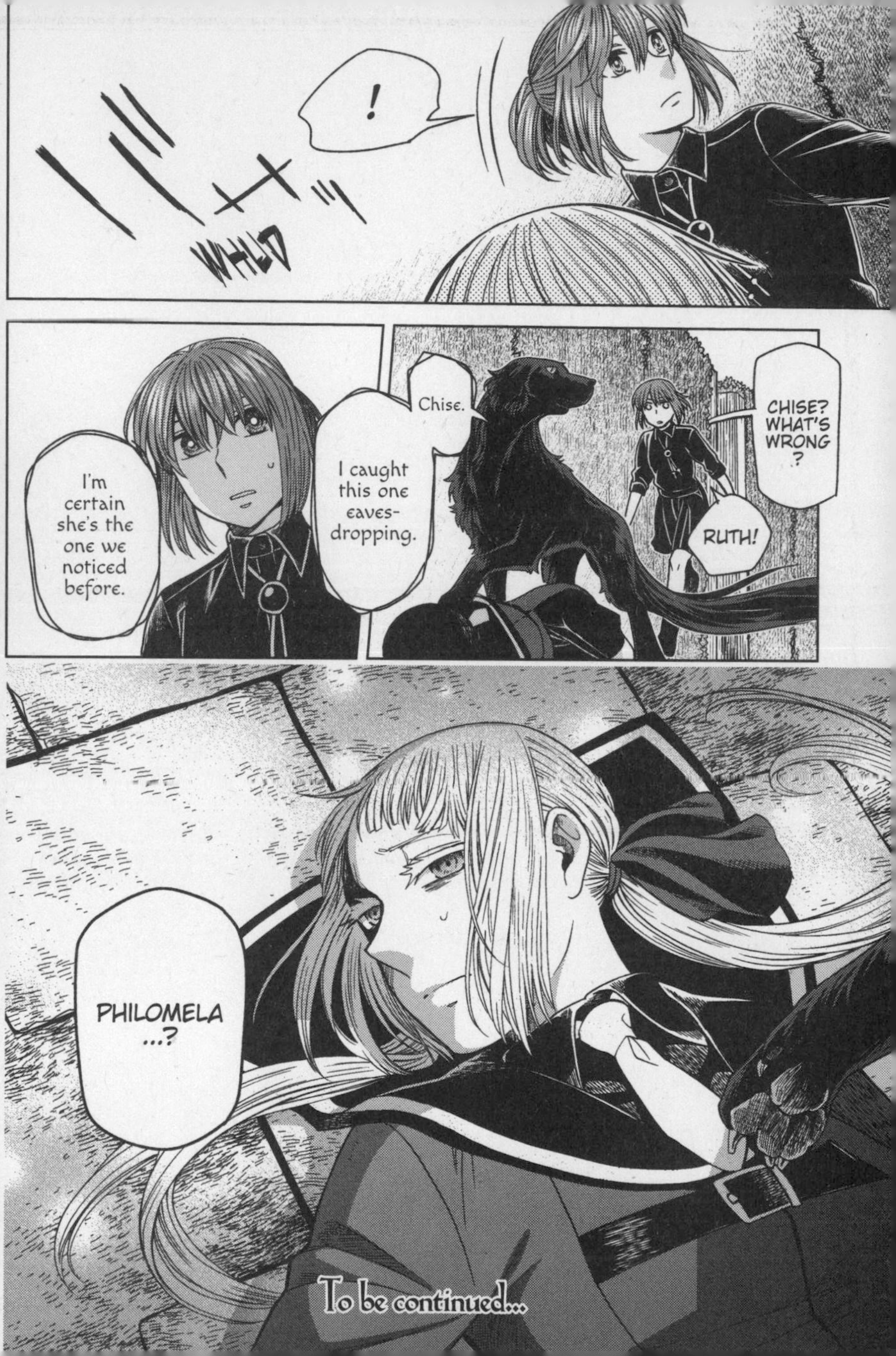
!
WHUD
CHISE? WHAT'S WRONG?
RUTH!
Chise.
I caught this one eaves-dropping.
I'm certain she's the one we noticed before.
PHILOMELA ...?
To be continued...

The Ancient Magus' Bride

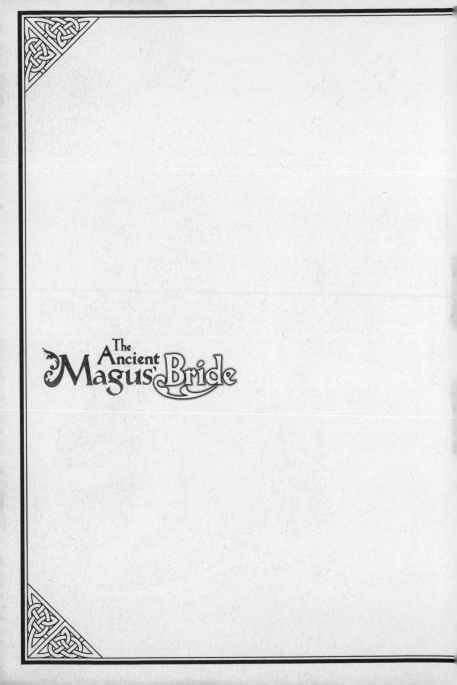

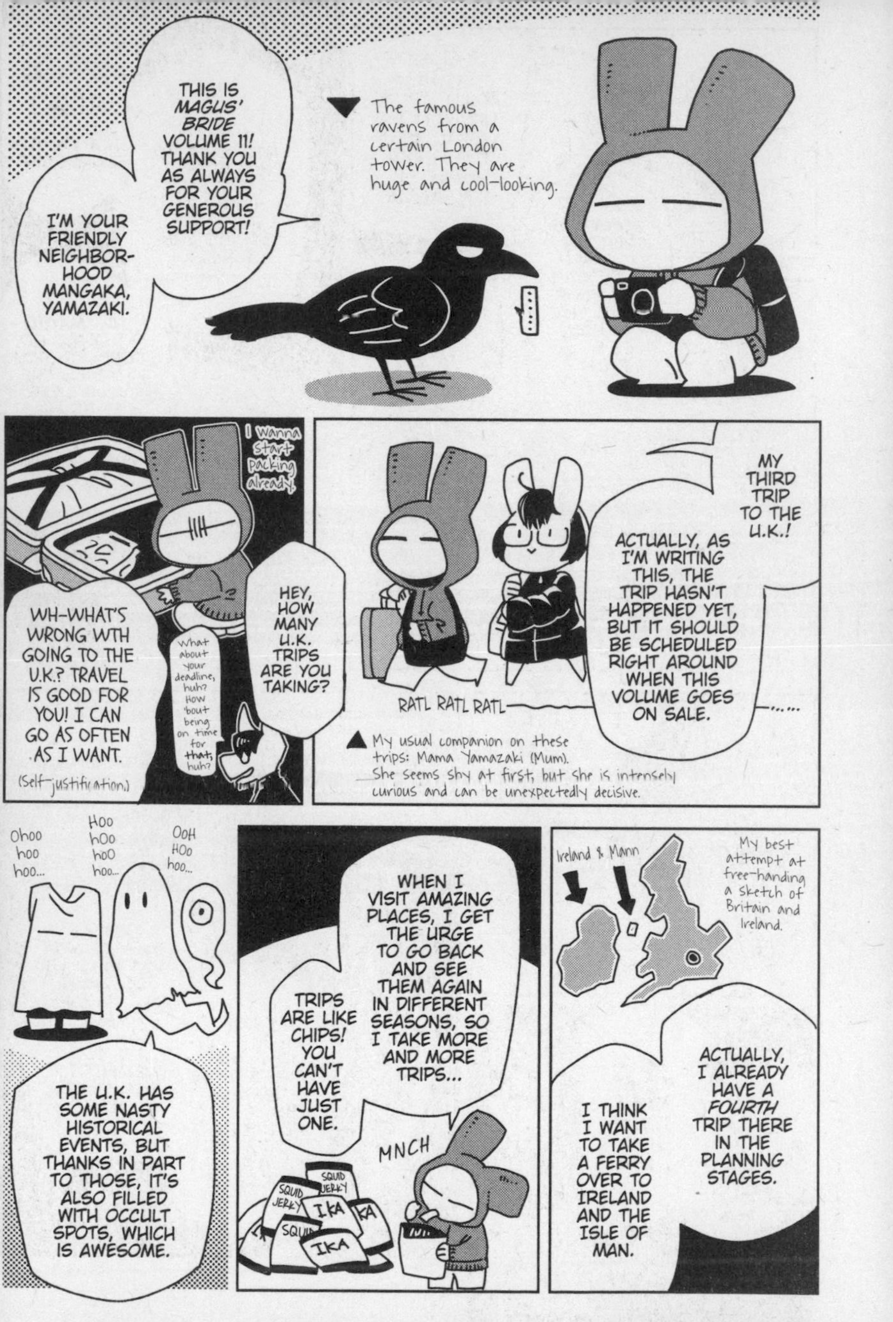
The famous ravens from a certain London tower. They are huge and cool-looking.
THIS IS *MAGUS' BRIDE* VOLUME 11! THANK YOU AS ALWAYS FOR YOUR GENEROUS SUPPORT!
I'M YOUR FRIENDLY NEIGHBOR-HOOD MANGAKA, YAMAZAKI.
MY THIRD TRIP TO THE U.K.!
ACTUALLY, AS I'M WRITING THIS, THE TRIP HASN'T HAPPENED YET, BUT IT SHOULD BE SCHEDULED RIGHT AROUND WHEN THIS VOLUME GOES ON SALE.
......
RATL RATL RATL
My usual companion on these trips: Mama Yamazaki (Mum). She seems shy at first, but she is intensely curious and can be unexpectedly decisive.
I wanna start packing already.
HEY, HOW MANY U.K. TRIPS ARE YOU TAKING?
What about your deadline, huh? How 'bout being on time for that, huh?
WH-WHAT'S WRONG WTH GOING TO THE U.K.? TRAVEL IS GOOD FOR YOU! I CAN GO AS OFTEN AS I WANT.
(Self justification.)
My best attempt at free-handing a sketch of Britain and Ireland.
Ireland & Mann
ACTUALLY, I ALREADY HAVE A *FOURTH* TRIP THERE IN THE PLANNING STAGES.
I THINK I WANT TO TAKE A FERRY OVER TO IRELAND AND THE ISLE OF MAN.
WHEN I VISIT AMAZING PLACES, I GET THE URGE TO GO BACK AND SEE THEM AGAIN IN DIFFERENT SEASONS, SO I TAKE MORE AND MORE TRIPS...
TRIPS ARE LIKE CHIPS! YOU CAN'T HAVE JUST ONE.
MNCH
SQUID JERKY
SQUID JERKY
IKA
IKA
OOH HOO hoo...
Hoo hOo hoO hoo...
Ohoo hoo hoo...
THE U.K. HAS SOME NASTY HISTORICAL EVENTS, BUT THANKS IN PART TO THOSE, IT'S ALSO FILLED WITH OCCULT SPOTS, WHICH IS AWESOME.

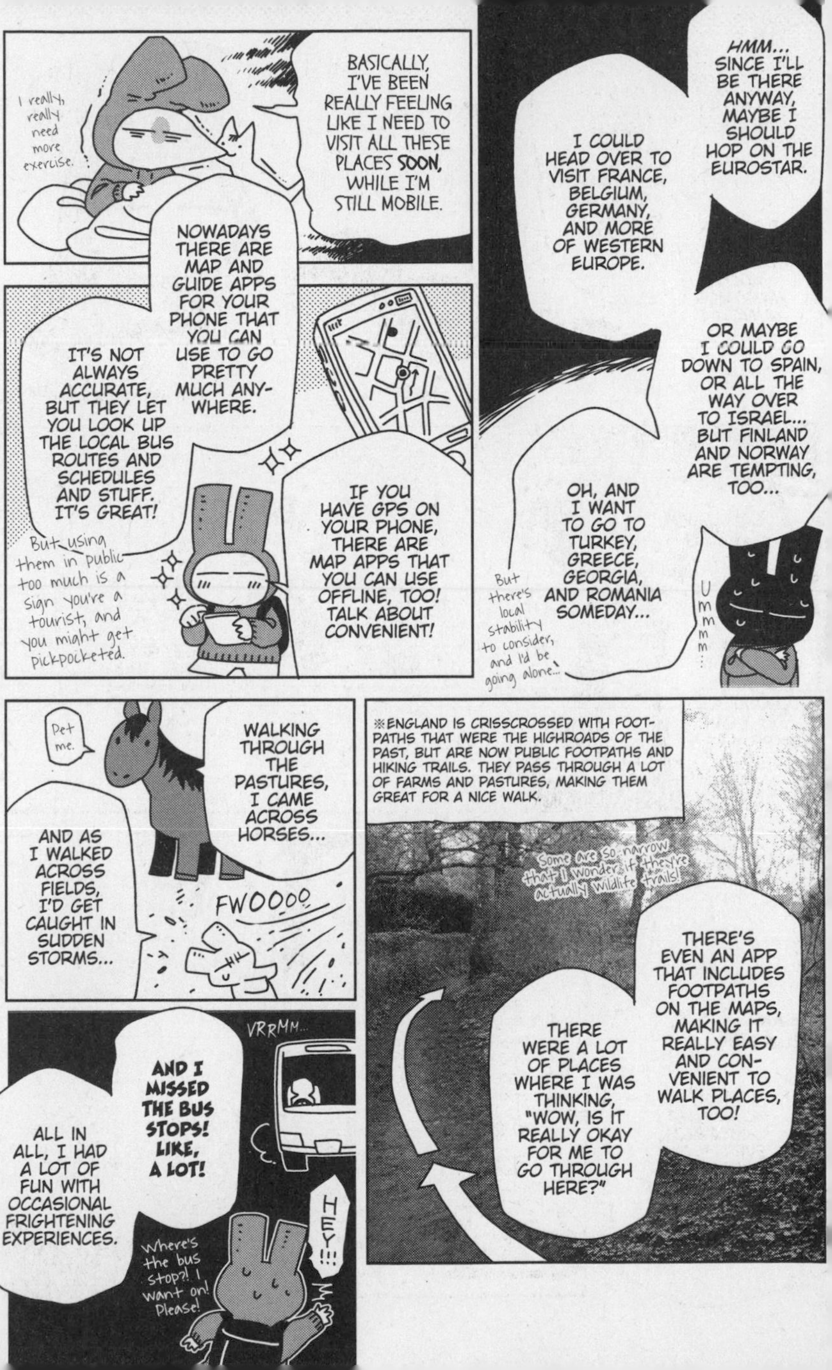
HMM... SINCE I'LL BE THERE ANYWAY, MAYBE I SHOULD HOP ON THE EUROSTAR.
I COULD HEAD OVER TO VISIT FRANCE, BELGIUM, GERMANY, AND MORE OF WESTERN EUROPE.
OR MAYBE I COULD GO DOWN TO SPAIN, OR ALL THE WAY OVER TO ISRAEL... BUT FINLAND AND NORWAY ARE TEMPTING, TOO...
OH, AND I WANT TO GO TO TURKEY, GREECE, GEORGIA, AND ROMANIA SOMEDAY...
But there's local stability to consider, and I'd be going alone...
Ummmm...
BASICALLY, I'VE BEEN REALLY FEELING LIKE I NEED TO VISIT ALL THESE PLACES SOON, WHILE I'M STILL MOBILE.
I really, really need more exercise.
NOWADAYS THERE ARE MAP AND GUIDE APPS FOR YOUR PHONE THAT YOU CAN USE TO GO PRETTY MUCH ANYWHERE.
IT'S NOT ALWAYS ACCURATE, BUT THEY LET YOU LOOK UP THE LOCAL BUS ROUTES AND SCHEDULES AND STUFF. IT'S GREAT!
IF YOU HAVE GPS ON YOUR PHONE, THERE ARE MAP APPS THAT YOU CAN USE OFFLINE, TOO! TALK ABOUT CONVENIENT!
But using them in public too much is a sign you're a tourist, and you might get pickpocketed.
※ENGLAND IS CRISSCROSSED WITH FOOTPATHS THAT WERE THE HIGHROADS OF THE PAST, BUT ARE NOW PUBLIC FOOTPATHS AND HIKING TRAILS. THEY PASS THROUGH A LOT OF FARMS AND PASTURES, MAKING THEM GREAT FOR A NICE WALK.
Some are so narrow that I wonder if they're actually wildlife trails!
THERE'S EVEN AN APP THAT INCLUDES FOOTPATHS ON THE MAPS, MAKING IT REALLY EASY AND CONVENIENT TO WALK PLACES, TOO!
THERE WERE A LOT OF PLACES WHERE I WAS THINKING, "WOW, IS IT REALLY OKAY FOR ME TO GO THROUGH HERE?"
WALKING THROUGH THE PASTURES, I CAME ACROSS HORSES...
Pet me.
AND AS I WALKED ACROSS FIELDS, I'D GET CAUGHT IN SUDDEN STORMS...
FWOOOO
VRRMM...
AND I MISSED THE BUS STOPS! LIKE, A LOT!
ALL IN ALL, I HAD A LOT OF FUN WITH OCCASIONAL FRIGHTENING EXPERIENCES.
HEY!!!
Where's the bus stop?! I want on! Please!

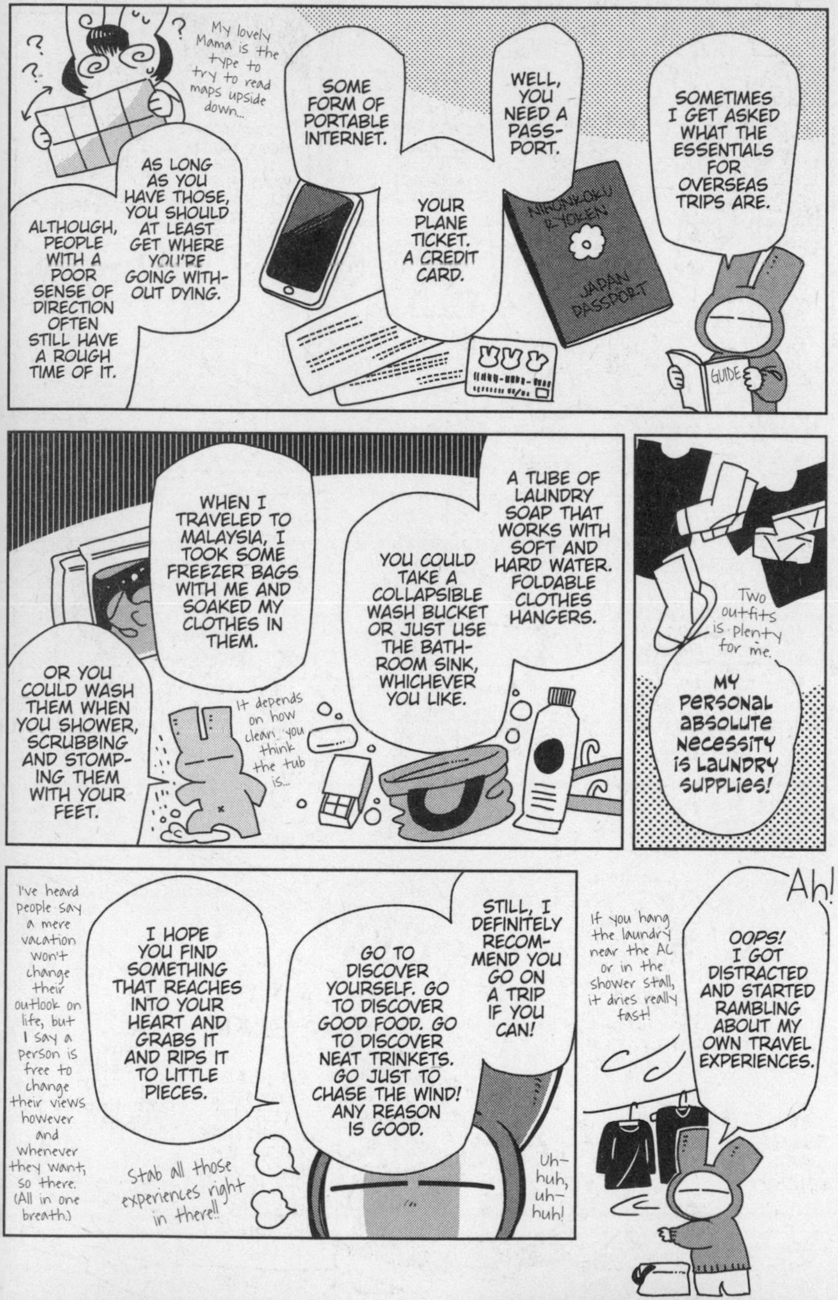
SOMETIMES I GET ASKED WHAT THE ESSENTIALS FOR OVERSEAS TRIPS ARE.
GUIDE
WELL, YOU NEED A PASS-PORT.
NIHONKOKU RYOKEN
JAPAN PASSPORT
YOUR PLANE TICKET. A CREDIT CARD.
SOME FORM OF PORTABLE INTERNET.
My lovely Mama is the type to try to read maps upside down...
AS LONG AS YOU HAVE THOSE, YOU SHOULD AT LEAST GET WHERE YOU'RE GOING WITH-OUT DYING.
ALTHOUGH, PEOPLE WITH A POOR SENSE OF DIRECTION OFTEN STILL HAVE A ROUGH TIME OF IT.
Two outfits is plenty for me.
MY PERSONAL ABSOLUTE NECESSITY IS LAUNDRY SUPPLIES!
A TUBE OF LAUNDRY SOAP THAT WORKS WITH SOFT AND HARD WATER. FOLDABLE CLOTHES HANGERS.
YOU COULD TAKE A COLLAPSIBLE WASH BUCKET OR JUST USE THE BATH-ROOM SINK, WHICHEVER YOU LIKE.
WHEN I TRAVELED TO MALAYSIA, I TOOK SOME FREEZER BAGS WITH ME AND SOAKED MY CLOTHES IN THEM.
It depends on how clean you think the tub is...
OR YOU COULD WASH THEM WHEN YOU SHOWER, SCRUBBING AND STOMP-ING THEM WITH YOUR FEET.
Ah!
OOPS! I GOT DISTRACTED AND STARTED RAMBLING ABOUT MY OWN TRAVEL EXPERIENCES.
If you hang the laundry near the AC or in the shower stall, it dries really fast!
STILL, I DEFINITELY RECOM-MEND YOU GO ON A TRIP IF YOU CAN!
GO TO DISCOVER YOURSELF. GO TO DISCOVER GOOD FOOD. GO TO DISCOVER NEAT TRINKETS. GO JUST TO CHASE THE WIND! ANY REASON IS GOOD.
Uh-huh, uh-huh!
I HOPE YOU FIND SOMETHING THAT REACHES INTO YOUR HEART AND GRABS IT AND RIPS IT TO LITTLE PIECES.
Stab all those experiences right in there!!
I've heard people say a mere vacation won't change their outlook on life, but I say a person is free to change their views however and whenever they want, so there. (All in one breath.)

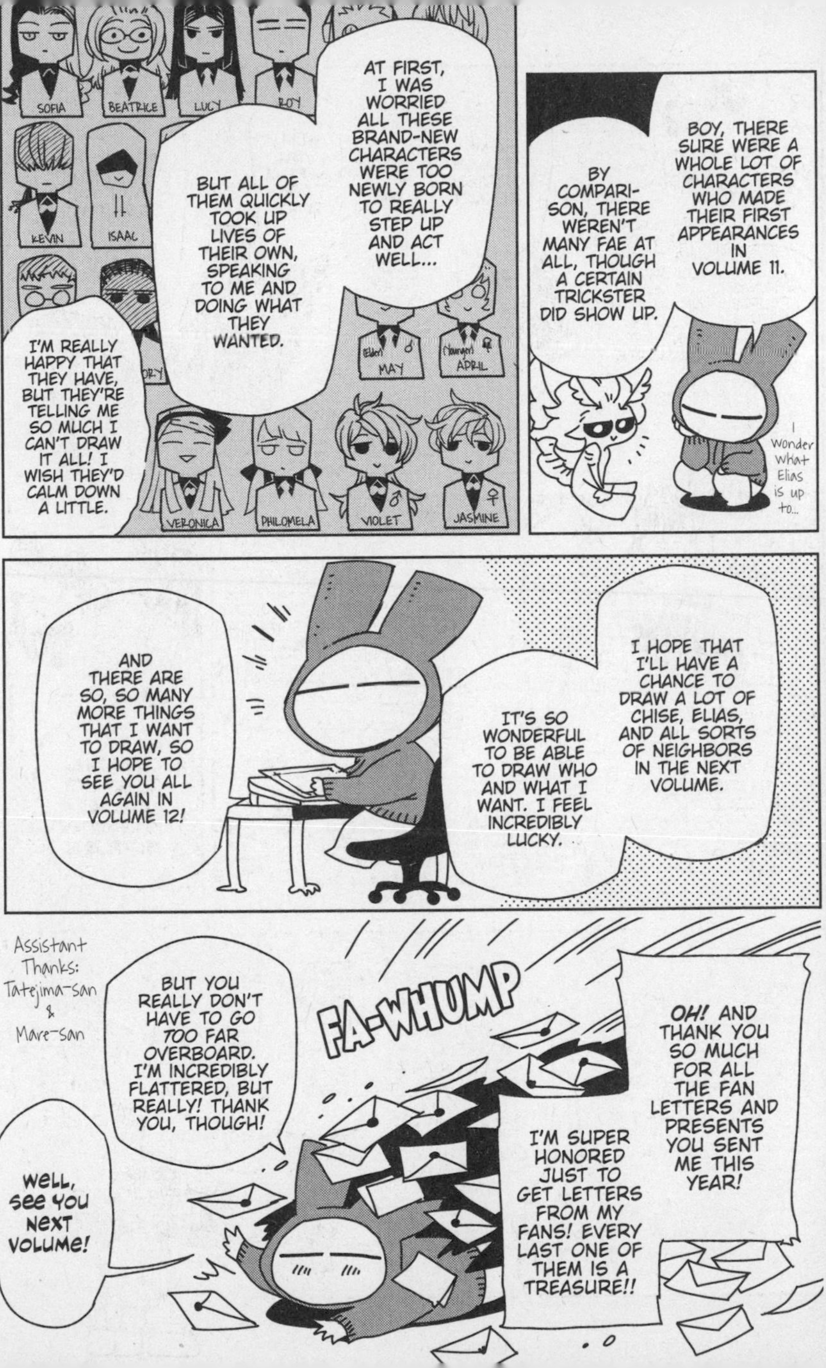
BOY, THERE SURE WERE A WHOLE LOT OF CHARACTERS WHO MADE THEIR FIRST APPEARANCES IN VOLUME 11.
BY COMPARISON, THERE WEREN'T MANY FAE AT ALL, THOUGH A CERTAIN TRICKSTER DID SHOW UP.
I wonder what Elias is up to...
AT FIRST, I WAS WORRIED ALL THESE BRAND-NEW CHARACTERS WERE TOO NEWLY BORN TO REALLY STEP UP AND ACT WELL...
BUT ALL OF THEM QUICKLY TOOK UP LIVES OF THEIR OWN, SPEAKING TO ME AND DOING WHAT THEY WANTED.
I'M REALLY HAPPY THAT THEY HAVE, BUT THEY'RE TELLING ME SO MUCH I CAN'T DRAW IT ALL! I WISH THEY'D CALM DOWN A LITTLE.
SOFIA
BEATRICE
LUCY
ROY
KEVIN
ISAAC
(Elder) MAY
(Younger) APRIL
VERONICA
PHILOMELA
VIOLET
JASMINE
I HOPE THAT I'LL HAVE A CHANCE TO DRAW A LOT OF CHISE, ELIAS, AND ALL SORTS OF NEIGHBORS IN THE NEXT VOLUME.
IT'S SO WONDERFUL TO BE ABLE TO DRAW WHO AND WHAT I WANT. I FEEL INCREDIBLY LUCKY.
AND THERE ARE SO, SO MANY MORE THINGS THAT I WANT TO DRAW, SO I HOPE TO SEE YOU ALL AGAIN IN VOLUME 12!
OH! AND THANK YOU SO MUCH FOR ALL THE FAN LETTERS AND PRESENTS YOU SENT ME THIS YEAR!
I'M SUPER HONORED JUST TO GET LETTERS FROM MY FANS! EVERY LAST ONE OF THEM IS A TREASURE!!
FA-WHUMP
BUT YOU REALLY DON'T HAVE TO GO TOO FAR OVERBOARD. I'M INCREDIBLY FLATTERED, BUT REALLY! THANK YOU, THOUGH!
WELL, SEE YOU NEXT VOLUME!

Assistant Thanks: Tatejima-san & Mare-san

What does Chise's presence bring to the College...?

The college's student body is made up of unique individuals with their own thoughts and agendas, and slowly, one step at a time, Chise finds her own niche with them. But then she hears rumors about Lucy's past...

This fairy tale with hints of otherworldly romance, set in England, continues in Volume 12!

SEVEN SEAS ENTERTAINMENT PRESENTS

DEC – – 2019

The Ancient Magus' Bride

VOLUME 11

story and art by KORE YAMAZAKI

TRANSLATION
Adrienne Beck

ADAPTATION
Ysabet Reinhardt MacFarlane

LETTERING AND RETOUCH
Lys Blakeslee

COVER DESIGN
Nicky Lim

PROOFREADER
Janet Houck

ASSISTANT EDITOR
J.P. Sullivan

PRODUCTION MANAGER
Lissa Pattillo

MANAGING EDITOR
Julie Davis

EDITOR-IN-CHIEF
Adam Arnold

PUBLISHER
Jason DeAngelis

THE ANCIENT MAGUS' BRIDE VOL. 11
© Kore Yamazaki 2019

Originally published in Japan in 2019 by MAG Garden Corporation, Tokyo.
English translation rights arranged through TOHAN CORPORATION, Tokyo.

Seven Seas press and purchase enquiries can be sent to Marketing Manager
Lianne Sentar at press@gomanga.com. Information regarding the distribution
and purchase of digital editions is available from Digital Manager CK Russell
at digital@gomanga.com.

Seven Seas and the Seven Seas logo are trademarks of
Seven Seas Entertainment. All rights reserved.

ISBN: 978-1-64275-101-7

Printed in Canada

First Printing: September 2019

10 9 8 7 6 5 4 3 2 1

FOLLOW US ONLINE: *www.sevenseasentertainment.com*

READING DIRECTIONS

This book reads from *right to left*, Japanese style.
If this is your first time reading manga, you start
reading from the top right panel on each page and
take it from there. If you get lost, just follow the
numbered diagram here. It may seem backwards at
first, but you'll get the hang of it! Have fun!!

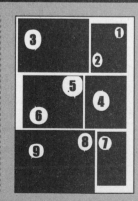